Lecture Notes in Computer Science

Commenced Publication in 1973
Founding and Former Series Editors:
Gerhard Goos, Juris Hartmanis, and Jan van Leeuwen

Thomas Bauschert (Ed.)

Advances in Communication Networking

19th EUNICE/IFIP WG 6.6 International Workshop
Chemnitz, Germany, August 28-30, 2013
Proceedings

 Springer

Volume Editor

Thomas Bauschert
Technische Universität Chemnitz
Professur Kommunikationsnetze
Reichenhainer Straße 70
09107 Chemnitz, Germany
E-mail: thomas.bauschert@etit.tu-chemnitz.de
Web: http://www.tu-chemnitz.de/etit/kn/

ISSN 0302-9743   e-ISSN 1611-3349
ISBN 978-3-642-40551-8   e-ISBN 978-3-642-40552-5
DOI 10.1007/978-3-642-40552-5
Springer Heidelberg New York Dordrecht London

Library of Congress Control Number: 2013946103

CR Subject Classification (1998): C.2.0-2, C.2, H.3.3-5, F.2.2, C.0, K.6, H.4

LNCS Sublibrary: SL 3 – Information Systems and Application, incl. Internet/Web
and HCI

Typesetting: Camera-ready by author, data conversion by Scientific Publishing Services, Chennai, India

Printed on acid-free paper

Springer is part of Springer Science+Business Media (www.springer.com)

Preface

It was a great honor for TU Chemnitz to host the 19th EUNICE Workshop on Advances in Communication Networking. EUNICE has a long tradition in bringing together young scientists and researchers from academia, industry, and government organizations to meet and to discuss their recent achievements. The single-track structure with sufficient time for presentations provides an excellent platform for stimulating discussions. The proceedings of the EUNICE workshops are published in Springer's LNCS series.

This year, the workshop focus was on "Advances in Communication Networking." Several keynote speakers from industry were invited to foster discussions between industry and academia about recent communication networking issues, trends, and solutions. Moreover, the original aim of the EUNICE-Forum was adopted by organizing a summer school on the dedicated topic of "Network Performance Evaluation and Optimization" co-located to the EUNICE workshop.

EUNICE 2013 received 40 paper submissions. According to the evaluations, the top 23 papers were selected for oral presentations. In addition, nine papers were selected for poster presentations. All of these papers appear in this proceedings volume.

On behalf of the Chair for Communication Networks of TU Chemnitz, I would like to express my thanks to everyone who actively participated in the organization of EUNICE 2013, in particular to the members of the Technical Program Committee, the reviewers, and last but not least the members of my team. Special thanks go to the keynote speakers from industry for contributing to the workshop as well as to the colleagues from academia for contributing to the summer school.

June 2013   Thomas Bauschert

Organization

EUNICE 2013 was organized by the Chair for Communication Networks, TU Chemnitz.

Executive Committee

Conference Chair
Thomas Bauschert   Chair for Communication Networks,
                                   TU Chemnitz, Germany

Local Organization
Thomas M. Knoll   TU Chemnitz, Germany

Technical Program Committee

Finn Arve Aagesen   NTNU Trondheim, Norway
Thomas Bauschert   TU Chemnitz, Germany
Piotr Cholda   AGH University Krakow, Poland
Jörg Eberspächer   TU München, Germany
Markus Fiedler   BIT, Blekinge, Sweden
Carmelita Görg   University of Bremen, Germany
Annie Gravey   TELECOM Bretagne, France
Yvon Kermarrec   TELECOM Bretagne, France
Thomas M. Knoll   TU Chemnitz, Germany
Paul Kühn   University of Stuttgart, Germany
Ralf Lehnert   TU Dresden, Germany
Matthias Lott   DOCOMO Euro-Labs München, Germany
Miquel Oliver   University Pompeu Fabra, Spain
Michal Pioro   Warsaw University of Technology, Poland
Aiko Pras   University of Twente, The Netherlands
Jacek Rak   Gdansk University of Technology, Poland
Burkhard Stiller   University of Zürich, Switzerland
Robert Szabo   Budapest University of Technology, Hungary
Andreas Timm-Giel   TU Hamburg-Harburg, Germany
Phuoc Tran-Gia   University of Würzburg, Germany
Christian Wietfeld   TU Dortmund, Germany
Adam Wolisz   TU Berlin, Germany

Sponsors

- EUNICE

- International Federation for Information Processing (IFIP)

- Informationstechnische Gesellschaft (ITG) im VDE

- Technische Universität Chemnitz

Table of Contents

Network Modeling and Design

Dynamic Resource Operation and Power Model for IP-over-WSON
Networks 1
    Uwe Bauknecht and Frank Feller

A Generic Multi-layer Network Optimization Model with Demand
Uncertainty 13
    Uwe Steglich, Thomas Bauschert, Christina Büsing, and
    Manuel Kutschka

Modeling and Quantifying the Survivability of Telecommunication
Network Systems under Fault Propagation 25
    Lang Xie, Poul E. Heegaard, and Yuming Jiang

Traffic Analysis

Analysis of Elephant Users in Broadband Network Traffic 37
    Péter Megyesi and Sándor Molnár

Evaluation of the Aircraft Distribution in Satellite Spotbeams 46
    Christoph Petersen, Maciej Mühleisen, and Andreas Timm-Giel

Network and Traffic Management

Self-management of Hybrid Networks – Hidden Costs Due to TCP
Performance Problems 54
    Giovane C.M. Moura, Aiko Pras, Tiago Fioreze, and
    Pieter-Tjerk de Boer

A Revenue-Maximizing Scheme for Radio Access Technology Selection
in Heterogeneous Wireless Networks with User Profile Differentiation ... 66
    Elissar Khloussy, Xavier Gelabert, and Yuming Jiang

Services over Mobile Networks

Mobile SIP: An Empirical Study on SIP Retransmission Timers
in HSPA 3G Networks 78
    Joachim Fabini, Michael Hirschbichler, Jiri Kuthan, and
    Werner Wiedermann

Addressing the Challenges of E-Healthcare in Future Mobile
Networks 90
    Safdar Nawaz Khan Marwat, Thomas Pötsch, Yasir Zaki,
    Thushara Weerawardane, and Carmelita Görg

Monitoring and Measurement

Evaluation of Video Quality Monitoring Based on Pre-computed Frame
Distortions 100
    Dominik Klein, Thomas Zinner, Kathrin Borchert, Stanislav Lange,
    Vlad Singeorzan, and Matthias Schmid

QoE Management Framework for Internet Services in SDN Enabled
Mobile Networks 112
    Marcus Eckert and Thomas Martin Knoll

A Measurement Study of Active Probing on Access Links 124
    Bjørn J. Villa and Poul E. Heegaard

Design and Evaluation of HTTP Protocol Parsers for IPFIX
Measurement 136
    Petr Velan, Tomáš Jirsík, and Pavel Čeleda

Security Concepts

IPv6 Address Obfuscation by Intermediate Middlebox in Coordination
with Connected Devices 148
    Florent Fourcot, Laurent Toutain, Stefan Köpsell,
    Frédéric Cuppens, and Nora Cuppens-Boulahia

Balanced XOR-ed Coding 161
    Katina Kralevska, Danilo Gligoroski, and Harald Øverby

Application of ICT in Smart Grid and Smart Home Environments

Architecture and Functional Framework for Home Energy Management
Systems 173
    Kornschnok Dittawit and Finn Arve Aagesen

Interdependency Modeling in Smart Grid and the Influence of ICT
on Dependability 185
    Jonas Wäfler and Poul E. Heegaard

Development and Calibration of a PLC Simulation Model
for UPA-Compliant Networks 197
    Ievgenii Anatolijovuch Tsokalo, Stanislav Mudriievskyi, and
    Ralf J. Lehnert

Data Dissemination in Ad-Hoc and Sensor Networks

Efficient Data Aggregation with CCNx in Wireless Sensor Networks   209
  Torsten Teubler, Mohamed Ahmed M. Hail, and Horst Hellbrück

EpiDOL: Epidemic Density Adaptive Data Dissemination Exploiting
Opposite Lane in VANETs   221
  Irem Nizamoglu, Sinem Coleri Ergen, and Oznur Ozkasap

Services and Applications

Advanced Approach to Future Service Development   233
  Tetiana Kot, Larisa Globa, and Alexander Schill

A Transversal Alignment between Measurements and Enterprise
Architecture for Early Verification of Telecom Service Design   245
  Iyas Alloush, Yvon Kermarrec, and Siegfried Rouvrais

DOMINO – An Efficient Algorithm for Policy Definition and Processing
in Distributed Environments Based on Atomic Data Structures   257
  Joachim Zeiß, Peter Reichl, Jean-Marie Bonnin, and Jürgen Dorn

Poster Papers

Performance Evaluation of Machine-to-Machine Communication on
Future Mobile Networks in Disaster Scenarios   270
  *Thomas Pötsch, Safdar Nawaz Khan Marwat, Yasir Zaki, and
  Carmelita Görg*

Notes on the Topological Consequences of BGP Policy Routing on the
Internet AS Topology.   274
  Dávid Szabó and András Gulyás

Graph-Theoretic Roots of Value Network Quantification   282
  Patrick Zwickl and Peter Reichl

A Publish-Subscribe Scheme Based Open Architecture
for Crowd-Sourcing   287
  Róbert L. Szabó and Károly Farkas

A Testbed Evaluation of the Scalability of IEEE 802.11s Light
Sleep Mode   292
  Marco Porsch and Thomas Bauschert

HTTP Traffic Offload in Cellular Networks via WLAN Mesh Enabled
Device to Device Communication and Distributed Caching   298
  Chris Drechsler, Marco Porsch, and Gerd Windisch

Protocol-Independent Detection of Dictionary Attacks 304
    Martin Drašar

Distributing Key Revocation Status in Named Data Networking 310
    Giulia Mauri and Giacomo Verticale

Test-Enhanced Life Cycle for Composed IoT-Based Services 314
    Daniel Kuemper, Eike Steffen Reetz, Daniel Hölker, and Ralf Tönjes

Author Index 321

Dynamic Resource Operation and Power Model for IP-over-WSON Networks

Uwe Bauknecht and Frank Feller

Institute of Communication Networks and Computer Engineering (IKR)
Universität Stuttgart, Pfaffenwaldring 47, 70569 Stuttgart, Germany
{uwe.bauknecht,frank.feller}@ikr.uni-stuttgart.de

Abstract. The power consumption of core networks is bound to grow considerably due to increasing traffic volumes. Network reconfiguration adapting resources to the load is a promising countermeasure. However, the benefit of this approach is hard to evaluate realistically since current network equipment does not support dynamic resource adaptation and power-saving features. In this paper, we derive a dynamic resource operation and power model for IP-over-WSON network devices based on static power consumption data from vendors and reasonable assumptions on the achievable scaling behavior. Our model allows to express the dynamic energy consumption as a function of active optical interfaces, line cards, chassis, and the amount of switched IP traffic. We finally apply the model in the evaluation of two network reconfiguration schemes.

Keywords: Dynamic Energy Model, Resource Model, IP-over-WDM Network, Multi-layer Network, Energy Efficiency.

1 Introduction

The continuous exponential growth of the traffic volume is driving an increase in the power consumption of communication networks, which has gained importance due to economic, environmental, and regulatory considerations. While the access segment has traditionally accounted for the largest share of the energy consumed in communication networks, core networks are bound to become predominant due to new energy-efficient broadband access technologies like FTTx [1,2].

Today, core network resources are operated statically whereas the traffic exhibits significant variations over the day, including night periods with as little as 20 % of the daily peak rate [3]. Adapting the amount of active, i. e. energy-consuming, resources to the traffic load could therefore significantly reduce power consumption. Since the paradigm of static operation has traditionally guaranteed the reliability of transport networks, research needs to thoroughly investigate both the benefits and the consequences of dynamic resource operation.

A first challenge is to determine the energy savings achievable by this approach. Current core network equipment neither allows the deactivation of components nor features state-of-the-art power-saving techniques (such as frequency

T. Bauschert (Ed.): EUNICE 2013, LNCS 8115, pp. 1–12, 2013.

scaling found in desktop processors). Hence, its power consumption hardly depends on the traffic load [4,5]. For the static operation of network equipment, researchers have derived power models from measurements [4] and product specifications or white papers [6]. These models are either intended as a reference for future research [6] or applied in power-efficient network planning studies [7].

Core network reconfiguration studies base on different power adaptation assumptions. Mostly, components (e. g. optical cross-connects, amplifiers, regenerators [8,9]; router interfaces, line cards [10,11]) or whole links and nodes [10] are switched off. Alternatively, the energy consumption is scaled with active capacity [12], link bit rate [13], or traffic load [14]. Restrepo *et al.* [15] propose load-dependent energy profiles justified by different power-saving techniques for components and also apply them to nodes. Lange *et al.* [16] derive a dynamic power model from a generic network device structure and validate it by measurements of one piece of power-saving enabled equipment. To our knowledge, however, there is no coherent reference model for the dynamic power consumption of current core network equipment assuming state-of-the-art power-scaling techniques. Such a model is highly desirable for network reconfiguration studies.

In this paper, we derive a dynamic resource operation and power model for Internet protocol (IP) over wavelength switched optical network (WSON) networks. We start by decomposing network nodes into their relevant hardware components, for which we obtain static power consumption values from reference models and publicly available manufacturer data. Based on their structure and functions, we identify applicable activation/deactivation patterns and power-scaling techniques and derive the operation state-dependent power consumption. We then aggregate the component behavior into a power model suitable for network-level studies. It features power values for optical circuits and electrically switched traffic. In addition, it takes the resource hierarchy of network nodes into consideration and describes their static power consumption. We finally illustrate the application of our model using reconfiguration schemes from [11,17].

2   Network Equipment Structure

The two layers of IP-over-WSON networks are reflected in the structure of the network nodes. The nodes typically consist of a router processing IP packets for the upper layer and a wavelength-selective optical circuit switch in the lower layer. Optical circuits interconnect arbitrary IP routers.

2.1   IP Routers

Large core routers like the Cisco CRS-3, Alcatel-Lucent (ALU) 7950 XRS, or Juniper T4000 have a modular structure as depicted in Fig. 1. Their basic element is the line card chassis (LCC), which features a passive backplane interconnecting card slots. The chassis is equipped with a number of elements to provide basic functionality. This comprises power supply and cooling units realized in a modular way for failure tolerance and step-wise upgrades. Power supply and cooling

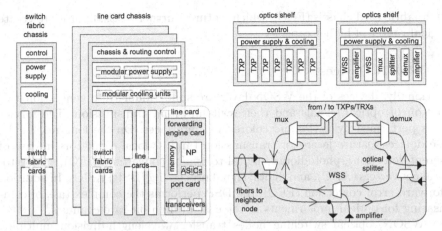

Fig. 1. IP layer device structure   **Fig. 2.** WSON node structure

are managed by the chassis control (CC) among other tasks. The routing engine (RE) exchanges routing protocol messages with other network nodes and builds a routing table. Essentially, the CC and RE modules are small general-purpose server systems. In the case of Cisco, one such system fulfills both functions.

Line cards (LC) perform the central role of the router: they terminate optical circuits and switch the traffic on the IP packet level. One can subdivide them according to these functions into port cards (PC) and forwarding engine cards (FE). The latter feature network processors (NP), further application specific integrated circuits (ASIC), and memory to process and store packets. NPs generally have highly parallel architectures[1]. Typically, one part of the memory is used for packet buffering, whereas a copy of the routing table occupies the rest.

PCs provide the connection between optical circuits and the electrical interfaces of FEs. One PC may terminate several circuits. Traditionally, PCs feature ports for pluggable optical transceiver (transmitter and receiver) modules such as SFP[2], XFP[3], or CFP[4]. These transceivers (TRX) are so-called short-reach transceivers (SR-TRX) of a limited optical reach (100 m to 100 km); they connect the LCs to transponders (TXP) converting the signal to a given wavelength for long-haul transmission. Alternatively, PCs can directly feature *colored* interfaces with long-reach transceivers (LR-TRX). This avoids the overhead of signal conversion, but currently restricts the number of interfaces per LC.

Switch fabric cards (SFC) comprising ASICs and buffer memory interconnect LCs over the passive backplane. They are essential for the forwarding of packets between different LCs. The total interconnection capacity between any pair of LCs is distributed over several SFCs, allowing graceful degradation in case of failures. It is likewise possible to interconnect several LCCs using a dedicated

---

[1] Cf. Cisco Quantum Flow Array [18], ALU FP3 [19], EZchip NPS-400 [20].
[2] Small form-factor pluggable, capable of 1 Gbps.
[3] 10 Gigabit small form-factor pluggable.
[4] C form-factor pluggable, capable of 100 Gbps.

switch fabric card chassis (FCC), which features further SFCs, in order to create a logical router of higher capacity.

2.2 WSON Devices

Functionally, devices of the WSON layer are subdividable into generation/termination of optical signals and their switching and transmission. The former task is performed by TXPs and colored LC interfaces. On the long-reach side, these devices feature lasers for transmission (and as local oscillators in case of coherent detection), photodiodes, digital-to-analog converters (DAC), analog-to-digital converters (ADC), and digital signal processing (DSP) ASICs. In addition to forward error correction (FEC), the DSP performs the complex task of compensating for optical impairments in the case of high bit-rate channels.

In WSON, optical switching nodes transfer wavelength-division multiplex (WDM) signals between fibers connecting to neighbor nodes and from/to local TXPs/TRXs. There exists a variety of configurations differing in functionality and complexity. We assume the setting depicted in the lower part of Fig. 2. It is *colorless* and *directionless*, meaning that any incoming WDM signal is switchable to any output fiber (as long as there is only one fiber pair to each neighbor node). Each wavelength may only be used once in the node. Key components are optical splitters relaying channels to neighbor nodes and wavelength selective switches (WSS), which are able to select any wavelength from either the local ring or the incoming fiber. In addition, WSSs act as multiplexer (mux) and demultiplexer (demux) to insert and drop locally terminated channels.

Optical (i. e. analog) signal amplification is not only needed at the input and output of the optical node, but also along the fibers. Typically, an optical line amplifier (OLA) is placed every 80 km. Introducing noise, this in turn limits the distance without electrical (i. e. digital) signal regeneration (essentially by two back-to-back TXPs) to between 800 km and 4000 km.

Like in the IP layer, the optical components present in nodes are organized in shelves providing power supply, cooling, and control (cf. Fig. 2, top). Such shelf systems are e. g. ALU 1830 Photonic Service Switch, ADVA FSP 3000 or Cisco ONS 15454 Multiservice Transport Platform.

3   Static Power Consumption Values

We derive our power model from static (maximum) power values for Cisco's CRS-3, ONS 15454 MSTP, and their respective components, as well as a stand-alone EDFA by Finisar. We mainly refer to Cisco equipment since to our knowledge, Cisco is the only vendor to publicly provide power values of individual components for both core router and WDM equipment. This also makes our work comparable to that of other researchers who use the same data for similar reasons [6,7,35]. Table 1 lists the static power values (along with variables referring to them in Sect. 4.2). They are largely identical to the ones in the Powerlib[5].

---

[5] Cf. http://powerlib.intec.ugent.be and [6].

Table 1. Static power values per component. Symbols are explained in section 4.

Component type	Power Consumption	Number installable	Source
FCC control per chassis	1068 W $/\eta := P_{SCC}$	1 for 9 LCC	[21]
Switch Fabric Card for FCC	229 W $/\eta := P_{S2SFC}$	8 for 3 LCC	[21]
Optical Interface Module	166 W $/\eta := P_{OIM}$	8 for 3 LCC	[21]
Chassis Control	275 W $/\eta := P_{CC}$	2 per LCC	[22]
Fan Tray	344 W $/\eta := P_{CU}$	2 per LCC	[6]
Switch Fabric Card for LCC	206 W $/\eta := P_{SFC}$	8 per LCC	[6]
140G Forwarding Engine	446 W $/\eta := P_{FE}$	1 to 16 per LCC	[6]
1x 100G LR-TRX	180 W $/\eta \in P_{TRX}$	1 per FE	[23]
2x 40G LR-TRX	150 W $/(2 \cdot \eta) \in P_{TRX}$	1 per FE	[6]
4x 10G LR-TRX	150 W $/(4 \cdot \eta) \in P_{TRX}$	1 per FE	[6]
1x 100G SR-port card	150 W $/\eta \in P_{PC}$	1 per FE	[6]
2x 40G SR-port card	185 W $/\eta \in P_{PC}$	1 per FE	[24]
4x 40G SR-port card	185 W $/\eta \in P_{PC}$	1 per FE	[25]
14x 10G SR-port card	150 W $/\eta \in P_{PC}$	1 per FE	[6]
20x 10G SR-port card	150 W $/\eta \in P_{PC}$	1 per FE	[6]
1x 100G SR-TRX (CFP)	12 W $/\eta \in P_{TRX}$	1 per 100G PC	[26]
1x 100G SR-TRX (CXP)	6 W $/\eta \in P_{TRX}$	1 per 100G TXP	[27]
1x 40G SR-TRX	8 W $/\eta \in P_{TRX}$	1 to 4 per 40G PC	[28]
1x 10G SR-TRX	3.5 W $/\eta \in P_{TRX}$	1 to 14 per 10G PC	[27]
1x 100G TXP (excl. SR-TRX)	133 W $/\eta \in P_{TXP}$	6 per 100G-Shelf	[29]
1x 40G TXP (incl. SR-TRX)	129 W $/\eta \in P_{TXP}$	6 per shelf	[30]
1x 10G TXP (excl. SR-TRX)	50 W $/\eta \in P_{TXP}$	12 per shelf	[6]
OLA standalone	50 W $/\eta := P_{OLA}$	1 every 80 km	[31]
OLA card	40 W $/\eta := P_{Amp}$	2 on every edge	[32]
WSS card	20 W $/\eta := P_{WSS}$	1 on every edge	[33],[6]
12-Port Optics Shelf	260 W $/\eta := P_{OS}$	-	[34],[33]
6-Port Optics Shelf (100G)	284 W	-	[34]

In the CRS-3, the components are combined as follows: One LCC houses one to eight power supply modules, which can reach an efficiency of about 95 % [21]. In addition, there are two fan trays and two CC cards (also acting as RE). The switch fabric is realized by an output-buffered Beneš network distributed on 8 parallel SFCs. A multi-chassis configuration requires an FCC with a set of control modules and eight special SFCs and optical interface modules (OIM) per group of three LCCs [7]. The LCCs then use a different type SFCs with a similar power consumption. We use the most powerful type of FE (or *Modular Services Card*) capable of 140 Gbps, which allows for PCs with a maximum of 1x 100G, 3x 40G or 14x 10G ports at full line rate. On the optical layer, we consider TXPs matching these performance values. While the 40G TXP has an integrated SR-interface, the 100G TXP and 10G TXP need additional SR-TRXs.

For the ONS 15454 MSTP version with 100G-capable backplane, Cisco lists a power consumption of 284 W for shelf, cooling, and controller card [34]. We estimate the power consumption of the larger 12-port version, for which no such reference is available, to 260 W, since both cooling and CC are slightly less power-hungry for this version (although exact numbers vary between references[6]). Contrary to the specification, we assume that the 12-port version can hold the 100G TXP as long as the backplane is not used. Unlike the stand-alone OLA, the OLA modules for the shelves are unidirectional. Consequently, two of them are deployed for each connection to another router. The WSS is Cisco's 80-channel WXC, which additionally comprises a passive beam splitter.

---

[6] Cf. tables A-1, A-4 and A-5 from [34] and table A-1 from [33].

4   Dynamic Resource Operation and Power Model

We derive a dynamic model for the momentary power consumption of a hypo-
thetical core network node with extended power saving features. For the application in network-level studies, we limit the scope of power scaling to adapting
processing capacity to the amount of packet-switched traffic and modifying optical circuits (along with the hierarchically required resources like LCs and LCCs).
The according scaling mechanisms operate at different time scales: To follow fast
fluctuations of the packet rate, processing capacity needs adaptation in the order
of microseconds. In contrast, establishing or tearing down an optical circuit takes
in the order of several minutes due to transient effects in OLAs. We assume that
this latter time scale enables the (de)activation of any electronic component.

   In the following, we discuss the power scaling possibilities of the node's components. We then describe the resulting model.

4.1   Dynamic Operation and Power Scaling Assumptions

Power Supply: We expect the CRS power supply modules to behave like the
most efficient Cisco models, which reach an efficiency of at least $\eta = 90\,\%$ in
a load range of 25 % to 90 % [36]. Since chassis are operable with a varying
number of such modules, we assume that we can switch modules off to stay in
the 90 % efficiency region. We accordingly derive the gross power consumption
by increasing all power values by a factor of $1/\eta \approx 1.11$.

Cooling: The affinity laws relate the power consumption P_i of fans at operation point i to their rotational speed N_i by $P_1/P_2 = (N_1/N_2)^3$. The normal operation range of CRS fans is 3300 RPM to 5150 RPM, with the maximum rated at 6700 RPM [37]. We obtain a net minimum power consumption of
$(3300/6700)^3 \approx 12\,\%$ of the total fan tray power. Accounting for driver overhead,
we estimate the static fraction at 20 % and let the remainder scale linearly with
the number of active LCs, since these produce the largest share of heat.

Chassis Controller Cards: Being a small general-purpose server system, the CC
can readily benefit from power saving features like dynamic voltage and frequency scaling (DVFS) or power-efficient memory [38]. We do however not model
the control workload and consequently consider that the CC consume constant
(maximum) power.

Switch Fabric: The interconnection structure prohibits the scaling of SFCs along
with LCs, and the signaling time overhead for SFC (de)activation impedes an
adaptation to the switched IP traffic. We therefore assume all SFCs to be active
when their LCC is so, and we disregard power scaling options of ASICs and
memory *on* SFCs. For multi-chassis routers, we allow active SFCs and OIMs in
the FCC to scale with LCCs in accordance with possible static configurations
(i. e. we switch blocks of eight SFCs and OIMs per group of three LCCs).

Forwarding Engine Cards: ASICs and NPs account for 48 % of the power budget of a LC, memory for 19 %; the remaining 33 % is spent on power conversion, control and auxiliary logic [39]. We assume the latter part to be static. The same applies to 9 % (out of the 19 %) of memory power consumption for the forwarding information base [40]. The remainder (10 % of the LC consumption) is for buffer memory, which is presumably dimensioned for the 140 Gbps capacity of the FE following the bandwidth-delay product (BDP) rule. We let the active buffer memory scale according to the BDP with the capacity of the active circuits terminated by the LC. Neglecting the residual power consumption in deep sleep state and the discrete nature of switchable memory units [40], we assume the buffer's power consumption to scale linearly with the active port capacity.

Recent NP designs support power saving by switching off unused components, e.g. cores [19,41,42]. In theory, deactivating and applying DVFS to NP cores alone can save more than 60 % in low traffic situations [43]. We therefore assume that 70 % of the power consumption of ASICs and NPs dynamically scales with processed IP traffic, while 30 % is static. In sum, we assign 33 % + 9 % + (30 % · 48 %) = 56.4 % statically to an active LC; we let 10 % scale with the active port capacity and 70 % · 48 % = 33.6 % with processed traffic.

Port Cards, Transceivers, Transponders: Like the latest hardware generation [16,41], we allow the dynamic deactivation of unused LC ports. We assume that a (multi-port) PC is active along with the FE as long as one of its ports is so. TRXs and TXPs are switched on and off with the respective circuits. We disregard more fine-grained power scaling proposals for TXP ASICs [44], but we do assume that the transmit and receive parts of a TXP may be activated separately[7]. In case of a PC with multiple colored interfaces, we distribute the total power consumption of the PC to the ports and let it scale with the circuits.

Optical Node: We consider the power consumption for cooling, power supply, and control of an optics shelf as static, since it is much less than the consumption of the respective LCC modules. The same applies to OLAs and WSSs. We do however allow the deactivation of TXP-hosting shelves when all TXPs are switched off.

4.2 Resulting Power Model

For the mathematical model, we use the following conventions: Capital letters without indexes represent equipment-specific constants. C_α denotes capacity in Gbps, P_α maximum power consumption and N_α the maximum installable quantity of component α. The set of all possible values for P_α is denoted by $\boldsymbol{P}_\alpha$. Indexed variables denote a specific component in a specific node. Variables of the type n_β represent dimensioning parameters describing the configuration of one node. Small letters indicate model parameters characterizing the dynamic configuration and load situation.

---

[7] The power distribution between the parts is of minor relevance since one of each is needed for one circuit.

A router may consist of a maximum of $N_{\text{LCC}} = 9$ LCCs; the actual number is $n_{\text{LCC}} \in \{1..N_{\text{LCC}}\}$. If the router has more than one LCC, a FCC is needed. In this case the first factor of (1) is nonzero, and so is $P_{\text{FCC,stat}}$.

A LCC is always equipped with $N_{\text{SFC}} = 8$ SFCs, $N_{\text{CC}} = 2$ CC cards and $N_{\text{CU}} = 2$ cooling units. We consider 20 % of the cooling power consumption as static, resulting in the total static LCC consumption in (2). The remaining 80 % of the cooling units gives the dynamic power consumption of LCC i with x_i active out of $n_{\text{LC},i} \in \{1..N_{\text{LC}}\}$ installed LCs according to (3). One LCC houses at most $N_{\text{LC}} = 16$ LCs. An active LC statically consumes 56.4% of P_{FE} and the total of the respective port card out of $\boldsymbol{P}_{\text{PC}}$. The power cost of the j-th LC in LCC i is thus given by (4). The power consumption per active port has two components: The packet buffers of the FE and the respective TRX $P_{\text{TRX},ij} \in \boldsymbol{P}_{\text{TRX}}$. For colored LC interfaces, $P_{\text{TRX},ij}$ is the consumption of the PC over the number of ports and $P_{\text{PC},ij} = 0$. The buffer's consumption (10 % of P_{FE}) is scaled to the capacity of one port $C_{\text{P},ij}$ ($C_{\text{FE}} = 140$ Gbps is the total capacity of the FE). The dynamic LC power share is obtained by multiplying these contributions by the number of active ports y_{ij}, (5). Equation (6) represents the traffic-dependent power consumption of a LC. The variable z_{ij} indicates the traffic demand in Gbps at LC j in LCC i.

In the optical layer, we assume a ring configuration according to Fig. 2. Each of the n_{d} links to a neighbor node requires one WSS module and two amplifiers. The router is connected through two additional WSS modules. WSS modules, amplifiers and TXPs each use one of 12 available slots in an optics shelf. This adds up to the static power of optical components $P_{\text{Opt,stat}}$ in (7), where n_λ is the maximum number of wavelengths needed on one link, $N_\lambda = 80$ the maximum number of wavelengths per fiber and P_{WSS}, P_{Amp} and P_{OS} are the power consumptions of a WSS module, OLA module and optics shelf respectively. n_{TXP} is the number of installed TXPs.

$$P_{\text{FCC,stat}} = \left\lceil \frac{n_{\text{LCC}} - 1}{N_{\text{LCC}}} \right\rceil \left(\left\lceil \frac{n_{\text{LCC}}}{3} \right\rceil \cdot 8(P_{\text{OIM}} + P_{\text{S2SFC}}) + P_{\text{SCC}} \right) . \quad (1)$$

$$P_{\text{LCC,stat}} = N_{\text{SFC}} \cdot P_{\text{SFC}} + N_{\text{CC}} \cdot P_{\text{CC}} + N_{\text{CU}} \cdot P_{\text{CU}} \cdot 20\% . \quad (2)$$

$$P_{\text{LCC,dyn},i}(x_i) = \frac{x_i}{N_{\text{LC}}} \cdot N_{\text{CU}} \cdot P_{\text{CU}} \cdot 80\% . \quad (3)$$

$$P_{\text{LC,stat},ij} = P_{\text{FE}} \cdot 56.4\% + P_{\text{PC},ij} . \quad (4)$$

$$P_{\text{LC,dyn},ij}(y_{ij}) = \left(\frac{P_{\text{FE}} \cdot 10\%}{C_{\text{FE}}} \cdot C_{\text{P},ij} + P_{\text{TRX},ij} \right) \cdot y_{ij} . \quad (5)$$

$$P_{\text{LC,traff},ij}(z_{ij}) = \frac{48\% \cdot 70\% \cdot P_{\text{FE}}}{C_{\text{FE}}} \cdot z_{ij} . \quad (6)$$

$$P_{\text{Opt,stat}} = \left\lceil \frac{n_\lambda}{N_\lambda} \right\rceil \cdot \left(n_{\text{d}} \cdot (P_{\text{WSS}} + 2 \cdot P_{\text{Amp}}) + 2 \cdot P_{\text{WSS}} \right) + \left\lceil \left(\left\lceil \frac{n_\lambda}{N_\lambda} \right\rceil \cdot (n_{\text{d}} \cdot 3 + 2) + n_{\text{TXP}} \right) \cdot \frac{1}{12} \right\rceil \cdot P_{\text{OS}} . \quad (7)$$

Equation (8) finally gives the dynamic consumption $P_{\text{Opt,dyn}}$ of the TXPs connected to LC j in LCC i.

$$P_{\text{Opt,dyn}}(y_{ij}) = \sum_{i=1}^{n_{\text{LCC}}} \sum_{j=1}^{n_{\text{LC},i}} P_{\text{TXP},ij} \cdot y_{ij} \ . \tag{8}$$

5   Application Example

We illustrate the application of the dynamic power model by evaluating the power savings achieved by different degrees of network reconfiguration assuming two different node configurations.

5.1   Scenario

Node Configuration. We assume WDM channels of 40 Gbps, which are terminated either by colored LC interfaces (*case A*) or by TXPs in a WDM shelf connected to LCs via short-reach optics (*case B*). While each LC can only feature one interface in case A, we serve up to three 40 Gbps channels with one LC in case B. In both cases, add/drop traffic is handled by 10 Gbps short-reach interfaces on dedicated tributary LCs (with up to 14 such interfaces). Unlike resources on the core network side, all tributary interfaces are constantly active. Table 2 gives the numerical power values. The port comprises TXP (and SR-TRX in case B) as well as the dynamic line card power share. Values for the optical equipment are used in (7) according to node dimensioning.

Network and Traffic. We present results for the 22-node Géant reference network (available from SNDLib [45]) using ten days out of demand traces collected in 2005 [46]. Assuming similar statistical properties in these ten days, we give 95 % confidence intervals for the metrics. To vary the network load, we linearly scale the demand traces and quantify this scaling based on a *peak demand matrix* containing the peak values of each node-to-node demand trace. We scale the traces such that the average of the values in the peak demand matrix ranges between 2 Gbps and 160 Gbps, corresponding to a total peak demand (sum over all values in the matrix) of 924 Gbps to 73.9 Tbps.

Resource Adaptation. We consider three operation schemes and evaluate the power consumption every 15 minutes: (*i*) In a static network configuration (regarding virtual topology and demand routes optimized for the peak demand matrix), we let active resources scale with the load. This corresponds to FUFL in [11]. (*ii*) We reconfigure the virtual topology by periodically applying the *centralized dynamic optical bypassing* (CDOB) scheme according to [17], using the actual power consumption as cost function with the simulated annealing-based solution method. (*iii*) The static operation of all resources dimensioned for the peak demand matrix serves as baseline.

Table 2. Power values (in Watts)

Component	Contribution	Case A	Case B
FCC	static if >1 LCC	1124	1124
SFC in FCC	per 3 LCC	3326	3326
LCC	if ≥ 1 LC on	2336	2336
LC	if ≥ 1 port on	286	471
Port	per circuit	163	150
Tributary LC	static	436	436
Tributary port	static	3.5	3.5
IP processing	per Gbps	1.07	1.07
Optics shelf	per 12 units	260	260
WSS+2Ampl.	static	100	100
2 WSS	static	40	40

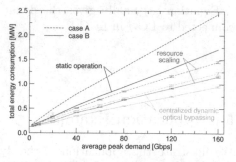

Fig. 3. Network-wide power consumption

5.2   Results

Fig. 3 plots the average power consumption of all devices in the network over the average peak demand for the different configuration cases and adaptation schemes. As one would expect, the power consumption increases with the load in all cases. We further observe that the power consumption is systematically higher for case A compared to the same adaptation scheme in case B: the savings due to the higher port density per LC and per LCC overcompensate the cost for additional short-reach optics.

Energy savings by resource adaptation in an otherwise static network config-uration range between 20 % for low average load and 40 % for high load in case A. The increasing benefits are explained by a higher number of parallel circuits allowing deactivation. CDOB likewise requires a certain amount of traffic to be effective and yields 10 additional percentage points of savings over the simple dynamic resource operation at maximum load. In case B, the achievable savings only range between 20 % and 33 % (resp. 44 % for CDOB), albeit at an alto-gether lower power consumption level. This effect is explained by the resource hierarchy: unlike in case A, LCs may need to remain active when only a fraction of their ports is used.

6   Conclusion

In this paper, we derived a dynamic power model for IP-over-WSON network equipment assuming the presence of state-of-the-art power-saving techniques in current network devices. Based on an in-depth discussion of the power scaling behavior of the components of the devices, we express the dynamic power con-sumption of a network node as a function of the optical circuits it terminates and the pieces of the hardware hierarchy (line cards, racks) required for this. In ad-dition, a smaller share of power scales with the amount of electrically processed traffic.

Lacking reliable data on power scaling options for optical switching equip-ment and amplifiers, we assume that the power consumption of these devices is independent of the load. While the model is open to improvement in this respect, the impact of this limitation is small given the predominance of the power consumption of IP layer equipment and transceivers.

By applying our power model to different network resource adaptation schemes in an example scenario, we found that dynamic resource operation can reduce the total power consumption of the network by 20 % to 50 %. However, generalizing these figures requires much caution since they strongly depend on the assumed resource dimensioning in the static reference case.

Future work could extend the dynamic power model in order to take new devices and trends into account. E. g., the power consumption of rate-adaptive transponders could be modeled. Likewise, different optical node variants could be included. Besides, the model awaits application in research on network reconfiguration.

Acknowledgments. The work presented in this paper was partly funded within the SASER project SSEN by the German Bundesministerium für Bildung und Forschung under contract No. 16BP12202.

References

1. Baliga, J., et al.: Energy consumption in optical IP networks. J. Lightwave Technol. 27(13) (2009)
2. Hinton, K., et al.: Power consumption and energy efficiency in the Internet. IEEE Netw. 25(2) (2011)
3. De-Cix: Traffic statistics (2013), http://www.de-cix.net/about/statistics/
4. Chabarek, J., et al.: Power awareness in network design and routing. In: Proc. INFOCOM (2008)
5. Hülsermann, R., et al.: Analysis of the energy efficiency in IP over WDM networks with load-adaptive operation. In: Proc. 12th ITG Symp. on Photonic Netw. (2011)
6. Van Heddeghem, W., et al.: Power consumption modeling in optical multilayer networks. Photonic Netw. Communic. 24 (2012)
7. Wang, L., et al.: Energy efficient design for multi-shelf IP over WDM networks. In: Proc. Computer Communic. Workshops at INFOCOM (2011)
8. Wu, Y., et al.: Power-aware routing and wavelength assignment in optical networks. In: Proc. ECOC (2009)
9. Silvestri, A., et al.: Wavelength path optimization in optical transport networks for energy saving. In: Proc. ICTON (2009)
10. Chiaraviglio, L., et al.: Reducing power consumption in backbone networks. In: Proc. ICC (2009)
11. Idzikowski, F., et al.: Dynamic routing at different layers in IP-over-WDM networks – maximizing energy savings. Optical Switching and Netw. 8(3) (2011)
12. Bathula, B.G., et al.: Energy efficient architectures for optical networks. In: Proc. London Commun. Symp. (2009)
13. Vasić, N., et al.: Energy-aware traffic engineering. In: Proc. e-Energy (2010)
14. Puype, B., et al.: Power reduction techniques in multilayer traffic engineering. In: Proc. ICTON (2009)
15. Restrepo, J., et al.: Energy profile aware routing. In: Proc. Green Communic. Workshops at ICC (2009)

16. Lange, C., et al.: Network element characteristics for traffic load adaptive network operation. In: Proc. ITG Symp. on Photonic Netw. (2012)
17. Feller, F.: Evaluation of centralized solution methods for the dynamic optical by-passing problem. In: Proc. ONDM (2013)
18. Ungerman, J.: IP NGN backbone routers for the next decade (2010), http://www.cisco.com/web/SK/expo2011/pdfs/SP_Core_products_and_technologies_for_the_next_decade_Josef_Ungerman.pdf
19. Alcatel-Lucent: New DNA for the evolution of service routing: The FP3 400G network processor (2011)
20. Wheeler, B.: EZchip breaks the NPU mold. Mircoprocessor Report (2012)
21. Cisco: CRS Carrier Routing System Multishelf System Description (2011)
22. Cisco: CRS 16-slot line card chassis performance route processor data sheet (2012)
23. Cisco: CRS 1-port 100 gigabit ethernet coherent DWDM interface module data sheet (2012)
24. Cisco: CRS 2-port 40GE LAN/OTN interface module data sheet (2013)
25. Cisco: CRS 4-port 40GE LAN/OTN interface module data sheet (2012)
26. Cisco: 100GBASE CFP modules data sheet (2012)
27. Cisco: Pluggable optical modules: Transceivers for the cisco ONS family (2013)
28. Cisco: 40GBASE CFP modules data sheet (2012)
29. Cisco: ONS 15454 100 Gbps coherent DWDM trunk card data sheet (2013)
30. Cisco: ONS 15454 40 Gbps CP-DQPSK full C-band tuneable transponder card data sheet (2012)
31. Finisar: Stand alone 1RU EDFA (2012)
32. Cisco: Enhanced C-band 96-channel EDFA amplifiers for the cisco ONS 15454 MSTP data sheet (2012)
33. Cisco: ONS 15454 DWDM Reference Manual – Appendix A. (2012)
34. Cisco: ONS 15454 Hardware Installation Guide – Appendix A. (2013)
35. Rizzelli, G., et al.: Energy efficient traffic-aware design of on–off multi-layer translucent optical networks. Comput. Netw. 56(10) (2012)
36. 80 PLUS: Certified power supplies and manufacturers – Cisco
37. Cisco: CRS Carrier Routing System 16-Slot Line Card Chassis System Description. (2012)
38. Malladi, K.T., et al.: Towards energy-proportional datacenter memory with mobile DRAM. In: Proc. ISCA (2012)
39. Epps, G., et al.: System power challenges (2006), http://www.cisco.com/web/about/ac50/ac207/proceedings/POWER_GEPPS_rev3.ppt
40. Vishwanath, A., et al.: Adapting router buffers for energy efficiency. In: Proc. CoNEXT (2011)
41. EZchip: NP-4 product brief (2011)
42. Ungerman, J.: Anatomy of Internet routers (2013), http://www.cisco.com/web/CZ/ciscoconnect/2013/pdf/T-VT3_Anatomie_Routeru_Josef-Ungerman.pdf
43. Mandviwalla, M., et al.: Energy-efficient scheme for multiprocessor-based router linecards. In: Proc. SAINT (2006)
44. Le Rouzic, E., et al.: TREND towards more energy-efficient optical networks. In: Proc. ONDM (2013)
45. Orlowski, S., et al.: SNDlib 1.0–Survivable Network Design Library. Netw. 55(3), 276–286 (2010)
46. Uhlig, S., et al.: Providing public intradomain traffic matrices to the research community. SIGCOMM Comput. 36 (2006)

A Generic Multi-layer Network Optimization Model with Demand Uncertainty

Uwe Steglich[1], Thomas Bauschert[1], Christina Büsing[2], and Manuel Kutschka[3]

[1] Chair for Communication Networks, Chemnitz University of Technology,
09107 Chemnitz, Germany
{uwe.steglich,thomas.bauschert}@etit.tu-chemnitz.de
[2] Lehrstuhl für Operations Research, RWTH Aachen University,
52062 Aachen, Germany
buesing@or.rwth-aachen.de
[3] Lehrstuhl II für Mathematik, RWTH Aachen University,
52062 Aachen, Germany
kutschka@math2.rwth-aachen.de

Abstract. In this work we introduce a mixed integer linear program
(MILP) for multi-layer networks with demand uncertainty. The goal is
to minimize the overall network equipment costs containing basic node
costs and interface costs while guarding against variations of the traffic demand. Multi-layer network design requires technological feasible
inter-layer connections. We present and evaluate two layering configurations, *top-bottom* and *variable*. The first layering configuration utilizes
all layers allowing shortcuts and the second enables layer-skipping. Technological capabilities like *router-offloading* and layers able to *multiplex*
traffic demand are also included in the model. Several case studies are
carried out applying the Γ-robustness concept to take into account the
demand uncertainties. We investigate the dependency of the robustness
parameter Γ on the overall costs and possible cost savings by enabling
layer-skipping.

Keywords: network, design, multi-layer, uncertainty, robustness.

1 Introduction and Motivation

Today's telecommunication networks utilize different technologies for transporting multiple services like voice calls, web-content, television and business services. The traffic transported in networks is steadily increasing and operators
have to extend their network capacities and migrate to new technologies. In the
competitive market operators want to reduce overall network costs as much as
possible. The nature of multi-layer networks allows a wide range of technological
possibilities for transporting traffic through its layers. Evaluating all technological feasible interconnections provides a great potential in capital expenditures
(CAPEX) savings. Also operational expenditures (OPEX) reductions are possible due to the different energy consumption of the network equipment of each
layer.

T. Bauschert (Ed.): EUNICE 2013, LNCS 8115, pp. 13–24, 2013.

The traffic demand influences network planning fundamentally. Conservative traffic assumptions lead to over provisioning and underestimated traffic values to a congested network. To strike a balance between these two extremes, concepts of uncertain demand modeling can be applied. The simplest way is to allocate a safety gap to the given traffic demand values. More sophisticated concepts are the Γ-robust approach by Bertsimas and Sim [1,2] and the hose model approach by Duffield et al. [3]. Other formulations use stochastic programming, chance-constraints or a network design with several traffic matrices. Appropriate uncertainty models incorporate statistical insight of available historical data e.g. mean and peak demand values.

A further network planning challenge is the determination which technologies should be used in a multi-layered network. Multi-layer networks offer a high flexibility regarding the possibility of traffic offloading. Note that, it is not necessary that all nodes support all technologies.

Investigations about single-layer networks with uncertainty were performed for example by Koster et al. in [4] or by Orlowski in [5]. They focus on a logical (demand) layer and one physical layer. Multi-layer network models without demand uncertainty were proposed for example by Katib in [6] or Palkopoulou in [7]. The former deals with a strict layer structure of Internet Protocol/Multiprotocol Label Switching (IP/MPLS) over Optical Transport Network (OTN) over Dense Wavelength-Division Multiplex (DWDM) and the latter evaluates the influence of multi-homing in a multi-layer networking scenario. A multi-layer network model with uncertainty was suggested in [8] by Belotti et al. The authors apply the Γ-robust optimization approach for a two-layer network scenario (MPLS, OTN) with demand uncertainty. In [9] Kubilinskas et al. propose three formulations for designing robust two-layer networks.

In this paper we deal with the following problem: Determine a cost optimal multi-layer network design allowing technology selection at each node and incorporating traffic demand uncertainty. Compared to other formulations, our proposed MILP formulation yields full flexibility regarding the number of layers and integrates layer-skipping and router offloading.

The paper is structured as follows: In Sect. 2 we shortly describe the relevant layers in today's communication networks. We present a generic multi-layer network optimization model and include traffic uncertainty constraints. Section 3 describes the input data used in the case studies: network topologies, traffic demand data, path sets and cost figures. The results of the multi-layer network optimization with demand uncertainty are presented in Sect. 4. Section 5 concludes the paper and gives an outlook on our future work.

2 Optimization Model

Generally, core networks may comprise the following technological layers: IP layer, MPLS layer, OTN layer and DWDM layer. With MPLS, network operators can establish explicit paths independently from the IP routing. OTN is specified in ITU-T G.709 [10] and defines optical network elements enabling transport, switching and multiplexing of client signals. OTN introduces different Optical Transport Units (OTU) which serve as optical channel wrapper for Optical Data Units (ODU) in several granularities. Beyond OTN the optical multiplexing of different wavelengths onto one single fiber is realized by DWDM technology.

The traffic demand and its fluctuation can be treated as a further, logical layer. Thus, in our investigations we deal with five different layers.

A generic multi-layer network model was proposed in [7] to evaluate different homing architectures. We apply some modifications to this model and extend it to cope with traffic demand uncertainty.

Given is a set of layers $\mathcal{L}$ and for all $\ell \in \mathcal{L}$ an undirected graph with node set $\mathcal{N}_\ell$ and edges $\mathcal{E}_\ell$. A path set $\mathcal{P}_{\ell,j}$ with candidate paths is introduced for each layer $\ell \in \mathcal{L}$ and all commodities j. The interaction of two layers is also modeled by an edge. In the set $I_{\ell,n}$ different basic node types per layer $\ell \in \mathcal{L}$ and per node $n \in \mathcal{N}_\ell$ are specified. We define $\delta_\ell(n)$ to be the set of neighboring nodes of node n in layer ℓ.

We define the notation of layer sets as follows: $\mathcal{L}_\ell$ specifies the set containing all layers below the current layer ℓ. With $\mathcal{L}^\ell$ the set of layers above the current layer ℓ is indicated. We denote the highest, logical layer (DEMAND) with $\ell_{\max}$ and the lowest, physical layer (DWDM) with ℓ_0. Layers with subinterfaces are contained in $\mathcal{L}_{\text{sub}}$.

The notation for the flow-variables $x_{\text{i,ii,iii,iv}}$ is as follows: i is the source layer, ii the destination layer, iii the commodity or edge and iv the candidate path. The demand parameter $\alpha_{\ell,e}$ specifies the nominal value and $\hat{\alpha}_{\ell,e}$ the deviation value (difference between peak and nominal) of all demands between a node pair j/edge e in layer ℓ.

2.1 Approach for Uncertainty

Traffic demand uncertainty is introduced in a general way. Fluctuations are described through the variables $\beta_{\ell,e}$ for all layers $\ell \in \mathcal{L}$ and edges $e \in \mathcal{E}_\ell$. As uncertainty can be handled in different ways this allows us a universal formulation for these uncertainty variables. The uncertain traffic demand is transported in fractions across different layers.

We apply edge-based flow conservation. The constraints (1) describe the flow conservation including the uncertainty. On the left hand side all demands from higher layers except the highest layer are summed up and have to be less or equal to the sum of all outgoing demands on the right hand side. The multiplexing factor $\mu_{o,\ell}$ converts capacity granularities between the source s and current layer ℓ. Variables $x_{s,\ell,j,p}$ contain the amount of traffic flowing in and $x_{\ell,s,e,p}$ out of the current layer. With $\beta_{\ell,e}$ we increase the amount of incoming demand by the uncertain demand. Via parameters $\alpha_{\ell,e}$ direct demand on a certain edge e in a layer ℓ is allowed.

$$\sum_{\substack{s\in\mathcal{L}^\ell\setminus\{\ell_{\max}\}, \\ j\in\mathcal{E}_s, p\in\mathcal{P}_{\ell,j}:\, e\in p}} \mu_{s,\ell}x_{s,\ell,j,p} + \alpha_{\ell,e} + \beta_{\ell,e} \leq \sum_{\substack{s\in\mathcal{L}_\ell, \\ p\in\mathcal{P}_{s,e}}} x_{\ell,s,e,p} \quad \forall \ell\in\mathcal{L}\setminus\{\ell_0\}, \forall e\in\mathcal{E}_\ell.$$

(1)

We decided to use the Γ-robust approach by Bertsimas and Sim [1,2] where the fluctuation variables $\beta_{\ell,e}$ contain the worst case demand variation. New supplementary flow variables $\bar{x}$ are introduced. Uncertain flows start from layer $\ell_{\max}$ and terminate at a subset of lower layers. This holds true for all paths p in layer ℓ and for all commodities j. The formulation (2) explains the concept of Γ-robustness. The binary variables $v_{j,p}$ are relaxed to $0 \leq v_{j,p} \leq 1$ and are used to select at most Γ fractional demands to be on their peak value. The maximization ensures that these Γ uncertain demand fractions are chosen which have the largest influence on the necessary edge capacity.

$$\text{maximize} \quad \sum_{\substack{j\in\mathcal{E}_s, \\ p\in\mathcal{P}_{\ell,j}:\, e\in p}} \hat{a}_j\bar{x}_{s,\ell,j,p}v_{j,p}$$
$$\text{s.t.} \quad \sum_{j\in\mathcal{E}_s} v_{j,p} \leq \Gamma \tag{2}$$
$$0 \leq v_{j,p} \leq 1$$
$$\forall s\in\mathcal{L}, \forall e\in\mathcal{E}_\ell, \forall \ell\in\mathcal{L}_{\ell_{\max}}$$

As proposed in [1,8] this linear program can be dualized. The dual problem (DP) of the optimization problem in (2) is shown in (3). Compared to (2) the new dual variables $\vartheta_{\ell,e}$ and $\pi_{\ell,e,j,p}$ are introduced.

$$\text{minimize} \quad \Gamma\vartheta_{\ell,e} + \sum_{\substack{j\in\mathcal{E}_s, \\ p\in\mathcal{P}_{\ell,j}:\, e\in p}} \pi_{\ell,e,j,p}$$
$$\text{s.t.} \quad \vartheta_{\ell,e} + \pi_{\ell,e,j,p} \geq \hat{a}_j\bar{x}_{s,l,j,p} \tag{3}$$
$$\vartheta_{\ell,e}, \pi_{\ell,e,j,p} \geq 0$$
$$\forall s\in\mathcal{L}, \forall e\in\mathcal{E}_\ell, \forall \ell\in\mathcal{L}_{\ell_{\max}}$$

We use the DP to limit the lower bound of $\beta_{\ell,e}$ in our multi-layer network optimization model with uncertainty as shown in constraints (4) and (5).

$$\Gamma\vartheta_{\ell,e} + \sum_{\substack{j\in\mathcal{E}_s, \\ p\in\mathcal{P}_{\ell,j}:\, e\in p}} \pi_{\ell,e,j,p} \leq \beta_{\ell,e} \quad \forall \ell\in\mathcal{L}\setminus\mathcal{L}_0, \forall e\in\mathcal{E}_\ell \tag{4}$$

$$\vartheta_{\ell,e} + \pi_{\ell,e,j,p} \geq \mu_{\ell_{\max},\ell}\hat{\alpha}_j\bar{x}_{\ell_{\max},\ell,j,p} \quad \forall j\in\mathcal{E}_{\ell_{\max}}, \forall p\in\mathcal{P}_{\ell,j}:\, e\in p \tag{5}$$

By constraints (6) the sum of all fractions of uncertain demand $\bar{x}$ are enforced to be one.

$$\sum_{\substack{\ell\in\mathcal{L}\setminus\{\ell_{\max}\},\\ p\in\mathcal{P}_{\ell,j}}} \bar{x}_{\ell_{\max},\ell,j,p} = 1 \quad \forall j \in \mathcal{E}_{\ell_{\max}} \tag{6}$$

Uncertainty also has to be applied to the inter-layer node capacities. The number of access interfaces h between the layers is influenced by the additional demand entering this specific layer. We introduce new constraints for the lower bound of access interfaces originating in the highest layer into all other layers. The Γ-robustness is introduced by additional dual variables $\nu_{\ell,n}$ and $\lambda_{\ell,n,j,p}$ and reused fractional variables $\bar{x}$. These extensions are shown in constraints (7) and (8).

$$\Gamma\nu_{\ell,n} + \sum_{\substack{j\in\delta_\ell(n),\\ p\in\mathcal{P}_{\ell,j}}} \lambda_{\ell,n,j,p} \le h_{\ell_{\max},\ell,n} \quad \forall \ell \in \mathcal{L}\setminus\{\ell_{\max}\}, \forall n \in \mathcal{N}_{\ell_{\max}} \tag{7}$$

$$\nu_{\ell,n} + \lambda_{\ell,n,j,p} \ge \eta_{\ell_{\max},\ell}\hat{\alpha}_j\bar{x}_{\ell_{\max},\ell,j,p}$$
$$\forall \ell \in \mathcal{L}\setminus\{\ell_{\max}\}, \forall n \in \mathcal{N}_{\ell_{\max}}, \forall j \in \delta_\ell(n), \forall p \in \mathcal{P}_{\ell,j} \tag{8}$$

With (1) and (4) to (8) all requirements for handling traffic demand uncertainty in the generic multi-layer network optimization model are specified.

2.2 MILP with Uncertainty Extension

The objective (9) is to minimize the overall costs in all layers $\ell \in \mathcal{L}$. Costs are induced by all basic nodes k_ℓ and deployed interfaces y_ℓ (access and network interfaces) in each layer ℓ.

$$\text{minimize} \quad \sum_{\ell\in\mathcal{L}}(k_\ell + y_\ell) \tag{9}$$

For the intra-layer demand the needed number of network interfaces $z_{\ell,e}$ are calculated by summing up all demands for all commodities in this layer — see constraints (10).

$$\sum_{\substack{j\in\mathcal{E}_\ell,\\ p\in\mathcal{P}_{\ell,j}:e\in p}} x_{\ell,\ell,j,p} \le z_{\ell,e} \quad \forall \ell \in \mathcal{L}, \forall e \in \mathcal{E}_\ell \tag{10}$$

The inter-layer node capacities for all demands not originating in the highest layer have to fulfill the constraints (11).

$$\sum_{\substack{j\in\delta_\ell(n),\\ p\in\mathcal{P}_{\ell,j}}} \eta_{s,\ell}x_{s,\ell,j,p} \le h_{s,\ell,n} \quad \forall \ell \in \mathcal{L}\setminus\{\ell_{\max}\}, \forall s \in \mathcal{L}^\ell\setminus\{\ell_{\max}\}, \forall n \in \mathcal{N}_s \tag{11}$$

Edges from and a specific node might be used and thereby require installation of network interfaces. For cost calculation the number of installed network interfaces at a node is needed. This is formulated in constraints (12). $z_{\ell,e}$ contains the number of network interfaces on edge e and $w_{\ell,n}$ the number of network interfaces at node n of layer ℓ.

$$\sum_{e \in \delta_\ell(n)} z_{\ell,e} \leq w_{\ell,n} \quad \forall \ell \in \mathcal{L}, \forall n \in \mathcal{N}_\ell \tag{12}$$

Some layers have a maximum demand limit per edge. This restriction is modeled in constraints (13) using parameter $\gamma_{\ell,e}$.

$$z_{\ell,e} \leq \gamma_{\ell,e} \quad \forall \ell \in \mathcal{L}, \forall e \in \mathcal{E}_\ell \tag{13}$$

For the node capacity constraints we have to distinguish between layers with and without subinterfaces. In both cases the node capacity is determined by the number of network interfaces $w_{\ell,n}$ and the access interfaces $h_{s,\ell,n}$ into this layer ℓ. In case of subinterfaces a conversion factor $\eta_{s,\ell}$ is used. This is shown in constraints (14) and (15).

$$w_{\ell,n} + \sum_{s \in \mathcal{L}^\ell} h_{s,\ell,n} \leq q_{\ell,n} \quad \forall \ell \in \mathcal{L} \backslash \mathcal{L}_{\text{sub}}, \forall n \in \mathcal{N}_\ell \tag{14}$$

$$w_{\ell,n} + \sum_{s \in \mathcal{L}^\ell} \eta_{s,\ell} h_{s,\ell,n} \leq q_{\ell,n} \quad \forall \ell \in \mathcal{L}_{\text{sub}}, \forall n \in \mathcal{N}_\ell \tag{15}$$

Finally, in constraints (16), the costs are calculated based on the number of interfaces deployed in all nodes. The parameters φ_ℓ for basic nodes in layer ℓ and $\chi_{s,\ell}$ for access interfaces between layer s and ℓ are input parameters from the applied cost model.

$$\sum_{n \in \mathcal{N}_\ell} \varphi_\ell w_{\ell,n} + \sum_{\substack{s \in \mathcal{L}^\ell, \\ n \in \mathcal{N}_\ell}} \chi_{s,\ell} h_{s,\ell,n} \leq y_\ell \quad \forall \ell \in \mathcal{L} \tag{16}$$

The parameter $\psi_{\ell,d}$ represents the basic node costs depending on the basic node size d and layer ℓ. A binary decision variable $r_{\ell,d,n}$ is used to decide whether this node type is used. The overall costs of all basic nodes k_ℓ in a specific layer ℓ are derived by applying constraints (17).

$$\sum_{\substack{n \in \mathcal{N}_\ell, \\ d \in I_{\ell,n}}} \psi_{\ell,d} r_{\ell,d,n} \leq k_\ell \quad \forall \ell \in \mathcal{L} \tag{17}$$

The maximum number of interfaces of a node is specified by the basic node type and its capacity. Constraints (18) give an upper bound for the total number of deployed interfaces $q_{\ell,n}$.

$$q_{\ell,n} \leq \sum_{d \in I_{\ell,n}} d r_{\ell,d,n} \quad \forall \ell \in \mathcal{L}, \forall n \in \mathcal{N}_\ell \tag{18}$$

We restrict the installation of basic nodes at a location to exactly one type. This is enforced by constraints (19).

$$\sum_{d \in I_{\ell,n}} r_{\ell,d,n} \leq 1 \quad \forall \ell \in \mathcal{L}, \forall n \in \mathcal{N}_\ell \tag{19}$$

All bounds and limitations of the optimization variables are listed in (20).

$$
\begin{aligned}
k_\ell, y_\ell &\geq 0 && \forall \ell \in \mathcal{L} \\
x_{s,\ell,j,p} &\geq 0 && \forall \ell \in \mathcal{L}, \forall s \in \mathcal{L}, \forall j \in \mathcal{E}_s, \forall p \in \mathcal{P}_{s,j} \\
\bar{x}_{\ell_{\max},\ell,j,p} &\geq 0 && \forall \ell_{\max} \in \mathcal{L}_{\max}, \forall \ell \in \mathcal{L}, \forall j \in \mathcal{E}_\ell, \forall p \in \mathcal{P}_{\ell,j} \\
z_{\ell,e} &\in \mathbb{Z}^+ && \forall \ell \in \mathcal{L}, \forall e \in \mathcal{E}_\ell \\
h_{s,\ell,n} &\in \mathbb{Z}^+ && \forall \ell \in \mathcal{L}, \forall s \in \mathcal{L}^\ell, \forall n \in \mathcal{N}_\ell \\
w_{\ell,n} &\geq 0 && \forall \ell \in \mathcal{L}, \forall n \in \mathcal{N}_\ell \\
q_{\ell,n} &\in \mathbb{Z}^+ && \forall \ell \in \mathcal{L}, \forall n \in \mathcal{N}_\ell \\
r_{\ell,d,n} &\in \{0,1\} && \forall \ell \in \mathcal{L}, \forall n \in \mathcal{N}_\ell, \forall d \in I_{\ell,n} \\
\vartheta_{\ell,e}, \pi_{\ell,e,j,p} &\geq 0 && \forall \ell \in \mathcal{L}, \forall j \in \mathcal{E}_{\ell_{\max}}, \forall p \in \mathcal{P}_{\ell,j} : e \in p \\
\nu_{\ell,n}, \lambda_{\ell,n,j,p} &\geq 0 && \forall \ell \in \mathcal{L} \setminus \{\ell_{\max}\}, \forall n \in \mathcal{N}_{\ell_{\max}}, \forall j \in \delta_\ell(n), \forall p \in \mathcal{P}_{\ell,j}
\end{aligned}
\tag{20}
$$

2.3 MILP Size Estimation

In order to compare the complexity of the non-robust model with the model that includes Γ-robustness, we perform an estimation of the model sizes. In the following n is the number of nodes in all layers and p the overall number of paths in all layers.

The order of the number of variables increases from n^2 to $n^2 p$ and the order of the created number of constraints increases from $n^2 p$ to $n^4 p$ for the model with uncertainty. This is caused by the dual variables and the required constraints for modeling the uncertainty in flow conservation and inter-layer node capacity.

The MILP size is a critical point in terms of computation time and optimality gap. A possible reduction of the model size can be achieved by merging layers, decreasing the set of candidate paths in selected layers and by omitting nodes in specific layers.

3 Input Data for the Case Studies

3.1 Example Network Topologies

It is assumed that all layers comprise the same node set. First of all, we define an artificial, small-scale 5-node network topology. It contains nodes A to E, bidirectional edges (A, B), (A, D), (A, E), (B, C), (C, D), (C, E) and has an average nodal degree of 2.40. Furthermore, we use the Abilene and Géant topologies from SNDlib [11]. Abilene is a reference for a mid-scale network containing 12 nodes (avg. nodal degree 2.50) and Géant is a large-scale network with 22 nodes (avg. nodal degree 3.27).

Table 1. Layer mapping configurations *top-bottom* and *variable*

configuration	layer ℓ	$\mathcal{L}^\ell$	$\mathcal{L}_\ell$
variable	DEMAND	$\emptyset$	IP
	IP	DEMAND	MPLS, OTN, DWDM
	MPLS	IP	OTN, DWDM
	OTN	IP, MPLS	DWDM
	DWDM	IP, MPLS, OTN	$\emptyset$
top-bottom	DEMAND	$\emptyset$	IP
	IP	DEMAND	MPLS
	MPLS	IP	OTN
	OTN	MPLS	DWDM
	DWDM	OTN	$\emptyset$

3.2 Traffic Demand

For the 5-node network we assume nominal demand values of $\alpha = 20$ GBit/s for all end-to-end node pairs. Overall 10 demand pairs exist in this network. The deviation of the demand values are assumed to be $\hat{\alpha} = 0.5 \cdot \alpha$ for node pairs (A, B), (A, D) and to be $\hat{\alpha} = 0.25 \cdot \alpha$ for the other node pairs.

For Abilene and Géant traffic measurement traces can be found in SNDlib [11]. We use the first week measurements and set α to the nominal value and $\hat{\alpha}$ to the maximum minus the nominal value. In total Abilene has 66 and Géant 462 demand pairs.

3.3 Network Layers

In our case studies we consider five network layers: One logical layer DEMAND and four technological layers IP, MPLS, OTN and DWDM. However, the MILP theoretically supports an unlimited number of layers.

In Table 1 technologically feasible mappings between the layers are shown. We distinguish between *variable* and *top-bottom* configuration. The top-bottom configuration is a worst case scenario in terms of overall costs as all layers have to be used by all demands. The variable configuration enables a technology selection by skipping some of the layers.

For our calculations it is assumed that all layers have a interface granularity of 40 GBit/s except the logical demand layer which has a granularity of 1 GBit/s.

3.4   Cost Model

We only consider CAPEX costs for our case studies. In [12] by Huelsermann et al. a CAPEX cost model for multi-layer networks is provided where the costs are separated into three main parts:

1. Basic node costs: chassis, power supplies, cooling, etc.
2. Interface costs: interfaces placed within one layer ℓ
3. Access interface costs: interfaces from a layer s to a layer ℓ

All costs are normalized to the costs of a single 10G long-haul transponder and without any reference to a specific vendor. Basic node costs depend on the number of available slots. For IP and MPLS 16, 32, 48 and 64 slots with corresponding costs of 16.67, 111.67, 140.83 and 170.0 are distinguished. The costs for IP and MPLS equipment are assumed to be equal.

3.5   Path Sets

In the DWDM layer k-shortest paths are calculated choosing $k = 5$ for small- to mid-scale and $k = 2$ for large-scale networks. The DWDM-paths are modified and extended to provide path sets for the higher layers.

In [7] different bypassing options *Unrestricted, Restricted, Opaque* and *Transparent* were proposed. These options create different candidate paths for an end-to-end connection within a single layer. We apply the Restricted, Opaque and Transparent option for non-DWDM path sets. In addition to the k-shortest paths (Opaque) also the direct connection between source and destination exists (Transparent, bypassing at all intermediate nodes). Further paths are introduced by the Restricted option where specific nodes are skipped after a specific node hop count is exceeded. By use of these path sets we allow, that specific nodes might be skipped and traffic is offloaded. We assume a fully meshed graph in the logical DEMAND layer.

4   Results

In this section we present the results of our case studies. The main target is to evaluate whether our multi-layer network optimization model with uncertainty is solvable for realistic problem sizes applying off-the-shelf solvers.

For our calculations we use a conventional PC with multi-core CPU (Intel® Core™ i7-3930K CPU @ 3.20GHz) and 64 GBytes of memory. Operating system is Ubuntu in version 11.04. AMPL is used in version 20111121 and IBM® ILOG® CPLEX® in version 12.5. For the MIP gap tolerance the CPLEX default value of $1e-4$ is used and the time limit is set to 86400s (1 day).

In [13] was shown that choosing Γ to about 6% of the number of demands is already sufficient to provide total robustness. Therefore, we perform a parameter study regarding Γ and increase it from 0 (no uncertainty) up to 10 (at most ten demands on peak value). With the *top-bottom* configuration the overall real-runtime for the 5-node network is 124.2s (user-runtime 1264.6s). As can be seen from Fig. 1 increasing Γ rises the CAPEX costs up to 23% and influences mainly the DWDM layer. The reason is that the traffic demand is in the range of 50% of the interface capacities. Already two demands on nominal value utilize the interfaces completely. The course of the curve for the *variable* configuration is similar, except that the MPLS and OTN layers are skipped. The cheapest solution is to apply IP-over-DWDM in this case. The calculation time for *variable* configuration is slightly smaller compared to *top-bottom* with a real-runtime of 73.6s (user-runtime 672.9s). CAPEX increases by 25.6% when Γ is varied from 0 to 10.

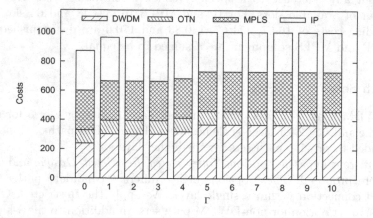

Fig. 1. CAPEX costs versus Γ uncertainty parameter for the 5-node network with *top-bottom* configuration

In case of the *variable* configuration the optimization results for Abilene and Géant are different compared to the 5-node network: the OTN layer is not skipped. The computing times and memory requirements increase substantially. For Abilene the computing time increases to a real-runtime of 218999.3s (user-runtime 1835679.0s) and for Géant to a real-runtime of 39625.0s (user-runtime 401265.4). The reason why Géant has a lower runtime is that only a set of $k = 2$ shortest paths are used compared to $k = 5$ for Abilene. If we use $k = 5$ also for Géant, CPLEX terminates with an out of memory exception.

In Fig. 2, for the Géant network a strong dependency on the parameter Γ can be observed. Already the step from no uncertainty to $\Gamma = 1$ raises CAPEX by 70.4%. For $\Gamma = 10$ a CAPEX increase of 117.2% is discovered.

The cost of the Abilene network does not change when introducing uncertainty. Independently from Γ the CAPEX costs are 1537.04 for the IP layer, 117.05 for the OTN layer and 86.76 for the DWDM layer. The MPLS layer is skipped. For none of the Abilene-runs the optimality gap was reached. Probably the reason is that the traffic demands do not match well to the granularity of the interface capacities yielding sufficient spare capacity to accommodate the traffic fluctuations. It is planned to perform further investigations on this issue.

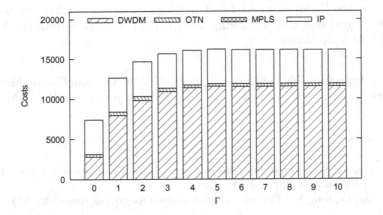

Fig. 2. CAPEX costs versus Γ uncertainty parameter for the Géant network with *variable* configuration

For both topologies (Abilene, Géant) the MPLS layer is skipped, but the OTN layer is used for grooming IP demands. This behavior is correct as the cost parameters of IP and MPLS are assumed to be equal.

5 Conclusion and Outlook

We introduced a generic multi-layer network optimization model with traffic uncertainty applying the Γ-robust approach. The model has full flexibility regarding the number of layers. Path sets are calculated with the special bypassing options *Unrestricted, Restricted* and *Opaque* or *Transparent*. These options allow router offloading and shortcuts for selected layers. Two possible layer mapping configurations *top-bottom* and *variable* are considered. The former yields a worst-case solution for passing all layers with shortcuts and the latter a cost minimal solution with shortcuts and layer-skipping.

We evaluated the MILP for different network sizes. Compared to the non-robust model the computing time for the robust model increases significantly. When using off-the-shelf solvers especially in mid- and large-scale networks todays computational power is still not sufficient to solve the problem to an optimality gap of $1e-4$. Hence, more advanced mathematical techniques for modeling and solving are needed.

By decreasing the size of the path sets for specific layers and the optimality gap for the multi-layer network model with uncertainty even large-scale networks remain solvable. Computing times are reasonable but the solver requires very large memory for improving the initial solution. Also modeling alternatives should be investigated for their potential to decrease the memory consumption for larger networks.

In our future work we will investigate several options to improve scalability and memory consumptions. We will analyze how different robustness metrics are influenced by the Γ parameter setting. Furthermore, we will continue our studies with an improved cost model allowing more realistic comparisons of the MPLS and the OTN layer options.

Acknowledgments. This work was supported by the German Federal Ministry of Education and Research (BMBF) via the research project ROBUKOM [14].

References

1. Bertsimas, D., Sim, M.: Robust discrete optimization and network flows. Mathematical Programming 95(1), 3–51 (2003)
2. Bertsimas, D., Sim, M.: The price of robustness. Operations Research 52(1), 35–53 (2004)
3. Duffield, N.G., Goyal, P., Greenberg, A., Mishra, P., Ramakrishnan, K.K., van der Merive, J.E.: A flexible model for resource management in virtual private networks. SIGCOMM Comput. Commun. Rev. 29(4), 95–108 (1999)
4. Koster, A.M.C.A., Kutschka, M., Raack, C.: Robust network design: Formulations, valid inequalities, and computations. Networks 61, 128–149 (2013)
5. Orlowski, S.: Optimal design of survivable multi-layer telecommunication networks. PhD thesis, Technische Universität Berlin (2009)
6. Katib, I.A.: IP/MPLS over OTN over DWDM multilayer networks: Optimization models, algorithms, and analyses. PhD thesis, University of Missouri (2011)
7. Palkopoulou, E.: Homing Architectures in Multi-Layer Networks: Cost Optimization and Performance Analysis. PhD thesis, Chemnitz University of Technology (2012)
8. Belotti, P., Kompella, K., Noronha, L.: A comparison of OTN and MPLS networks under traffic uncertainty. IEEE/ACM Transactions on Networking (2011)
9. Kubilinskas, E., Nilsson, P., Pioro, M.: Design models for robust multi-layer next generation Internet core networks carrying elastic traffic. Journal of Network and Systems Management 13(1), 57–76 (2005)
10. Telecommunication Standardization Sector of ITU: ITU-T Recommendation G.709: Interfaces for the optical transport network. International Telecommunication Union (2009)
11. Orlowski, S., Wessäly, R., Pióro, M., Tomaszewski, A.: SNDlib 1.0—survivable network design library. Networks 55(3), 276–286 (2010)
12. Huelsermann, R., Gunkel, M., Meusburger, C., Schupke, D.A.: Cost modeling and evaluation of capital expenditures in optical multilayer networks. Journal of Optical Networking 7(9), 814–833 (2008)
13. Koster, A.M.C.A., Kutschka, M., Raack, C.: Towards robust network design using integer linear programming techniques. In: 2010 6th EURO-NF Conference on Next Generation Internet (NGI), pp. 1–8. IEEE (2010)
14. Koster, A.M.C.A., Helmberg, C., Bley, A., Grötschel, M., Bauschert, T.: BMBF project ROBUKOM: Robust communication networks. In: Euro View 2012, Berlin, Offenbach. VDE-Verlag (2012)

Modeling and Quantifying the Survivability of Telecommunication Network Systems under Fault Propagation

Lang Xie, Poul E. Heegaard, and Yuming Jiang

Department of Telematics,
Norwegian University of Science and Technology,
7491 Trondheim, Norway
{langxie,Poul.Heegaard,jiang}@item.ntnu.no

Abstract. This paper presents a generic state transition model to quantify the survivability attributes of a telecommunication network under fault propagation. This model provides a framework to characterize the network performance during the transient period that starts after the fault occurrence, in the subsequent fault propagation, and until the network fully recovers. Two distinct models are presented for physical fault and transient fault, respectively. Based on the models, the survivability quantification analysis is carried out for the system's transient behavior leading to measures like transient connectivity. Numerical results indicate that the proposed modeling and analysis approaches perform well in both cases. The results not only are helpful in estimating quantitatively the survivability of a network (design) but also provide insights on choosing among different survivable strategies.

Keywords: survivability, analytical models, fault propagation.

1 Introduction

Telecommunication networks are used in diverse critical aspects of our society, including commerce, banking and life critical services. The physical infrastructures of communication systems are vulnerable to multiple correlated failures, caused by natural disasters, misconfigurations, software upgrades, latent failures, and intentional attacks. These events may cause degradations of telecommunication services for a long period. Understanding the functionality of a network in the event of disasters is provided by survivability analysis. Here, qualitative evaluation of network survivability may no longer be acceptable. Instead, we need to quantify survivability so that a network system is able to meet contracted levels of survivability.

1.1 Fault Propagation

An undesired event is an event which impacts system normal operation. It triggers faults, which cause an error. When the error becomes visible outside the

T. Bauschert (Ed.): EUNICE 2013, LNCS 8115, pp. 25–36, 2013.

system boders, we have a failure, i.e., the system does not behave as specified. An excellent explanation of fault, error, failure pathology is given in [12]. The types of such events include operational mistakes, malicious attacks, and large-scale disasters.

When multiple network elements (e.g. nodes or links) go down simultaneously due to a common event, we have multiple correlated failures. Different from single random link or node failure, multiple failures are often caused by natural disasters such as hurricane, earthquake, tsunami, etc., or human-made disasters such as electromagnetic pulse (EMP) attacks and weapons of mass destruction (WMD) [8]. Correlated failures can be cascading where the initial failures are followed by other failures caused by some propagating events. Therein, a network system may be vulnerable to a time sequence of single destructive faults. It starts by an initial event on a part of network and spreads to another part of the network. The propagation continues in a cascade-like manner to other parts. This phenomena is denoted as fault propagation. As few examples: the power outages and floods caused by 2005 US hurricane Katrina resulted in approximately 8% of all customarily routed networks in Louisiana outaged [9]; in the March 2011 earthquake and tsunami in east Japan, almost 6720 wireless base stations experienced long power outage [10]. Also, some studies warn that risk of WMD attacks on telecommunication networks is rising [8].

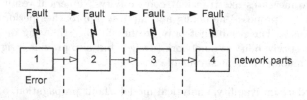

Fig. 1. Comparison of fault propagation and error propagation

Different from error propagation, fault propagation does not necessarily occur among interconnected network equipments. Since a fault may be an external event, it can occur in isolated parts of a network. The difference between fault propagation and error propagation is illustrated in Fig. 1. With the aim of developing a more realistic survivability model, fault propagating phenomena must be taken into account.

1.2   Related Work

Survivability is defined as the system's ability to continuously deliver services in compliance with the given requirements in the presence of failures and other undesired events [3]. Most of the literature on network survivability quantificaiton has been done on combating single-link or node failures [1],[2],[4]. Only a few studies have considered multiple failures. A state transition model for base station exposed to channel failures and disastrous failures was proposed in [11].

Nevertheless, this model only considers one base station without multiple or correlated base station failures. Our previous work [5] uses a continuous-time Markov chain (CTMC) to model and analyze the survivability of an infrastructure-based wireless network in the presence of disastrous failures and repairs. However, it considers only a single disaster scenario where failures are not correlated.

Very few studies have considered the quantification of network survivability against correlated failures caused by some propagating events. Therefore, there exists a critical need for appropriate quantitative, model-based evaluation techniques to address this limitation. In our previous work [6], we propose an approximative survivability model to take a disaster propagation scenario into account. To the best of our knowledge, this is the first work to quantify the survivability and the failure and repair rate tradeoffs of networks. However, such model does not distinguish the state of system before and after repair. We further relax these approximations and develop a more realistic mode in [7]. However, only a particular case of a three-subnetwork system is considered in this work.

In this paper we generalize our previous work in [7]. The resulting model turns out to be a general model that considers the fault propagation among n $(n > 0)$ sub-networks. Specifically, transient failures are integrated into the proposed model. The analysis results are helpful in estimating quantitatively the survivability, in terms of certain chosen performance metrics of a network (design). Further, they provide insights on specifying the values of repair rates required to achieve a con-tracted service performance and availability. Our goals are providing some critical inputs for network design and operation. For example, in network deployment in coastal areas, which are vulnerable to specific disaster types like flooding as well as hurricanes, the knowledge of network survivability is useful.

The rest of the paper is organized as follows. In Section 2, we develop Markov models for a system from the survivability quantificaiton view point. Section 3 analyzes the models that may be used to find the transient probabilities leading to the computation of transient survivability measures. Numerical results of the analysis performed on the models are presented in Section 4. Finally, Section 5 gives the conclusions along with some future directions in this area.

2 Markov Model for Survivability Quantification

A network system that is survivable consists of network design and management procedures to mitigate the effects of failures on the network services. To analyze and quantify the survivability attributes of such a network system, we have to take into account the propagating behavior of a fault as well as the network sys-tem's response to the fault propagation. Therefore, we would require a composite survivability model that incorporates the behavior of both these elements.

2.1 Network View

The network can be viewed as a directed graph consisting of nodes and directed edges. A node can be a single network equipment or a subnetwork. The directed edges denote the directions of possible disaster propagation among various nodes. We suppose the number of subnetworks in the networked system is n $(n > 0)$. Furthermore, we assume a disastrous event initially occurred on one subnetwork and then propagated from the affected subnetwork to another within a random time period. The process continues until no more subnetwork failures occur. Here, we mainly consider the multiple failures caused by some events such as natural disasters, intentional attacks, etc, which are among the main reasons that trigger fault propagation.

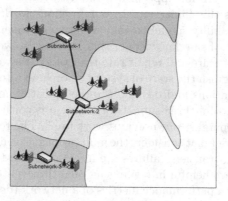

Fig. 2. Network example with three subnetworks

To illustrate the above view, we use a wireless network example. As depicted in Fig. 2, it consists of n (e.g. $n = 3$) subnetworks. The view shows the actual geographic layout of the network elements, such as cell site, radio network controller (RNC), mobile switching center (MSC) and so on. Assume a disastrous event occurs in subnetwork-1 at the beginning. Then the disastrous event propagates its effect to subnetwork-2, subnetwork-3 in successive steps. For the sake of illustration, the number of network elements in the figure does not necessarily equal to the real number. Our objective is to investigate the network performance during the transient period that starts after the disaster occurrence, in the subsequent disaster propagation and until the network fully recovers. For this, we define the (i) *undesired events* to be disastrous events, (ii) *service* to be the connections between access points and subscribers, (iii) *service requirement* to be a minimum number of access points that need to be operational for the service. It is remarked that our focus is "connectivity" and our focus is not about how to obtain the performance metric at a real network or network component. Thus we do not consider the dynamics brought by routing and traffic flows further in this paper.

We need a methodology to capture the transient variation of performance under fault propagation, as well as tractable. In what follows, we introduce a phased recovery model to quantify the survivability of network under fault propagation caused by disaster. The model is constructed stepwise, starting with only permanent hardware failures and gradually extending it to include software and transient hardware failures. The discussion here is not limited into a wireless network. We believe the methods and analysis presented can be applied to other telecommunication networks such as a public switched telephone network (PSTN), a data network, or an optical network.

2.2 Model I: Permanent Hardware Failures

The first model only considers failures that require manual repair, i.e., permanent hardware failures caused by the disasters (e.g. hurricanes, tornados, floods, earthquakes, and tsunamis) and environment (e.g. power outages).

A fault always tries to bring a network system into a failure state. This requires the fault to spend time and effort. In general, this time or effort is best modeled as a random variable. Once a fault is detected, the system needs to initiate appropriate recovery actions. The basic nature of this response would be to try to make the system move back to a normal state from a failure state. This movement requires time or effort on the system. As before, this time or effort is best modeled as a random variable that is described by a suitable probability distribution function. The system's response to a fault may be described by the states and transitions between these states. In order to analyze the survivability attributes of a network system, we need to consider the actions undertaken by a fault as well as the system's response to a fault. The transient period of our interest is assumed to evolve as a continuous-time stochastic process $\{X(\tau) : \tau \geq 0\}$. The state X of the n-subnetworks at any time τ can be completely described by the collection of the state of each subnetwork. That is, a n-dimensional vector

$$X(\tau) = (X_1(\tau), X_2(\tau), \cdots, X_n(\tau)), \qquad \tau \geq 0, \tag{1}$$

where for each subnetwork $X_l(\tau) = p$ (l is discrete; $l = 1, \cdots, n$) represents the state that a permanent hardware failure has occurred on the l-th subnetwork at time τ, $X_l(\tau) = o$ in the case when the l-th subnetwork works normally at time τ, and $X_l(\tau) = r$ if the l-th subnetwork has been repaired at time τ. Here, it is assumed that the service in state r restores to the same value as in normal state o.

The propagation is assumed to have 'memoryless' property: the probability of disastrous events spreading from one given subnetwork to another depends only on the current system state but not on the history of the system. The affected subnetwork can be repaired in a random period. Moreover, all the times of the disaster propagation and repair are exponentially distributed.

With the above assumptions, the transient process $X(\tau)$ can be mathematically modeled as a continuous-time Markov chain (CTMC) with state space $\Omega = \{(X_1, X_2, \cdots, X_n) : X_1, X_2, \cdots, X_n \in \{p, o, r\}\}$. The transition rate matrix of $X(\tau)$ is $\mathbf{Q}$.

In brief, the following summarizes the model:

- the state of each subnetwork at time t lies within the set $\{p, o, r\}$,
- at the initial time $t = 0$, a disastrous event hits the 1-st subnetwork, which changes the system state to $(p, o, \cdots, o)$,

- the disaster propagates from the subnetwork l (l is discrete; $l = 1, \cdots, n$) to subnetwork $l+1$ according to Poisson processes with rate $\lambda_{p(l+1)}$,
- a disastrous event can occur on only one subnetwork at a time,
- each subnetwork has a specific repair process which is *all at once* and the repair time of subnetwork l is exponentially distributed with mean $1/\mu_{pl}$,
- subnetworks with permanent failure are not repaired before all subnetworks are affected by the disaster,
- the propagation or repair transition is determined only by the current state, not on the path until reaching the current state.

Table 1. Transition generation rules for $\mathbf{Q}$

Condition	Q_{ab}	$a \rightarrow b$
Propagation phases:		
$'r' \notin a \&\& 'r' \notin b, a[0] = b[0] =' p'$	λ_{p2}	$(p,o,\cdots,o) \rightarrow (p,p,o,\cdots,o)$
	$\vdots$	$\vdots$
	λ_{pn}	$(p,\cdots,p,o) \rightarrow (p,\cdots,p)$
Repair phases:		
$f(b) = f(a) + 1, a[i] = b[j] =' r',$	μ_{pj}	
$i,j \in 1\cdots n, j \neq i$		

*Note: 1. f is the function to return
the number of 'r' in the state;
2. state $(r,\cdots,r) = (o,\cdots,o)$.

Our previous work [7] has provided a 3-subnetwork example in Section 2.1. Here we make a further step in constructing a general model for a network with n subnetworks. We consider the transition from one certain state a to b with rate Q_{ab}, where the state is represented as a vector as the form in Eq. (1). To distinguish the states in repair phases, we use a function f to counter the number of $'r'$ in the state. Table. 1 summarises the rules in constructing the infinitesimal generation matrix of model I for a network with a general number of subnetworks n ($n > 0$; n is discrete).

2.3   Model II: Transient Failures

Transient failure is a brief malfunction that often occurs at irregular and unpredictable times, which has in most systems a significant impact on the reliability and survivability. Some examples of transient failures are electromagnetic interference and radiation, noise on a transmission line and alpha-particles passing through RAM flipping bits. The restoration after a transient failure does not require manual maintenance and repair, it is often the case that the automatic reboot fix the problem. As an important type of failure, transient failure is largely overlooked in network survivability modeling. In the following, we will integrate the impact of transient failures into the system model.

It is necessary to distinguish between permanent and transient failures. We add a new value to the state space, that is, $X_l(t) = t$ represents the state that a transient failure has occurred on the l-th subnetwork at time τ. The following summarizes the increased model assumptions:

- the state of each subnetwork at time τ lies within the set $\{p, t, o, r\}$,
- the disaster propagates from the subnetwork l (l is discrete; $l = 1, \cdots, n$) to subnetwork $l + 1$ according to Poisson processes with rate $\lambda_{p(l+1)}$,
- transient failures occur according to a Poisson process of intensity λ_t,
- the restoration of a transient failure does not require manual repair, it is assumed that the automatic reboot (with mean rate μ_t) fix the problem, which implies a shorter repair/restoration time, i.e., $\mu_t > \mu_p$,
- each subnetwork has a specific repair process which is *all at once* and the repair time of subnetwork l is exponentially distributed with mean $1/\mu_{pl}$,
- a subnetwork with a permanent failure cannot fail due to transient failures,
- a subnetwork with a transient failure can fail due to a permanent failure,
- when a subnetwork is repaired both permanent and transient failures are removed.

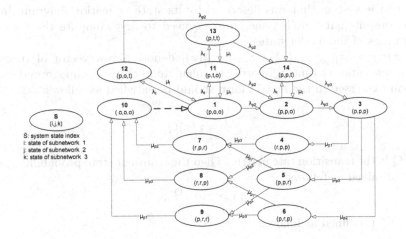

Fig. 3. A state transition diagram for model II

For the sake of illustration, we use the wireless network example in Section 2.1. The state transition model considering transient failures is presented in Fig. 3. This diagram is an extension of the model I example which has been presented in [7]. Given the initial state is (p, o, o), the CTMC may jump to state (p, p, o) if the propagation occurs with rate λ_{p2}; or it may jump to state (p, t, o) or (p, o, t) with rate λ_t due to transient failures. Time to restart to fix the transient failures is assumed to be exponentially distributed with rate μ_t. Similarily, on state (p, p, o), the CTMC may jump to state (p, p, p) if the propagation continues with rate λ_{p3}; or it may jump to state (p, p, t) with rate λ_t for transient failures. As for the other transition structures, model II is the same with model I.

On state (p, p, p), the CTMC may jump to three possible states: firstly, it may jump to state (p, p, r) if the subnetwork-3 is recovered (this occurs with rate μ_{p3}); secondly, it may jump to state (r, p, p) if the subnetwork-1 is recovered (this occurs with rate μ_{p1}); and thirdly, the CTMC may jump to state (p, r, p) if the subnetwork-2 is recovered (this occurs with rate μ_{p2}).

It should be observed that the frequency of the initial event is not considered in the survivability model because the focus is: given that an undesired event has occurred what is the nature of performance degradation just after such event until the system stabilizes again. This is indicated by the dashed line in Fig. 3.

Section 3 will discuss the use of the Markov model and transient probabilities to arrive at the transient suvivability model analysis.

3   Model Analysis

In this section we discuss and derive survivability attributes based on the Markov models presented in the previous section. It was explained earlier that to carry out the survivability quantification analysis, we need to analyze the Markov model of the system that was described by its state transition diagram. In order to compute survivability measure, we need to first compute the transient probabilities of the model states.

Let $\pi(\tau) = [\pi_{(p,o,\cdots,o)}(\tau) \cdots \pi_{(o,o,\cdots,o)}(\tau)]$ denote a row vector of transient state probabilities at time τ. In order to calculate $\pi(\tau)$, the Kolmogorov-forward equation expressed in the matrix form should be satisfied as follows:

$$\frac{d\pi(\tau)}{d\tau} = \pi(\tau)\mathbf{Q}, \tag{2}$$

where $\mathbf{Q}$ is the transition rate matrix. Then the transient state probability vector can be obtained as follows:

$$\pi(\tau) = \pi(0)e^{\mathbf{Q}\tau}, \tag{3}$$

where $e^{\mathbf{Q}\tau}$ is defined as follows:

$$e^{\mathbf{Q}\tau} = \sum_{i=0}^{\infty} \mathbf{Q}^i \frac{\tau^i}{i!}. \tag{4}$$

The simplest method to compute Eq. (4) is to truncate the summation to a large number (e.g., K), which can be expressed as follows:

$$e^{\mathbf{Q}\tau} = \sum_{i=0}^{K} \mathbf{Q}^i \frac{\tau^i}{i!}. \tag{5}$$

The other common alternative methods to obtain the transient probability vector $\pi(\tau)$ include uniformization [13], matrix exponential approach [14]. Here we take uniformization approach as the model analysis example. Let q_{ii} be the diagnoal element of $\mathbf{Q}$ and $\mathbf{I}$ be the unit matrix, then the transient state probability vector is obtained as follows:

$$\pi(\tau) = \pi(0) \sum_{i=0}^{\infty} e^{-\beta\tau} \frac{(\beta\tau)^i}{i!} \mathbf{P}^i, \tag{6}$$

where $\beta \geq max_i |q_{ii}|$ is the uniform rate parameter and $\mathbf{P} = \mathbf{I} + \mathbf{Q}/\beta$. Truncate the summation to a large number (e.g., K), the controllable error ϵ can be computed from

$$\epsilon = 1 - e^{-\beta\tau} \sum_{i=0}^{K} \frac{(\beta\tau)^i}{i!}. \tag{7}$$

Whenever the system is in state $i \in \Omega$, a reward is assigned at a rate $\Upsilon(i)$, where Υ denotes a reward function. Since Υ_i is the reward rate associated with state i, and so Υ_i can take any of the $|\Omega|$ values. The vector of reward rates associated with the state is expressed as $\Upsilon = [\Upsilon_1, \Upsilon_2, ..., \Upsilon_{|\Omega|}]$. Here, the reward rate can be many types, such as economic return vector or cost vector in business continuity preparedness planning.

We currently equate survivability performance with connectivity, *the percentage of users connected successfully*. Based on the above calculated transient probabilities, the measure of interest is obtained as reward measures from the CTMC model. Then, the expected instantaneous reward rate $E[\Upsilon_{X(\tau)}]$ gives the average connectivity of the system at time t, which is expressed as follows:

$$E[\Upsilon_{X(\tau)}] = \Upsilon \cdot \pi^T(\tau). \tag{8}$$

As stated in Section 2 complete description of this Markov model requires the knowledge of various model parameters. Clearly for the model to be accurate, it is important to estimate the model parameters accurately. In this paper, our focus is more on developing a methodology for analyzing quantitatively the survivability attributes of a network rather than model parameterization.

4   Numerical Example

In this section, we perform numerical experiments for the case study in Section 2.1. First, we apply and compare model I and model II in this network example for different values of fault propagation rates. Then we study the impact of differents repair rates on model II's performance.

For the parameters setting of the proposed models, we refer to the data from Japan 2011 earthquake situation report [10]. In doing so, our model parameters fall in ranges which represent the typical real system's behavior. Our experimental setup consists of three subnetworks and the disaster occurs at subnetwork-1 initially. We set the transition rates as follows: $\lambda_{p2} = \lambda_{p3} = 0.67$, $\lambda_t = 50$, $\mu_t = 100$, $\mu_{p1} = \mu_{p2} = \mu_{p3} = 0.097$, given in units of events per day. For simplicity, the average number of users per each base station is assumed to be the same.

Table 2. Rewards: fraction of available base stations

Parameter	Value	Parameter	Value
Υ_1	0.560	Υ_8	0.871
Υ_2	0.429	Υ_9	0.611
Υ_3	0.040	Υ_{10}	1.000
Υ_4	0.429	Υ_{11}	0.430
Υ_5	0.483	Υ_{12}	0.130
Υ_6	0.169	Υ_{13}	0.040
Υ_7	0.560	Υ_{14}	0.040

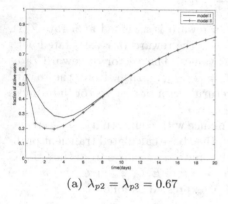
(a) $\lambda_{p2} = \lambda_{p3} = 0.67$

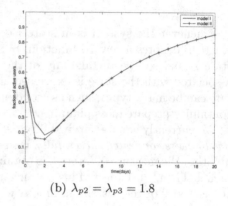
(b) $\lambda_{p2} = \lambda_{p3} = 1.8$

Fig. 4. Comparison of the fraction of connected users in model I and II for different values of fault propagation rates

Then the percentage of connected users is equal to the fraction of available base stations. The rewards at each model state are shown in Table 2.

First, we compare model I and model II in this network example for different values of fault propagation rates. In fig. 4, when $\lambda_{p2} = \lambda_{p3} = 0.67$, there is a gap between model I and model II curves. Compared to model I, the fraction of active users in model II decreases more sharply. On the other hand, as expected, when fault propagation rates increase, i.e., $\lambda_{p2} = \lambda_{p3} = 1.8$, then model I and model II curves are close to each other. The impact of transient failure and repair is not as evident as in former case.

Then we study the impact of different repair rates on model II's performance. We vary the transient and permanent failure repair rate values, and the results are summarized in Fig. 5. Consider the scenario in which the permanent failure repair rate is low ($\mu_{p1} = \mu_{p2} = \mu_{p3} = 0.3$). In this scenario, the fraction of active users is low (roughly 0.3, 2 hours after the failure when $\mu_t = 10$). However, when the permanent failure repair rates are relatively higher ($\mu_{p1} = \mu_{p2} = \mu_{p3} = 3$), the fraction of active users sharply increases. In both figures, the effect of the transient failure repair rate is not as evident for longer observation time (after 8 hours). As shown in 5(b), the value of transient failure repair rate μ_t which makes the fraction of active users achieve 60% in two days is $\mu_t > 100$.

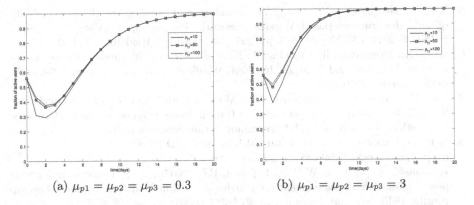

(a) $\mu_{p1} = \mu_{p2} = \mu_{p3} = 0.3$ (b) $\mu_{p1} = \mu_{p2} = \mu_{p3} = 3$

Fig. 5. Impact of repair rates on the fraction of connected users in model II

5   Conclusions and Future Work

In this paper we have presented an approach for quantitative assessment of network survivability against fault propagation. First, we considered the case where physical fault propagation is considered. Second, we considered the case in which both physical and transient fault are incorporated. The impact of different parameters, such as fault propagation rates, repair rates were studied. Users can choose different models depending on the real cases. For example, if both physical and transient faults occurred, model II is more appropriate; otherwise, model I is enough for the requirement. The main goal of this paper is to construct the models, rather than model parameterization.

One of the goals of our future work is to collect more real data. This information should provide us with a better understanding of the behavior exhibited by faults, help us to refine its stochastic description and lead to better estimates of the model parameters. Another goal of our future work is to consider geographic factors. We will extend the system state by adding more dimensions representing geographical characterizations.

References

1. Zolfaghari, A., Kaudel, F.J.: Framework for network survivability performance. IEEE Journal on Selected Areas in Communications 5, 46–51 (1994)
2. Yun, L., Menditta, V.B., Kishor, S.T.: Survivability analysis of telephone access network. In: IEEE 15th International Symposium on Software Reliability Engineering, pp. 367–377. IEEE Press, Bretagne (2004)
3. Heegaard, P.E., Kishor, S.T.: Network survivability modeling. Comput. Netw. 53, 1215–1234 (2009)
4. Fei, X., Wenye, W.: On the Survivability of Wireless Ad Hoc Networks with Node Misbehaviors and Failures. IEEE Transactions on Dependable and Secure Computing 7, 284–299 (2010)

5. Xie, L., Heegaard, P.E., Jiang, Y.: Modeling and Analysis of the Survivability of an Infrastructure-Based Wireless Network. In: Szabó, R., Vidács, A. (eds.) EUNICE 2012. LNCS, vol. 7479, pp. 227–238. Springer, Heidelberg (2012)
6. Lang, X., Heegaard, P.E., Yuming, J.: Network Survivability under Disaster Propagation: Modeling and Analysis. In: IEEE Wireless Communications and Networking Conference (2013)
7. Lang, X., Yuming, J., Heegaard, P.E.: Modelling and Analysis of the Survivability of Telecommunication Network. In: International Symposium on Performance Evaluation of Computer and Telecommunication Systems (2013)
8. Reuters: Experts Warn of Substantial Risk of WMD Attack, http://research.lifeboat.com/lugar.htm
9. Kwasinski, A., Weaver, W.W., Chapman, P.L., Krein, P.T.: Telecommunications power plant damage assessment for Hurricane Katrina - site survey and follow-up results. IEEE Systems Journal 3(3), 277–287 (2009)
10. Adachi, T., Ishiyama, Y., Asakura, Y., Nakamura, K.: The restoration of telecom power damages by the Great East Japan Earthquake. In: Proc. IEEE Telecomm. Energy Con. (INTELEC), Amsterdam, Netherlands (2011)
11. Jindal, V., Dharmaraja, S., Kishor, S.T.: Analytical survivability model for fault tolerant cellular networks supporting multiple services. In: IEEE International Symposium on Performance Evaluation of Computer and Telecommunication Systems, pp. 505–512. IEEE Press, Calgary (2006)
12. Avizienis, A., Laprie, J.C., Randell, B.: Landwehr,C.: Basic concepts and taxonomy of dependable and secure computing. IEEE Transactions on Dependable and Secure Computing 1, 11–33 (2004)
13. Jensen, A.: Markoff chains as an aid in the study of Markoff processes. Skand. Aktuarietiedskr 36, 87–91 (1953)
14. Trivedi, K.S.: Probability and Statistics with Reliability, Queueing, and Computer Science Applications, 2nd edn. (2001)

Analysis of Elephant Users
in Broadband Network Traffic

Péter Megyesi and Sándor Molnár

High Speed Networks Laboratory,
Department of Telecommunications and Media Informatics,
Budapest University of Technology and Economics,
1117, Magyar tudósok körútja 2.,
Budapest, Hungary
{megyesi,molnar}@tmit.bme.hu

Abstract. *Elephant and mice* phenomena of network traffic flows have been an interesting research area in the past decade. Several operational broadband measurement results showed that the majority of the traffic is caused by a small percentage of large flows, called the *elephants*. In this paper, we investigate the same phenomenon in regards of users. Our results show that even though the packet level statistics of *elephant users* and *elephant flows* show similar characteristics, there is only a small overlap between the two phenomena.

Keywords: traffic measurement, traffic analysis, elephant flows, elephant users.

1   Introduction

Traffic profiling is a crucial objective for network monitoring and management purposes. Flow characterization has been given a large attention by the research community in the past decade. Flows has been classified by their size of traffic (as *elephant and mice*) [1] [2] [3], by their duration in time (as *tortoise and dragonfly*) [4], by their rate (as *cheetah and snail*) [5] and by their burstiness (as *porcupine and stingray*) [5]. Several studies were written about the correlation between these flow behaviors [6] [7].

However, current literature lacks in profiling users in such regards. In this paper we investigate the *elephant and mice* phenomena regarding Internet users. We analyzed two recent measurements taken from high speed operational networks and found that *elephant users* show similar packet level characteristics to *elephant flows*. We also determined that there is a much smaller overlap between these two phenomena that one would expect. We found that only a small portion (10%-30%) of *elephant flows* are generated by *elephant users* and also the generation of *elephant flows* is not a necessary condition for being an *elephant user*. These results indicate that further investigation of user characterization could aid network operators in the future to apply different services or charging policies for different users.

T. Bauschert (Ed.): EUNICE 2013, LNCS 8115, pp. 37–45, 2013.

The contribution of this paper is threefold. First, to our knowledge, our study is the first that presents the discussed characteristics of *elephant users*. Second, we point out that there is only a small overlap between *elephant flows* and *elephant users*. Finally, our measurements from recent networks show that the *elephant and mice* phenomena of flows and users are still present in todays networks.

This paper is organized as follows. Section 2 presents the related work. In Section 3 we give the definition of *elephants* and the properties of the two datasets we used for our research. Section 4 presents the results of our measurements. Finally, in Section 5 we conclude our work.

2   Related Work

There are several different definitions for *elephant flows* in the literature. In [2] authors propose two techniques to identify *elephants*. The first approach is based on the heavy-tail nature of the flow bandwidth distribution, and one can consider a flow as an *elephant* if it is located in this tail. The second approach is more simple, *elephants* are the smallest set of flows whose total traffic exceeds a given threshold. Estan and Varghese [3] used a different definition. They considered a flow as an *elephant* if its rate exceeds the 1% of the link utilization.

However, the definition given by Lan and Heidemann [5] become a rule of thumb in later literature (e.g. both [7] and [8] use this definition). They define *elephant flows* as flows with a size larger than the average plus three times the standard deviation of all flows. They use the same idea for categorize flows by their duration, rate and burstiness as *tortoise, cheetah* and *porcupine*, respectively. [5] was also the first study that presented the *cheetah and snail* and the *porcupine and stingray* classifications. *Tortoise and dragonfly* properties of traffic flows were first investigated in [4]. Here, the authors considered a flow as *tortoise* simply if its duration was lager than 15 minutes. Given the generality and the rule of thumb nature of the definition by Lan and Heidemann [5] we will use the same definition for *elephants* later in this paper.

In [9] Sarvotham et al. present a comprehensive study that traffic bursts are usually caused by only few number of high bandwidth connections. They separate the aggregated traffic into two components, *alpha* and *beta* by their rate in every 500ms time window. If the rate of the flow is greater than a given threshold (mean plus three standard deviations) than the traffic is *alpha*, otherwise it is *beta*. Authors determine that while the *alpha* component is responsible for the traffic bursts, the *beta* component has similar second order characteristics to the original aggregate.

The term *elephant user* appears in [10] where the authors calculate the Gini coefficient for the user distribution. The Gini coefficient is usually used in economics for measuring statistical dispersion of a distribution. They calculate the value of the Gini coefficient for the distribution of the number of bytes generated by the users as 0.7895 but no further discussion is presented.

In [11] authors investigate application penetration in residential broadband traffic. They calculate the results separately for the top 10 *heavy-hitters* (the top 10 users that generated the most traffic) in their measurement data. Besides pointing out the fact that the majority of the data is generated by a small group of users the paper does not tackle any further issues about *elephant users*.

3   Methodology

In this section we present the source of the two network traces we used in this study. We also give the definition of *elephants* and the metrics we used to analyze them.

3.1   Datasets

The first trace was measured by the The Cooperative Association for Internet Data Analysis (CAIDA) [13] in a 10 Gbit/s backbone link between Chicago and San Jose. They periodically take measurements on this link and make them available for the research community upon request in an anonymous format (removed payload and hashed IP addresses). We analyzed multiple subsets of these data and since we found similar result we chose one given time period to present our findings. This trace was recorded on 13:15 (UTC), 20th of December 2012 and contains four minutes of network traffic. Furthermore, we refer to this measurement as *CAIDA Trace*.

The second measurement was taken in the campus network of the Budapest University of Technology and Economics (BME) on 16:31 (CET), 18th of December 2012 and contains six minutes of traffic. The measured link was a 10Gigabit Ethernet port of a Cisco 6500 Layer-3 switch which transfers the traffic of two buildings on the campus site to the core layer of the university network. This measurement is not available to the public. However, we consider the results relevant to present since our findings are similar to the *CAIDA Trace* even though the nature of network is different. We refer to this measurement as *BME Trace*.

Table 1 presents the basic statistics of the two traces. Generally, the *CAIDA Trace* contains more data than the *BME Trace* by one order of magnitude.

3.2   Measuring Elephants

During the identification of *elephant users and flows* we use the definition presented in [5]: a user or a flow is considered an *elephant* if its flow size or traffic volume is grater than the average plus three times the standard deviation of all the flow sizes or traffic volumes of flows and users, respectively. Table 1 presents the values of these threshold for the two traces. The *elephant and mice* phenomena clearly exist: less than a thousandth of the users and flows are responsible for roughly 60%-80% of the total traffic.

In the next section we firstly show that the *elephant* phenomenon also exist with different threshold levels by plotting the cumulative distribution of user and flow sizes against theirs cumulative proportion of the total traffic. Furthermore, we present the comparison of the following three packet level metrics, (1) byte

Table 1. Statistics of the two traces used for analysis

	CAIDA Trace	BME Trace
Number of packets	105444780	6804958
Number of users	680300	63668
Number of flows	3876982	264117
Total traffic	65.6 Gbyte	5.66 Gbyte
Elephant user threshold	15.9 Mbyte	13.7 Mbyte
Number of elephant users	661	56
Proportion of elephant users	0.097%	0.088%
Total traffic of elephant users	71.5%	84.5%
Elephant flow threshold	2.3 Mbyte	4.96 Mbyte
Number of elephant flows	2714	151
Proportion of elephant flows	0.07%	0.057%
Total traffic of elephant flows	61.7%	83.41%

and packet throughput, (2) packet size distribution and (3) inter packet time distribution. We chose these metrics because they are the most frequently used packet level characteristics for comparing traffic traces [12]. Additionally, we investigate presence of both *elephant* and *non-elephant flows* in the traffic of *elephant users*.

4   Measurement Results

4.1   User and Flow Sizes

In Figure 1 one can investigate the *elephant and mice* phenomena for both traces. Here we plotted the cumulative distribution of user traffic volumes and flow sizes

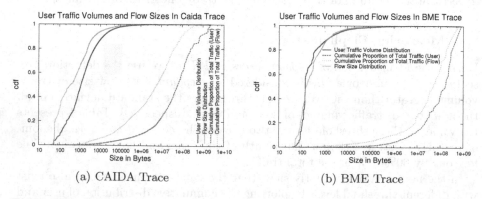

(a) CAIDA Trace   (b) BME Trace

Fig. 1. The *elephant and mice* phenomena presented by cumulative distribution of user traffic volume and flow sizes and their cumulative proportion of the total traffic

Table 2. Proportion of *elephants* with different thresholds

Threshold in Mbyte	CAIDA Trace				BME Trace			
	Users		Flows		Users		Flows	
	Ratio	Traffic	Ratio	Traffic	Ratio	Traffic	Ratio	Traffic
0.1	2.17%	95.48%	1.21%	85.29%	1.21%	98.75%	0.53%	94.84%
0.5	0.8%	92.44%	0.29%	74.21%	0.53%	96.97%	0.16%	91.08%
1	0.54%	90.55%	0.18%	69.56%	0.37%	95.66%	0.11%	89.46%
2	0.37%	88.17%	0.11%	63.71%	0.23%	93.45%	0.08%	87.04%
5	0.23%	83.48%	0.04%	52.03%	0.14%	89.96%	0.06%	83.23%
10	0.13%	76.92%	0.02%	42.87%	0.1%	86.35%	0.03%	73.56%
15	0.1%	72.2%	0.017%	37.25%	0.08%	83.96%	0.025%	70.65%
20	0.08%	68.78%	0.011%	32.09%	0.06%	80.91%	0.02%	66.67%
50	0.03%	53.55%	0.003%	17.88%	0.03%	68.12%	0.007%	47.93%

against theirs cumulative proportion of the total traffic. In Table 2 we collected the complementary values in percentage (1 minus the actual value) of the curves in Figure 1 for different thresholds. *Ratio* presents the proportion of users and flows whose traffic was larger than the *Threshold* value and *Traffic* represents their total share from the aggregated traffic.

4.2 Byte and Packet Throughput

In Figure 2 the traffic of *elephant users* and *elephant flows* are plotted against the original traffic. The relative difference are also presented. In case of the *BME Trace* the *elephants* are responsible for sufficient amount of the total traffic (80%-85%), while in the *CAIDA Trace* this ration is a bit smaller (60%-70%). Since the traffic of *elephants* seems to follow the bursts in the original traffic (the relative

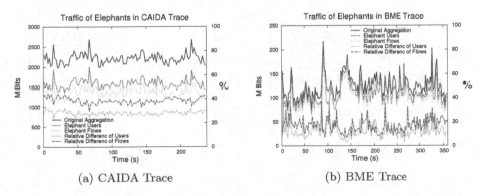

(a) CAIDA Trace   (b) BME Trace

Fig. 2. Traffic of *elephants*

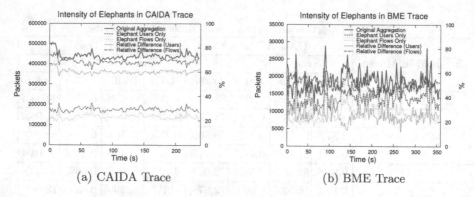

(a) CAIDA Trace   (b) BME Trace

Fig. 3. Intensity of *elephants*

differences are also smaller at these peaks), the results suggests that *elephant users* are main cause for traffic burstiness.

Figure 3 present the number of packets in every one second time interval. Here, the relative difference is much higher than in case of the byte throughput. In the *CAIDA Trace elephants* are responsible for only roughly 30%-40% of the total packets, while in case of the *BME Trace* this number is ratio is 50%-70%. Intensity of *elephants* are also following the packet burst of the original aggreagte since the relative difference is smaller in traffic peaks.

4.3   Packet Sizes

Packet size distributions of the two measurements is given in Figure 4. The joint property in both traces is that ratio of maximum and minimum sized packets is larger in *elephants* than in the original aggregate. Packets with intermediate size share similar proportion. We collected a few numerical example to Table 3 to present this phenomenon.

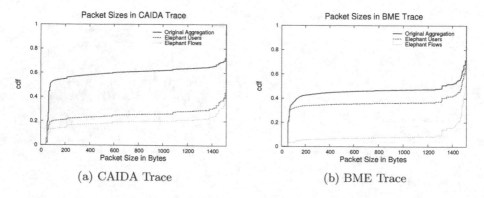

(a) CAIDA Trace   (b) BME Trace

Fig. 4. Packet size distributions of *elephants*

Table 3. Packet proportions under different conditions

Condition	CAIDA Trace			BME Trace		
	Original Aggregate	Elephant Users	Elephant Flows	Original Aggregate	Elephant Users	Elephant Flows
PS <= 54 Byte	18.9%	11.9%	7.4%	20.9%	21.0%	2.9%
PS <= 66 Byte	44.3%	16.7%	9.9%	30.1%	29.4%	3.3%
PS >= 1450 Byte	32.8%	66.3%	72.8%	44.8%	54.6%	79.1%
PS = 1514 Byte	27.6%	54.2%	61.4%	28.5%	33.9%	49.7%

Table 4 present the ratio of number of packet in *elephants* compared to the number in the original aggregate under different conditions. It is clear from the values that *elephants* contains the majority of maximum sized packet and *elephant flows* exclude the majority of minimum sized packets. The ratio of minimum sized packets in *elephant users* shows different behavoir in the two measurements.

4.4   Inter Packet Times

Inter arrival time between consecutive packets corresponding the *elephant users or flows* are presented in Figure 5. The curves show similar characteristics for *elephant users* and *elephant flows*. The *cdf* curves of *elephants* are increasing slower than the original aggregate's which is an expected behavior since traffic of *elephants* are the rarefaction of the original packet stream.

4.5   Elephant and Non-elephant Flows in Elephant Users

In Figure 6 every dot represents an *elephant user* according to the generated number of *elephant flows* and *mice flows*. These results indicate that there is no correlation between the number of *elephant flows* and *mice flows* generated by an *elephant users*. Furthermore, a user can be an *elephant* without generating any *elephant flows*. There was 53 *elephant users* in the *CAIDA Trace* who did

Table 4. Ratio of number of packets in *elephants* compared to the original

Condition	CAIDA Trace		BME Trace	
	Elephant Users	Elephant Flows	Elephant Users	Elephant Flows
PS <= 54 Byte	25.0%	12.3%	74.7%	6.8%
PS <= 66 Byte	15.0%	7.0%	71.0%	5.3%
PS >= 1450 Byte	80.6%	70.2%	90.2%	88.6%
PS = 1514 Byte	81.2%	70.3%	88.4%	87.8%

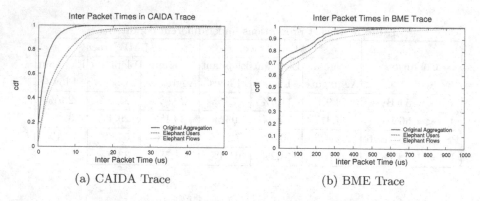

(a) CAIDA Trace   (b) BME Trace

Fig. 5. Inter Packet Time distributions of *elephants*

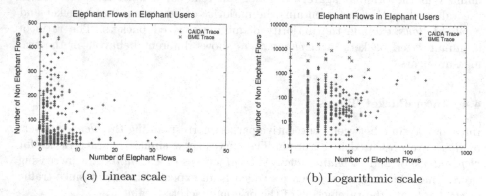

(a) Linear scale   (b) Logarithmic scale

Fig. 6. The number of *elephant* and *non-elephant flows* generated by *elephant users*

not generated any *elephant flow*. They account for 8% of all *elephant users* in the *CAIDA Trace*. In the *BME Trace* this number is only 3, but since there were only 56 *elephant users* in that measurement their share is 5%.

Another interesting result is that in case of the *CAIDA Trace* only the 9.13% of *elephant flows* were generated by *elephant users*. In case of the *BME Trace* this value is higher, namely 37.85%. These result clearly indicate that the overlap between the *elephant user* and *elephant flow* phenomenons could be much smaller in some cases that one would expect.

5 Conclusion

In this paper we investigated the *elephant and mice* phenomena of Internet users in recent broadband network measurements. We found that *elephant users* show similar packet-level characteristics to the well-investigated *elephant flow* phenomenon. However, we pointed out that only a small portion (10%-30%) of *elephant flows* were generated by *elephant users*. We also found that the generation of *elephant flows* by a user is not a necessary condition for being an *elephant user*.

As future work we would like to further analyze the *elephant user* phenomenon in the same way that *elephant flows* were analyzed in [5] [9]. Such study would aid us in the understanding of how particular users are affecting the second-order characteristics of network traffic.

Acknowledgments. The authors would like to thank CAIDA for granting access to the measurement data that was analyzed in this paper. The research was supported by OTKA-KTIA grant CNK77802.

References

1. Thompson, K., Miller, G., Wilder, R.: Wide Area Internet Traffic Patterns and Characteristics. IEEE Network Magazine 11(6), 10–23 (1997)
2. Papagiannaki, K., Taft, N., Bhattacharyya, S., Thiran, P., Salamatian, K., Diot, C.: A pragmatic definition of elephants in internet backbone traffic. In: Proceedings of the 2nd ACM SIGCOMM Workshop on Internet Measurement (IMW 2002), Marseille, France, pp. 175–176 (2002)
3. Estan, C., Varghese, G.: New directions in traffic measurement and accounting: Focusing on the elephants, ignoring the mice. ACM Transactions on Computer Systems 21(3), 270–313 (2003)
4. Brownlee, N., Claffy, K.: Understanding Internet traffic streams: dragonflies and tortoises. IEEE Communications Magazine 40(10), 110–117 (2002)
5. Lan, K., Heidemann, J.: A measurement study of correlations of Internet flow characteristics. Computer Networks 50(1), 46–62 (2006)
6. Markovich, N., Kilpi, J.: Bivariate statistical analysis of TCP-flow sizes and durations. Annals of Operations Research 170(1), 199–216 (2009)
7. Molnár, S., Móczar, Z.: Three-Dimensional Characterization of Internet Flows. In: Proceedings of IEEE International Conference on Communications (ICC 2011), Kyoto, Japan (2011)
8. Callado, A., Kamienski, C., Szabo, G., Gero, B., Kelner, J., Fernandes, S., Sadok, D.: A Survey on Internet Traffic Identification. IEEE Communications Surveys & Tutorials 11(3), 37–52 (2009)
9. Sarvotham, S., Riedi, R., Baraniuk, R.: Connection-level analysis and modeling of network traffic. In: Proceedings of the 1st ACM SIGCOMM Internet Measurement Workshop (IMW 2001), San Francisco Bay Area, CA, USA, pp. 99–103 (2001)
10. Liu, P., Liu, F., Lei, Z.: Model of Network Traffic Based on Network Applications and Network Users. In: International Symposium on Computer Science and Computational Technology (ISCSCT 2008), Shanghai, China, pp. 171–174 (2008)
11. Pietrzyk, M., Plissonneau, L., Urvoy-Keller, G., En-Najjary, T.: On profiling residential customers. In: Domingo-Pascual, J., Shavitt, Y., Uhlig, S. (eds.) TMA 2011. LNCS, vol. 6613, pp. 1–14. Springer, Heidelberg (2011)
12. Molnár, S., Megyesi, P., Szabó, G.: How to Validate Traffic Generators. In: Proceedings of the 1st IEEE Workshop on Traffic Identification and Classification for Advanced Network Services and Scenarios (TRICANS 2013), Budapest, Hungary (2013)
13. The Cooperative Association for Internet Data Analysis, http://www.caida.org

Evaluation of the Aircraft Distribution in Satellite Spotbeams

Christoph Petersen, Maciej Mühleisen, and Andreas Timm-Giel

Institute of Communication Networks
Schwarzenbergstr. 95, 21073 Hamburg, Germany
{chr.petersen,maciej.muehleisen,timm-giel}@tuhh.de
http://www.tuhh.de/comnets

Abstract. Upcoming inflight entertainment and other onboard data services request broadband data connections during long- and short-haul flights all over the world. To cope with this amount of traffic, especially over oceanic areas where no ground infrastructure is available, satellite systems offer broadband satellite links for avionic purpose.

This work analyzes the distribution of aircraft traffic for selected satellite spotbeams for intercontinental, rural and urban scenarios. For this, the statistic properties of the number of arriving and departing aircraft within a time interval are analyzed. Our results show, that the law of small number and therefore a Poisson distribution is only applicable to areas with low air traffic. Aircraft arrivals to- and departures from satellite spotbeams can be modeled using the negative binomial distribution, as proven by presented results.

1 Introduction

Aircraft are fast and popular conveyances today. For safety and passenger comfort, broadband data communication links are often installed. In some regions, but only over terrain, direct air to ground links are maintained, e.g. Aircell GoGo in the United States of America. Other avionic data links as VHF or HF do not offer high bandwidth, are highly congested and very expensive, so they are not used for services requesting high data rates. Therefore, the most widely used worldwide available avionic broadband data communication are satellite links. Fields of application range from inflight entertainment to maintenance or even flight recorder data transmission. To assess the performance of current satellite systems and estimate the capacity demands, reliable information about the number of aircraft inside specific areas are required.

In order to estimate the aggregated capacity demands, the actual offered data traffic load needs to be analyzed. It is feasible to assume the offered data traffic load being proportional to the number of aircraft in that area. Although traces of aircraft densities are available, analytical models allow more general conclusions about offered traffic loads and help to become independent from large data sets of aircraft positions. Also conclusions about areas where no aircraft position information are available may be drawn. These models are also suitable to

T. Bauschert (Ed.): EUNICE 2013, LNCS 8115, pp. 46–53, 2013.

extrapolate prospective situations or determine system performance for extraordinary situations, e.g. aviation distress. Furthermore, an analytical model can be used for systems simulation.

The same methods were applied to derive realistic vehicular traffic models. Examplarily in [1], a model for car arrivals on higways around the city of Madrid, Spain, is developed. The analysis of the arrival process identifies two different types of vehicles to be further investigated: Cars that drive together in a bursty way and isolated ones without any dependencies e.g. in traveling speed. Therefore, a Gaussian-exponential mixture model is proposed to handle bursty traffic with Gaussian distributed interarrival times and isolated traffic with exponential distributed interarrival times. For sparse vehicular traffic, [2] comes to the same result of exponential distributed vehicular interarrival times and therefore Poisson distributed vehicle arrival rates.

In [3] the German Aerospace Center (Deutsches Zentrum fuer Luft- und Raumfahrt - DLR) developed an aircraft distribution model to evaluate aircraft-to-aircraft communication. In [4] the feasibility of that approach is shown, based on data from the airline flight schedule database published by the International Air Transport Association (IATA) and therefore, assuming all aircraft being equipped with ad-hoc communication equipment. The analysis presented in the following is based on more realistic aircraft position data derived from Flightradar24 [5].

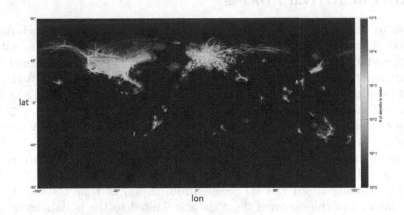

Fig. 1. Two weeks of captured Flightradar24 data

2   Captured Data Set and scope

Flightradar24 captures and visualizes Automatic Dependant Surveillance Broadcast (ADS-B) messages from aircrafts, received by the Federal Aviation Administration (FAA) and a community of people privately operating ADS-B receivers. The available aircraft position data does not cover the whole globe. In fact, oceanic areas are very rarely covered as visible in Figure 1, showing all observed

aircraft position during a two week period. Conclusions regarding aircraft densities over the ocean can be derived from aircraft position data close to the ocean shore. This is visible in Figure 2, representing the observed aircrafts with scope over the United States of America.

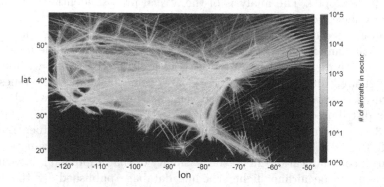

Fig. 2. Spotbeam over Newfoundland

3   Aircraft Arrival Process

In order to derive worst case capacity demands, the busy hour of each day is analyzed. The area of interest for this model is a satellite spotbeam with a satellite system specific radius. Considering one particular day, the quadruple $d = \{lat, lon, t, id\}$ represents one data record with the unique aircraft ID, the aircraft position in geographic coordinates lat, lon at time instance t. The set $\mathbb{D}_t$ contains all data records worldwide at time t, whereas the subset $\mathbb{D}_{t,A} \subset \mathbb{D}$ is reduced to the records inside the satellite spotbeam area A, defined by a radius r around its center point lat_C, lon_C. Furthermore, the subset $\mathbb{D}_{t,A,H} \subset \mathbb{D}_{t,A}$ describes all data records of $\mathbb{D}_{t,A}$ within the given busy hour of an arbitrary day in this area. To identify the aircraft arrivals and departures, the set $\mathbb{X}_{t,A,H}$ is created containing all aircraft ID records from $\mathbb{D}_{t,A,H}$ of time instance t. The update interval of the captured flight data is limited to the update interval of Flightradar24 being $\Delta t = 10s$. Therefore, a time-discrete model describing the aircraft arrivals and departures during one time instance Δt is developed. With $\mathbb{X}_{t,A,H}$ and $\mathbb{X}_{t+\Delta t,A,H}$ as the set of aircraft for the next time instance,

$$a(t) = |\mathbb{X}_{t+\Delta t,A,H} \setminus \mathbb{X}_{t,A,H}| \tag{1}$$

is the number of aircrafts (IDs) being in that area at time instance $t + \Delta t$ but not at time instance t. Hence, $a(t)$ is the number of aircraft arrivals in area A during that update interval. Analogously, the number of departures from the area is defined as

$$d(t) = |\mathbb{X}_{t,A,H} \setminus \mathbb{X}_{t+\Delta t,A,H}| \tag{2}$$

The data for a and d is collected and analyzed for several weeks. Figure 3 shows the distribution of aircraft arrivals inside a $200km$ radius of Newfoundland. It allows the hypothesis that the number of aircraft arrivals follow a Poisson distribution. This hypothesis is verified using the Chi Square test.

4   Scenarios

Several scenarios for the Iridium [6],[7] low earth orbit satellite systems are further investigated. The aircraft arrival process for one spotbeam is analyzed. Depending on its position inside the overall satellite footprint, the area of the spotbeam equates to a circle becoming oval towards the border of the footprint. In this work, a circle with radius r and according area A is assumed. The system specific radius is $r_{Iridium} = 200km$ for the Iridium system.

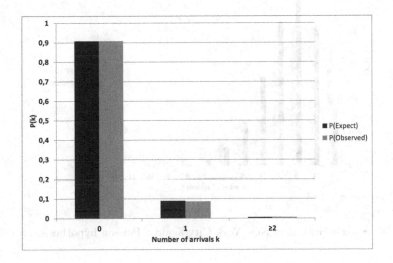

Fig. 3. Observed arrivals over Newfoundland against Poisson hypothesis, $r = 200km$

The parameters for the model differ depending on the flight scenario and e.g. the used communication system. As flight scenarios, data for urban, rural or intercontinental areas is analyzed. The transition beetween these scenarios is smooth, but as typical representatives a spotbeam over New York City has been chosen for the urban scenario, over Omaha in Nebraska for the rural scenario and over the ocean shore of Newfoundland as intercontinental scenario.

5   Results

Figure 3 shows the distribution of aircraft arrivals over Newfoundland for the intercontinental scenario as well as the theoretical distribution according to a

Poisson distribution. For Chi Square testing, k classes are defined and the class number, except for the last class k, represents the number of arrivals during a time instance. The empirical rate parameter $\hat{\lambda}$ is set to the average number of arrivals within the considered timeframe and busy hours. The kth class summarizes the occurences of even more or equal than $k - 1$ arrivals to avoid classes with to few arrivals.

As visible in the figure, only a few aircraft pass this area. The result is based on two weeks of flight data in December 2012. The Chi Square test supports the hypothesis of aircraft arrivals being Poisson distributed with 95% confidence.

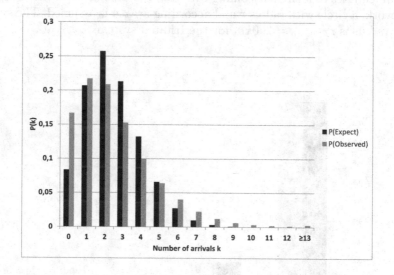

Fig. 4. Observed arrivals over New York City against Poisson hypothesis, $r = 200km$

Aircraft arrivals in the urban scenario over New York City are not following a Poisson distribution according to the Chi Square test. The empiric distribution and the Poisson distribution with the same mean value is shown in Figure 4. Both distributions are obviously different. The Chi Square test value exceeds the critical value by far, as shown in Table 1. As the hypothesis of arrivals and departures following a Poisson distribution must be rejected, a new one is formulated. Further suitable distributions are examined with focus on generalization of the Poisson distribution. The negative binomial distribution is a generalization of the Poisson distribution with a second parameter allowing to independently select the mean and variance. The Probability Density Function (PDF) of a negative binomial distribution is stated in Equation 3

$$P(X = x) = \begin{cases} p^n(1-p)^x \binom{n+x-1}{n-1} & x \geq 0 \\ 0 \end{cases} \tag{3}$$

Therefore, the hypothesis for the Chi Square test is changed and the data set is tested against the negative binomial distribution. As shown in [8], the negative binomial distribution is a mixture of Poisson distributions. Whereas for the Poisson distribution hypothesis only the mean value has to be estimated, for the negative binomial hypothesis an additional estimation of the variance is needed. Hence, the degree of freedom for the Chi Square test is increased by one. As visible in Figures 5, 6 and Table 2, the aircraft arrivals follow a negative binomial distribution.

Table 1. Overview: Chi Square test results against Poisson hypothesis

Scenario	$r_{Spotbeam}$ [km]	Mean arrivals / Interval	Chi Square test value	Critical value	Test result
Intercontinental	200 km	0,1275	3,0836	3,84	pass
Rural	200 km	0,4052	367,82	7,82	fail
Urban	200 km	2,49	5960	19,68	fail

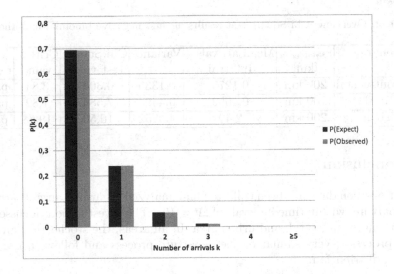

Fig. 5. Observed arrivals over Omaha against negative binomial hypothesis, $r = 200km$

The results show that inside the observed areas, the aircraft arrivals and departures follow a negative binomial distribution. It is therefore suitable to assume a negative binomial for aircraft arrivals and departures in those areas. As the three investigated areas cover representative flight scenarios, it can be assumed that this model can also be applied for air traffic in other areas. Even the first assumption of poissonian aircraft arrivals remains valid since the Poisson distribution is a special case of the negative binomial distribution.

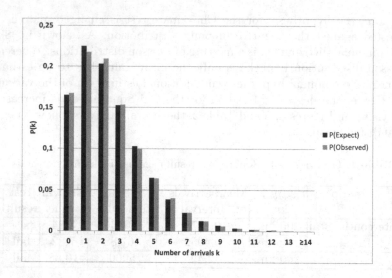

Fig. 6. Observed arrivals over New York City against negative binomial hypothesis, $r = 200km$

Table 2. Overview: Chi Square test results against negative binomial hypothesis

Scenario	$r_{Spotbeam}$ [km]	Mean arrivals / Interval	Variance	Chi Square test value	Critical value	Test result
Intercontinental	200 km	0,1275	0.1339	0.3044	3,84	pass
Rural	200 km	0,4052	0.4494	7.5867	7,82	pass
Urban	200 km	2,49	4.4252	16,505	19,68	pass

6   Conclusion

Aircraft position data has been collected and analyzed regarding aircraft arrivals and departures within time intervals of $\Delta t = 10s$. The investigations focussed on an intercontinental, rural, and urban area. In all areas, the stochastical aircraft arrival process is very similar to the departure process and follows a negative binomial distribution.

7   Future Work

In this work, we found out that the aircraft arrivals and departures inside a satellite spotbeam follow a negative binomial distribution. Future work should further clarify the reasons for this. Inside one spotbeam, especially in urban areas, arrival and departure rates of different aircraft types occur. While long range flights often just pass by, the impact of short haul flights e.g. by take off or landing is higher inside an urban spotbeam. This would also be an explanation for the varying results of the Chi Square test against the Poisson hypothesis.

For futher validation of the hypothesis more regions have to be investigated. Thereby, generally valid distribution parameter (mean value and variance) can be determined.

References

1. Gramaglia, M., Serrano, P., Hernandez, J.A., Calderon, M., Bernardos, C.J.: New insights from the analysis of free flow vehicular traffic in highways. In: 2011 IEEE International Symposium on World of Wireless, Mobile and Multimedia Networks (WoWMoM), pp. 1–9 (2011), http://dx.doi.org/10.1109/WoWMoM.2011.5986384
2. Wisitpongphan, N., Bai, F., Mudalige, P., Sadekar, V., Tonguz, O.: Routing in sparse vehicular ad hoc wireless networks. IEEE Journal on Selected Areas in Communications 25(8), 1538–1556 (2007), http://dx.doi.org/10.1109/JSAC.2007.071005
3. Medina, D., Hoffmann, F., Rossetto, F., Rokitansky, C.-H.: A geographic routing strategy for north atlantic in-flight internet access via airborne mesh networking. IEEE/ACM Transactions on Networking (TON) 20(4), 1231–1244 (2012)
4. Medina, D., Hoffmann, F., Ayaz, S., Rokitansky, C.H.: Feasibility of an aeronautical mobile ad hoc network over the north atlantic corridor. In: 5th Annual IEEE Communications Society Conference on Sensor, Mesh and Ad Hoc Communications and Networks, SECON 2008, pp. 109–116 (2008), http://dx.doi.org/10.1109/SAHCN.2008.23
5. Flightradar24 real time flight tracking service, http://www.flightradar24.com
6. Fossa, C.E., Raines, R.A., Gunsch, G.H., Temple, M.A.: An overview of the IRID-IUM (r) low earth orbit (LEO) satellite system. In: Proceedings of the IEEE 1998 National Aerospace and Electronics Conference, NAECON 1998, pp. 152–159 (1998), http://dx.doi.org/10.1109/NAECON.1998.710110
7. Walke, B.: Mobilfunknetze und ihre Protokolle 2, pp. 433–493. Springer DE (2001)
8. Hofmann, M.: Uber zusammengesetzte poisson-prozesse und ihre anwendungen in der unfallversicherung. Ph.D. dissertation, Diss. Math. ETH Zurich, Nr. 2511, 0000. Ref.: Saxer, W., Korref.: Nolfi, P. (1955)

Self-management of Hybrid Networks – Hidden Costs Due to TCP Performance Problems

Giovane C.M. Moura, Aiko Pras, Tiago Fioreze, and Pieter-Tjerk de Boer

University of Twente
Centre for Telematics and Information Technology
Faculty of Electrical Engineering, Mathematics and Computer Science
Design and Analysis of Communications Systems (DACS)
Enschede, The Netherlands
{g.c.m.moura,a.pras,t.fioreze,p.t.deboer}@utwente.nl

Abstract. Self-management is one of the most popular research topics in network and systems management. Little is known, however, regarding the costs, in particular with respect to performance, of self-management solutions. The goal of this paper is therefore to analyze such hidden performance costs. Our analysis will be performed within the context of a specific example, namely automatically moving elephant flows from the routed IP layer to optical light-paths (lambdas) in hybrid networks. The advantage of moving elephant flows to light-paths is that such flows will experience lower delays, lower jitter and lower loss, thus better Quality of Service (QoS), while reducing the load at the IP-level, which means that the remaining flows will also experience better QoS. The lower delay at the optical level may cause temporary reordering of packets, however, since the first packet over the light-path may arrive at the receiver side before the last routed IP packet has arrived. Such reordering may lead to short but severe performance problems at the TCP level. We systematically analyze under which conditions such TCP performance problems occur, and how severe these problems are. Although our conclusions are specific to self-management of hybrid networks, it demonstrates by means of an example that self-management solutions may also introduce new problems, which must further be investigated before conclusions can be drawn regarding the pros and cons of self-management.

1 Introduction

One of the most popular research topics within the network management community is *self-management* [1–5]. The key idea behind self-management is to develop computer systems that are able to manage their own operation without (or with little) human intervention. Although self-management is often seen as a solution for many problems, little is known about the hidden costs in terms of potential new problems that may result from self-management. Such problems may vary from case to case, and therefore need to be investigated within the context of specific examples.

T. Bauschert (Ed.): EUNICE 2013, LNCS 8115, pp. 54–65, 2013.

To get a better understanding of such hidden problems, this paper tackles the example of hybrid networks in which routed flows at the IP level can be moved to the optical level. In such networks, IP packets can be forwarded either through a chain of IP routers, or through an end-to-end lightpath. Such a "lightpath" uses optical switching technology, either at the level of entire fibers, a wavelength within a fiber (lambda), or a TDM-based channel (SONET/SDH) within a wavelength; in any case, switching delays will be smaller, and data rates may well be higher than at the IP level. Moving large flows from the routed IP level to a direct optical lightpath thus enables these flows to experience a faster and more reliable service, while at the same time reducing the load on the IP level equipment, which is typically much more expensive than lightpath equipment.

Current approaches to manage such hybrid networks mostly rely on human operators in order to: (*i*) select the flows to be moved to the optical level, and (*ii*) create and release the necessary lightpaths. Since these decisions can be slow and error prone, we envision a move towards self-management approaches, which automatically move IP flows to lightpaths on the fly [6–8]. Network operators would only be required to initially configure the self-management process with decision policies, such as setting thresholds and priorities. After this initial setup, the self-management process runs by itself. For more details, see [9].

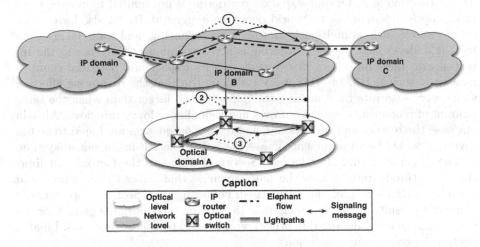

Fig. 1. Self-management of lightpaths in hybrid optical and packet networks: in step 1, the elephant flows are identified; in step 2 the optical switches are informed about the decision to move a flow; and in step 3, the optical switches establish the lightpath.

Self-management of hybrid networks can result in performance problems at the TCP level, however. In a manual process, a lightpath is established a-priori, before the start of the flow (note that within this paper the term "flow" relates to a single TCP connection). Since our self-management process cannot rely on human intelligence to identify a-priori which flows should be transferred over a lightpath, it should analyze existing flows at the IP level to find those flows that are worthwhile to be moved to the optical level. Flows are thus moved *on the fly*, which means that the first packets of a flow may be forwarded at the IP level, whereas later packets can be moved to the lightpath. The lower delay at the optical level may cause temporary reordering of packets however, since the first packet over the lightpath may arrive at the receiver side before the last packet has arrived via the IP level. Under certain conditions, such reordering may lead to short, but severe performance problems at the TCP level.

The goal of this paper is to investigate the potential performance problems at the TCP level, to gain a better understanding of the potential hidden costs of self-managing hybrid networks. With 'cost', we do not necessarily mean monetary costs, but more generally problems and disadvantages (although those may well translate into monetary costs for a commercial network operator). Also, we will not look at the direct costs such as the costs of (re)configuring the equipment when moving a flow.

The approach taken in this paper is to first identify the factors that may limit the throughput of a TCP flow, and define four scenarios to cover these factors, thus extending a previous paper [10] in which we analyzed only one scenario. We will then use the *ns-2* network simulator [11] to investigate, for each scenario, the effect of moving TCP flows on the fly.

As noted above, the essence of the problem is the reordering of packets and TCP's reaction to it. Of course, packet reordering is not limited to moving flows to the optical domain, or to hybrid networks in general. It can also have many other causes, such as multipath routing, load balancing, and route changes. In fact, [12] shows that packet reordering is a very common occurrence in the Internet, and there have been many studies on its impact and potential counter-measures, such as [13, 14]. Our study is different in that the reordering affects a single very high rate flow, making the impact much larger than when the same amount of reordering is spread out over many smaller or lower rate flows. Also, in our case the reordering is intentional, and if its consequences are found to be too severe, it would be an argument against the use of the self-management system.

The paper structure is as follows. Section 2 discusses the factors that limit the TCP throughput, defines the four scenarios that cover these factors, and introduces the ns-2 simulation setup used. Following that, Section 3 presents the simulation results for all four scenarios. In Section 4, the insights gained for the four scenarios are generalized to other scenarios and transport protocols. Finally, Section 5 presents our conclusions.

2   Simulation Setup

This section discusses the simulation setup: we discuss the topology, the relevant thoughput limiting factors, the TCP variant to be used, and the simulator.

Network Topology. Figure 2 shows our simulation topology. It consists of three routers (r1, r2, and r3) and two nodes (Sender and Receiver) connected by two different paths: the IP path (r1-r2-r3) and the optical path (r1-r3).

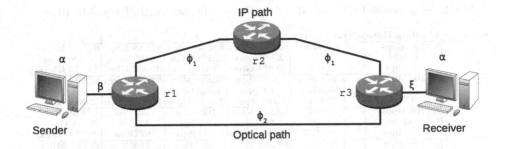

Fig. 2. Topology used in the simulations and limiting factors (Greek letters)

The simulation starts with the sender opening a single TCP connection to the receiver and sending data, forwarded via the IP path. After reaching a predefined throughput value, the decision is made to move that flow to the optical path: from that moment on, router r1 will forward all subsequent data to the receiver via the optical path. Note that this only affects the data direction (sender → receiver), while the acknowledgment packets continue to use the IP path. For a short period of time after the switch – the *transient phase* – there will be data packets on both the IP and optical paths; after this phase, all data packets are on the optical path.

Simulation Scenarios. Although many factors can limit the throughput of TCP [15], since the scope of this paper is on self-management of network configurations, we focus on those factors that relate to the configuration of the network, namely the capacity of network links and the size of the TCP buffers. Thus, we have identified the following scenarios:

– **Scenario A**: the size of the TCP buffers (α in Figure 2) are the limiting factors for the TCP throughput.
– **Scenario B**: the capacity of the sender's local link (β in Figure 2) is the limiting factor for the TCP throughput.
– **Scenario C**: the capacity of the core links (ϕ_1 and ϕ_2 in Figure 2) acts as the limiting factor. We distinguish between the cases where the capacity of IP links is equal to that of the optical links ($\phi_1 = \phi_2$) and where the capacity of the optical links is larger than that of the IP links ($\phi_2 > \phi_1$).
– **Scenario D**: the receiver local link is the limiting factor (ξ in Figure 2).

For each scenario we simulate three limiting data rates: 100 Mbps, 1 Gbps, and 10 Gbps. In each simulation, the flow is moved to the optical path once the actual throughput reaches the limiting rate. We simulate three base RTT values, namely 10, 100 and 1000 ms, with corresponding optical path RTTs of 6, 60 and 600 ms, respectively. Table 1 summarizes the values of the parameters used in our simulation scenarios for RTT=10 ms; an equal number of simulations was conducted for 100 ms and 1000 ms RTT, with α in Scenario A scaled accordingly.

Table 1. Scenarios and values used for the limiting factors for RTT equal to 10 ms

Scenario	Limiting Rate	α (rtt=10ms)	β	ϕ_1	ϕ_2	ξ
A	100 Mbps	0.125 MB	622.08 Mbps	622.08 Mbps	622.08 Mbps	622.08 Mbps
	1 Gbps	1.25 MB	2.488 Gbps	2.488 Gbps	2.488 Gbps	2.488 Gbps
	10 Gbps	12.5 MB	39.813 Gbps	39.813 Gbps	39.813 Gbps	39.813 Gbps
B	100 Mbps	1.16 GB	100 Mbps	622.08 Mbps	622.08 Mbps	622.08 Mbps
	1 Gbps	1.16 GB	1 Gbps	2.488 Gbps	2.488 Gbps	2.488 Gbps
	10 Gbps	1.16 GB	10 Gbps	39.813 Gbps	39.813 Gbps	39.813 Gbps
C1	100 Mpbs	1.16 GB	622.08 Mbps	100Mbps	100Mbps	622.08Mbps
	1 Gbps	1.16 GB	2.488 Gbps	1 Gbps	1 Gbps	2.488 Gbps
	10 Gbps	1.16 GB	39.813 Gbps	10 Gbps	10 Gbps	39.813 Gbps
C2	100 Mbps	1.16 GB	622.08 Mbps	100 Mbps	622.08 Mbps	622.08 Mbps
	1 Gbps	1.16 GB	2.488 Gbps	1 Gbps	2.488 Gbps	2.488 Gbps
	10 Gbps	1.16 GB	39.813 Gbps	10 Gbps	39.813 Gbps	39.813 Gbps
D	100 Mbps	1.16 GB	622.08 Mbps	622.08 Mbps	622.08 Mbps	100 Mbps
	1 Gbps	1.16 GB	2.488 Gbps	2.488 Gbps	2.488 Gbps	1 Gbps
	10 Gbps	1.16 GB	39.813 Gbps	39.813 Gbps	39.813 Gbps	10 Gbps

TCP Version and Simulator. For this study, we decided to use TCP CU-BIC (version 2.1) [16], since it is adapted to links with a large bandwidth-delay product (as is the case in our scenarios), and nowadays widely used because it is the default in Linux. For the simulations we use the ns-2 network simulator, version 2.33, which can run the actual TCP CUBIC code from Linux [17].

3 Simulation Results

In this section, we show some simulation results for all four scenarios, illustrating the various problems that may occur.

3.1 Scenario A: TCP Buffers as the Limiting Factor

In this scenario we configured the TCP buffers to act as the limiting factor of the TCP throughput, as discussed earlier in [10]. This is done by setting the other potentially limiting factors (link capacities β, ϕ, and ξ) high enough, as presented in Table 1. The TCP buffers were set equal to the bandwidth-delay product, calculated from the limiting flow rate (100 Mbps, 1 Gbps or 10 Gbps) and the RTT *before* the switchover.

For all cases of Scenario A, only one type of behavior was seen, independent of RTT and buffer sizes: after the switchover, the TCP throughput increases without any packet loss. Figures 3(a) and 3(b) show the throughput as a function of time for the 1 Gbps case, before and after the switch at $t = 0$ (vertical line).

These graphs differ in their "granularity", i.e., the time interval over which the data rate is averaged. This is a compromise between cluttering the picture at too small granularity, and masking interesting effects at coarse granularity. We henceforth show only graphs for a granularity of 1000 ms; if this hides any interesting effects, these are discussed in the text.

As can be seen, before switchover the flows present a stable rate of 1 Gbps, limited only by the TCP buffers. After the switchover, CUBIC's throughput increases quickly to the expected new theoretical value of 1.667 Gbps (i.e., the buffer size divided by the new RTT).

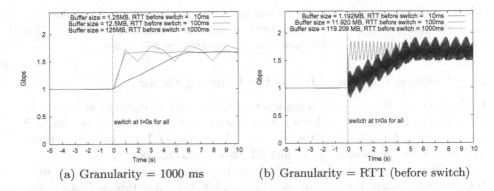

(a) Granularity = 1000 ms   (b) Granularity = RTT (before switch)

Fig. 3. Throughput of TCP flows in Scenario A (1 Gbps limiting rate)

3.2 Scenario B – Sender's Local Link as the Limiting Factor

In Scenario B, the sender's local link is the limiting factor for TCP throughput. Intuitively, one might expect that in this case, the optical switch has no influence, since the bottleneck does not change. However, this is not true; Figure 4 shows that there is a brief decrease of the throughput immediately after the switch (solid line), compared to the case without switching (dotted line).

With a finer granularity, one can also see a *peak* of 1.3 Gbps in the first 0.1 s after the switch. This is due to packets arriving from both the IP and optical paths during this transient phase. The packets arriving via the optical path have a higher sequence number than the ones coming from the IP path, because of the optical path's lower delay. This causes the receiver to perform reordering and

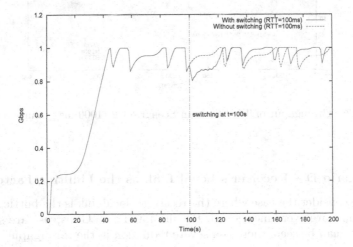

Fig. 4. Throughput of TCP flows in scenario B for RTT=100 ms, $\beta = 1$ Gbps and granularity equal to 1000 ms

ask for retransmissions (through a total of 14186 duplicate ACKs), resulting in the reduction of the congestion window and thus a throughput reduction. This can be seen at $t = 102$ s, where the throughput reaches 803 Mbps.

3.3   Scenario C – Core Link as the Limiting Factor

In this scenario, the core link is the limiting factor, and we distinguish two cases: C1 with the IP and optical links having the same capacity ($\phi_1 = \phi_2$), and C2 with the optical link being faster ($\phi_2 > \phi_1$). In scenario C1, the behaviour turns out essentially the same as in scenario B, so we focus on scenario C2.

In scenario C2, similar behavior was seen as in scenarios C1 and B during the transient phase: throughput oscillation. However, after this oscillation, the throughput increases significantly, using the optical path's higher capacity. This is shown in Figure 5 for a 10 Gbps IP link and a 39.813 Gbps optical link, at RTTs of 10 and 100 ms. In either case, we see a mostly linear[1] growth of the throughput until the IP link is fully utilized; then the switch to the optical domain is made, and mostly linear growth resumes until the optical link speed is reached.

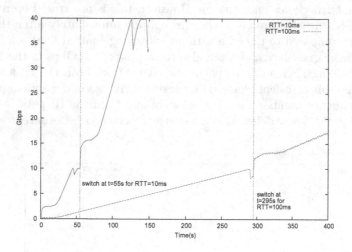

Fig. 5. Throughput of TCP flows in Scenario C2 (1000 ms granularity)

3.4   Scenario D – Receiver's Local Link as the Limiting Factor

Finally, we consider the case where the receiver's local link is the bottleneck and all other links are overdimensioned. Results for the 10 Gbps case are shown in Figure 6. As can be seen, there is a severe reduction in the throughput after the switchover.

---

[1] One might expect cubic rather than linear growth; however, version 2.1 of TCP CUBIC had an upper bound on the growth rate. This was removed in version 2.2 [16].

Like in the other scenarios, after the switchover router r3 temporarily receives data via both the IP and the optical links simultaneously, for a total of 20 Gbps. However, unlike in the other scenarios, the link from this router to the destination was already fully loaded at 10 Gbps, and cannot cope with this temporary double data flow. Queueing all these packets is not possible either (in our simulation, r3 has a 500 packet buffer), causing many packets to be dropped (335107 packets in the first 200 ms after the switchover in the 10ms RTT case). This in turn causes the receiver to send a massive number of duplicate ACKs, which leads the sender to reduce its congestion window, causing the throughput to drop to a minimum value of 1.6 Gbps.

Figure 7 shows how r3's queue size changes in time. Since TCP CUBIC (like most other TCP versions) measures the available bandwidth on the path by increasing its congestion window until packet loss occurs, the queue also builds up at other moments than the switchover, for example at $t = 46s$. When the optical switchover occurs at $t = 55$ s, the queue already contains 343 packets due to TCP CUBIC probing for bandwidth. After the switchover, packets arrive from both paths, causing the queue to fill up very quickly and resulting in a massive discarding of packets, as discussed above. The queue increases at later times are again due to CUBIC's normal bandwidth probing.

Note that the problem seen here is fundamentally different from that seen in scenarios B and C. In either case, temporarily two streams of packets (namely via the IP path and via the optical path with less delay) are merged, causing reordering. However, in scenarios B and C, no packets were dropped, whereas in the current scenario many packets are dropped. This causes a much larger reduction in throughput, and recovery from this also takes much more time.

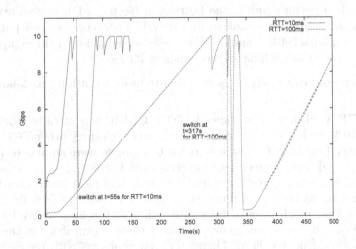

Fig. 6. Throughput of TCP flows for Scenario D (1000 ms granularity)

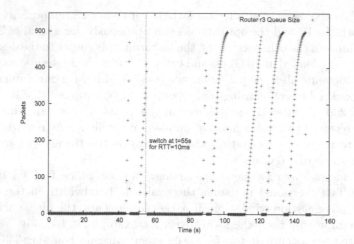

Fig. 7. Router r3 Queue Size for 10Gbps case with RTT = 10ms

4   Discussion and Generalization

In the previous section, we have seen three types of behaviour when switching a TCP flow from the IP to the optical path:

- When the TCP buffers were the limiting factor (scenario A), nothing unto-ward happens: the system converges quickly to the new higher throughput made possible by the lower RTT.
- When the sender's link or the IP and optical paths are the bottleneck (scenarios B and C), temporarily packets from both paths arrive at the receiver, causing reordering but no loss. We have seen that TCP reacts to this rather benignly, with only a small (< 20%) and short-lived reduction in throughput.
- When the receiver's link is the bottleneck (scenario D), it gets overloaded due to the temporary simultaneous arrival of packets via both paths. This causes much packet loss and a severe (> 80%) reduction of throughput, from which recovery takes longer (thousands of RTTs).

These conclusions can easily be generalized to other situations, as follows.

Other TCP Variants. The choice for TCP CUBIC was already motivated in Section 2. Still, we have done similar experiments with three other TCP variants (Reno, Vegas, Compound). The results for Compound were similar to those for CUBIC reported here, sometimes recovering even faster.

Reno and Vegas performed far worse: due to their at most linear growth of the congestion window, they need much more time to recover. In fact, for the same reason they need much time to fully utilize link with a large delay bandwidth product even before the changeover, making them unsuitable for the kind of elephant flows considered here. Therefore, their problems with recovering from the optical switchover can be safely ignored.

Other Protocols. Although TCP is the dominant transport protocol in the internet, there are others, such as UDP, SCTP and DCCP. Clearly, after the switchover they will experience the same packet reordering and loss as TCP.

UDP does not by itself have a congestion control mechanism, so the reordering and loss will not directly affect its throughput. However, the reordering and loss will be passed on to the application, so detailed knowledge of the application would be needed to predict the effects for the user.

New transport protocols such as SCTP (Stream Control Transmission Protocol) [18]) and DCCP (Datagram Congestion Control Protocol) [19] have congestion control mechanisms that are directly based on TCP variants [20]. Therefore we can expect them to behave similarly to TCP, with possibly additional application layer effects like with UDP.

Other Scenarios. In the scenarios considered so far, the same parameter was the limiting factor before and after the switchover. Of course, in reality after the switchover a different parameter can be the limiting factor. What happens in those cases will generally be a mixture of the "pure" behaviours studied here.

Also the numerical values of parameters (link speeds etc.) can be different. Clearly, such changes will change the outcomes quantitatively (e.g., recovery will take longer or shorter), but no qualitative differences are to be expected.

One might hope that installing a large buffer at the output router would prevent the massive packet loss in scenario D, but this is not true. TCP's congestion control algorithm would have filled such a buffer (because TCP needs to detect loss to know when to back off), so there would not be space to temporarily accept the extra packets when the flow is moved to the lightpath.

5   Conclusions

In this paper we investigated hidden costs of self-management within the specific context of hybrid networks. In particular we analyzed the performance problems that may result if an elephant TCP flow at the IP level is moved on the fly to the optical level using ns-2 simulations for four different scenarios. During such move, a temporary but massive reordering of packets occurs since the first packets transferred over the optical level will arrive before the last packets arrive at the IP level.

We found three qualitatively different behaviours. In case the TCP throughput of the elephant flow was limited by the size of the TCP send and receive buffers, the throughput *increases* substantially due to the lower RTT of the optical path. In case the throughput was limited by the sender's local link or by the backbone links, TCP reacts benignly to the reordering, with only a small and short-lived reduction of throughput. On the other hand, if the throughput was limited by the receiver's local link, a *significant drop* in the throughput occurs for a relatively long period. In this case, the router at the receiver side needs to drop a large number of packets when they arrive simultaneously via both links, because its outgoing link was already fully used.

The significant throughput drop and long recovery period observed in the last scenario can be very noticable to the end user, and thus is something the operator of the network might want to avoid. However, whether or not this problem is going to occur depends on the bottleneck in the receiver's network, which may well be out of sight of the operator of the hybrid network, making this truly a *hidden* cost of implementing self-management.

The conclusion that can be drawn from the hybrid networks case presented in this paper, is that self-management mechanisms may introduce unexpected side-effects, which require further analysis before such self-management mechanisms can be widely adopted. Research on self-management mechanisms should therefore not be performed in isolation, but always consider the context in which these mechanisms will be applied, to fully understand their pros and cons.

Acknowledgments. The research reported in this paper is supported by the FP7 ICT UniverSelf project (#257513). The authors would like to thank Wouter Kooij for his work on extending the simulations presented in this paper to other TCP flavors – Vegas, Reno, and Compound.

References

1. Pras, A., Schönwälder, J., Burgess, M., Festor, O., Pérez, G., Stadler, R., Stiller, B.: Key Research Challenges in Network Management. IEEE Communications Magazine 45(10), 104–110 (2007)
2. Jennings, B., van der Meer, S., Balasubramaniam, S., Botvich, D., Foghlu, M., Donnelly, W., Strassner, J.: Towards Autonomic Management of Communications Networks. IEEE Communications Magazine 45(10), 112–121 (2007)
3. Lupu, E., Dulay, N., Sloman, M., Sventek, J., Heeps, S., Strowes, S., Twidle, K., Keoh, S.L., Schaeffer-Filho, A.: AMUSE: Autonomic Management of Ubiquitous e-Health Systems. Concurr. Comput.: Pract. Exper. 20(3), 277–295 (2008)
4. Cheng, L., Galis, A., Mathieu, B., Jean, K., Ocampo, R., Mamatas, L., Rubio-Loyola, J., Serrat, J., Berl, A., de Meer, H., Davy, S., Movahedi, Z., Lefevre, L.: Self-organising Management Overlays for Future Internet Services. In: van der Meer, S., Burgess, M., Denazis, S. (eds.) MACE 2008. LNCS, vol. 5276, pp. 74–89. Springer, Heidelberg (2008)
5. Derbel, H., Agoulmine, N., Salaün, M.: ANEMA: Autonomic Network Management Architecture to Support Self-configuration and Self-optimization in IP networks. Comput. Netw. 53(3), 418–430 (2009)
6. Fioreze, T., Granville, L., Sadre, R., Pras, A.: A Statistical Analysis of Network Parameters for the Self-management of Lambda-Connections. In: Sadre, R., Pras, A. (eds.) AIMS 2009 Enschede. LNCS, vol. 5637, pp. 15–27. Springer, Heidelberg (2009)
7. Fioreze, T., Pras, A.: Self-management of Lambda-connections in Optical Networks. In: Bandara, A.K., Burgess, M. (eds.) AIMS 2007. LNCS, vol. 4543, pp. 212–215. Springer, Heidelberg (2007)
8. Fioreze, T., van de Meent, R., Pras, A.: An Architecture for the Self-management of Lambda-Connections in Hybrid Networks. In: Pras, A., van Sinderen, M. (eds.) EUNICE 2007. LNCS, vol. 4606, pp. 141–148. Springer, Heidelberg (2007)

9. Fioreze, T.: Self-Management of Hybrid Optical and Packet Switching Networks. PhD thesis, Universiteit Twente (February 2010)

10. Moura, G.C.M., Fioreze, T., de Boer, P.-T., Pras, A.: Optical switching impact on TCP throughput limited by TCP buffers. In: Nunzi, G., Scoglio, C., Li, X. (eds.) IPOM 2009. LNCS, vol. 5843, pp. 161–166. Springer, Heidelberg (2009)

11. The Network Simulator NS-2, http://nsnam.isi.edu/nsnam/index.php/Main_Page

12. Bennett, J., Partridge, C., Shectman, N.: Packet reordering is not pathological network behavior. IEEE/ACM Transactions on Networking 7(6), 789–798 (1999)

13. Zhang, M., Karp, B., Floyd, S., Peterson, L.: RR-TCP: a reordering-robust TCP with DSACK. In: 11th IEEE International Conference on Network Protocols, pp. 95–106 (November 2003)

14. Karlsson, J., Hurtig, P., Brunstrom, A., Kassler, A., Di Stasi, G.: Impact of multi-path routing on TCP performance. In: IEEE International Symposium on a World of Wireless, Mobile and Multimedia Networks (WoWMoM), pp. 1–3 (June 2012)

15. Timmer, M., de Boer, P., Pras, A.: How to Identify the Speed Limiting Factor of a TCP Flow. In: 4th IEEE/IFIP Workshop on End-to-End Monitoring Techniques and Services, pp. 17–24 (April 2006)

16. Ha, S., Rhee, I., Xu, L.: CUBIC: a new TCP-friendly high-speed TCP variant. SIGOPS Oper. Syst. Rev. 42(5), 64–74 (2008)

17. Wei, D.X., Cao, P.: NS-2 TCP-Linux: an NS-2 TCP Implementation with Congestion Control Algorithms from Linux. In: WNS2 2006: The 2006 Workshop on NS-2: The IP Network Simulator. ACM, New York (2006)

18. Steward, R. (ed.): Stream Control Transmission Protocol (SCTP). RFC 4960 (2007)

19. Kohler, E., Handley, M., Floyd, S.: Datagram Congestion Control Protocol (DCCP). RFC 4340 (2006)

20. Floyd, S., Kohler, E.: Profile for Datagram Congestion Control Protocol (DCCP) Congestion Control ID 2: TCP-like Congestion Control. RFC 4341 (2006)

A Revenue-Maximizing Scheme for Radio Access Technology Selection in Heterogeneous Wireless Networks with User Profile Differentiation

Elissar Khloussy[1], Xavier Gelabert[2], and Yuming Jiang[1]

[1] Department of Telematics, NTNU, Norway
[2] Huawei Technologies Sweden AB, 16440 Kista, Sweden
{khloussy,jiang}@item.ntnu.no, xavier.gelabert@huawei.com

Abstract. In this paper, the problem of radio access technology (RAT) selection in heterogeneous wireless networks (HWNs) is tackled from an operator's perspective, with the objective of maximizing the generated revenue. Two user profiles are considered with different priority levels. An integrated 3GPP Long Term Evolution (LTE) and Wireless Fidelity (WiFi) network is considered as an example of HWN, where LTE is used mainly for the high-priority class, while a portion of its resources, defined by a load threshold, can be shared by the low-priority class. A Markovian model is defined and validated by simulation. Subsequently, the value of the load threshold for resource sharing in LTE is investigated, and an optimization problem is formulated to find the optimal threshold for which the revenue is maximized.

Keywords: Heterogeneous Wireless Networks, Resource Management, Revenue Maximization.

1 Introduction

With the tremendous evolution of wireless network technologies and the ever increasing demand from users to be always best connected, various radio access technologies (RATs) have been standardized and deployed. It has become very likely to encounter geographical areas covered by more than one RAT, each with different characteristics in terms of latency, coverage, and link capacity. By providing more connection options than a single-RAT network, a heterogeneous wireless network (HWN) offers the operator additional tuning knobs to meet the users' needs and at the same time generate higher revenues.

In this paper, we consider the scenario of a HWN that is run by a single operator and where two RATs are integrated, namely 3rd Generation Partnership Project (3GPP) Long Term Evolution (called LTE hereafter) and Wireless Fidelity (WiFi). This network scenario is rather practical and can be found from real networks. Moreover, mobile devices and smartphones supporting both technologies are now available in the market. With these factors combined, it becomes of interest to investigate mechanisms that allocate users' connections effectively, allowing an efficient utilization of the system resources.

T. Bauschert (Ed.): EUNICE 2013, LNCS 8115, pp. 66–77, 2013.

In order to take advantage of the combined features of the different coexisting RATs in a HWN, a good coordination among these RATs is required. This involves the adoption of common radio resource management (CRRM) strategies, a critical factor for the success of HWNs. Among the various CRRM functionalities [1], RAT selection is known to be most fundamental. It can be *user-centric* or *operator-centric*. Typically, a user-centric RAT selection scheme considers the user's preferences as objective, such as signal strength and access cost. An operator-centric one is oriented towards maximizing the operator's interests, e.g. the overall HWN capacity, and takes into consideration the network-related parameters such as RATs' loads and capabilities as well as the existing service types [1]. In this paper, we address an *operator-centric* RAT selection with specific objective of maximizing the operator's revenue.

A thorough analysis and classification of the recently proposed radio resource management procedures in HWNs can be found in [1, 2]. In [1], the authors provided a case study that illustrated the potential gain offered by CRRM especially in terms of capacity enhancement. In [3], a CRRM scheme that minimizes the vertical handover rate and service cost while achieving the desired quality of service (QoS) was proposed. In CRRM, RAT selection functionality has gained a particular attention in the literature. For example, Gelabert et al. provided in [4] a framework to allocate services in HWNs with the help of Markov chain. The model was used to compare and evaluate the performance of various RAT selection policies that fall into three categories: service-based, load-balancing based and multi-mode terminal driven strategies. However, the users' perceived QoS was the main focus of most of the proposed RAT selection algorithms e.g., [5–7].

Very few *operator-centric approaches with the objective of maximizing the operator's revenue* can be found. In [8], a fuzzy neural based CRRM strategy was presented. Both techno-economic cognitive mechanisms and user differentiation concepts were investigated, with the aim of guaranteeing the user satisfaction maintained at a certain target level, while also considering the network's generated revenue. However, the proposed CRRM strategy, based on a fuzzy neural network, is complex for implementation in real networks. In our early work [9], CRRM strategies based on call admission control and vertical handover were presented and compared. It was shown that a significant increase of revenue could be incurred by the adoption of CRRM policies. However, the evaluation in [9] was only based on simulation. Other admission control where decisions are taken dynamically to maximize the operator's revenue can also be found in the literature [10, 11].

In this paper, we propose a new scheme for RAT selection that is intuitive and easy to implement. In addition, the proposed approach is devised to work at a different level in the sense of providing the operator with the initial setting of an important parameter i.e., the load threshold in LTE, at the early planning phase of the system. With an appropriate setting of the load threshold, system resources can be used efficiently and the revenue be maximized. To demonstrate its use, a specific example of HWN, which is an integrated LTE/WiFi network, is considered. Also, for practical reasons, only two user profiles with different priority levels are offered and a load threshold is defined in LTE to reserve resources to the high-priority users. Importantly, an analytical model for the proposed scheme is presented and validated by simulation. In addition, we investigate the impact of the choice of the load threshold on the revenue and solve the corresponding optimization problem.

The paper is organized as follows. Sec. 2 describes the system model and the proposed RAT selection scheme. In Sec. 3, the different elements of the Markovian model are introduced. Sec. 4 presents the results obtained by the model and the simulation. In Sec. 5 we introduce and solve the optimization problem for finding the optimal threshold value, and Sec. 6 concludes the paper.

2 The System Model and User Profile-Based RAT Selection

We consider an integrated LTE/WiFi heterogeneous network. While WiFi offers broadband data transmission for a limited coverage area at low cost and simple control plane, LTE provides more efficient services and better QoS with wider coverage area, at bandwidth and cost comparable to that of the WLAN [12, 13].

In the considered scenario, a user can be either residing in an area covered by LTE only, or in a dual coverage area with a probability P_{dual}. Two user profiles C_1 and C_2 are provided. Class C_1 has higher priority than class C_2. Practically, the prioritized class C_1 targets the business sector, known to be more sensitive to the perceived QoS than the charged price. The low-priority class C_2 targets the individual users who care mainly about the access cost, and don't have strict requirements with respect to the QoS. Naturally, C_1 users get faster connection speed by paying higher connection fees as compared to users belonging to C_2 class. In terms of admission to LTE, C_1 users have a privilege in using LTE resources over C_2. For this purpose, a load threshold θ is defined as the percentage of LTE capacity that the low-priority users are allowed to share with C_1 users.

The RAT selection block, as illustrated in Fig. 1, requires mainly two types of inputs: network parameters (LTE and WiFi loads and the value of θ), and user parameters (the user's class of service, and whether the user is in a dual-coverage area or not). It generates as output the decision of admitting or blocking the arriving session, as well as the selected RAT in the case where the admission of the session is successful.

Based on the RATs characteristics and the considered user profile differentiation, we propose the following RAT selection strategy:

- When a new C_1 session arrives, it is admitted to LTE as long as LTE has enough available resources. This policy reflects the operator's willingness to offer better QoS for C_1 users whose contribution, in terms of generated revenue, is more significant than C_2 users.
- When a new C_2 session arrives, the RAT selection module tries to admit this session into WiFi first. This way, the operator benefits from WiFi capacity

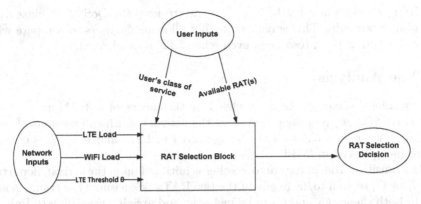

Fig. 1. RAT selection block

to accommodate sessions belonging to the low-priority profile, keeping more
resources in LTE available for C_1 class. In the case where the admission of
the new C_2 session to WiFi is not possible (user out of WiFi coverage or
WiFi is overloaded), and with traffic load in LTE below the threshold θ, the
RAT selection module allows the admission of the new C_2 session to LTE.
– When the load in LTE exceeds θ, only C_1 sessions are admitted.

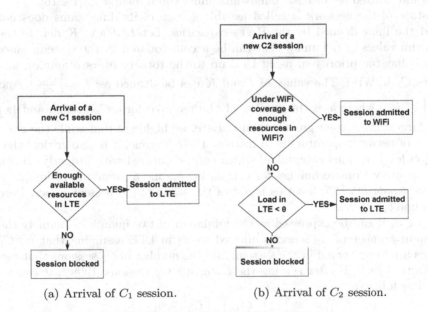

(a) Arrival of C_1 session.   (b) Arrival of C_2 session.

Fig. 2. Algorithm for RAT selection

Corresponding to the above strategy, Fig. 2 illustrates the RAT selection
algorithm. Note that though the proposed RAT selection scheme gives higher

priority to C_1 class in using LTE, it also tries to keep the QoS of C_2 class from degrading drastically. This is realized by not allowing C_1 users to compete with C_2 users in using WiFi resources, even when LTE is overloaded.

3   The Analysis

The considered scenario can be modeled by the means of a 3D Markov chain. Each state $S(i,j,k)$ represents a state of the network in which i sessions of class C_1, and j sessions of class C_2 are being served in LTE, and k sessions of class C_2 are being served in WiFi.

The transition from one state to another is initiated upon the arrival/departure of a C_1 or C_2 session to/from any of the two RATs. We assume the traffic generated in both classes C_1 and C_2 to be inelastic, and arriving according to Poisson processes with rates λ_1 and λ_2 respectively. As for the session holding times, they follow exponential distributions with mean values $1/\mu_1$ and $1/\mu_2$ for classes C_1 and C_2 respectively. We would like to stress that, at the session level, these assumptions are rather realistic [14].

3.1   The Set of Feasible States

In the proposed scenario, we assume a fixed total bandwidth for each of the RATs, namely C_{lte} and C_{wifi} for LTE and WiFi respectively, each being partitioned into a fixed set of basic bandwidth units (bbu) as in, e.g. [15, 16].

A state of the network is called feasible if each of its dimensions does not exceed the limit defined by the RATs capacities. Let I, J and K denote the maximum values of i, j and k that can be accommodated by the system. Since C_1 class has the priority in using LTE up to the totality of its resources, and so does C_2 in WiFi, The values of I and K can be defined as: $I = \left\lfloor \frac{C_{lte}}{b_1} \right\rfloor$, and $K = \left\lfloor \frac{C_{wifi}}{b_2} \right\rfloor$, where b_i is the number of bbu required for a C_i session, and $\lfloor x \rfloor$ is the largest integer not greater than x. Here, we highlight that while the main interest of network operators is to increase their revenue, it is also critical that the QoS level remains acceptable, which can be ensured with properly chosen b_i. There are various techniques for calculating b_i, and a promising technique is *effective bandwidth* [17], but this is out of the scope of the present paper. Here we assume b_i is given.

As for J, it can be expressed as the minimum of two quantities, namely the maximum number of C_2 sessions allowed to be in LTE assuming that no C_1 sessions are being served in the system, and the number of C_2 sessions that can be admitted to LTE after serving the i ongoing C_1 sessions. Hence, J can be defined as follows:

$$J(i) = min(\left\lfloor \theta \frac{C_{lte}}{b_2} \right\rfloor, \left\lfloor \frac{C_{lte} - b_1 \cdot i}{b_2} \right\rfloor). \tag{1}$$

Hence, the set of feasible states in the proposed system can be written as:

$$S = \{S(i,j,k) | 0 \le i \le I, 0 \le j \le J(i), 0 \le k \le K\}. \tag{2}$$

Table 1. Transition rates from generic state $S(i, j, k)$

To State	Rate	Condition
$S(i+1, j, k)$	λ_1	$i < I$
$S(i-1, j, k)$	$i.\mu_1$	$i > 0$
$S(i, j, k+1)$	$\lambda_2.P_{dual}$	$k < K$
$S(i, j, k-1)$	$k.\mu_2$	$k > 0$
$S(i, j+1, k)$	$\lambda_2.(1 - P_{dual})$	$j < J(i) \wedge k < K$
	λ_2	$j < J(i) \wedge k = K$
$S(i, j-1, k)$	$j.\mu_2$	$j > 0$

3.2 State Transitions

Having defined the set of feasible states, we need to specify the transitions between the different states in order to build the transition rate matrix $\mathbf{Q}$. The transition rates from a given state $S(i, j, k)$ to any of its neighboring states are provided in Table 1. After creating $\mathbf{Q}$ matrix, the next step is to find the stationary probability vector. This can be obtained with the help of numerical methods, and specifically we use the Successive Overrelaxation Method (SOR) [18]. The steady state probability allows us to derive the needed performance metrics as shown in the following subsection.

3.3 Performance Metrics

Average Number of Sessions. The average number of sessions admitted in the system for both classes is defined as follows:

$$E[x] = \sum_{S(i,j,k) \in S} x \cdot P_{(i,j,k)}, x \in \{i, j, k\}. \tag{3}$$

where $E[x]$ is the average value of x, and $P_{(i,j,k)}$ is the steady state probability for the state $S(i, j, k)$.

Blocking Probability. By (3), the average number of users is found, which also represents the carried traffic in the system. This latter can be computed as the portion of the offered traffic A ($A = \lambda/\mu$) that has been admitted successfully to the system as follows:

$$E[x] = A_\gamma \cdot (1 - P_{b,\gamma}), \gamma \in \{1, 2\}. \tag{4}$$

where $P_{b,\gamma}$ is the blocking probability of class C_γ, $x = i$ for $\gamma = 1$, and $x = j + k$ (with $E[j + k] = E[j] + E[k]$) for $\gamma = 2$. Therefore, the blocking probability of class C_γ is computed as:

$$P_{b,\gamma} = 1 - \frac{E[x]}{A_\gamma}, \gamma \in \{1, 2\}. \tag{5}$$

Table 2. System Parameters

Parameter	Symbol	Value
Capacity of LTE	C_{lte}	10
Capacity of WiFi	C_{wifi}	5
Number of bbu required per C_1 session	b_1	2
Number of bbu required per C_2 session	b_2	1
Throughput per bbu in LTE	r_{lte}	1Mbps
Throughput per bbu in WiFi	r_{wifi}	1Mbps
Arrival rate of C_1 class	λ_1	$1/60\ s^{-1}$
Arrival rate of C_2 class	λ_2	$1/30\ s^{-1}$
Session holding time of C_1 class	$1/\mu_1$	200 s
Session holding time of C_2 class	$1/\mu_2$	150 s
Dual coverage probability	P_{dual}	0.6

Throughput. The throughput of a certain class of service is the product of its carried traffic by the throughput of the total allocated bbu for this class in the serving RAT. Hence, the throughput for service class C_γ can be defined as:

$$Th_\gamma = \sum_\alpha E[x] \cdot b_\gamma \cdot r_\alpha \,, \gamma \in \{1, 2\}. \tag{6}$$

where: r_α is the throughput (in Mbps) per bbu of RAT α, $x = i$ for $\gamma = 1$, $x = j$ for $(\gamma = 2 \wedge \alpha = \text{LTE})$, and $x = k$ for $(\gamma = 2 \wedge \alpha = \text{WiFi})$.

4   Validating the Analysis

To validate the analytical model, a system-level simulation has been conducted in Matlab. The simulation was run for 5000 time units, and the same simulation repeated 100 times to get its average performance. The applied RAT selection policy in simulation follows the state feasibility conditions imposed for the Markov model. For ease of presentation, we used the settings in Table 2 to analyze the performance of the proposed RAT selection policy. The analysis may be further extended for other more realistic settings. The results are plotted in Fig. 3 and Fig. 4, with the 95% confidence intervals provided. the results show a good matching between the model and the simulation, proving the validity of our proposed Markovian model.

Fig. 3 depicts the blocking probabilities for classes C_1 and C_2, considering different values of θ, ranging from 0 i.e., no C_2 sessions can be admitted to LTE, to 1 where the whole capacity of LTE can be shared by traffic of both classes. It is shown that, when the admission to LTE is restricted to C_1 class solely, the low-priority class suffers from extremely high blocking probability. This is a consequence of the limited coverage and smaller capacity of WiFi as compared to LTE. Therefore, denying the access of C_2 sessions to LTE decreases their probability of being admitted to the system. However, when the admission of C_2 class to LTE is allowed, through an increase of the value of θ, the blocking probability

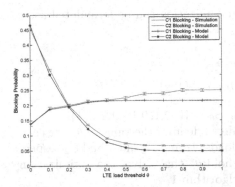

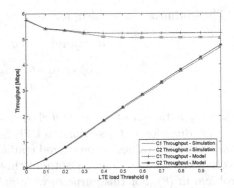

Fig. 3. C_1 and C_2 blocking probabilities for different values of θ

Fig. 4. C_1 and C_2 throughput variations for different values of θ

of C_2 class drops fast, leading to an enhancement of the QoS perceived by the low-priority users. On the other hand, the blocking probability of class C_1 is not severely affected by the admission of C_2 sessions to LTE.

Another performance metric is depicted in Fig. 4, namely the throughput. With the increase of the value of θ, the throughput of C_2 sessions increases fast. This is directly related to the decrease of the blocking probability of C_2 class in similar conditions as discussed earlier. Also, even when C_2 sessions are allowed to share the entire capacity of LTE, this does not cause a dramatical decrease of the throughput of C_1 sessions, which are granted the double number of bbu per session as compared to C_2 class.

5   Revenue Maximization

In the previous sections, a RAT selection strategy in HWNs with profile differentiation has been proposed, and several performance metrics have been derived with the help of a Markovian model. According to the proposed scenario, the number of users that can be admitted to LTE is directly related to the value of the load threshold θ. Therefore, the parameter θ plays a key role in determining the revenue generated in the overall system, and any variation of its value can cause an increase or decrease of the operator's profit. In this section, we aim to find the optimal value of θ that leads to maximizing the network revenue, while guaranteeing that the user's perceived QoS in terms of blocking probability stays below a predefined threshold β.

Let R_1 and R_2 denote the prices that users pay for C_1 and C_2 connections respectively, with $R_1 > R_2$. A simple way to formulate the operator's average revenue is:

$$Avg\_Rev = R_1 \cdot E[i] + R_2 \cdot (E[j] + E[k]) \tag{7}$$

where the detailed expressions of $E[i]$, $E[j]$ and $E[k]$ are given by (3) with $x = i$, $x = j$ and $x = k$ respectively.

The optimization problem for revenue maximization can be formulated as:

$$\underset{\theta}{\text{maximize}} \quad Avg\_Rev$$

$$\text{subject to} \quad \theta \in S_\theta \tag{8}$$

$$P_{b,i} \le \beta_i \,, i \in \{1,2\}.$$

where S_θ is the set of values of θ chosen as: $S_\theta = \{0, 0.1, 0.15, 0.2, .., 1\}$.

The admission of C_2 sessions to LTE is dependent on the value of θ. For each combination of values of the offered traffic loads A_1 and A_2 of C_1 and C_2 respectively, we intend to find the optimal threshold θ^* that solves the optimization problem in (8). For this purpose, we use Algorithm 1.

Algorithm 1. Algorithm for finding the optimal threshold θ^*

Input: A_1, A_2
Output: θ^*, Avg_Rev^*
Initialize: $sol \leftarrow 0$, $Avg\_Rev^* \leftarrow 0$
for all θ in S_θ **do**
  Find $P_{b,1}$, $P_{b,2}$, Avg_Rev
  if $(P_{b,1} \le \beta_1) \wedge (P_{b,2} \le \beta_2)$ **then**
    $sol \leftarrow 1$
    if $Avg\_Rev > Avg\_Rev^*$ **then**
      $Avg\_Rev^* \leftarrow Avg\_Rev$
      $\theta^* \leftarrow \theta$
    end if
  end if
end for
if sol=1 {a solution has been found} **then**
  Return θ^*, Avg_Rev^*
end if

As shown in Algorithm 1, to find θ^* for some given values of the offered load traffic of C_1 and C_2 profiles, we first start with the smallest value of θ (i.e. $\theta = 0$), and keep increasing it until we find the value that provides a feasible solution for the considered optimization problem. Once found, we keep increasing the value of θ to check if highest revenue could be achieved without violating the blocking probability constraints. If there are more than one value of θ that ensure the same highest revenue, we have interest in choosing the smallest θ^*, as it corresponds to a smaller blocking probability for the high-priority class.

Fig. 5 depicts the selected values of θ^* for different traffic loads of C_1 and C_2 classes. It shows that, for small values of A_1, C_2 class can share up to 60% of C_{LTE}. When A_1 increases, the value of θ^* decreases, and it becomes less likely to find a θ^* that solves the optimization problem.

Finding the optimal threshold has an important impact on the generated revenue. This can be deduced from Fig. 6 that depicts the revenue of the network for arbitrary load thresholds compared to the revenue achieved with the optimal

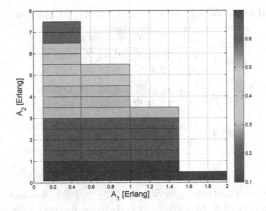

Fig. 5. Optimal threshold value for $\beta_1 = 5\%$ and $\beta_2 = 10\%$

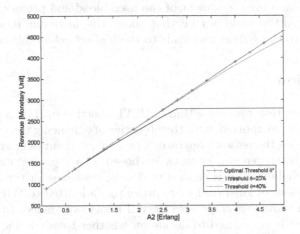

Fig. 6. Revenue for arbitrary and optimal load thresholds, $A_1 = 0.8$ Erlang

threshold, for an offered traffic $A_1 = 0.8$ of class C_1. Fig. 6 clearly shows that the optimal threshold always achieves the highest revenue.

When the offered traffic for C_2 is low, e.g. $A_2 = 1.5$, an arbitrary threshold of 25% or 40% provide the same revenue as θ^*. However, for a load traffic of C_2 profile exceeding the value of 3, a threshold of 25% is no more sufficient. It leads to significantly lower achieved revenue than the optimal threshold, because it cannot satisfy the QoS constraint for C_2 profile. This choice of the threshold results in blocking C_2 sessions, and hence deprives the operator from the profit that could be achieved from the potential admittance of the blocked C_2 sessions if a proper choice of the load threshold was initially made. These results are indeed consistent with the ones given by Fig. 5. Similarly, when choosing the value of 40% for the LTE load threshold, less revenue could be achieved due to blocking of C_2 sessions when the traffic load of this latter is high. The blocking probabilities $P_{b,1}$ and $P_{b,2}$ for the same values of θ are presented in Table 3. For

Table 3. Values of $P_{b,1}$ and $P_{b,2}$, $A_1 = 0.8$ Erlang

		$\theta = 25\%$	$\theta = 40\%$	θ^*
$A_2 = 1.1$	$P_{b,1}$	0.33 %	0.36 %	0.31 %
	$P_{b,2}$	2.2 %	0.77 %	2.52 %
$A_2 = 3.1$	$P_{b,1}$	0.55 %	0.99 %	0.99 %
	$P_{b,2}$	**11.3 %**	1.52 %	1.52 %
$A_2 = 4.1$	$P_{b,1}$	0.61 %	1.34 %	1.30 %
	$P_{b,2}$	**16 %**	3.44 %	3.7 %

targeted blocking probabilities $\beta_1 = 5\%$ and $\beta_2 = 10\%$, a choice of threshold of 25% will cause unacceptable blocking probabilities for C_2 class when the load of this latter exceeds the value of 3. Therefore, the network operator has interest in knowing, based on a pre-assessment of the users' load and profiles, the optimal setting of the load threshold in LTE that allows the maximum number of users to be admitted to the system and leads to the highest achievable revenue.

6   Conclusion

In this paper, we present an algorithm for RAT selection in HWNs where different user profiles are supported, with the objective of enhancing the system capacity and maximizing the network operator's revenue, without degrading the QoS. An LTE/WiFi heterogeneous network is chosen as a representative of HWN, and a load threshold in LTE is defined to reserve resources for the high-priority user profile. Sessions of low-priority are preferably admitted to WiFi, unless the user was not in a dual-coverage area or WiFi was overloaded. In these latter cases, LTE's load is considered to decide on whether to admit the low-priority session to LTE or reject it. A 3-D Markov model is defined to study and analyze the proposed RAT selection scheme that is further validated by simulation. Then, an optimization problem is presented, and a solution is provided in order to find the optimal load threshold that ensures the highest achievable revenue, while satisfying the blocking probability constraints. Finally, the importance of defining the optimal value of the load threshold is highlighted.

References

1. Da Silva, A.P., et al.: Common Radio Resource Management for Multiaccess Wireless Networks. In: Cavalcanti, F., Andersson, S. (eds.) Optimizing Wireless Communication Systems, pp. 233–265. Springer (2009)
2. Piamrat, K., et al.: Radio Resource Management in Emerging Heterogeneous Wireless Networks. Computer Communications 34, 1066–1076 (2011)
3. Hasib, A., Fapojuwo, A.: Analysis of Common Radio Resource Management Scheme for End-to-End QoS Support in Multiservice Heterogeneous Wireless Networks. IEEE Trans. Vehic. Tech. 57, 2426–2439 (2008)

4. Gelabert, X., et al.: A Markovian Approach to Radio Access Technology Selection in Heterogeneous Multiaccess/Multiservice Wireless Networks. IEEE Trans. Mobile Comput. 7, 1257–1270 (2008)
5. Song, W., et al.: Resource Management for QoS Support in Cellular/WLAN Interworking. IEEE Network Magazine 19, 12–18 (2005)
6. Niyato, D., Hossain, E.: A NonCooperative Game-Theoretic Framework for Radio Resource Management in 4G Heterogeneous Wireless Access Networks. IEEE Trans. Mobile Comput. 7, 332–345 (2008)
7. Falowo, O.E., et al.: Dynamic Pricing for Load-Balancing in User-Centric Joint Call Admission Control of Next-Generation Wireless Networks. Int'l. J. Comm. Syst. 23, 335–368 (2010)
8. Giupponi, L., et al.: An Economic-Driven Joint Radio Resource Management with User Profile Differentiation in a Beyond 3G Cognitive Network. In: IEEE Globecom (2006)
9. Khloussy, E., et al.: Maximizing Network Revenue Through Resource Management in Heterogeneous Wireless Networks. IEEE Symp. Comp. and Comm. (2011)
10. Yu, F., Krishnamurthy, V.: Optimal Joint Session Admission Control in Integrated WLAN and CDMA Cellular Networks with Vertical Handoff. IEEE Trans. Mobile Comput. 6, 126–139 (2007)
11. Chen, H., et al.: Guard-Channel-Based Incremental and Dynamic Optimization on Call Admission Control for Next-Generation QoS-Aware Heterogeneous Systems. IEEE Trans. Veh. Tech. 57, 3064–3082 (2008)
12. Kim, D.K., et al.: A New Call Admission Control Scheme for Heterogeneous Wireless Networks. IEEE Trans. Wirel. Comm. 9, 3000–3005 (2010)
13. The 3rd Generation Partnership Project, http://www.3gpp.org/lte-advanced
14. Bonald, T., Roberts, J.W.: Internet and the Erlang formula. ACM SIGCOMM Comput. Commun. Rev. 42, 23–30 (2012)
15. Falowo, O.E., Chan, H.A.: Multiple-RAT Selection for Reducing Call Blocking/Dropping Probability in Cooperative Heterogeneous Wireless Networks. J. on Wirel. Comm. and Netw. (2012)
16. Nasser, N., Hassanein, H.: Dynamic Threshold-Based Call Admission Framework for Prioritized Multimedia Traffic in Wireless Cellular Networks. Globecom 2, 644–649 (2004)
17. Kelly, F.: Notes on effective bandwidths in Stochastic Networks: Theory and Applications, Royal Statistical Society. Lecture Notes Series, vol. 4. Oxford University Press (1996)
18. Stewart, W.J.: Probability, Markov Chains, Queues and Simulation (2009)

Mobile SIP: An Empirical Study on SIP Retransmission Timers in HSPA 3G Networks

Joachim Fabini[1], Michael Hirschbichler[1],
Jiri Kuthan[2], and Werner Wiedermann[3]

[1] Institute of Telecommunications, Vienna University of Technology,
Favoritenstr. 9/E389, 1040 Wien
[2] iptelorg GmbH, Am Borsigturm 11, 13507 Berlin
[3] Telekom Austria Group, Lassallestrasse 9, 1020 Wien

Abstract. Mobile packet-switched voice must replace mobile circuit-switched voice latest with the large-scale deployment of LTE. However, short-term full-area LTE coverage is highly unlikely, handover to and interworking with 3G HSPA networks being a must. This raises the question of how the Session Initiation Protocol SIP performs in today's HSPA networks.

Relying on live SIP provider monitoring data and active HSPA measurements, this paper demonstrates that default SIP retransmission timers are inappropriate for real-world deployments of packet switched voice over today's 2G and 3G networks including HSPA. Main reason for this deficiency is the reactive, demand-driven resource allocation strategy of HSPA which results in huge uplink delays. These delays eventually lead to a high number of unnecessary SIP message retransmissions which load networks and servers. SIP clients for mobile devices should therefore implement adaptive, user-configurable SIP retransmission timers and provide appropriate default values for these timers to enable seamless SIP operation in mobile cellular networks.

1 Introduction

From a standardization point of view, the Session Initiation Protocol (SIP) [1] is currently considered to be the most promising candidate for implementing Voice over IP (VoIP) in converged fixed and wireless networks. However, the SIP design and base standard is more than ten years old, being focused on providing best-effort services in deterministically behaving wired networks. During the last years, driven by requirements for deploying SIP in carrier-grade infrastructures, the research community has started to publish and discuss severe SIP deficiencies with respect to unstable behavior in high-load or overload situations.

Latest with the replacement of mobile circuit-switched voice technology with packet-switched-only capable LTE networks, IP-based signaling must operate in the mobile domain. In this paper we demonstrate by means of representative SIP server log files and measurements in state-of-the-art HSPA networks that default SIP timers as recommended by RFC 3261 are inappropriate for SIP operation

T. Bauschert (Ed.): EUNICE 2013, LNCS 8115, pp. 78–89, 2013.

in mobile 3G networks. This observation is valid for all SIP messages which are sent after seconds of inactivity, outside of ongoing data sessions, i.e., particularly for registrations and SIP presence related messages. SIP server statistics evaluations show that these SIP message types account for the majority of the overall SIP traffic. Our HSPA measurement results demonstrate that due to the highly reactive nature of HSPA uplink, timers of mobile SIP user agents will deterministically trigger SIP retransmissions, which generate redundant traffic and waste considerable resources in the network and in servers. This is a severe drawback, aggravated by the fact that mobile applications reduce user-configurable options to an absolute minimum and typically do not implement user-configurable timer values.

1.1 Related Work

The SIP protocol and SIP retransmission timers are defined in RFC 3261[1], whereas SIP performance metrics for registration request delay are standardized in RFC 6076[8]. C. Egger et. al. discuss in [5] and [7] the inherent problem of SIP retransmissions and their negative impact on SIP proxy performance and networks, proposing to manipulate SIP retransmission timers to handle SIP overload situations. The authors of [6] conclude that SIP overload control mechanisms are an absolute MUST, implicit overload control being subject to lower overhead but explicit overload control behaving more deterministic in situations of high overload. Vingarzan et. al. discuss in [9] the latency impact of various wireless network technologies, including 2G, 3G, and WiFi onto end-to-end SIP performance for IMS, concluding that GPRS networks are not appropriate for IMS signaling, whereas IEEE 802.11b,g, and CDMA networks can handle IMS traffic adequately in terms of delay and loss. The contribution of different network components (user equipment, NodeB and RNC) on HSUPA end-to-end delay is analyzed in [10], inferring on 30 ms delay for 1 kbyte packets. In earlier work ([12] and [13]) we have dissected difficulties and uncertainty factors to be expected when measuring mobile network delay, focusing on randomness in terms of inter-packet delay and payload size as key factor to reveal load-dependent network behavior.

1.2 Structure of This Paper

The remainder of this paper is structured as follows: section 2 reviews the SIP registration procedure and discusses the methodology used for iptel.org SIP registrar log evaluation and for HSPA measurements. Building on this information, section 3 presents and discusses SIP registrar log and measurement results from live HSPA networks. The paper ends with summary and conclusions in section 4.

2   Protocols and Setup

Adoption of SIP by the 3rd Generation Partnership Project (3GPP) as main signaling protocol for the IP Multimedia Subsystem (IMS) has significantly boosted the world wide use of SIP. Due to high scalability and freely available standards, several free, open-source SIP client and server implementations are available for download. In the following we restrict discussions to plain SIP registration, arguing that 3GPP SIP signaling messages are typically larger than plain SIP signaling messages because of 3GPP-specific SIP extensions and headers. Therefore, delays are likely to increase for 3GPP IMS signaling even more, plain SIP delays offering a lower boundary on propagation delays in mobile networks. Even if SIP signaling compression is deployed as mandated by 3GPP for the use on wireless cellular networks, compression is unlikely to offer significant delay reductions for sporadically sent messages like SIP registrations.

2.1   SIP Basics: Registration

SIP is a simple, plain-text message based request-reply protocol. Fundamental to SIP is the registration process. During registration a terminal, the so-called SIP user agent, registers the user's generic SIP address – the so called SIP URI – and its current transport address with its assigned SIP server, the SIP registrar. Using the transport address binding stored during the user's registration process, SIP registrars can then forward incoming calls via IP routing to the terminal(s) where the specific user is currently logged in.

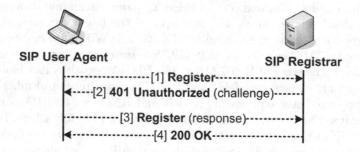

Fig. 1. SIP Registration message flow

Fig. 1 illustrates the message sequence required for an authenticated SIP registration. The first registration request (1) is rejected by the registrar using a 401, unauthorized reply (2). This reply message includes a random value, the so-called nonce, which is encrypted by the user agent on receiving the reply using a secret key shared with the registrar. This response is appended as SIP authentication header to a new registration request (3) sent to the registrar. On receiving the authenticated registration request, the registrar repeats the user agent's processing, i.e., encodes the random value with its pre-shared secret. If the result matches the response sent by the user agent in its registration request, the registering user is supposed to be authenticated. The registrar can safely store the binding between the client's SIP URI and its contact (transport) address and confirm successful authentication to the client by sending a 200 OK response (message 4 in fig. 1).

Registrations expire, raising the need for periodical registration message re-transmissions to refresh the registration state. The interval between successive re-registrations is always a trade-off between the user agent's reachability for incoming calls, i.e., up-to-date registrar information, and the amount of required signaling load. In a mobile cellular context, mobility and radio provisioning are two factors which can result in IP address changes and therefore demand for relatively small registration intervals. Moreover, mobile firewalls and/or private IP address NAT devices in some cases use these re-registrations as keep-alive messages to maintain their internal bindings. Consequently, re-registration intervals for mobile SIP clients should be in the order of tens of minutes, compared to wired SIP terminals which typically re-register every hour or several hours. However, this high registration frequency causes a high data volume for SIP over mobile networks.

2.2 SIP Registrar Logging

iptelorg GmbH offers free SIP-based IP Telephony services. Users can request their free personal SIP URI @iptel.org and use this URI to register their SIP user agents with the SIP registrar iptel.org. The core functionality behind the iptel.org registrar is implemented by the open source SIP Express Router (SER)[14], which offers complex and detailed logging facilities. The results published in this paper base on 27 hours of anonymized, representative iptel.org SER logs acquired during a typical business day in spring 2012. During these 27 hours, the log has recorded a total of 9,980,000 SIP requests including retransmissions which scales down to an effective traffic of 7,400,000 SIP requests and 7,500,000 SIP replies when eliminating SIP message retransmissions. Prior to evaluation, all SIP messages have been categorized into several orthogonal classes, focusing on the SIP registration process.

First, all SIP requests have been categorized according to their type. A second category differentiates between the user agent classes "fixed" and "mobile" by comparing logged SIP User-Agent headers against a list of well-known user agent strings. Subclass "mobile" aggregates smartphone clients, i.e., software SIP clients for iOS and Android which might face limitations in terms of computing ressources. However, "mobile" does not infer on any specific kind of network connectivity, on the contrary. One of our conclusions in this paper is, that the majority of these mobile clients connect using Wireless LAN networks rather than using cellular technologies. As second option, the subclass "fixed" groups hard-phones, SIP-routers and -proxies, as well as soft-phones for desktop operating systems which typically have abundant ressources available.

Table 1 summarizes the SIP registrar log, classifying SIP requests according to their request type for fixed clients (Fixed), mobile clients (Mobile), and aggregated (Total), considering only first requests (i.e., eliminating all retransmissions). Registrations dominate this statistic, accounting for more than 40% of all requests (3,090,000 registrations in absolute numbers). This confirms our assumption that SIP registration requests generate significant load in mobile and fixed networks. However, in a server-based enterprise infrastructure featuring

Table 1. SIP request distribution (no retransmissions)

Request	Total	Fixed	Mobile
INVITE	0.19%	0.29%	0.03%
BYE	0.05%	0.08%	0.01%
REGISTER	41.50%	51.45%	25.39%
SUBSCRIBE	2.77%	3.46%	1.65%
NOTIFY	17.81%	28.82%	0.001%
OPTIONS	37.22%	15.21%	72.85%
Others	0.46%	0.70%	0.07%

server-based presence services we predict a load shift towards notify and sub-scribe requests. As third category, because of their distinct handling and re-sponse time within the SIP registrar, SIP registration requests must be divided into registrations *without* authentication information (message 1 in fig. 1) and registrations *with* authentication information (message 3 in fig. 1).

More, detailed registration request statistics can be found in the following measurement results section.

2.3   HSPA Measurement Setup

For measuring one-way (OWD) and round-trip delay (RTD) in mobile cellular networks we have used operational High Speed Packet Access (HSPA) networks.

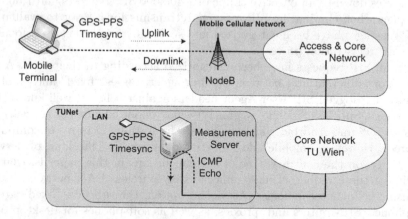

Fig. 2. Measurement Setup for Accurate OWD Measurements

Fig. 2 depicts the setup used for active end-to-end delay measurements in pub-lic HSPA networks. Measurement server and mobile terminal are both running Ubuntu Linux 12.04 using a custom-compiled Kernel 3.4.0 at 1 kHz kernel tick with Pulse-per-second (PPS) functionality activated. The measurement server is equipped with an Intel Q6600 CPU at 2.4 GHz and 4 Gbyte of RAM, connected using its on-board Ethernet interface to the public Internet. The mobile client is a

Dell Latitude D630 laptop with an Intel T7100 processor at 1.8 GHz and 2 Gbyte of RAM, connected to the mobile network using a Huawei E870 HSPA Express-Card 34. For accurate OWD measurements, mobile client and server are both time-synchronized using the network time protocol daemon (NTPD) and local EM 406A based GPS-PPS time sources as recommended by [11]. The maximum measured deviation from global time is below 50 μs, which is sufficiently accurate for our measurements. From a measurement methodology point of view we have followed and extended the recommendations of the IP Performance Metrics Framework[2] to avoid correlation with periodic network behavior. The measurement traffic is random with respect to send time and payload size. ICMP echo request packets of representative random payload size are sent at random time intervals, triggering corresponding ICMP echo replies.

3 Measurement Results

This section presents the iptel.org SIP server log analysis and HSPA delay measurement results for sporadic SIP registration traffic designed according to the iptel.org log evaluation. As main criterion for representativeness we have used the live traces from iptel.org, such that the packet size of our measurement traffic matches the size of real registration messages.

3.1 SIP Registrar Statistics

As mentioned in subsection 2.2, the monitored SIP traffic totals 27 hours of traffic. Out of the 7.4 million unique SIP requests 4.6 million requests are from fixed clients and 2.8 million from mobile clients conforming to the mobile-fixed categorization presented in section 2.2. Table 2 illustrates that mobile clients

Table 2. Total register requests vs. registrations which require retransmission

	Register Requests	Register Requests w Retransmissions	Ratio
Fixed	2,365,404	167,467	7.08%
Mobile	721,303	161,111	22.34%

retransmit SIP registration requests almost three time as frequent as fixed clients. In average, every fifth register request is retransmitted due to firing of SIP retransmission timer T1 (500 ms). Retransmission messages are evenly distributed over all mobile clients and request sizes, which excludes that this problematic behavior is initiated by one specific user or user-agent implementation. It must be emphasized once again that "mobile" client is NOT a synonym for 3G connectivity. On the contrary, more detailed iptel.org log evaluation indicates that the majority of mobile clients connects using WLAN or faster non-3G technologies.

As presented in section 2.1 in fig. 1, an authenticated SIP registration requires two SIP register requests. The second request (message 3) differs from the first

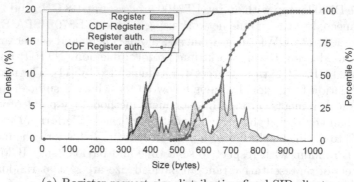

(a) Register request size distribution fixed SIP clients

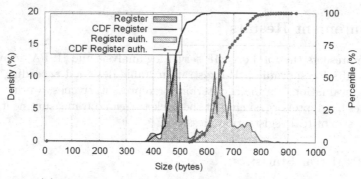

(b) Register request size distribution mobile SIP clients

Fig. 3. SIP REGISTER size distribution with and without authentication header

one (message 1) by the additional SIP authentication header. Fig. 3(a) and
fig. 3(b) show the distribution of SIP register request size with and without
authentication header for fixed and mobile clients, respectively. Accordingly,
the authentication header is increasing SIP request size in average by about
200 bytes.

To eliminate SIP server or core network performance as potential delay sources
we have evaluated processing duration of SIP registration requests with and without authentication. Using metrics from [8], nearly 99% of all "401 Unauthorized"
responses are sent within 1 ms and 98% of all "200 OK" within 2 ms of registration request arrival. Both values are well below the SIP retransmission timer T1
value of 500 ms, such that SIP server delay can be excluded as reason for timer
T1 expiry.

3.2   HSPA Measurement Results

Based on the evaluation of iptel.org's SIP server log we have built a prototypical
signaling data stream at IP layer using ICMP messages to measure accurate
round-trip (RTD) and one-way uplink (UL) and downlink (DL) delay measurements for SIP signaling traffic in live HSPA networks. Main motivation of these

HSPA delay measurements was to determine the impact and feasibility of VoIP on top of mobile HSPA networks. HSPA was selected as mobile cellular technology because back in Q2 2012, when acquiring iptel.org traces for this publication, no LTE capable terminals have been available on the market. Therefore it is unlikely that mobile clients have accessed iptel.org in spring 2012 using a more advanced technology than HSPA. Today, one year later, Long Term Evolution (LTE) networks are operational in many countries worldwide but typically still limited in their coverage to high-traffic areas.

Using the setup presented in section 2, an extended Internet Control Message Protocol (ICMP) packet generator and an artificial, random signaling data traffic we have measured end-to-end RTD and OWD in public live Austrian HSPA networks. As mentioned earlier, measurement representativeness has been increased by following the recommendations of the IPPM Framework [2] and of its associated metrics for OWD [3] and RTD [4] when designing the measurement traffic. In particular we have created a scenario consisting of 10,000 single ICMP measurement packets. Based on iptel.org log's payload size distribution for mobile clients as depicted in fig. 3(b), the measurement traffic's payload range is uniform distributed between 400 and 800 byte. The measurement traffic's interpacket interval is uniformly distributed between 1 and 10 seconds, totaling more than 15 measurement hours. The selected delay range has been chosen as a minimum period of mobile network inactivity. We argue this period to be exceeded in most cases for registration requests while the terminal is idle, i.e., has no ongoing packet-switched voice or data sessions.

Figure 4 shows the resulting diagrams and statistics for RTD measurements. The x-y scatter plot in fig 4(a) depicts delay as a function of payload size. Any one of the almost 10,000 dots in the figure correspond to the delay value of one single measurement packet. Only 3 packets out of the 10,000 were lost, meaning that loss can be excluded for the large number of retransmission of mobile clients. The corresponding cumulative distribution function (CDF) in fig 4(c) reveals that – ignoring potential processing overhead and delay in SIP Registrars - slightly more than one third (36.2%) of all measurement samples arrive in less than 500 ms. Accordingly, almost two thirds (63.8%) of the requests will trigger retransmissions. More than 10% of all requests will exceed 1500 ms and trigger at least two retransmissions.

As mentioned earlier in section 2.1 SIP re-registrations must be sent periodically. We argue that there is a high likelihood that intervals of mobile network inactivity preceding a SIP Registration are significantly larger than one second. We have therefore selected from all 10,000 measurement samples the 5441 ones which have inter-packet delays – i.e., network inactivity period before sending the packet – between 5 and 10 seconds. The resulting scatter plot is depicted in fig 4(b) and the distribution function in fig 4(d), respectively.

The result is alarming with respect to user experience, network load and server load. Considering exclusively network delay, less than 4% of all measurement samples arrive within the expected timeframe of 500 ms to avoid SIP retransmissions. More than 96% of all SIP requests will therefore trigger at least one,

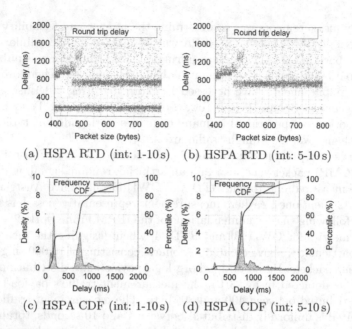

(a) HSPA RTD (int: 1-10 s)   (b) HSPA RTD (int: 5-10 s)

(c) HSPA CDF (int: 1-10 s)   (d) HSPA CDF (int: 5-10 s)

Fig. 4. RTD dependence on inter-packet send interval for HSPA networks

8% will exceed the default limit of 1500 ms and trigger at least two retransmissions. These results show that in a passive state with no ongoing call, mobile SIP devices on HSPA networks will effectively – at least – double the effective load on the network and on the registrar. Although resource allocation and - release in HSPA networks depends significantly on operator-specific parameters, measurements in other mobile HSPA networks suggest that the figures we have obtained are relevant with respect to the order of magnitude. It is important to note that these findings are not restricted to Voice over IP but can be generalized for other SIP-based services as Presence or Instant Messaging, too, which all use the default timer T1 value of 500 ms.

For isolating an accurate origin of the large RTD we have dissected measured round-trip-delay samples into UL and DL delay as displayed in fig 5. The figures confirm that the major delay uncertainty factor is HSPA UL. The reason for the high end-to-end delay experienced by a mobile client following a period of network inactivity is intrinsic to HSPA's architecture. Mobile clients must send signaling messages over the wireless link to the network-based scheduler to switch from inactivity or to request allocation of additional capacities in the wireless network. These round-trip messages delay the sending of first messages, whereas subsequent messages can be transmitted much faster due to already allocated capacities.

Comparing one-way UL delay diagrams for 1-10 s inter-packet delay in fig 5, left (5(a) and 5(d)), with the corresponding diagrams with larger inter-packet delay of 5-10 s shown in fig 5, center (5(b) and 5(e)), reveals that the ratio of requests which unconditionally run into SIP retransmission timeouts increases to more than 90% after more than 5 seconds of inactivity.

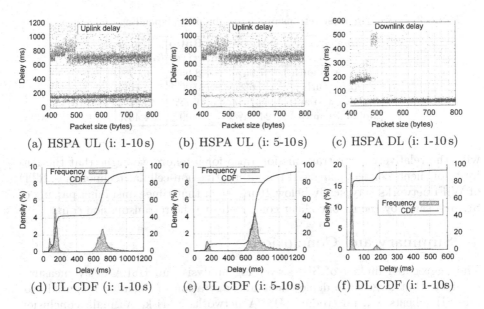

(a) HSPA UL (i: 1-10 s)   (b) HSPA UL (i: 5-10 s)   (c) HSPA DL (i: 1-10 s)

(d) UL CDF (i: 1-10 s)   (e) UL CDF (i: 5-10 s)   (f) DL CDF (i: 1-10s)

Fig. 5. UL and DL delay dependence on inter-packet send interval for HSPA networks

The DL delay depicted in fig. 5(c) and 5(f) recovers much faster from inactivity. On DL data arrival the scheduler is located in the wired network domain and can act instantaneously, which saves time-consuming round-trip signaling messages over the wireless link. More than 80% of DL samples are below 50 ms and more than 90% below 200 ms end-to-end delay.

3.3 Discussion

Two main factors may originate SIP retransmissions: mobile client limitations in terms of software and hardware or reactive HSPA UL behavior. Diving deeper into iptel.org's server log details reveals that a) mobile client limitations can be one main reason for increased retransmission ratio on iptel.org and b) as of today few mobile clients use 2G or 3G technologies to connect to iptel.org. These statements can be concluded from table 3 which shows SIP retransmission ratio depending on a presumed mobile link state. Based on the finding of section 3.2 that HSPA clients experience an increased delay after more than 5 seconds of network inactivity, mobile client registrations have been split into two categories. A mobile client's network connection is supposed to be *active* when iptel.org has logged a message from the client's socket within 5 seconds before arrival of the request, or *inactive* otherwise.

Comparing total registration request retransmission ratio for mobile clients with and without authentication in table 3 reveals that more register requests *with* authentication are retransmitted than *without*. This result conflicts with our HSPA delay measurement results, where 96% of requests sent with inactive mobile network are retransmitted but only 63% of the active ones. Combined

Table 3. Register request retransmission probability depending on load history

Connection	Ratio (total)	Ratio (inactive)	Ratio (active)
Fixed (w/o auth.)	7.95%	8.65%	6.07%
Fixed (w auth.)	3.63%	0.00%	4.10%
Mobile (w/o auth.)	18.70%	11.95%	45.11%
Mobile (w auth.)	24.34%	0.00%	24.46%

with the relatively low retransmission ratio for iptel.org we argue that the majority of clients connect using WiFi or alternative non-cellular technologies. RTD of WiFi networks is typically below 10 ms, such that time-consuming parsing of SIP messages by the mobile client contributes to the retransmission count.

4   Summary and Conclusions

The aggregated finding of SIP server log analysis and HSPA delay measurements is that large-scale deployment and operation of default-configured mobile SIP clients will put today's HSPA networks at risk. As main conclusion of iptel.org SIP server log and HSPA measurement results we recommend all mobile SIP clients to offer user-configurable SIP retransmission timer values. The application-configured default values for HSPA networks must be at least double of the default SIP timer T1 value of 500 ms, i.e. 1 second. For a detailed discussion on retransmission timer effects and fine-tuning we refer the reader to [5]. Alternatively, SIP clients could ideally support automated, mobile-network-technology-dependent values for T1. Using cross-layer information on the network technology which the mobile device currently uses (e.g., WiFi or 3G), mobile SIP clients could configure appropriate SIP timer values to minimize the likelihood of unnecessary retransmissions.

Latest with large-scale deployment of SIP clients in mobile cellular networks, network and SIP server operators will be forced to over-dimension their infrastructure by orders of magnitude and to implement SIP overload control mechanisms. The authors of [7] have demonstrated the catastrophic impact that short-term SIP network overloads can have onto network stability. A SIP retransmission flooding triggered by a short-term overload period eventually can end up in a congestion collapse state for SIP servers and networks. Recovery from SIP congestion collapse requires appropriate algorithms and substantial load reduction. For safeguarding acceptable user experience of SIP in mobile cellular networks it is highly desired to prevent congestion collapse scenarios, adequate SIP timer handling being a first, mandatory step.

Acknowledgment. The authors would like to thank their colleagues Markus Laner and Philipp Svoboda for their work and support in implementing reliable, affordable solutions for accurate GPS-PPS based measurement clock synchronization. The views expressed in this paper are those of the authors and do not necessarily reflect the views of their employers.

References

1. Rosenberg, J., Schulzrinne, H., Camarillo, G., et al.: SIP: Session Initiation Protocol Network Working Group RFC 3261 (June 2002)
2. Paxson, V., Almes, G., Mahdavi, J., Mathis, M.: Framework for IP Performance Metrics Network Working Group RFC 2330 (May 1998)
3. Almes, G., Kalidindi, S., Zekauskas, M.: A One-way Delay Metric for IPPM Network Working Group RFC 2679 (September 1999)
4. Almes, G., Kalidindi, S., Zekauskas, M.: A Round-trip Delay Metric for IPPM Network Working Group RFC 2681 (September 1999)
5. Egger, C., Hirschbichler, M., Reichl, P.: Enhancing SIP Performance by Dynamic Manipulation of Retransmission Timers. In: Wolfinger, B., Heidtmann K. (Hrg.) Leistungs- Zuverlaessigkeits- und Verlaesslichkeitsbewertung von Kommunikationsnetzen und Verteilten Systemen Universitaet Hamburg, Fachbereich Informatik, Vogt-Koelln-Strasse 30, D-22527 Hamburg, Bericht 298, pp. 47–54 (2011)
6. Happenhofer, M., Fabini, J., Egger, C., Hirschbichler, M.: An Architectural and Evaluative Review of Implicit and Explicit SIP Overload Handling. International Journal of Measurement Technologies and Instrumentation Engineering (IJMTIE) 1(4), 12–27 (2011)
7. Egger, C., Happenhofer, M., Fabini, J., Reichl, P.: Collapse Detection and Avoidance for SIP Architectures. Praxis der Informationsverarbeitung und Kommunikation (PIK) 35(2), 91–100 (2012) ISSN 0930-5157
8. Malas, D., Morton, A.: Basic Telephony SIP End-to-End Performance Metrics Network Working Group RFC 6076 (January 2011)
9. Vingarzan, D., Weik, P.: End-to-end performance of the IP multimedia subsystem over various wireless networks. In: IEEE Wireless Communications and Networking Conference, WCNC 2006 (2006)
10. Laner, M., Svoboda, P., Hasenleithner, E., Rupp, M.: Dissecting 3G uplink delay by measuring in an operational HSPA network. In: Spring, N., Riley, G.F. (eds.) PAM 2011. LNCS, vol. 6579, pp. 52–61. Springer, Heidelberg (2011)
11. Laner, M., Caban, S., Svoboda, P., Rupp, M.: Time Synchronization Performance of Desktop Computers. In: 2011 International IEEE Symposium on Precision Clock Synchronization for Measurement Control and Communication, ISPCS (2011)
12. Fabini, J., Karner, W., Wallentin, L., Baumgartner, T.: The Illusion of Being Deterministic – Application-Level Considerations on Delay in 3G HSPA Networks. In: Fratta, L., Schulzrinne, H., Takahashi, Y., Spaniol, O. (eds.) NETWORKING 2009. LNCS, vol. 5550, pp. 301–312. Springer, Heidelberg (2009)
13. Fabini, J., Wallentin, L., Reichl, P.: The Importance of Being Really Random: Methodological Aspects of IP-Layer 2G and 3G Network Delay Assessment. In: IEEE International Conference on Communications 2009, ICC 2009 (2009)
14. SIP Express Router (SER), http://www.iptel.org/ser/

Addressing the Challenges of E-Healthcare
in Future Mobile Networks

Safdar Nawaz Khan Marwat[1], Thomas Pötsch[1], Yasir Zaki[2],
Thushara Weerawardane[3], and Carmelita Görg[1]

[1] ComNets, University of Bremen, Bremen, Germany
[2] New York University Abu Dhabi, Abu Dhabi, United Arab Emirates
[3] Sir John Kotelawala Defense University, Ratmalana, Sri Lanka
{safdar,thp,cg}@comnets.uni-bremen.de,
yz48@nyu.edu, tlw@kdu.ac.lk

Abstract. Machine-to-Machine (M2M) communication is expected to play a major role within the coming years towards the development of e-healthcare applications. The design of cellular networks, such as Long Term Evolution (LTE), is optimized to serve the data traffic of human-based communication with broadband requirements. E-healthcare traffic has different characteristics such as small packet sizes, narrowband requirements and huge number of devices. The focus of this work is to investigate the impact of e-healthcare traffic on LTE cellular networks. We develop a possible future scenario of electrocardiography (ECG) devices performing remote monitoring of patients with mobility support in our LTE simulation model. Regular LTE traffic is also deployed in the network and the influence of the varying ECG traffic is examined. The simulation results indicate that the e-healthcare related data traffic has a drastic influence on regular LTE traffic.

Keywords: e-healthcare, M2M, LTE, throughput.

1 Introduction

Machine-to-Machine (M2M) communication is a global and rapidly developing research area for interconnecting different devices without human intervention. The growth of this area is not only restricted to the diversity and number of future M2M devices, but also the mobile data traffic is expected to grow significantly in future communications [1].

The "Internet of Things" is a new paradigm for interconnecting devices, and the M2M communication is a key area in this field. The authors of [2] anticipate that the "Internet of Things" would extend the existing Internet with a large variety of connected devices. As a result, several application domains would benefit from this concept, for instance supervision in logistical processes, smart metering and monitoring, intelligent transport systems etc.

Recently, researchers have shown an increasing interest in remote monitoring of homes, vehicles and places with M2M devices [3,4,5]. Examples are energy, traffic

T. Bauschert (Ed.): EUNICE 2013, LNCS 8115, pp. 90–99, 2013.

and environmental monitoring. Nowadays, whenever connectivity is debated, the next issue that comes to mind is mobility. Mobile connectivity is almost synonymous with cellular communications. The costs of cellular services experienced dramatic decrease and cellular broadband connectivity became ubiquitous in the recent past. The decrease in the costs and sizes, and the increase of power capabilities of devices with integrated sensors, network interfaces, etc. has paved the way for manufacturers to offer diverse applications and services. Various implementation areas, where those applications can be deployed, benefited from this development.

Long Term Evolution (LTE) and LTE-Advanced (LTE-A) are expected to be the future technologies for providing M2M services. These cellular systems are expected to offer a diverse range of services to M2M applications. M2M applications are generally based on narrowband applications transmitting data frequently or infrequently. The development of LTE was primarily aimed for broadband data services. With narrowband M2M applications, LTE may not achieve spectrum and cost efficiency. Therefore, the integration of M2M communication, with their rather low data rates and small packet sizes but higher number of devices, might have a substantial impact on the LTE system performance.

The concept of e-healthcare is based on establishing a relationship between a healthcare organization and a patient through M2M communication [6]. E-healthcare is defined by the Health Information and Management Systems Society (HIMSS) [7] as "the application of Internet and other related technologies in the healthcare industry to improve the access, efficiency, effectiveness, and quality of clinical and business processes utilized by healthcare organizations, practitioners, patients, and consumers in an effort to improve the health status of patients".

The motivation behind the work of this paper is to study the challenges of providing e-healthcare facilities in future mobile networks. The usage of mobile network resources by mobile e-healthcare devices to monitor the health condition of a patient can have a significant impact on the performance of regular data traffic such as voice, video and file transfer. This paper illustrates the impact of M2M traffic on LTE regular traffic performance by comparing the simulation results of scenarios with varying M2M (e-healthcare) traffic load.

2   Future Mobile Networks and E-Healthcare

LTE and LTE-A are the recent standards of wireless communication developed by the Third Generation Partnership Project (3GPP) to fulfill the data volume requirements of cellular mobile users. The objectives of these standards are to increase the peak user throughput, enhance spectral efficiency and reduce latency for broadband services as compared to the previous standards. These recent standards are based on a packet-oriented transmission scheme. The original design goal was to serve cellular devices with data rates of up to 100 Mbps [8]. The access network of LTE, also termed as the Evolved UMTS Terrestrial Radio Access Network (E-UTRAN), consists of only two types of nodes; the eNodeB and the User Equipment (UE). In the radio access network, time and frequency resources are allocated to UEs by the

Medium Access Control (MAC) layer scheduler of the eNodeB. The scheduler is generally designed to allocate resources for downlink and uplink transmission of regular LTE traffic according to the data buffer sizes of the UEs.

The evolution of mobile networks has led to the notion of providing healthcare and patient monitoring facilities outside the hospital and dispensary premises. Traditionally, the health condition of a patient, suffering from a disease which requires regular check-ups, is monitored on the hospital bed. The patient's temperature, blood pressure, heartbeat rate, etc. are monitored by the staff of the designated hospital ward. Hospital beds and staff are valuable but scarce public resources. The allocation management of these resources has routinely been a challenging task for healthcare organizations, even in advanced countries.

With the recent technological advancements, the topic of patient monitoring from remote locations has been investigated by employing Wireless Local Area Networks (WLANs). The patients can be monitored while at home wearing sensors connected to a WLAN for transferring the health status to the hospital; for example, sending the temperature, electrocardiography (ECG) data, or electronic images of the patient from a remote location using a sensor belt wrapped around the patient's chest. This arrangement provides ease, not only to the healthcare organizations but also, to the patients by significantly decreasing the waiting time in the hospital. Moreover, the domestic routine activities of the patients are not disturbed if they stay at home. The healthcare organizations are expected to take measures for patient treatment only when the sensors detect an unusual health status. This saves healthcare resources. An additional advantage for the patient is to stay away from the hospital environment and reduce the risk of infections and other diseases.

As explained above, mobility is a very special feature of cellular networks and mobility support is a major requirement of several M2M applications. E-healthcare is no exception. It is usually advisable for patients to keep themselves involved in outdoor physical activities like jogging, walking, exercises, etc. In order to perform such activities, the patients are required to leave their home (or office) WLAN coverage areas. In daily life, patients may also be expected to travel by vehicles to go for shopping, picnicking, as well as visiting their relatives and friends; or in critical cases, being taken to hospital by ambulance. In such situations, it is apparent that the home WLAN is not a practicable solution for providing e-healthcare services. In these scenarios, the role of mobile networks becomes vital. The monitoring of patient conditions in mobility scenarios is the focus of this research work.

3   Literature Review

Most of the literature available on e-healthcare technologies focuses on indoor scenarios of patient monitoring. The authors in [9] have highlighted the security issues of e-healthcare over mobile networks, and have proposed an architecture to facilitate doctors' and patients' mobility within the hospital. In [10], various M2M implementation scenarios including e-healthcare have been discussed. The authors underline the use of capillary networks and enhanced LTE architecture for M2M communications. In [11], the issues of energy efficiency, reliability and security are elaborated for M2M communications and e-healthcare. In [12], the authors suggest a system design for body parameter sensing over GSM/GPRS (Global System for Mobile Communication/General Packet Radio Service) via a modem capable of sending and receiving SMS (Short Message Service). In [13], the authors propose mobile sensor agent and adapter for intelligent M2M communication in e-healthcare. In [14], the integration of vehicular networking and e-healthcare technologies is studied with Bluetooth devices employed at the roadside. The mobile network requirements and issues related to e-healthcare and patient monitoring are discussed in [15]. In [16], two major types of network architectures for e-healthcare are elaborated, i.e. home-oriented architecture and hospital-oriented architecture.

A review of the available literature on this topic reveals that most of the e-healthcare based research is focused on home or hospital scenarios. Only few authors discuss the issues of mobile networks. The discussion on mobile networks is also limited to GSM/GPRS. Our paper highlights the issues of mobile networks under the paradigm of LTE and LTE-A.

4   Remote Health Monitoring

The health status of a patient can be monitored by providing belts or straps equipped with sensors, to be worn by the patient. The sensors would read the health parameters of the patient regularly and transmit the information over a communication medium to the e-healthcare organization. Based on the received information, the e-healthcare service provider takes remedial actions according to patient conditions. The transmission of health parameters at hospital and home scenarios is possible with the help of capillary networks like WLAN, ZigBee, etc.. However, if the patient is walking down the street or driving a vehicle, the capillary network may not be an appropriate solution for e-healthcare. In such cases, the cellular networks can play a significant role.

The usual health parameters which are frequently required for the evaluation of patient health status are temperature, blood pressure, heartbeat rate, etc. The temperature and blood pressure monitoring is usually performed approximately every half hour. From the mobile network point of view, these parameters have very low throughput requirements. However, the ECG for heartbeat monitoring requires continuous network resources. ECG is a "tracing representing the heart's electrical action derived by amplification of the minutely small electrical impulses normally generated by the heart" [17]. Each beat of the heart is triggered by an electrical impulse normally generated from special cells in the upper right chamber of the heart [18]. An ECG records these electrical signals as they travel through the heart.

The British Heart Foundation (BHF) offers ECG tests where patients are monitored for 24 hours [19]. The electrodes are placed on the chest and the attached wires are connected to a small portable recorder. The test can also be performed while walking on a treadmill or cycling an exercise bike. In special cases, Implantable Loop Recorders (ILRs) are implanted under the patient's skin to monitor the heart activity for up to 14 months. In such cases, it is eminent that the patient would be mobile on several occasions. The ECG data recorder could be provided with mobile connectivity for continuous patient diagnosis. The digital data generated by an ECG recorder for transmission over a network is 9.6 kbps according to [20].

5   Simulation Settings and Results

The modeling methodology behind our simulation model is to focus primarily on the user plane and evaluate the end-to-end performance. The model is developed using the OPNET simulation environment [21]. In Fig. 1, a number of network elements, e.g. access Gate-Way (aGW), Packet Data Network Gate-Way (PDN GW), eNodeB and the UEs, are depicted. Additionally, some ECG devices are also deployed in the simulation environment. All these network nodes contain the complete protocol stack implementation according to the 3GPP release 8 specifications. The details of our LTE simulation model are provided in [22], [23]. The OPNET simulations are performed under the parameter settings illustrated in Table 1. Since the ECG data requires uplink radio resources, the Bandwidth and QoS Aware (BQA) LTE uplink scheduler proposed in [24] is used for resource allocation.

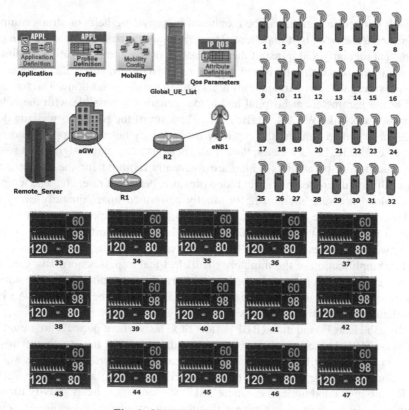

Fig. 1. OPNET LTE simulation model

Table 1. Simulation Parameters

Parameter	Setting
Cell layout	1 eNodeB, 3 cells
System Bandwidth	5 MHz (~25 PRBs)
Frequency reuse factor	1
Cell radius	375m
Device velocity	3kmph, 120kmph
Max UE power	23dBm
Path loss	$128.1+37.6\log_{10}(R)$, R in km
Slow fading	Log-normal shadowing, 8dB standard deviation, correlation 1
Fast fading	Jakes-like method [25]
Mobility Model	Random Way Point (RWP)
UE buffer size	Infinite
Power Control	Fractional PC, $\alpha = 0.6$, $P_0 = -58$dBm
Traffic environment	Loaded
LTE Uplink Scheduler	BQA [24]
Voice traffic model (Priority 1)	
Silence/ talk spurt length	Exponential(3 sec)
Encoder scheme	GSM EFR
Video traffic model (Priority 2)	
Frame size	1200 Bytes
Frame inter-arrival time	75ms
Mobile point-of-sale traffic model (Priority 3)	
Page size	100 KBytes
Page inter-arrival time	12 sec
FTP traffic model (Priority 4)	
File size	20 MBytes
File inter-request time	Uniform distribution, min 80 sec, max 100 sec
ECG traffic model (Priority 1)	
Frame size	1200 Bytes
Frame inter-arrival time	1 sec

The performance of different e-healthcare traffic load scenarios is compared by analyzing the QoS performance of mobile devices with regular LTE uplink traffic. The simulations are carried out by considering four types of LTE uplink traffic, i.e., voice, video, mobile point-of-sale (POS) and file transfer; and one e-healthcare traffic type. The POS traffic has characteristics similar to web browsing, but in uplink direction. So each mobile POS device acts as a web server. The voice and ECG traffic is treated as highest priority traffic by the scheduler. Video traffic has the next highest priority. POS comes after video in terms of priority and web browsing is the best effort traffic with lowest priority. The regular LTE traffic load is kept constant and the ECG data traffic load is varied in the scenarios. In all scenarios, the number of voice, video, mobile POS and file transfer users is 8 each. In the first scenario, there are no

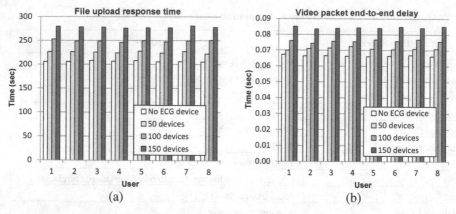

Fig. 2. (a) Average file upload time (b) Average video user packet end-to-end delay

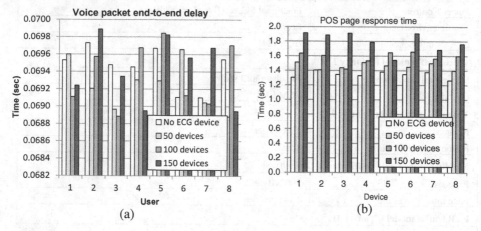

Fig. 3. (a) Average voice user packet end-to-end delay (b) Average POS page upload time

ECG devices; whereas in the subsequent scenarios, the number of devices is incremented by 50. During the simulations, the velocity of mobile devices and half of the ECG devices deployed in the cell is 120 kmph, whereas half of the ECG devices are moving at 3 kmph.

The simulation results of LTE regular traffic users are depicted in Fig. 2 (a), Fig. 2 (b) and Fig. 3 (a) for user file upload time, user video packet end-to-end delay and user voice packet end-to-end delay respectively. Fig. 3 (b) illustrates the results for mobile POS devices in terms of device page upload time. There is a clear increase in the traffic delay times of the file upload user, video users and POS devices. The voice user results, however, do not reveal any substantial impact of increasing the ECG traffic load within the LTE cell. The cause that voice traffic is not influenced by the increase in load is that the LTE uplink scheduler [24] gives strict priority to delay sensitive voice traffic. However, the priority of ECG data traffic is higher than other traffic classes. The low priority traffic classes are greatly influenced by the increasing ECG traffic, as evident from the overall average cell QoS results in Fig. 4 (a). Clearly,

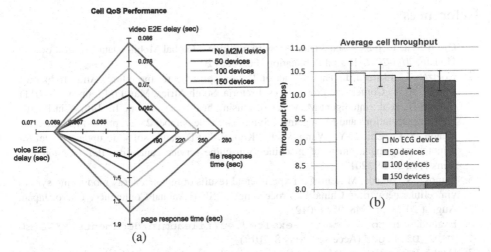

Fig. 4. (a) Cell QoS performance comparison with varying load (b) Average cell throughput

the increasing load of ECG traffic drastically degrades the performance of the video, file transfer and POS traffic. Even in such scenarios with low LTE traffic, ECG devices are already causing hindrance in their QoS performance. The results for average cell throughput in Fig. 4 (b) also indicate performance degradation with increasing e-healthcare load.

6   Conclusion and Outlook

We conducted a feasibility study in this work to highlight the influence of the new and challenging topic of e-healthcare over the future mobile networks. Though the design of LTE fits the wideband traffic demands, it is not proven how LTE handles the massive deployment of e-healthcare communicating devices. Contrary to the idea that the low M2M traffic might have a negligible impact on future wireless communication systems, we demonstrated in this work that the M2M traffic can have drastic impact on the performance of regular LTE traffic in terms of QoS and throughput.

In future, network operators have to find ways to deal with the issue of increasing M2M and e-healthcare devices; and minimize its influence on the regular LTE traffic. Despite the fact that the performance of voice users remained unaffected by the additional M2M traffic in our simulations, other LTE traffic experienced a considerable increase in delay. We also intend to evaluate the system performance for other kinds of M2M traffic, such as smart metering, intelligent transport, emergency alerting etc. and propose ways to deals with the expected M2M traffic growth in coming years.

Acknowledgement. We are grateful to the International Graduate School for Dynamics in Logistics, University of Bremen, Germany and University of Engineering and Technology, Peshawar, Pakistan for supporting this research work financially. We are also thankful to Dr. Haroon Ahmed Khan, Post Graduate Trainee, Department of General Surgery, Saidu Teaching Hospital, Swat, Pakistan for his assistance in understanding several e-healthcare aspects and ECG functionalities.

References

1. Cisco Systems Inc., Cisco Visual Networking Index: Global Mobile Data Traffic Forecast Update, 2011-2016. Digital Publication (February 2012)
2. Coetzee, L., Eksteen, J.: The Internet of Things - promise for the future? An introduction. In: IST-Africa Conference Proceedings, Pretoria, South Africa, May 11-13, pp. 1–9 (2011)
3. Shin, S.H., et al.: Intelligent M2M network using healthcare sensors. In: 14th Asia-Pacific Network Operations and Management Symposium, September 25-27, pp. 1–4 (2012)
4. Chang, Y.-C., Chi, T.-Y., Wang, W.-C., Kuo, S.-Y.: Dynamic software update model for remote entity management of machine-to-machine service capability. IET Communications 7(1), 32–39 (2013)
5. Yunoki, S., Takada, M., Liu, C.: Experimental results of remote energy monitoring system via cellular network in China. In: Proceedings of SICE Annual Conference, Tokyo, Japan, August 20-23, pp. 948–954 (2012)
6. Exalted, http://www.ict-exalted.eu/fileadmin/documents/EXALTED _WP2_D2.1.pdf (Accessed: May 8, 2013)
7. Health Information and Management Systems Society, http://himss.files.cms-plus.com/HIMSSorg/Content/files/ehealth_whitepaper.pdf (Accessed: May 8, 2013)
8. 3GPP Technical Specification 25.913 V 9.0.0, Requirements for Evolved UTRA (E-UTRA) and Evolved UTRAN (E-UTRAN), (December 2011)
9. Nguyen, T.-D., AI-Saffar, A., Huh, E.-N.: A dynamic ID-based authentication scheme. In: Sixth International Conference on Networked Computing and Advanced Information Management, Suwon, South Korea, August 16-18, pp. 248–253 (2010)
10. LTE for Devices: Requirements, Deployment Phases and Target Scenarios. In: 11th European Wireless Conference 2011 - Sustainable Wireless Technologies, Vienna, Austria, April 27-29, pp. 1-6 (2011)
11. Lu, R., Li, X., Liang, X., Shen, X., Lin, X.: GRS: The green, reliability, and security of emerging machine to machine communications. IEEE Communications Magazine 49(4), 28–35 (2011)
12. Suganthi, J., Umareddy, N.V., Awasthi, N.: Medical alert systems with TeleHealth & telemedicine monitoring using GSM and GPS technology. In: Third International Conference on Computing Communication & Networking Technologies, Coimbatore, India, July 26-28, pp. 1–5 (2012)
13. Shin, S.H., et al.: Intelligent M2M network using healthcare sensors. In: 14th Asia-Pacific Network Operations and Management Symposium, Seoul, South Korea, September 25-27, pp. 1–4 (2012)
14. Imadali, S., et al.: eHealth service support in IPv6 vehicular networks. In: IEEE 8th International Conference on Wireless and Mobile Computing, Networking and Communications, Barcelona, Spain, October 8-10, pp. 579–585 (2012)
15. Chen, H., Jia, X.: New requirements and trends of mHealth. In: IEEE 14th International Conference on e-Health Networking, Applications and Services, Beijing, China, October 10-13, pp. 27–31 (2012)
16. Poenaru, E., Poenaru, C.: Networking architectures for healthcare wireless sensor networks comparison of architectures used for remote patient monitoring. In: 11th Roedunet International Conference, Sinaia, Romania, January 17-19, pp. 1–6 (2013)
17. The Free Medical Online Dictionary, http://medical-dictionary.thefreedictionary.com/ECG (Accessed: May 15, 2013)

18. MayoClinic.com, http://www.mayoclinic.com/health/electrocardiogram/ MY00086 (Accessed: May 15, 2013)
19. British Heart Foundation, http://www.bhf.org.uk/heart-health/tests/ ecg.aspx (Accessed: May 15, 2013)
20. Keong, H.C., Yuce, M.R.: Low data rate ultra wideband ECG monitoring system. In: 30th Annual International Conference of the IEEE Engineering in Medicine and Biology Society, Vancouver, Canada, August 20-25, pp. 3413–3416 (2008)
21. OPNET Modeler, http://www.opnet.com (Accessed: May 15, 2013)
22. Zaki, Y., Weerawardane, T., Goerg, C., Timm-Giel, A.: Long Term Evolution (LTE) model development within OPNET simulation environment. In: OPNET Workshop, Washington, D.C., USA, August 29-September 1 (2011)
23. Zaki, Y., Zahariev, N., Weerawardane, T., Goerg, C., Timm-Giel, A.: Optimized Service Aware LTE MAC Scheduler: Design, Implementation. In: OPNET Workshop, Washington, D.C., USA, August 29-September 1 (2011)
24. Marwat, S.N.K., Weerawardane, T., Zaki, Y., Goerg, C., Timm-Giel, A.: Performance evaluation of bandwidth and qoS aware LTE uplink scheduler. In: Koucheryavy, Y., Mamatas, L., Matta, I., Tsaoussidis, V. (eds.) WWIC 2012. LNCS, vol. 7277, pp. 298–306. Springer, Heidelberg (2012)
25. Cavers, J.K.: Mobile Channel Characteristics. Kluwer Academic Publishers (2002)

Evaluation of Video Quality Monitoring Based on Pre-computed Frame Distortions

Dominik Klein[1], Thomas Zinner[1], Kathrin Borchert[1], Stanislav Lange[1],
Vlad Singeorzan[2], and Matthias Schmid[2]

[1] University of Würzburg
[2] Infosim GmbH & Co. KG, 97076 Würzburg

Abstract. A large fraction of the current Internet traffic is caused by video streaming. Due to the growing expectations of video consumers, monitoring video applications is getting more and more important for network and service providers. In a previous work, we proposed a video quality monitoring solution which utilizes the full reference SSIM metric to improve the monitoring in the network by distributing pre-computed distortion information induced by frame losses. To improve scalability, we introduced a less complex algorithm which infers the distortion for higher loss scenarios from single loss scenarios and inter-frame dependencies. In this work, we evaluate the accuracy of our algorithm by comparing it with the exact calculation of the SSIM metric for different frame loss scenarios. We further consider different high definition test video sequences and group of picture structures and investigate the influence on the accuracy of our proposed approximation.

1 Introduction

Among the currently popular Internet applications, video streaming is responsible for the largest fraction of the global Internet traffic and is said to keep its pace within the next years [1]. This trend underlines the growing importance of video streaming in current and future networks. In parallel, technologies like software defined networking or network virtualization enable the development of application-specific virtual networks which fulfill the special requirements of applications like video streaming. Virtual networks introduce new management mechanisms [2] to optimize the virtual network towards the hosted application but require an accurate monitoring solution to assess the effects of applied management mechanisms with respect to the perceived service quality of end customers. In [3], we proposed a monitoring solution that uses a full reference metric to pre-compute the distortion per group of pictures (GOP) for different frame loss scenarios. This pre-computed information is used to improve the accuracy of the monitoring in the network, which infers the video quality from lost frames. In particular, video dependencies are included in our approach as they are captured by the video quality assessment (VQA) metric, in our case the structural similarity (SSIM) [4] metric. However, including all possible frame loss combinations per GOP introduces a large number of frame loss scenarios and hence, excessive computing power is required. To achieve a better scalability of our approach, higher frame loss scenarios are approximated by adding the

T. Bauschert (Ed.): EUNICE 2013, LNCS 8115, pp. 100–111, 2013.

distortion of single frame loss scenarios. Hence, only the distortions for single frame loss scenarios need to be pre-computed. This approach however reduces the accuracy compared to the exact SSIM metric.

In this work, we evaluate the accuracy of our solution by comparing it with the exact calculation of the SSIM metric for different frame loss scenarios. We further consider different high definition test video sequences and GOP structures and investigate the influence on the accuracy of our proposed approximation. The remainder is structured as follows. In Section 2, we discuss similar approaches. Section 3 briefly introduces our proposed monitoring framework and in Section 4, we explain the setup of the evaluation. In Section 5, we assess the accuracy of our approach and investigate the influence of different video structures. Finally in Section 6, we conclude the paper and present future work.

2 Related Work

The quality of experience (QoE) of consumers has several influence factors like the physical and social context, the expectation and usage history of the human user, and the technical system itself [5]. Despite the technical network parameters, these factors are hard to measure. Another important factor is the video quality itself and there are several monitoring solutions which try to infer the video quality from technically measurable parameters. The most simple mechanisms is to define a packet loss threshold for the IPTV service and assume the video quality as acceptable as long as the threshold is not exceeded. This technique does not take any video and content information into account. While a lost packet will produce a large error in regions with medium motion, it may produce no sizable error in regions with low motion. The mechanism introduced by Reibman et al. [6] focuses on no reference methods which estimate the video quality on network level and, if possible, on codec level. The estimation on codec level includes for instance spatio-temporal information and effects of error propagation. Tao et al. [7] propose a relative quality metric, rPSNR, which allows the estimation of the video quality against a quality benchmark provided by the network. The introduced system offers a lightweight video quality solution. Naccari et al. [8] introduce a no reference video quality monitoring solution which takes spatio-temporal error propagation as well as errors produced by spatial and temporal concealment into account. The results are mapped to SSIM and compared to results gained by computing the SSIM of the reference video and the distorted video. All these video quality monitoring mechanisms work on no reference or reduced reference metrics for estimating the video quality. A brief overview on current research questions within the area of IPTV monitoring can be found in [9].

3 Proposed Monitoring Solution

In this section, we give a brief overview to our proposed video monitoring solution. The idea of our proposed monitoring solution is to distribute pre-computed distortion information induced by losing frames to monitoring agents in the network. The agents monitor lost frames in the video streams and utilize the pre-computed distortion information to infer the distortion of multiple frame losses within a GOP based on the distortion of single frame losses and the frame dependencies. The distortion per frame for the single frame loss scenarios and the frame dependencies are extracted on a per GOP basis during a SSIM-based video analysis prior to the video streaming process. More details to the different building blocks are provided in the following.

3.1   Precomputation of Distortion

The distortion values are computed according to the SSIM metric and we define the distortion as the dissimilarity of two frames. For each frame within a GOP, the video analysis generates a loss scenario where only this specific frame is dropped and the resulting distortion on all frames within that group is investigated. Therefore, we directly compare the undistorted image f_{Good} with the distorted image f_{Bad} via the SSIM method and hence obtain, how different the undistorted and distorted image are. The SSIM metric yields values between 0 and 1 and the distortion value per frame d_{Frame} is defined in Equation 1.

$$d_{Frame} = 1 - SSIM(f_{Good}, f_{Bad}) \tag{1}$$

The distortion value per single frame d_{Frame} hence has a maximum of 1 which means two completely different pictures. However, only I-frames are completely independent of other frames and constitute fixed pictures. All other frame types are dependent on other frames and if these frames are lost, the dependent frames cannot be decoded. Hence, a single frame can have a much higher distortion value in case a lot of other frames are dependent on this frame. To normalize the distortion per group d_{GOP}, we divide it by the number of frames per group. To get the dependencies between the frames in a GOP, we also investigate in the above emulated loss scenarios which other frames are also distorted in the currently considered GOP if a specific frame is lost.

3.2   Calculation of Video Distortion

The distortion value is calculated per GOP and once the agent sees the next GOP in the stream, the old distortion value of the former GOP is sent to the monitoring database and the value is reset to 0 for the next group. For each lost frame per group, the monitoring agent updates the distortion value d_{GOP}. First, the monitoring agent checks whether the lost frame is dependent on other frames. If the lost frame is independent, the agent looks up the distortion value for the lost frame d_{Frame} and adds this value to the distortion value of the currently considered GOP (d_{GOP}) and the update process is finished. If otherwise the lost frame is dependent on other frames, the agent needs to check whether these frames are also lost. If the currently considered frame requires another frame which is also lost, the distortion of the current frame is already included and can be ignored. In this case, no update of the d_{GOP} value is required. If in contrast the required frame is not lost, the distortion of the currently considered lost frame is not yet included and hence, the distortion d_{Frame} is added to the d_{GOP} value.

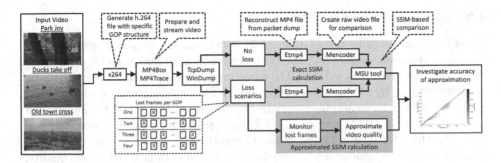

Fig. 1. Flow chart showing the different steps during the evaluation

3.3 Mapping from Distortion to Video Quality

After the distortion per GOP d_{GOP} has been calculated, the monitoring needs to map the distortion to a proper metric showing the actual video quality. For our approach, the distortion is mapped to the MOS value according to [10] and then to the video quality according to [5]. There the authors have shown via subjective tests for web services that 90 % of the users already accept a fair video quality (MOS 3). A distortion per GOP $d_{GOP} \leq 0.12$ corresponds to MOS values equal or larger than MOS 3. Hence, our monitoring solution rates GOPs with a distortion $d_{GOP} \leq 0.12$ as good or accepts the video quality and rates GOPs with a distortion $d_{GOP} > 0.12$ as bad or rejects the video quality.

4 Evaluation Setup

In this section, we first describe the test video sequences and GOP structures which have been considered for the evaluation. Second, we explain the evaluation setup and the used tools.

4.1 Test Video Sequences

In the following, we introduce the considered videos for the evaluation. The videos have been selected so that different amounts of temporal and spatial information are represented. Temporal information includes the motion between consecutive frames while spatial information includes the amount of details per single frame, as introduced in ITU-T Recommendation P.910 [11]. Our evaluation was performed using free available high definition 1080p test video sequences from the Xiph.org Test Media website [12]. The videos are listed in descending order according to the amount of temporal and spatial information and correspond to different content types such as high or low motion and high or low detail. The considered sequences are *Park Joy, Ducks Take Off,* and *Old Town Cross.* Screenshots for the three different videos are shown on the left-hand side in Figure 1.

4.2   Assessed GOP Structures

In addition to the influence of different types of videos, we also investigate how well our proposed monitoring solution behaves for different GOP structures. Therefore, we have analyzed the GOP structures currently used for live streaming of video content by two prominent German IPTV broadcasters, i.e. the German Telecom and the German public service broadcasters (ARD/ZDF). The German Telecom offers an IPTV service called T-Entertain which can be booked in addition to the DSL Internet connection. Entertain runs in a separate VLAN and provides access to various TV channels in high and standard definition quality. The GOP structure for Entertain in HD quality is $M = 8, N = 64$, whereas M denotes the distance between P-frames and N the distance between I-frames. Hence, for Entertain HD, there are 7 B-frames after an I- or P-frame and between two I-frames, there are 63 P- and B-frames. This kind of GOP structure reduces the amount of transmitted information but the encoding and playout order of frames is different which increases the complexity at decoder side. For the ARD/ZDF live TV stream in contrast, the GOP structure is different. There are no B-frames at all and also the length of the GOP is variable and not fixed. A possible explanation for the variable GOP length is that the length is adaptive to the video content to reduce the video bit rate. Such an approach is for example proposed in [13]. Hence, the GOP structure for the ARD/ZDF life stream can be written as $M = 1, N = variable$. This kind of structure has an increased video bitrate compared to the structure with B-frames but the encoding and playout order of frames is the same.

Table 1. Considered GOP structures

Label	Size	Length	Structure
IBP	M=4	N=16	IBBBPBBBPBBBPBBB
IPP	M=1	N=16	IPPPPPPPPPPPPPPP

For our evaluation, we use slightly adapted GOP structures considering the high definition video test sequences. The GOP length for both structures has been set to 16 frames and is not dependent on the video content anymore so that both structures are comparable. For the structure with B-frames, we have reduced the GOP size to 4 which results in 3 B-frames in between I- and P-frames. The resulting modified GOP structures can be seen in Table 1. For convenience, the structure with B-frames is denoted as *IBP* structure in the following and the structure without B-frames is denoted as *IPP* structure.

4.3   Evaluation Methods

For the evaluation of the accuracy of our proposed monitoring solution, we compare our approximated SSIM values with the exact SSIM values for different frame loss scenarios. The overall setup as well as the different steps during the evaluation can be seen in Figure 1. In the first step, the x264 tool [14] is used to create a h.264 file with a specific GOP structure (see Table 1) for the three different input videos. In the second step, we use the MP4Box tool [15] and the MP4Trace tool from the EvalVid framework [16] to create a video stream which is dumped in the next step using either TcpDump [17] or WinDump [18]. To evaluate different frame loss scenarios, we create a lossy dump file in the next step by removing certain frames from the dump file. This way, we generate different dump files for loss scenarios where exactly one, two, three, or four frames are lost per GOP. This results in $\binom{16}{i}$ scenarios in case exactly i frames are lost per GOP. Evaluating all frame loss combinations results in a high number of scenarios which requires excessive computing power. Hence, we limit our evaluation to at most four frame loss scenarios and show that higher loss scenarios are not required to demonstrate the accuracy of our approach. After the different dump files have been created, we use the Etmp4 tool from the EvalVid framework [16] to reconstruct the MP4 file from the dump file and create raw video files by using the MEncoder tool [19]. In the last step, we use the MSU tool [20] to compare the lossy video file with the original video file by calculating the exact SSIM values. These values are then used as reference and we evaluate the induced error due to our approximation of the SSIM metric. Therefore, the information about the lost frames is used by our proposed monitoring solution to calculate the approximated SSIM values (see lower part of Figure 1). The approximated SSIM values are then compared with the exact SSIM values calculated by the MSU tool.

5   Evaluation of Video Quality Monitoring

In this section, we show the accuracy of our approach with respect to the exact SSIM metric. First, we investigate which frame loss scenarios are relevant and which higher scenarios cannot deliver a good video quality anymore. Second, we assess the influence of the different video types and GOP structures on our approach and show, how our metric can be optimized for certain GOP structures. Third, we further investigate the error due to our approximation and finally, we show the sensitivity of our approach with respect to the acceptance threshold for the video quality.

5.1   Relevant Frame Loss Scenarios

In this subsection, we investigate which loss scenarios lead to a large fraction of GOPs where the video quality is still acceptable. For these scenarios, our proposed monitoring solution needs to be accurate. For loss scenarios where a large fraction of GOPs has a high distortion and hence a very bad quality, accuracy is not that important. According to Section 3.3, our mapping rates the video quality of a GOP acceptable if the distortion per GOP $d_{GOP} \leq 0.12$.

The resulting percentage of GOPs with a distortion less than 0.12 for the three different videos is shown in Figure 2. Figure 2a shows the results for the *IBP*

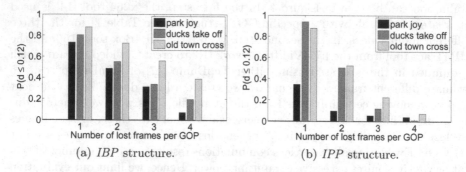

(a) *IBP* structure.   (b) *IPP* structure.

Fig. 2. Number of GOPs with distortion value less than 0.12

structure and Figure 2b shows the corresponding results for the *IPP* structure. In both figures, the x-axis shows the number of lost frames per GOP and the different colored bars denote the three different videos.

Concerning the *IBP* structure in Figure 2a, we see that the fraction of GOPs with acceptable quality decreases for the higher loss scenarios. This is in line with the expectations because the more frames are lost, the worse is the overall video quality per GOP. However, there are strong differences between the different types of video which can be explained due to the amount of spatial and temporal information. The Park Joy video sequence has the highest amount of information and is hence more susceptible to frame loss than the other two videos which have a higher number of acceptable GOPs in all loss scenarios. Even if four frames are lost within a GOP, about 40 % of the GOPs for the Old Town Cross test sequence still have an acceptable video quality. However, for five and six frame loss scenarios, the percentage of GOPs with good quality drops to 24.3 % and 13.32 % respectively. Hence, it would be necessary to take five and six frame loss scenarios into account. However, due to the high computational complexitiy we omit these scenarios for the video clip Old Town Cross.

For the *IPP* structure depicted in Figure 2b, similar observations are made. However, the fraction of acceptable GOPs is much smaller for all videos in the higher loss scenarios. Due to the absence of B-frames, the overall importance per frame is higher and hence, this structure is more susceptible to frame loss than the *IBP* structure. If we directly compare the number of accepted GOPs for the four frame loss scenario, we see that the *IPP* structure in the right figure has a much lower fraction as the *IBP* structure on the left figure. Overall, also for the *IPP* structure, it is sufficient to consider only loss scenarios where at most four frames are lost per GOP. For higher loss scenarios, our approach indicates an unacceptable video quality with a high probability.

5.2   Qualitative Evaluation of Accuracy

In this subsection, we plot our approximated distortion values against the distortion values calculated by the exact SSIM metric to show the accuracy of our monitoring solution. The evaluation does only consider loss scenarios where

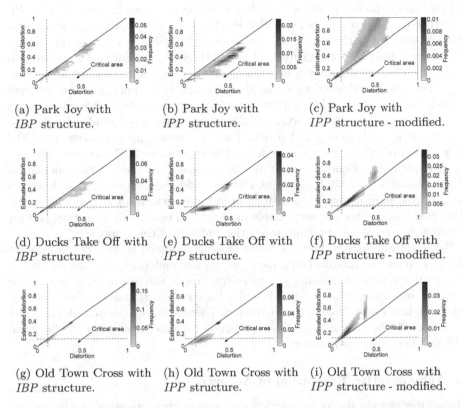

(a) Park Joy with
IBP structure.

(b) Park Joy with
IPP structure.

(c) Park Joy with
IPP structure - modified.

(d) Ducks Take Off with
IBP structure.

(e) Ducks Take Off with
IPP structure.

(f) Ducks Take Off with
IPP structure - modified.

(g) Old Town Cross with
IBP structure.

(h) Old Town Cross with
IPP structure.

(i) Old Town Cross with
IPP structure - modified.

Fig. 3. Scatter plots showing estimated distortion against exact distortion values

exactly two, three, and four frames are lost. One frame loss scenarios are not considered as for those scenarios, our approximation yields the same results as the exact SSIM metric. The results for the different video test sequences and GOP structures can be seen in Figure 3. Figures 3a-3c show the results for the Park Joy sequence, Figures 3d-3f show the results for the Ducks Take Off sequence, and 3g-3i show the results for the Old Town Cross sequence. All figures are plotted as scatter plots where the x-axis denotes the exact distortion values and the y-axis denotes the estimated distortion values. All plots also contain the 0.12 threshold lines for the estimated and exact distortion values as well as the identity line through the origin. Estimated distortion values which lie on the line through the origin perfectly match the exact distortion values.

Considering the IBP structure (see Figures 3a, 3d, and 3g) for the three different videos, we see that our approach performs best for the Old Town Cross video which has the lowest spatial and temporal information. For the other two video sequences, our approximation still performs very well in the critical area around the video quality acceptance threshold of 0.12 and only deviates in the higher distortion areas. There however, our monitoring does not accept GOPs with a bad video quality or a distortion value higher than the acceptance threshold and hence, no error occurs. A different observation can be seen for the *IPP* structure (see Figures 3b, 3e, and 3h). For this structure, our proposed approximation does not perform well and underestimates the distortion in the critical area around the acceptance threshold for all three videos. For this structure, all subsequent frames are always dependent on their precedent frames and errors in earlier frames influence all subsequent frames. Our approximation however ignores the distortion values for frames which are dependent on earlier frames (see Section 3.2) as the distortion of dependent frames is included in the distortion value of their required frame. This is a good approximation for GOP structures with minor inter-frame dependencies like the *IBP* structure but not for *IPP* structure. Hence, to improve our approach, we modify the calculation of the distortion per GOP d_{GOP} and always add the distortion of lost frames d_{Frame} instead of ignoring the distortion of frames which are dependent on another lost frame. This is a very simple modification to our initial metric. But for the specific use case, the results prove the viability of this approach.

Figures 3c, 3f, and 3i show the results for the modified version of our approximation. With the modified approach, we do not underestimate the distortion in the critical area. Accordingly, a large fraction of the estimations lies on the identity line through the origin. For the higher distortion area, our modified approach now overestimates the distortion. There however, our monitoring does not reject GOPs with a good video quality or an exact distortion smaller than 0.12 and hence, no error occurs.

5.3   Quantitative Evaluation of Accuracy

The scatter plots in the former section give a basic understanding about how our unmodified and modified metric perform for the different videos and GOP structures. However, for a quantitative statement, CDF plots are more suitable. Hence in Figure 4 and 5, we plot the CDF for the error e between the estimated and the exact distortion values. The error e is defined as the exact distortion minus the estimated distortion. A negative error means that our proposed approximation overestimates the distortion and positive error means an underestimation of distortion. From the perspective of a network provider, a positive error is more serious because the monitoring underestimates the distortion and hence recognizes a bad video quality too late or even not at all.

Regarding the *IBP* structure, we again see that our proposed monitoring solution performs best for the Old Town Cross sequence. For that video, all GOPs have an error e < 0.05. For the other two videos, about 80 % of the GOPs have an error e < 0.05. However, as we have seen in Figure 3, the larger error occurs in a distortion range where accuracy is less important.

For the *IPP* structure, it can be seen that the unmodified approach always significantly underestimates the distortion and hence is not suitable for this structure. In contrast, the modified approach mostly overestimates the distortion and only a very small fraction of GOPs has a positive error e. The modified approach is hence more suitable for the *IPP* structure as the GOPs with a high negative error e have a very high distortion and are rejected anyway.

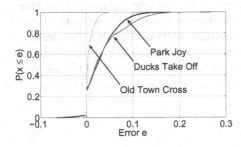

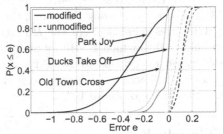

Fig. 4. Error depicted as CDF for *IBP* structure

Fig. 5. Error depicted as CDF for *IPP* structure

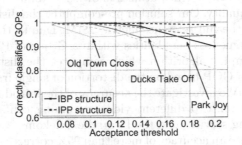

Fig. 6. Sensitivity with respect to acceptance threshold

5.4   Sensitivity with Respect to Acceptance Threshold

In the former evaluation of the accuracy of our proposed monitoring solution, we have used an acceptance threshold of 0.12 for the video quality. The video quality of GOPs is only accepted if the corresponding distortion is less than this threshold. However, this threshold was chosen according to [5], where the authors have shown via subjective tests for web services that 90 % of the users accept a fair service quality (MOS 3). If due to new findings in future work this threshold needs to be adapted, our monitoring solution should still be accurate. Hence in the following, we investigate how the percentage of correctly classified GOPs behaves for different acceptance thresholds. The corresponding results are shown in Figure 6. The x-axis shows different values for the acceptance threshold and the y-axis shows the percentage of correctly classified GOPs. The solid lines denote the results for the *IBP* structure and the dashed lines denote the results for the *IPP* structure. For the *IPP* structure, only the results with the modified approach are shown.

For all structures and videos, a threshold close to 0 leads to 100 % correctly classified GOPs. In that case, both metrics always reject the video quality for a GOP if the distortion is larger than 0 which is not a reasonable approach as such a monitoring would be far too pessimistic. For the chosen threshold of 0.12, our monitoring classifies about 98 % of the GOPs correctly. Only the *IBP* structure for the Old Town Cross sequence experiences a slightly lower classification rate of 93 %. For an increasing threshold, the classification rate for nearly all videos and structures decreases. For the *IBP* structure, the classification rate does not drop below 90 % which is still an acceptable result. For the *IPP* structure, the classification rate drops to 80 % for the Old Town Cross video. Overall, our monitoring still achieves a high correct classification of GOPs even in the higher dirstortion range of about 0.2.

6   Conclusion

In this work, we presented an evaluation of our proposed monitoring solution for IP video streaming services which utilizes knowledge about the video content to predict the service quality. Our solution pre-computes the distortion induced by losing frames using the full reference metric SSIM. Due to the high complexity for computing all frame loss possibilities within a Group of Pictures (GOP), we introduce a less complex algorithm which computes the distortion of multiple frame losses within a GOP based on the distortion of single frame losses and the frame dependencies. We investigate the accuracy of the introduced approximated monitoring solution for two different video streaming configurations used by German broadcasting services and the Deutsche Telekom.

Our results indicate an accuracy of more than 95% correctly classified GOPs of the proposed approximative distortion computations as compared to the correct values. At the same time the number of required computation is significantly reduced, since only single frame losses within a GOP have to be computed. Future work will focus on the comparison of the proposed solution with other monitoring approaches from literature with respect to the trade-off between monitoring costs, scalability, and accuracy. This also includes subjective user surveys which can be used as a metric for the comparison, and also to improve the accuracy of the proposed video monitoring solution.

Acknowledgment. The authors would like to thank Prof. Tran-Gia for the fruitful discussion and the support in this work.

References

1. C. S. Inc., Cisco visual networking index: Forecast and methodology, 2011-2016 (June 2012), http://www.cisco.com/en/US/solutions/collateral/ns341/ns525/ns537/ns705/ns827/white_paper_c11-481360.pdf
2. Meier, S., Barisch, M., Kirstädter, A., Schlosser, D., Duelli, M., Jarschel, M., Hoßfeld, T., Hoffmann, K., Hoffmann, M., Kellerer, W., Khan, A., Jurca, D., Kozu, K.: Provisioning and Operation of Virtual Networks. In: Electronic Communications of the EASST, Kommunikation in Verteilten Systemen 2011, vol. 37 (March 2011)
3. Klein, D., Zinner, T., Lange, S., Singeorzan, V., Schmid, M.: Video Quality Monitoring based on Precomputed Frame Distortions. In: IFIP/IEEE International Workshop on Quality of Experience Centric Management (QCMan), Ghent, Belgium (May 2013)

4. Wang, Z., Bovik, A., Sheikh, H., Simoncelli, E.: Image Quality Assessment: From Error Visibility to Structural Similarity. IEEE Transactions on Image Processing 13, 600–612 (2004)
5. Schatz, R., Hoßfeld, T., Janowski, L., Egger, S.: From Packets to People: Quality of Experience as a New Measurement Challenge. In: Biersack, E., Callegari, C., Matijasevic, M. (eds.) Data Traffic Monitoring and Analysis. LNCS, vol. 7754, pp. 219–263. Springer, Heidelberg (2013)
6. Reibman, A., Vaishampayan, V., Sermadevi, Y.: Quality monitoring of video over a packet network. IEEE Transactions on Multimedia 6(2) (April 2004)
7. Tao, S., Apostopoloulos, J., Guerin, R.: Real-Time Monitoring of Video Quality in IP Networks. IEEE Transactions on Networking 16(6) (December 2008)
8. Naccari, M., Tagliasacchi, M., Tubaro, S.: No-Reference Video Quality Monitoring for H.264/AVC Coded Video. IEEE Transactions on Multimedia 11(5) (August 2009)
9. Apostolopoulos, J., Reibman, A.: The Challenge of Estimating Video Quality in Video Communication Applications [In the Spotlight]. IEEE Signal Processing Magazine 29(2), 160–158(2012)
10. Wang, Z., Lu, L., Bovik, A.C.: Video quality assessment using structural distortion measurement. In: International Conference on Image Processing, vol. 3, pp. 65–68 (2002)
11. I. T. Union, ITU-T Recommendation P.910: Subjective video quality assessment-methods for multimedia applications (April 2008), http://www.itu.int/rec/T-REC-P.910/en
12. xiph.org, Derf's test media collection (March 2013), http://media.xiph.org/video/derf/
13. Zatt, B., Porto, M., Scharcanski, J., Bampi, S.: Gop structure adaptive to the video content for efficient H.264/AVC encoding. In: 2010 17th IEEE International Conference on Image Processing (ICIP), pp. 3053–3056 (September 2010)
14. x264 - h264/avc encoder, http://www.videolan.org/developers/x264.html
15. G. Multimedia open source project, Mp4box, http://gpac.wp.mines-telecom.fr/mp4box/
16. Klaue, J., Rathke, B., Wolisz, A.: EvalVid - A Framework for Video Transmission and Quality Evaluation. In: Kemper, P., Sanders, W.H. (eds.) TOOLS 2003. LNCS, vol. 2794, pp. 255–272. Springer, Heidelberg (2003)
17. tcpdump/libcap, http://www.tcpdump.org/
18. windump/winpcap, http://www.winpcap.org/windump/
19. T. M. Project, Mencoder, http://mplayerhq.hu/design7/news.html.
20. Graphics and M.S.U. Media Lab, CMC department, Msu video quality measurement tool

QoE Management Framework for Internet Services in SDN Enabled Mobile Networks

Marcus Eckert and Thomas Martin Knoll

Chemnitz University of Technology,
Reichenhainer Str. 70, 09126 Chemnitz, Germany
{marcus.eckert,knoll}@etit.tu-chemnitz.de

Abstract. In order to achieve acceptable service quality, the broad spectrum of Internet services requires differentiated handling and forwarding of the respective traffic flows in particular within increasingly overloaded mobile networks. The 3GPP procedures allow for such service differentiation by means of dedicated GPRS Tunnelling Protocol (GTP) tunnels, which need to be specifically set up and potentially updated based on the client initiated service traffic demand. The Software Defined Networking (SDN) enabled QoE monitoring and enforcement framework for Internet services presented in this paper is named ISAAR (Internet Service quality Assessment and Automatic Reaction) framework and will be abbreviated as ISAAR herein. It augments existing quality of service functions in mobile as well as software defined networks by flow based network centric quality of experience monitoring and enforcement functions. The following chapters state the current situation followed by the explanation of the ISAAR architecture in chapter 3 and its internal realisation in chapters 4, 5 and 6. In chapter 7 the summary and outlook are given.

Keywords: ISAAR, QoE framework, QoE, quality of experience, QoS, quality of service, measurement, estimation, monitoring, enforcement, DPI classification, traffic manipulation, flow-based QoE enforcement, Software Defined Networking, SDN, OpenFlow.

1   Introduction

Internet based services have become an essential part of private and business life and the user experienced quality of such services is crucial for the users' decision to subscribe and stay with the service or not. However the experienced service quality results from the whole end-to-end line-up from participating entities. It starts from the service generation, covers potentially several transport entities and finishes up in the application displaying or playing the result on the end device's screen or audio unit. However, the contributing performances of the individual service chain parties can often not be separately assessed from the end user perspective. Sluggish service behaviour can thus stem from slow server reaction, transport delay or losses due to congestion along the forwarding path as well as from the end device capabilities and load situation during the information processing and output. More insight can be gained

T. Bauschert (Ed.): EUNICE 2013, LNCS 8115, pp. 112–123, 2013.

from the mobile network perspective, which potentially allows for a differentiated assessment of the packet flow transport together with a transparent and remote Quality of Experience (QoE) estimation for the resulting service quality on the end device.

User satisfaction and user experienced service quality are strongly correlated and lead - from an Internet service provider point of view - either to an increase in subscription numbers or to customer churn towards competitors. Neither the capabilities and load situations on end devices nor the performance of content provider server farms nor the transport performance on transit links can be influenced by the operator of a mobile network. Therefore, this QoE framework will concentrate on the monitoring and enforcement capabilities of today's mobile networks in terms of differentiated packet flow processing and potentially SDN (Software Defined Networking) enabled forwarding. Since all competing providers will face similar conditions on either end of the service chain, the emphasis on the provider own match between service flow requirements and attributed mobile network resources in a cost efficient manner will be key for the mobile operator business success. That applies especially for SDN enabled networks, where a split between control and data path elements is made. This way, functions traditionally realized in specialised hardware can now be abstracted and virtualized on general purpose servers. Due to this virtualization, network topologies as well as transport and processing capacities can be easily and quickly adopted to the service demand needs under energy and cost constraints. One of the SDN implementation variants is the freely available OpenFlow (OF) standard [1]. With OF the path of packets through the network can be defined by software rules. OF is Ethernet based and implements a split architecture between so called OpenFlow Switches and OpenFlow controllers. A switch with OF control plane is referred to as "OpenFlow Switch". The switch consists of the specialised hardware (Flow Tables), the Secure Channel for communication between switch and OF controller and the OF protocol which provides the interface between them [2].

The Internet Service quality Assessment and Automatic Reaction (ISAAR) quality of experience framework takes this situation into account and leverages the packet forwarding and traffic manipulation capabilities available in modern mobile networks. It focuses on LTE and LTE Advanced networks, but is applicable to the packet domains in 3G and even 2G mobile networks as well. Since different services out of the broad variety of Internet services will ideally require individual packet flow handling for all possible services, the ISAAR framework will focus only on the major service classes for cost and efficiency reasons. The set of tackled services is configurable and should sensibly be limited to only the major contributing sources in the overall traffic volume or the strong revenue generating services of the operator network. The current Sandvine Internet statistic report [3] for instance shows that only HTTP, Facebook and YouTube services alone cover about 65% of the overall network traffic.

2   State of the Art

The standardization of mobile networks inherently addresses the topic of Quality of Service (QoS) and the respective service flow handling. The 3GPP defined architecture is called Policy and Charging Control (PCC) architecture, which started in Release 7 and applies now to the Evolved Packet System (EPS) [4]. The Policy and

Charging Rules Function (PCRF) is being informed about service specific QoS demands by the Application Function (AF). Together with the Traffic Detection Function (TDF) or the optionally available PCRF intrinsic Application Detection and Control (ADC), traffic flow start and end events are detected and indicated to the PCRF. This in turn checks the Subscription Profile Repository (SPR) or the User Data Repository (UDR) for the permission of actions as well as the Bearer Binding and Event Reporting Function (BBERF) for the current state of already established dedicated bearers. As can be seen here, the 3GPP QoS control relies on the setup of QoS by reserving dedicated bearers. These bearers need to be setup, torn down for service flows or modified in their resource reservation, if several flows are being bundled into the same bearer [5]. Nine QoS Class IDs (QCI) have been defined by 3GPP for LTE networks, which are associated with such dedicated bearers. Today, IP Multimedia Subsystem (IMS) based external services and or provider own services make use of this well-defined PCC architecture and setup dedicated service flow specific reservations by means of those bearers. Ordinary Internet services, however, are often carried in just one (default) bearer without any reservations and thus experience considerable quality degradations for streaming and real time services.

Therefore, network operators need to address and differentiate service flows besides the standardized QoS mechanisms of the 3GPP. HTTP based adaptive streaming video applications currently amount the highest traffic share (see [3]). They need to be investigated for their application behaviour and appropriate actions should be incorporated in any QoS enhancing framework architecture. An overview of HTTP based streaming services can be found in [7].

There are many approaches found in the literature, which address specific services and potential enhancements. HTTP Adaptive Streaming Services (HAS) [8] for instance is a new way to adapt the video streaming quality based on the observed transport quality.

Other approaches target the increasing trend of Fixed-Mobile Convergence (FMC) and network sharing concepts, which inherently require the interlinking of PCRF and QoS architecture structures and mechanisms (see e.g. [9]). This architectural opening is particularly interesting for the interlinking of 3GPP and non-3GPP QoS concepts, but has not yet been standardized for close QoS interworking. The proposed interworking of WiMAX and LTE networks [10] and the Session Initiation Protocol (SIP) based Next Generation Network (NGN) QoE Controller concept [11] are just examples of the recent activities in the field.

The ISAAR framework presented in this paper follows a different approach. It aims for service flow differentiation either within single bearers without PCRF support or PCRF based flow treatment triggering dedicated bearer setups using the Rx interface. This way it is possible to use ISAAR as a standalone solution as well as aligned with the 3GPP PCRF support.

The following chapters document the ISAAR framework structure and work principle in detail.

3   QoE Framework Architecture

The logical architecture of the ISAAR framework is shown in Figure 1. The framework architecture is 3GPP independent but closely interworks with the 3GPP PCC. If available, it also can make use of flow steering in SDN networks using OpenFlow. This independent structure generally allows for its application in non-3GPP mobile networks as well as in fixed line networks. ISAAR provides modular service specific quality assessment functionality for selected classes of services combined with a QoE rule and enforcement function. The assessment as well as the enforcement is done for service flows on packet and frame level. It incorporates PCC mechanisms as well as packet and frame prioritisation in the IP, Ethernet, and the MPLS layer. MPLS as well as OpenFlow can also be used to perform flow based traffic engineering to direct flows in different paths. Its modular structure in the architecture elements allows for later augmentation towards new service classes as well as a broader range of enforcement means as they are defined and implemented. Service Flow Class Index and Enforcement Database register the available detection, monitoring and enforcement capabilities to be used and referenced in all remaining components of the architecture.

ISAAR is divided into three functional parts which are the QoE Monitoring (QMON) unit, the QoE Rules (QRULE) unit and the QoE Enforcement (QEN) unit. These three major parts are explained in detail in the following chapters.

The interworking with 3GPP is mainly realized by means of the Sd interface [10] (for traffic detection support), the Rx interface (for PCRF triggering as application function and thus triggering the setup of dedicated bearers) and the Gx / Gxx interface [12] (for reusing the standardized Policy and Charging Enforcement Function (PCEF) functionality as well as the service flow to bearer mapping in the BBERF).

Since ISAAR is targeting default bearer service flow differentiation also, it makes use of DiffServ Code Point (DSCP) markings, Ethernet prio markings, MPLS Traffic Class (TC) markings as well as OpenFlow priority changes as available. This is being enforced within the QEN by Gateway and Base Station (eNodeB) initiated packet header priority marking on either forwarding direction inside as well as outside of the potentially deployed GTP tunnel mechanism. This in turn allows all forwarding entities along the packet flow path through the access, aggregation and backbone network sections to treat the differentiated packets separately in terms of queuing, scheduling and dropping.

The modular structure of the three ISAAR units (QMON, QRULE and QEN) allow for a centralized as well as a decentralized deployment and placement of the functional elements.

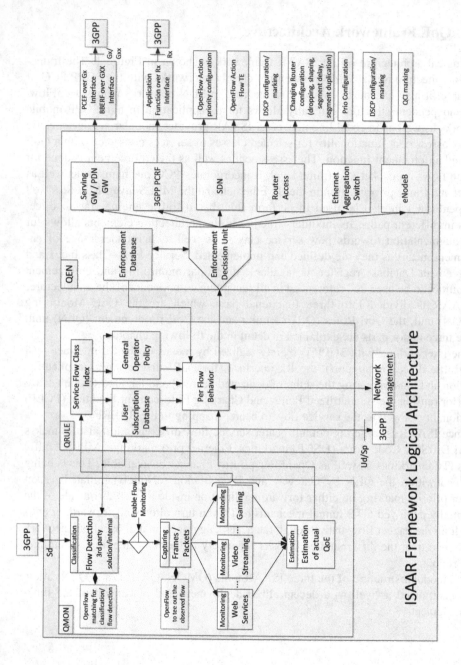

Fig. 1. SDN enabled ISAAR framework

4   QoE Monitoring (QMON)

Today's mobile networks carry a mix of different services. Each traffic type has its own network transport requirements in order to live up to the user expectation. To observe the achieved transport quality and its resulting user service experience, network operators need to monitor the QoE of the respective services. Since the quality of service experienced by the user is not directly measurable within the network, a new method is required, which can calculate a QoE Key Performance Indicator (KPI) value out of measurable QoS parameters. The most challenging and at the same time most rewarding service QoE estimation method is the one for video streaming services. Therefore, the paper will focus on video quality monitoring and estimation, not limiting the more general capabilities of ISAAR for all sorts of service KPI tracking. YouTube is the predominant video streaming service in mobile networks and ISAAR is consequently delivering a YouTube based QoE solution first. Within this YouTube monitoring we are able to detect and evaluate the QoE of MP4, Flash Video (FLV) as well as WebM video in Standard Definition (SD) and High Definition (HD) format. There are some client based video quality estimation approaches around (e.g. the YoMo application [13]), but we consider such end device bound solutions as being cumbersome and prone to manipulation. Therefore, ISAAR will not incorporate client-side solutions but concentrates on simple, transparent and network-based functionality only.

Some other monitoring solutions follow a similar way of estimation, like the Passive YouTube QoE Monitoring for ISPs approach [14]. However, they are not supporting such a wide range of video encodings as well as container formats.

Another approach is the Network Monitoring in EPC [15] system, but this does not focus on flow level service quality.

The flow monitoring which is used in the ISAAR framework is explained in chapter 4.2 Flow Monitoring). However, before the QoE of a service can be estimated, the associated data flow needs to be identified. Chapter 4.1 Flow Classification) explains the flow detection and classification in detail.

4.1   Flow Classification

The ISAAR framework is meant to work with and without support of an external Deep Packet Inspection (DPI) device. Therefore it is possible to use a centralized DPI solution like the devices provided by Sandvine [16]. For unencrypted and more easily detectable traffic flows the cheaper and more minimalist DPI algorithm which is built in the ISAAR framework can be used. In the first demo implementation, the build in classification is limited to TCP traffic, focussing on YouTube video stream detection within the operator's network. Extended with SDN support there is a third possibility: given the proper configuration, the matching function from OpenFlow could be used to identify the supported service flows within the traffic mix.

In the centralized architecture the flow detection and classification is most suitably done by a commercial DPI solution. In this case the QoE monitoring units have to be informed, that a data stream was found and the classification unit has also to tell them the data stream specific "five tuple". Contained in the five tuple are the source and destination IP address as well as the source and destination port and the used transport protocol. The QoE measurement starts, as soon as the flow identification information (five tuple) is available.

Due to the new SDN features provided by OpenFlow it is not only possible to identify specific data flows within the Internet. OpenFlow is also capable of teeing out a stream which matches a specific pattern. Thereby, the QoE estimation could be distributed to different monitoring units e.g. depending on the specific Internet application. OpenFlow disposes the right flows to the right monitoring unit.

4.2   Flow Monitoring

In the ISAAR framework the flow monitoring is application specific, i.e. for each service, which should be monitored, a specific measurement algorithm has to be provided. Our current implementation comprises the YouTube Video QoE estimation. It works transparently and independently from the user's end device. Therefore, no tools have to be installed and no access on the end device has to be granted. Our QoE estimation method relies on video stalling events and their re-buffering timings as a quality metric for the video QoE instead of fine grained pixel and block structure errors. To determine the number and duration of re-buffering events it is necessary to comprehend the fill level of the play out buffer at the client, but without access to the end device QMON has to estimate the fill level out of the accessible TCP information within the operator network. Note, that focusing on YouTube video incurs TCP encoded HTTP streaming transport. The detailed description of the method can be found in [17] and [18]. Three variants of the method exist - an exact method, an estimation-based method and a combination of the two.

4.3   Location Aware Monitoring

Due to the fact that it is probably not possible to measure all streams within an operator network, a subset of flows has to be chosen either randomly or in a policy based fashion. For example, the samples could be drawn based on the tracking area the flow goes to. If it is possible to map the eNodeB cell IDs to a tracking area, the samples also can be drawn in a regionally distributed fashion. With that, it could be decided whether a detected flow is monitored or not due to the respective destination region. Over the time, this sample selection procedure can shift the policy focus to regions with poor QoE estimation results in order to narrow down the affected regions and network elements.

5   QoE Policy and Rules (QRULE)

In this chapter the QoE Policy and Rules entity of the ISAAR framework is presented. The QRULE gets the flow information and the estimated QoE of the corresponding stream form the QMON entity. It also contains a service flow class index in which all measurable service flow types are stored. The enforcement actions for the required flow handling are determined based on information from the subscriber Database and the general operator policy. Also the enforcement database within the QEN is taken into account. Combining all this information the QRULE maps the KPIs to the Per Flow Behaviour (PFB) for each data stream managed by ISAAR. PFBs are defined by appropriate marking of packets and frames. Each PFB has to be specified. Table 1 shows an example of PFB settings for video streaming, voice traffic and Facebook traffic.

Table 1. Per Flow behaviour settings (example)

Media Type	Key Perform- ance Indicator	IP DSCP	OpenFlow Actions	Ethernet Prio	MPLS Traffic Class	3GPP QCI	Action
Video	Buffer Level in Sec. Th1 < t < Th2	CS5 101 000	set normal priority	101	101	6	Mark in S/P-GW and eNodeB with high priority
	Buffer Level in Sec. t < Th1	"Expedited Forwarding (EF)" 101 110	Change path + set high priority	111	111	4	Mark in S/P-GW and eNodeB with highest priority
	Buffer Level in Sec. Th2 < t	"Best Effort (BE)" 000 000 or even "Lower Effort (LE)" 001 000	set low priority	000	000	9	Mark in S/P-GW and eNodeB with default priority or even start drop- ping packets
Voice	Delay in ms	EF 101 110	Choose best path + set high priority	111	111	4 & 1 or 2	Mark in S/P-GW and eNodeB with highest priority or even Create dedicated bearer with QCI 1 or 2
Face- book	Page load time	CS5 101 000	Choose best effort path + set normal priority	101	101	6	Mark in S/P-GW and eNodeB with high priority
...							

For video streams three possible PFBs (corresponding to three different markings) are provided. These PFPs depend on the buffer fill level. In the example (Figure 2) two buffer fill level thresholds are defined: th1 = 20 seconds and th2 = 40 seconds. If the QoE is poor, i.e. the video buffer fill level is below threshold 1 (t < th1), the EF class (101110) should be used. If the fill level is between threshold 1 and 2 (th1 < t < th2) a DSCP value like CS5 (101 000) should be chosen, because the video QoE is suffi- cient. Finally if the fill level exceeds threshold 2 (th2 < t) a DSCP value with a lower priority like BE (000 000) or LE (001 000) is taken, so that other flows might get preferred access to the resources.

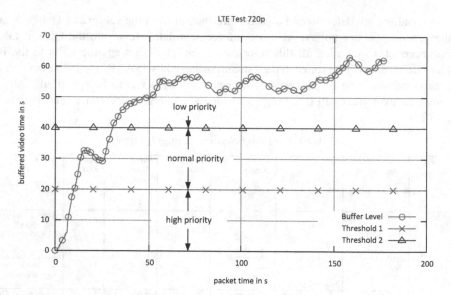

Fig. 2. Per flow behaviour dependent on the buffer fill level (YouTube example)

QRULE also decides which kind of marking is deployed depending on the networking technology. It is possible to apply IP DiffServ, Ethernet priority, MPLS traffic class marking and QCI tunnel mapping for GTP. The rules unit has to ensure that there are no oscillating effects in the network. Oscillating could occur on flow level if one flow that is lifted up in priority causes quality impairments for the neighbouring flows. Thus, the second flow will also require enforcement actions, which in turn causes the first one to deteriorate again. To overcome this effect QRULE has to consider which flows were manipulated and in which location they are. Continuous action triggering is an early indication for such race conditions, which results in QRULE dampening of enforcement actions. That is, the transport impairment are such, that ever increasing priority is simply not solving the issue. Oscillating could also occur not only on flow level but on local area level within the network. Thus regional impairment mitigation should not cause increased levels of impairments in neighbouring regions. If this is being detected by location aware QMON, QRULE should also dampen enforcement actions. Close interworking of ISAAR with network management systems fosters this detection of oscillation situations and provides vital information for root cause analysis. If the majority of the traffic would need to be precedented in priority, ISAAR has simply hit its limitation.

If there are OpenFlow enabled switches within the network it is also possible to influence the priority of the frames belonging to a critical flow by changing the OpenFlow Actions for that stream. As these mechanisms are often used in combination, there must be a consistent mapping between them. This mapping is also performed by the QRULE. Further details on the mapping can be found in [19].

For future investigation ISAAR is prepared to incorporate the interworking of GTP and MPLS LSPs in a transparent fashion. Further details on the interworking can be found in [20].

6   QoE Enforcement (QEN)

The third functional block in the ISAAR framework is the QoE Enforcement (QEN) where the flow manipulation is performed. For data streams with estimated low QoE QRULE changes the PFBs and QEN reacts accordingly by applying suitable mechanisms to influence the transmission of the involved data frames or packets.

One possibility to influence the data transmission is to use the PCRF/PCEF and trigger the setup of dedicated bearers via the Rx interface.

A second option is to deploy layer 2 and layer 3 frame/packet markings. Based on these markings a differentiated frame/packet handling (scheduling, dropping) is enforced in the network elements which are traversed by the frames/packets (per hop behaviour). The marking is realized via IP DiffServ, Ethernet priority, MPLS traffic class priority and QCI for GTP tunnels. In case a consistent marking scheme across all layers and technologies is ensured by the QRULE entity, the QEN does not need to change the existing configuration of the network elements.

In the case of a mobile network with GTP tunnelling the marking has to be performed within the GTP tunnel as well as outside. The outside marking enables routers to apply differentiated packet handling also on GTP encapsulated flows without requiring a new configuration. For IPsec encrypted GTP the marking also has to be included into the IPsec header to avoid per hop decryption/encryption. The inner and outer IP markings are set in downstream direction by the SGW/PGW and in upstream direction by the eNodeB based on the flow information (five tuple) and the PFB obtained from QMON. During handover the five tuple and the PFB are automatically transferred to the new eNodeB that is known from the Mobility Management Entity (MME).

As a third option - in case that the predefined packet handling configuration of the routers should not be used - the ISAAR framework is also able to perform a fully automated router configuration [21]. With that, the QEN may explicitly change the router packet handling behaviour (e.g. packet scheduling and dropping rules) to influence the flows.

With the SDN approach there is a fourth possibility to influence data flows by using OpenFlow features. For example, the priority of a flow can be changed in the forwarding configuration directly in an OpenFlow switch action list configuration. Furthermore, flow-specific traffic engineering could be realized. In order to use the OpenFlow features for flow enforcement ISAAR is connected to the control interfaces of the SDN enabled switches.

7   Summary

The ISAAR framework presented in this paper addresses the increasingly important quality of experience management for Internet based services in mobile networks. It takes the network operator's position to optimize the transport of packet flows belonging to most popular video streaming, voice, Facebook and other web services in order to satisfy the customer's service quality expectations. The framework is aware of the 3GPP standardized PCC functionality and tries to closely interwork with the PCRF and PCEF functional entities. However, 3GPP QoS control is mainly based on dedicated bearers and observations in today's networks reveal that most Internet services are carried undifferentiated within the default bearer only.

ISAAR therefore sets up a three component logical architecture, consisting of a classification and monitoring unit (QMON), a decision unit (QRULE) and an enforcement unit (QEN) in order to selectively monitor and manipulate single service specific flows with or without the standardized 3GPP QoS support. This is mainly achieved by priority markings on (potentially encapsulated) service flow packets making use of the commonly available priority and DiffServ capabilities in layer two and three forwarding devices. In the case of LTE networks, this involves the eNodeBs and SGWs/PGWs for selectively bidirectional marking according to the QRULE determined service flow behaviour.

More sophisticated mechanisms for location aware service flow observation and steering as well as direct router respectively OpenFlow switch configuration access for traffic engineered flow routing are optionally available within the modular ISAAR framework.

Due to the strong correlation between achieved video streaming QoE and customer satisfaction for mobile data services, the high traffic volume share of YouTube video streaming services are tackled first in the on-going ISAAR implementation activity. An optimized network-based precise video QoE estimation mechanism is coupled with automated packet flow shaping and dropping means guided by a three level play out buffer fill level estimation. This way, a smooth play out with reduced network traffic demand can be achieved. To prove the functionality of the network based video QoE estimation a demonstrator has been implemented which is capable of offline packet trace analyses from captured traffic as well as real time online measurements.

Since ISAAR is able to work independently of 3GPP's QoS functionality, it can be used with reduced functionality in any IP based operator network. In such setups, the service flow QoS enforcement would rely on IP DiffServ, Ethernet priority and MPLS LSP traffic class marking as well as SDN based flow forwarding only.

References

1. The OpenFlow Switch Specification, http://OpenFlowSwitch.org
2. IBM; OpenFlow: The next generation in networking interoperability (2011)
3. Sandvine: Global Internet Phenomena Report (2011)
4. 3GPP: TS 23.203 Policy and Charging Control Architecture. 3GPP standard (2012), http://www.3gpp.org/ftp/Specs/archive/23_series/23.203/23203 -b60.zip
5. Ekström, H.: QoS Control in the 3GPP Evolved Packet System. IEEE Communications Magazine, 76–83 (February 2009)
6. Balbas, I.-J.P., Rommer, S., Stenfelt, J.: Policy and Charging Control in the Evolved Packet System. IEEE Communications Magazine, 68–74 (February 2009)
7. Ma, K.J., Bartos, R., Bhatia, S., Naif, R.: Mobile Video Delivery with HTTP. IEEE Communications Magazine, 166–175 (April 2011)

8. Oyman, O., Singh, S.: Quality of Experience for HTTP Adaptive Streaming Services. IEEE Communications Magazine, 20–27 (April 2012)
9. Ouellette, S., Marchand, L., Pierre, S.: A Potential Evolution of the Policy and Charging Control/QoS Architecture for the 3GPP IETF-Based Evolved Packet Core. IEEE Communications Magazine, 231–239 (May 2011)
10. Alasti, M., Neekzad, B., Hui, L., Vannithamby, R.: Quality of Service in Wi-MAX and LTE Networks. IEEE Communications Magazine, 104–111 (May 2010)
11. Sterle, J., Volk, M., Sedlar, U., Bester, J., Kos, A.: Application-Based NGN QoE Controller. IEEE Communications Magazine, 92–101 (January 2011)
12. 3GPP: TS 29.212 Policy and Charging Control (PCC) over Gx/Sd reference point. 3GPP standard (2011)
13. Wamser, F., Pries, R., Staehle, D., Staehle, B., Hirth, M.: YoMo: A YouTube Application Comfort Monitoring Tool (March 2010)
14. Schatz, R., Hossfeld, T., Casas, P.: Passive YouTube QoE Monitoring for ISPs. In: 2nd International Workshop on Future Internet and Next Generation Networks, Palermo, Italy (June 2012)
15. Wehbi B., Sankala J.: Mevico D5.1. Network Monitoring in EPC, Mevico Project (2009-2012)
16. Sandvine Incorporated ULC: Solutions Overview (2012), http://www.sandvine.com/solutions/default.asp
17. Rugel, S., Knoll, T.M., Eckert, M., Bauschert, T.: A Network-based Method for Measurement of Internet Video Streaming Quality. In: European Teletraffic Seminar Poznan University of Technology, Poland (2011), http://ets2011.et.put.poznan.pl/index.php?id=home
18. Knoll, T.M., Eckert, M.: An advanced network based method for Video QoE estimation based on throughput measurement. In: EuroView 2012 (2012), http://www.euroview2012.org/fileadmin/content/euroview2012/abstracts/05_04_abstract_eckert.pdf
19. Knoll, T.M.: Cross-Domain and Cross-Layer Coarse Grained Quality of Service Support in IP-based Networks, http://archiv.tu-chemnitz.de/pub/2009/0165/
20. Windisch, G.: Vergleich von QoS- und Mobilitätsmechanismen in Backhaul-Netzen für 4G Mobilfunk (2008)
21. Eckert, M.: Analyse und automatisierte Konfiguration klassenbasierter Paketvermittlung (2010)

A Measurement Study of Active Probing on Access Links

Bjørn J. Villa and Poul E. Heegaard

Department of Telematics,
Norwegian Institute of Science and Technology, 7491 Trondheim, Norway
{bjorn.villa,poul.heegaard}@item.ntnu.no

Abstract. This paper presents a measurement study of two different methods for active probing of cross traffic on access links. The categories used in the study are packet pair probing and one-way-delay probing. The first approach uses measured increase in packet spacing as indicator of cross traffic presence, while the latter uses increase in one-way-delay for probe packets as indicator. These methods have been chosen because they are fundamentally different in terms of requirements, benefits and challenges. The main novelty of this paper is the presentation and discussion of measurement results from an access network using an adaptive video service as cross-traffic. The findings clearly illustrate the potential strengths of a probing method based on one-way-delay measurements, under the condition that the required timing accuracy is achieved and delay characteristics is available for the involved network path. The benefit of using Precision Time Protocol instead of Network Time Protocol is illustrated, even in networks of limited size.

Keywords: Packet Pair probing, One-Way-Delay probing, Access links.

1 Introduction

The dynamics of Internet traffic on different levels, ranging from per session, per user and up to backbone traffic aggregates is a topic of great interest in the research community. The reasons for performing such studies are diverse and so are also the techniques and methods applied. One obvious reason for studying Internet traffic dynamics on an aggregated level is the need for knowledge about how to best design and scale the future Internet as a whole. Another reason, on a lower level, is the growing amount of adaptive services on the Internet, which is characterized by their ability to change their requirements according to varying network conditions. Such services would obviously benefit from being able to obtain accurate views of different network- and traffic metrics in real-time.

Obtaining information about Internet traffic is best done by means of passive measurements performed in a non-intrusive way on the network links of interests. However, in some cases such passive measurements are not possible due to e.g. lack of access to the relevant links or involved equipment. In these cases, the use of active measurements is an alternative to consider. Such measurements are based on injecting probe traffic into the network between end-points and then study how this specific

T. Bauschert (Ed.): EUNICE 2013, LNCS 8115, pp. 124–135, 2013.

traffic is treated. Based on the findings for the probe traffic, one can then make some statements about the traffic conditions along the same path as the probe traffic followed. Examples of such statements could be related to e.g. packet loss or delay, described by basic mean value considerations or higher order statistical views.

In this paper we compare two active probing methods for estimating cross-traffic amount on access links by means of theoretical discussions and measurements in a controlled lab environment. The metric of interest describing the cross traffic amount is based on buffering time observations for injected probe traffic. These observations can then be analyzed over certain periods and used for different purposes. The methods used in our study are based on sequences of packet pairs and single packets, at different rates. The way buffering time observations are extracted for these two methods are quite different and will be further described later in this paper.

The measurement part of our study is done in a controlled lab environment reflecting a typical broadband access network, and using a high quality video streaming service as the cross traffic component. The reason for focusing on the access link part is that this is where we quite often encounter the bottleneck across a network path. The choice of video as cross traffic component is based on the growing popularity of this service type on the Internet.

The structure of this paper is as follows. Section 2 provides an overview of related work; Section 3 describes the active probing methods; Section 4 presents the measurement setup; Section 5 provides the results and an analysis; Section 6 provides the conclusions and an outline of future work is given in Section 7.

2   Related Work

There is a lot of research in the field of active probing addressing different research questions ranging from the application layer down to the physical layer. In the context of our work, i.e. estimating the amount of cross traffic (measured by increased buffering time for probe traffic) on an access link – the most related research are found in the domain of methods for available bandwidth estimations. For this purpose there are several approaches, most of which fall into either the Probe Rate Model (PRM) or Probe Gap Model (PGM) categories [1]. The PRM approach is based on the principle of self-induced congestion and by this detecting available capacity, while the PGM approach uses observed inter-arrival time (IAT) variations [2][3] for probe packets to estimate the current level of cross traffic. However, the original idea of using probe packets as basis for active measurements was suggested in [4] where back-to-back packets were sent to detect the capacity of bottlenecks.

The use of one-way-delay (OWD) observations [5][6] for probe packets through a network can also be used for estimating available bandwidth as per the PGM approach. However, as the computation of OWD is based on time information from different nodes in the network it has very strict requirements in terms of clock accuracy and synchronization [7]. As described in [8] the main protocols for distributing clock information across as network, NTP (Network Time Protocol) and PTP (Precision Time Protocol) have different capabilities in this regard. The latter is stated to give accuracy in the order of µs, while the former in the order of ms. However, it should be noted that this depends a lot on the specific hardware and software used. In a recent work [9] the performance of the Linux PTP daemon was evaluated and their findings were in line with [8]. What concerns NTP there are also improvements in this provided by the NTPv4 [10] which could bring the accuracy down into the µs region in certain cases.

As presented in [11] there are many sources of delay components along a network path and not all of them are influenced by cross traffic. This represents as source of error for all delay based probing methods.

3   Active Probing

The metric of interest to be measured by the active probing is amount of cross traffic present, represented by introduced additional buffering time for the probe traffic over some time interval. In Fig. 1 a simplified model for an access link as a basic queuing system is presented. The service rate λ_{out} corresponds to access capacity (bits/s), the λ_{cross} corresponds to the uplink capacity for the access node and V_B is the configurable buffer size (bytes) for a specific access. The indicated time parameters t_a and t_b represents time between packets in a packet pair and time between packet pairs as sent, while $t_{a*,i}$ and $t_{b*,i}$ are the corresponding values when probe traffic is received on the client side. The $t_{s,i}$ and $t_{r,i}$ parameters are timestamps for when a packet was sent and received.

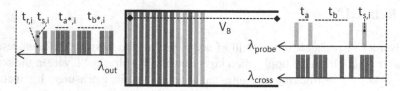

Fig. 1. Access Link Buffer Model

In the zero cross-traffic case the client side will in theory receive the probe traffic with $t_{a*,i} = t_a$, $t_{b*,i} = t_b$ and a constant $t_{s,i} - t_{r,i}$. When cross-traffic is introduced there will be time variations in the received probe traffic, caused by additional buffering time for the probe packets in the access link buffer.

When using packet pairs, the original time between the packets (t_a, t_b) is assumed known by the receiver. Thus, any changes to this would be caused either by cross-traffic or fluctuations in processing load on involved network components. By calculating the difference between packet spacing as received and sent – a series of samples is produced. An important benefit of this method is that there is no need for accurate time synchronization of sender and receiver side. Another benefit is that an increasing amount of probe traffic does not lead to potentially an over-sampling scenario, i.e. the registration of a certain buffering time component more than once. However, the method has a weakness in the sense that cross-traffic may delay the first packet in a pair, and thereby reduce the spacing between the packet pairs [12]. One way to handle this is to consider both packet pair spacing and the time between packet pairs by summarizing this into packet pair period samples $t_{pp,i}$ as given in Eq.1.

$$t_{pp,i} = [t_{a^*,i} - t_a]^+ + [t_{b^*,i} - t_b]^+ \tag{1}$$

In addition, some computation is required on the period sample time series as presented in our submitted work [13] in order to carry forward a time shift component to the next $t_{a^*,i}$ or $t_{b^*,i}$ observation. However, for the purpose of comparing the two active probing methods in this paper we have left this computational correction out. It is further important to note that for this method to be able to capture delay components higher than just the buffer output time of a single cross-traffic packet T_p, it is a requirement that the arrival rate λ_{cross} towards the bottleneck is higher than the service rate λ_{out}. This can be seen from Eq. 2 where the maximum value for observed time between packets in a packet pair $t_{a^*,Max}$ is expressed.

$$t_{a^*,Max} = \frac{(\lambda_{cross} t_a)}{\lambda_{out}} + T_p, \quad for \quad t_a \leq V_B/\lambda_{out} \tag{2}$$

In a real life network the condition $\lambda_{cross} > \lambda_{out}$ would normally apply since an access node typically is served by at least a gigabit connection and each customer connection would be in the order of tens of Mbps. One could also claim that the approach of using packet pairs has a drawback in the sense that is requires two probe packets to produce a single cross traffic sample. However, if both packet pair spacing and time between packet pairs are considered, this is no longer applicable.

When using a sequence of single probe packets it is the OWD for each packet which is used to obtain buffering time samples. The sender adds a time stamp to each packet when sent $t_{s,i}$, and the receiver adds his own timestamp to the packet when received $t_{r,i}$. If we then know the reference OWD during times of zero cross traffic $T_{owd,0}$, we can for each probe packet when received - compute a sample $t_{owd,i}$ for buffering time induced by cross-traffic.

$$t_{owd,i} = [(t_{r,i} - t_{s,i}) - T_{owd,0}]^+ \tag{3}$$

This approach has the benefit of that each probe packet gives one cross-traffic sample, and all samples are independent. However, even though the samples are independent they may actually lead to a degree of oversampling if more than one probe packet is in the buffer at the same time. The reason is that each probe packet will be delayed according to the total amount of packets ahead of it in the buffer, even if there are other probe packets as well there. Investigation of the over-sampling issue is left for future work. Further on, as the method uses timestamps from different sources (sender and receiver) it requires a high degree of accuracy in time synchronization. The use of NTP or even PTP may not be accurate enough. The challenge of actually knowing the reference OWD when no cross-traffic is present is also a significant challenge.

4   Measurement Setup

In order to perform a comparison of the two active probing methods, an access network testbed was established (cf. Fig. 2). In order to minimize cross process impacts on the client and server side, both the probe generator and the probe receiver were put on dedicated nodes. In a real life, this may be more integrated at least on the client side – but this depends on the specific application.

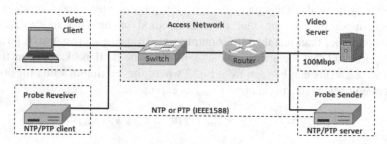

Fig. 2. Access Network Testbed

As probe traffic generator and receiver the Rude/Crude tool [14] was used. This has the capability of generating IP packets according to trace files, describing both packet size and time between packets. It also provides application level time stamping which is easily available on the receiver side. The accuracy of this tool has been shown in [15] to be in the area of $2\mu s$. The cross-traffic used in the measurements was a video stream operating at 5Mbps based on the MS Smooth Streaming platform [16]. In our earlier work [17] the nature of this traffic is described in more detail with special focus on its burst oriented nature. Based on this, we can state that a video server of this type connected on a 100Mbps link will send bursts of data towards the client at rates close to its link speed, independent of what the average video stream bitrate is. Thus, we have that the earlier stated $\lambda_{cross} > \lambda_{out}$ requirement for packet probing method is met. The access capacity towards the client was configured using the QoS mechanisms provided by the Cisco switch used. This configuration gives the λ_{out} and also the buffer size V_B available for the specific access.

For the purpose of time synchronization of probe sender and receiver both NTPv4 and PTPv2 [18] were used in the measurements. The NTP configuration was made so that the probe receiver used the probe sender as NTP server, in order to maximize timing accuracy when using this protocol. When using PTP as synchronization protocol, the same direct relationship between the probe sender and receiver was made. The probe sender in PTP master role and the probe receiver in PTP slave role.

The operating systems used on the video client and server side were MS Windows 7 Professional, while probe sender and receiver were using Linux Ubuntu 12.04.

All processing of measurement data was done post-experiment in order to keep the cross-process impact for each node as low as possible.

4.1   Measurement Scenarios

A range of different probe traffic patterns was used in the measurements. The parameters subject for change were the intra-packet time values t_a and t_b, while the probe packet size was fixed at 100Byte in all cases. When using packet pair probing, t_a was always smaller than t_b, thus reflecting the time between packets in a pair. In the case with a sequence of single probe packets and measurement of OWD, t_a was set equal to t_b. The sum of t_a and t_b gives the period in the probe pattern and thereby also the probing rate in pps and bps. Ideally, the probing rate should be kept as low as possible, in order to minimize the chances of self-induced congestion or other undesirable service impact.

Table 1. Configuration parameters

V_B [MB]	Packet Pair			One-Way-Delay		
	t_a [ms]	t_b [ms]	pps	t_a [ms]	t_b [ms]	pps
256/500/1000	0.55/0.65/0.75	4.6/4.5/4.4	388	2,60	2,60	383
256/500/1000	0.55/0.65/0.75	3.7/3.6/3.5	470	2,13	2,13	468
256/500/1000	0.55/0.65/0.75	3.0/2.9/2.8	562	1,78	1,78	559
256/500/1000	0.55/0.65/0.75	2.5/2.4/2.3	654	1,53	1,53	650
256/500/1000	0.55/0.65/0.75	2.1/2.0/1.9	752	1,33	1,33	747

The parameters given in Table 1 represent the range of different scenarios included in our measurements, for which we compared the two methods of active probing. For each scenario, measurements were done for a period of 10 minutes both with and without the cross-traffic (i.e. the 5Mbps video stream). The capacity on the access link was set to 10Mbps for all scenarios, but with different buffer (V_B) settings configured in the router.

5   Results

In this section, a selection of the measurement results is presented. The specific scenario for packet pair probing where $V_B=256/t_a=0.55/t_b=4.6$, and for OWD probing where $V_B=256 / t_a=t_b=2.6$ is presented in detail. The presentation of the results are mainly given by means of graphical summaries, and especially by estimated probability density function (PDF) plots and the corresponding cumulative distribution function (CDF). The differences in distributional properties for the received probe traffic with and without cross-traffic present are quite well presented by this. Whenever appropriate, interesting numerical indicators are also included.

The effect of time synchronization method used (NTP, PTP) is only presented for the OWD probing method. The reason for this is that the packet pair method only uses receiver side time information, and therefore is not affected by this.

5.1   Packet Pair Probing Results

For the packet pair probing method, the difference between the PDF for probe packets received when there is no cross-traffic present, and when the video stream is introduced is clear in terms of the reduced distribution peak for the latter case. In addition, it is interesting to note the appearance of a small peak in the distribution for $t_{a*,i}$ (cf. Fig 3, left side) in the low value region in the case when cross-traffic is present. The source of this effect is the occurrence of $t_{b*,i} > t_b$ samples, which delays the first packet in the next packet pair – as discussed in section 4. The result of this is the low value group of $t_{a*,i} < t_a$ observations.

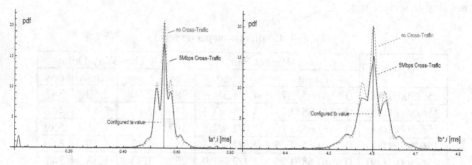

Fig. 3. PDF view of Packet Pair Results at t_a=0.55ms, t_b=4.6ms and V_B=256

By viewing the same measurements using a CDF plot rather than PDF, it is even easier to see that the packet pair probing is able to detect the cross-traffic (cf. Fig 4). The CDF for $t_{a*,i}$ observations are lifted in the low region, and reduced in the high region. The similar effect is also seen in the CDF for $t_{b*,i}$ observations. Thus, both $t_{a*,i}$ and $t_{b*,i}$ observations detect cross-traffic, but at the same time they have a negative impact on each other (as indicated by the low region CDF lift).

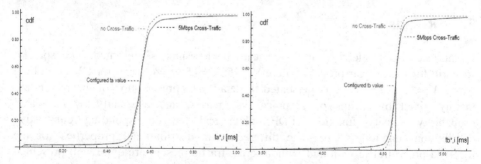

Fig. 4. CDF view of Packet Pair Results at t_a=0.55ms, t_b=4.6ms and V_B=256

Common for both the PDF and CDF view of the packet pair method is that even in the no Cross-Traffic scenario the received probe traffic has some deviations from the original pattern. This represents a significant source of error, which could be critical depending on how the results of the probing are to be applied.

5.2   One-Way-Delay Probing Results

For the OWD probing method, the difference between the PDF for probe packets received with and without cross-traffic present is quite significant in terms of shape (cf. Fig 5, left side). The dominating peak is shifted upwards when cross-traffic is present, which also contributes to a higher mean value.

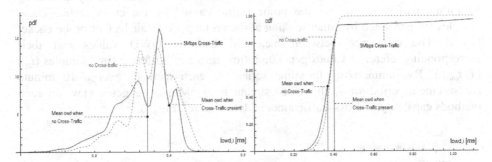

Fig. 5. PDF and CDF view of OWD results at $t_a=t_b=2.6$ms, $V_B=256$ and NTP

The effect on the CDF (cf. Fig 5, right side) illustrates the difference even better, as the two graphs follow each other up to the ~90% level and then the cross-traffic graph flattens out. This indicates that the high ~10% amount of values differ significantly in magnitude. Same as for the packet pair probing method, both the PDF and CDF view of the measurements show variations even in the no Cross-Traffic scenario.

5.3   Effect of NTP versus PTP on One-Way-Delay Results

The effect of using PTP as time synchronization protocol between the probe sender and receiver instead of NTP can be illustrated by a PDF and CDF plot for OWD observations as given in Fig. 6.

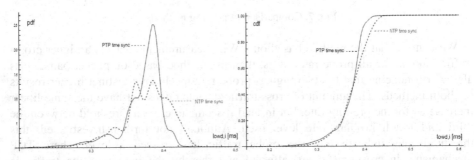

Fig. 6. PDF and CDF view of OWD results at $t_a=t_b=2.6$ms and no Cross-Traffic, NTP and PTP

The use of using PTP instead of NTP clearly gives a sharper peak in the PDF function and an increased function derivate in the mid region of the CDF function. These are both indications of more accurate sync. The difference in mean value for the observations when using NTP and PTP is about 6μS, which may increase the error in each probe sample value collected.

5.4   Cross Traffic Amount Detection

The active probing methods generate samples for cross-traffic amount by measuring additional buffering time for the probe traffic caused by the cross-traffic. These samples are generated by either looking at the probe packet pair IAT or probe packet OWD. The difference between measured IAT or OWD values and their corresponding reference values generate a time series of buffering time samples ($t_{pp,i}$ or $t_{owd,i}$). By summarizing the time series for each method, over a 10 minute measurement period while the video stream is at 5Mbps, we get a view on each methods capability of cross-traffic amount detection (cf. Fig. 7).

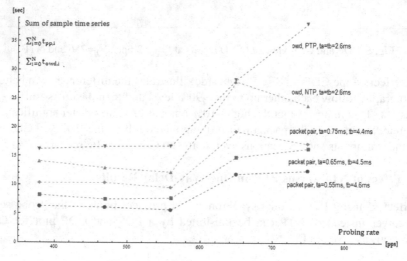

Fig. 7. Comparison of probing methods

We can see that the method based on OWD measurements detects a higher cross-traffic amount for all probe rate levels, than the method based on packet pairs. It is also worth noticing that the two highest probe rate levels give distinct higher results for both methods. The amount of cross-traffic detected does not have the same linear increase as for the probing rate, but instead it seems to cross a threshold between the third and fourth probing rate level used. Although not further investigated, this threshold may indicate that the probe traffic has crossed a level where TCP mechanisms in cross-traffic are affected and thereby the nature of the traffic is changing.

For the packet pair method and the different t_a values used (cf. Table 1) there are also quite noticeable differences. The highest t_a value gives the higher cross-traffic amount detection across all probe rate levels.

For the OWD based method it is clear that the use of PTP for time synchronization instead of NTP has a significant effect, as it always gives a higher cross-traffic estimate. The graph for the PTP case also has a more logical profile than in the NTP case, as the cross-traffic volume consistently increases with increasing probing rate. The NTP graph starts with a moderate decrease, followed by a significant peak before dropping again. Repeated experiments shows that the results for the NTP case fluctuate more than in the PTP case, which is expected due to clock drift.

The presence of potential oversampling for the OWD measurements was not investigated. However, as the trend for both packet pair probing and OWD probing is quite similar across all probing rate levels we believe that this error factor did not contribute much to the measurement results.

6   Conclusions

The measurement based comparison of packet pair and OWD probing presented in this paper highlights strengths and weaknesses for both methods. The objective of the comparison was not to make a statement about which one is better, as this would have to be done in the context of a specific application. However, in a scenario such as the one we used in our measurements, it is clear that the OWD based method is able to detect more of the cross-traffic than the packet pair method.

Concerning the packet pair method, we believe that our findings related to dependencies between t_{a*} and t_{b*} observations have significance for a range of suggested probing methods based on the packet pair principle, e.g. in the area of available bandwidth estimation. To our knowledge, this specific dependency has not been documented earlier. We further believe that our findings related to sensitivity for parameter values t_a and t_b selected are of interest. Finding the optimal parameter selection for a complex traffic mix is foreseen to be quite challenging, but an approach where a range of values are used may be a beneficial approach.

The most interesting finding for the OWD method is the significant impact of using PTPv2 instead of NTPv4. Keeping in mind that our access network lab is of a much smaller size than what a real network would be, it clearly demonstrates the shortcomings of using a NTP based synchronization for purposes like this. Another interesting finding is the challenge to establish a reference point for OWD when no cross-traffic is present. The variations observed even in the small access network lab were higher than what we expected.

7   Future Work

To further analyze the capabilities of active probing methods it would be interesting to also make measurements using other tools than Rude/Crude, and also use different operating systems and even HW components. Reason being that one can never neglect the possibilities when doing measurements that some of the things which are being observed have underlying reasons not related to the topic investigated.

The implementation of time synchronization between probe sender and receiver should also be closer investigated. The specific implementation of NTPv4 in Ubuntu 12.04 may have flaws, or there could even be some not obvious configuration options with a positive impact on accuracy. In a scenario with at least μs accuracy of time synchronization between hosts on the Internet, active probing using OWD measurements becomes very attractive.

The cross-traffic used in our measurements was of a specific type, operated at a specific quality (bitrate) level. A more composed and potentially complex cross-traffic profile would also be interesting to include in a measurement study. However, the burst oriented nature of the video service used gives a very challenging traffic pattern. Thus, we do not think a more composed cross-traffic scenario will make the research question significantly harder.

References

[1] Prasad, R., Dovrolis, C., Murray, M., Claffy, K.: Bandwidth estimation: Metrics, measurement techniques, and tools. IEEE Network 17(6), 27–35 (2003)
[2] Strauss, J., Katabi, D., Kaashoek, F.: A measurement study of available bandwidth estimation tools. In: Proceedings of the 3rd ACM SIGCOMM Conference on Internet Measurement, IMC 2003, pp. 39–44. ACM, New York (2003)
[3] Goldoni, E., Schivi, M.: End-to-end available bandwidth estimation tools, an experimental comparison. In: Ricciato, F., Mellia, M., Biersack, E. (eds.) TMA 2010. LNCS, vol. 6003, pp. 171–182. Springer, Heidelberg (2010)
[4] Keshav, S.: A control-theoretic approach to flow control. In: Proceedings of the Conference on Communications Architecture & Protocols, SIGCOMM 1991, pp. 3–15. ACM, USA (1991)
[5] Jain, M., Dovrolis, C.: Pathload: A measurement tool for end-to-end available bandwidth. In: Proceedings of Passive and Active Measurements (PAM) Workshop, pp. 14–25 (2002)
[6] Huang, Y.C., Lu, C.S., Wu, H.K.: Available bandwidth estimation via one-way delay jitter and queuing delay propagation model. In: Wireless Communications and Networking Conference, vol. 1, pp. 112–121 (2006)
[7] Shin, M., Park, M., Oh, D., Kim, B., Lee, J.: Clock synchronization for one-way delay measurement: A survey. In: Kim, T.-h., Adeli, H., Robles, R.J., Balitanas, M. (eds.) ACN 2011. CCIS, vol. 199, pp. 1–10. Springer, Heidelberg (2011)
[8] De Vito, L., Rapuano, S., Tomaciello, L.: One-way delay measurement: State of the art. IEEE Transactions on Instrumentation and Measurement 57(12), 2742–2750 (2008)
[9] Kovacshazy, T., Ferencz, B.: Performance evaluation of ptpd, a ieee 1588 implementation, on the x86 linux platform for typical application scenarios. In: 2012 IEEE International Instrumentation and Measurement Technology Conference (I2MTC), pp. 2548–2552 (2012)
[10] Mills, D., Martin, J., Burbank, J., Kasch, W.: Network Time Protocol Version 4: Protocol and Algorithms Specification. RFC 5905 (Proposed Standard), IETF (June 2010)
[11] Hernandez, A., Magana, E.: One-way delay measurement and characterization. In: Proceedings of the Third International Conference on Networking and Services, ICNS 2007, p. 114. IEEE Computer Society, Washington, DC (2007)

[12] Hu, N., Member, S., Steenkiste, P., Member, S.: Evaluation and characterization of available bandwidth probing techniques. IEEE Journal on Selected Areas in Communications 21, 879–894 (2003)

[13] Villa, B.J., Heegaard, P.E.: Estimating available bandwidth on access links by means of stratified probing. In: Proceedings of the 6th International Conference on Computer and Electrical Engineering Conference (ICCEE 2013) (October 2013)

[14] Laine, J., Saaristo, S., Prior, R.: Real-time udp data emitter (rude) and collector for rude (crude) (January 2000), http://rude.sourceforge.net/

[15] Ubik, S., Smotlach, V., Saaristo, S., Laine, J.: Low-cost precise qos measurement tool. CESNET Tech report number 7/2001

[16] Zambelli, A.: IIS smooth streaming technical overview. Tech. Rep. (March 2009), http://www.microsoft.com/silverlight/

[17] Villa, B.J., Heegaard, P.E.: Group based traffic shaping for adaptive http video streaming. In: Proceedings of the 27th IEEE International Conference on Advanced Information Networking and Applications (AINA 2013) (March 2013)

[18] IEEE Standard for a Precision Clock Synchronization Protocol for Networked Measurement and Control Systems 1588-2008, IEEE Std. 1588 (2008)

Design and Evaluation of HTTP Protocol Parsers for IPFIX Measurement

Petr Velan, Tomáš Jirsík, and Pavel Čeleda

Institute of Computer Science, Masaryk University,
Brno, Czech Republic
{velan,jirsik,celeda}@ics.muni.cz

Abstract. In this paper we analyze HTTP protocol parsers that provide
a web traffic visibility to IP flow. Despite extensive work, flow meters
generally fall short of performance goals due to extracting application
layer data. Constructing effective protocol parser for in-depth analysis is a challenging and error-prone affair. We designed and evaluated
several HTTP protocol parsers representing current state-of-the-art approaches used in today's flow meters. We show the packet rates achieved
by respective parsers, including the throughput decrease (performance
implications of application parser) which is of the utmost importance
for high-speed deployments. We believe that these results provide researchers and network operators with important insight into application
visibility and IP flow.

Keywords: HTTP, protocol, parser, traffic, measurement, flow, IPFIX.

1   Introduction

Flow monitoring technologies, such as NetFlow or IPFIX, are widely used in
large-scale networks to provide situational awareness. They provide information
about *who* communicates with *whom, when, how long,* using *what protocol* and
service and also *how much data* was transferred. Acquired flow data is based on
IP headers (network and transport layer) and it does not include any payload
information. On the other hand, we observe that HTTP protocol [6] became a
"new Transmission Control Protocol" (TCP). More and more applications rely
on HTTP protocol, e.g. Web 2.0 content, audio and video streaming, instant
messaging etc. HTTP traffic (TCP port 80) can usually pass through most firewalls and therefore presents a standard way of transporting/tunneling data. The
versatility, ubiquity and amount of HTTP traffic makes it easy for an attacker
to hide malicious activities. Missing application layer visibility renders standard
NetFlow and IPFIX to be ineffective for HTTP monitoring.

Network and security devices use application layer analysis to provide application visibility, monitoring and traffic control. For example, Cisco Application
Visibility and Control (AVC) [4] solution uses next-generation deep packet inspection (NBAR2) and flexible NetFlow to identify, classify and report on over
1,000 applications. HTTP information elements are supported by YAF [8] and

T. Bauschert (Ed.): EUNICE 2013, LNCS 8115, pp. 136–147, 2013.

nProbe [5] flow meters and are exported in IPFIX format. Most intrusion detection systems extract application layer data for in-depth analysis.

Deep Packet Inspection (DPI) predominates for application layer analysis. While it is possible for small and medium sized networks to effectively deploy the DPI, the amount of traffic in large (10+ Gb/s) networks makes the inspection of every packet a challenging problem. The performance and results that can be achieved depend on a number of factors including flow meter configuration and analyzed traffic distribution. Due to the complexity and sheer number of application protocols, it is hard to compare different environments/platforms and derive conclusions on which solution is the best.

Our research attempts to answer following question: *What are the impacts of application layer analysis of HTTP protocol on flow meters and flow monitoring process?* The contribution of our work is threefold: *(i)* We designed and evaluated several HTTP protocol parsers representing current state-of-the-art approaches used in today's flow meters. *(ii)* We introduced a new flex-based HTTP parser. *(iii)* We report on the throughput decrease (performance implications of application parser) which is of the utmost importance for high-speed deployments.

The paper is organized as follows. Section 2 describes related work. Section 3 contains a description of the HTTP inspection algorithms and the framework that was used to test the algorithms. Section 4 describes the methodology used for HTTP parsers performance comparison. Section 5 presents the performance evaluation of the individual algorithms. Finally, Section 6 contains our conclusions.

2   Related Work

Application layer protocol parsers are an integral part of many network monitoring tools. We explored the source code of the following frameworks to see how the HTTP parsing is implemented. nProbe uses standard glibc [2] functions like *strncmp* (compare two strings) and *strstr* (locate a substring). YAF uses Perl Compatible Regular Expressions (PCRE) [1] to examine HTTP traffic. Suricata [14] and Snort [18] are both written in C. Suricata uses LibHTP [17] library which does HTTP parsing using custom string functions while Snort does its parsing using glibc functions. httpry [3] is another HTTP logging and information retrieval tool which is also written in C and uses its own built-in string functions. These HTTP parsers are hand-written.

Other approach is taken by Bro [16] authors. They use binpac [15], a declarative language and compiler designed to simplify the task of constructing robust and efficient semantic analyzers for complex network protocols. They replaced some of Bro existing analyzers (handcrafted in C++) and demonstrated that the generated parsers are as efficient as carefully hand-written ones.

In this paper, we try to determine whether these approaches to HTTP parsing can handle large traffic volumes. Besides the above approaches, we propose to use the Fast Lexical Analyzer (Flex) [11] to design a new HTTP parser. Flex converts expressions into a lexical analyzer that is essentially a deterministic finite automaton that recognizes any of the patterns. The algorithm that converts a regular expression directly to deterministic finite automaton is described in [10] and [13].

There are other works that inspect the HTTP protocol headers. In [19] the authors use statistical flow analysis to differentiate traditional HTTP traffic and Web 2.0 applications. In [21] the authors identify HTTP sessions based on flow information. In both cases a ground truth sample is needed, which is a topic addressed by [22]. In [7] and [12] the authors use DPI to obtain information from the HTTP headers. Our approach is orthogonal to these works, since we are interested in extending IP flow records with HTTP data.

3   Parser Design

HTTP protocol [6] has a number of properties that can be monitored and exported together with IP flow data. The most commonly monitored ones are present in almost every HTTP request or response header. Based on the properties monitored by the state-of-the-art DPI tools we selected the following ones for our parsers: *HTTP method, status code, host, request URI, content type, user agent and referer*. Keeping track of every bidirectional HTTP connection is too resource consuming on high speed networks, thus we focus on evaluation of each individual packet. This approach is more common for flow meters since it is more resistant to resource depletion attacks.

We implemented and evaluated three different types of parsing algorithms. The first algorithm (*strcmp* approach) loops the HTTP header line by line and searches each line for given fields. It uses standard glibc string functions like *memchr, memmem* and *strncmp*. The simplified pseudocode is shown in Algorithm 1. The second algorithm (*pcre* approach) uses several regular expressions taken from YAF to search the packet for specific patterns indicating HTTP header fields. The pseudocode for the *pcre* algorithm is shown in Algorithm 2. We designed the third algorithm (*flex* approach) to handle each packet as a long string. It uses finite automaton to find required HTTP fields and the Flex lexer is used to process the packets. The automaton design is shown in Fig. 1.

Since the Flex is a generic tool, its initialization before scanning each packet is quite an expensive operation. Therefore we decided to remove all unnecessary dynamic memory allocations and costly initializations to see whether the performance can be increased. We named the new version *optimized flex*. The disadvantage of Flex is that it has to keep the data in its own writable buffer. Therefore the received data must be copied to such a buffer, which adds to the processing costs significantly. The advantage of the *flex* parser is its simple maintenance and extension possibilities. The framework can be modified to parse any other application layer protocol just by changing the set of regular expression rules. The *strcmp* parser would have to be rewritten from a scratch.

The *strcmp* implementation also offers a space for further improvement. Algorithm 3 shows an *optimized strcmp* version of the code that features a better processing logic. The optimized version searches for specific strings by comparing

Algorithm 1. *strcmp*
1: **if** first line contains "HTTP" **then**
2:    **while not** end of HTTP header **do**
3:       **for** every parsed HTTP field **do**
4:          **if** field matches the line **then**
5:             store the value of the line
6:          **end if**
7:       **end for**
8:       move to the next line
9:    **end while**
10:    **return** HTTP packet
11: **else**
12:    **return not** HTTP packet
13: **end if**

Algorithm 2. *pcre*
1: **if** first line contains "HTTP/x.y" **then**
2:    **for all** PCRE rules **do**
3:       **if** rule matches **then**
4:          store the matched value
5:       **end if**
6:    **end for**
7:    **return** HTTP packet
8: **else**
9:    **return not** HTTP packet
10: **end if**

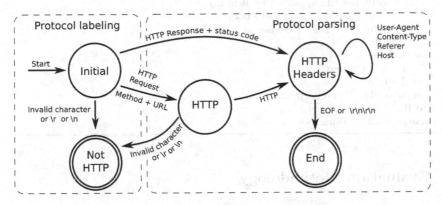

Fig. 1. *flex* algorithm schema

several bytes at once, which is done by casting the character pointer to integer pointer. The number that is compared to the string is computed from ASCII codes of the characters and converted to network byte order. The size of the used integer depends on the length of the string; longer integers offer better performance.

To focus only on the HTTP parsing algorithms we decided to let the FlowMon exporter [9] handle the packet preprocessing. We used a benchmarking (input) plugin that reads packets from PCAP file to memory at start-up. Then it supplies the same data continuously for further processing. This approach allows us to focus on benchmarking the algorithms without the necessity of considering the disk I/O operations. We provide the source code of implemented algorithms and used packet traces at the paper homepage [20].

Algorithm 3. *optimized strcmp*

```
 1: if payload begins with "HTTP" then
 2:     store status code
 3:     while not end of HTTP header do
 4:         for every parsed response HTTP field do
 5:             if line starts with field name then
 6:                 store the value of the line
 7:             end if
 8:         end for
 9:         move to the next line
10:     end while
11:     return  HTTP response packet
12: end if
13: if payload begins with one of GET, HEAD, POST, PUT,
        DELETE, TRACE, CONNECT then
14:     store request URI
15:     while not end of HTTP header do
16:         for every parsed request HTTP field do
17:             if line starts with field name then
18:                 store the value of the line
19:             end if
20:         end for
21:         move to the next line
22:     end while
23:     return  HTTP request packet
24: end if
25: return  not HTTP packet
```

---

4   Evaluation Methodology

In this section we define a methodology of HTTP protocol parsers evaluation. We focus on parsing performance (number of processed packets per second) of the algorithms described in Section 3 from several different perspectives.

The first perspective focuses on the performance comparison with respect to analyzed traffic structure. The second perspective covers the impact of the number of HTTP fields supported by parser. The third perspective describes the effect of a Carriage Return (CR or '\r') and a Line Feed (LF or '\n') control characters distribution in packet payload.

A common technique of increasing network data processing performance is processing only important part of each packet. Therefore, we perform each of the tests in two configurations. In the first configuration the parsers are given whole packets. This is achieved by setting limit on packet size to 1500 bytes, which is the most common maximum transmission unit value on most Ethernet networks. In the second configuration the parsers are provided with truncated packets of length 384 bytes, which is the minimum packet length recommended for DPI by authors of the YAF exporter [8].

To test the performance of the parsers, we created an HTTP traffic trace (testing data set). Our requirements on the data set were as follows: preserve the characteristics of HTTP protocol, reflect various HTTP traffic structures and have no side effects on the flow meter. In order to meet these requirements we decided to create synthetic trace.

The HTTP protocol is a request/response protocol. To preserve the characteristics of HTTP protocol during the testing a random request, response and binary payload packet was captured from the network. To omit the undesirable bias of the measurement only these three packets were used to synthesize test trace. The final test trace consists of 200 packets. In order to reflect various traffic structures, we suggested following ratio:

$$r = \frac{\#\text{request packets} + \#\text{response packets}}{\#\text{all packets}} * 100 \qquad (1)$$

where $r \in [0, 100]$ and created a test set for each integer ratio from the interval. Further, we created two packets with modified payload. One packet contained the CR and LF control characters only at the very *beginning* of the packet payload, the other one only at the *end*. For both of the modified packets and for the *unchanged* packet the test trace for each integer ratio was created.

Having defined the test trace, we propose the following case studies to cover all evaluation perspectives. The case studies are carried out for both full and truncated packets. Moreover, we measure the performance of the flow meter without an HTTP parser (*no HTTP* parser). This way we can estimate the performance decline caused by increased application layer visibility.

1. *Performance Comparison*: This case study compares the parsing performance of implemented parsers. Moreover, we report on the flow meter performance without an HTTP parser (*no HTTP* parser).
2. *Parsed HTTP Fields Impact*: This case study shows a parser performance with respect to the number of supported HTTP fields. We incrementally add support for new HTTP fields and observe the impact on the parser performance.
3. *Packet Content Effect*: The result of this study presents the influence of the CR and LF control characters position in a packet payload on the parser performance. The test traces containing modified payload packets are used to perform the measurement.

The performance evaluation process employs the benchmarking input plugin (see Section 3) to obtain the number of processed packets per second. In order to avoid influencing the results, the plugin uses separate thread and CPU core for the accounting. The plugin counts the number of the processed packets in ten second interval and then computes the packets per second rate. We have operated the benchmark plugin for fifty seconds for each test trace and computed a number of packets processed and a standard error of the measurement. The parsed HTTP header fields impact and packet content effect was assessed in a similar way. All measurements were conducted on a server with the following configuration: Intel Xeon E5410 CPU at 2.33 GHz, 12 GB 667 MHz DDR2 RAM and Linux kernel 2.6.32 (64 bit).

5 Parser Evaluation

In this section, we present results of HTTP parser evaluation. First we describe the parser performance comparison, then we investigate the impact of supported HTTP header fields. Finally, the effect of the packet content on HTTP parsing performance is shown.

Performance Comparison. This case study uses the standard version of each parser that supports seven HTTP fields. The data set containing the unmodified payload packets is used and the parsers are tested both on full and truncated packets. Fig. 2 shows the result for full packets case study and Fig. 3 shows performance evaluation for truncated packets.

First we discuss the Fig. 2. The *no HTTP* meter is capable of parsing more than 11 million packets per second. This result is not influenced by the application data carried in the packet, since the data is not accessed by the *no HTTP* parser. Employing event the fastest of the HTTP parsing algorithms the performance drops to the nearly one half of parsed packets per second. All of the HTTP parsers show the decrease in the performance as the ratio r increases since the amount of request and response packets, which are more time demanding to parse, grows.

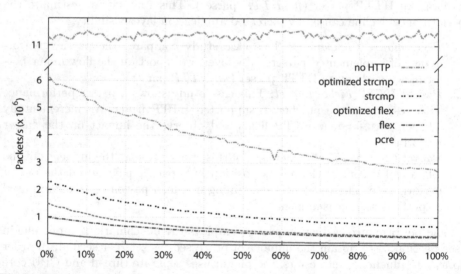

Fig. 2. Parser performance comparison with respect to HTTP proportion (0 % - no HTTP, 100 % - only HTTP headers) in the traffic - full packets 1500 B.

The best performance is achieved by *optimized strcmp* parser, which uses application protocol and code level optimizations. The parser takes into account the HTTP header structure, the difference between HTTP request and response headers and looks only for header fields that can be found in the specific header type. The code level optimizations include converting static strings into integers and matching them against several characters at once, which can be done in one processor instruction. The *strcmp* parser performance is the second best, although the throughput is less than half of the *optimized strcmp* parser.

The main difference between *flex* and *optimized flex* parsers is in the automaton initialization process. By rewriting the initialization process we achieved slight performance improvement, which is noticeable mainly in the ⟨0 %, 20 %⟩ interval, where the actual HTTP parsing time is short. There is one other important factor affecting the *flex* parser performance. The flex automaton is designed to work with its own writable buffer, since it marks end of individual parsed tokens directly into the buffer. For this reason a copy of the packet payload must be created before the actual parsing can start. To measure the impact of the copying, we created another two parser plugins called *empty* and *copy*. First we measured the flow meter throughput with *empty* plugin which performs no data parsing, then with *copy* plugin which only copies packet payload to static buffer. From the results we estimate the throughput the *optimized flex* parser would have without the memory copying. The performance of the *optimized flex* parser would be about 2.4 million packets per second for 0 % and 0.33 million packets per second for 100 % HTTP packets. This shows that the actual HTTP parsing, when compared to *strcmp* parser, is slightly faster for binary payload packets and slower for HTTP header packets.

The performance of the *pcre* parser is the lowest. The PCRE algorithm converts the regular expression to a tree structure and then performs a depth-first search while reading the input string. In case there is no match in current tree branch, the algorithm backs up and tries another one. Therefore, for a complex regular expression the pattern matching is not that fast as simple string search using functions like *strcmp*. Another reason why the *pcre* parser is not fast is that it performs all searches on whole packet payload. The other algorithms are processing the data sequentially.

Fig. 3 shows the results for truncated packets. The *optimized strcmp* and *no HTTP* are only slightly faster since the truncating of the packets has positive impact on CPU data cache utilization. The *strcmp* algorithm is flawed since its throughput on HTTP packets deteriorates rapidly. This shows the disadvantage of hand-written parsers, as they are more error-prone than the generated ones. The *pcre* parser performance is almost doubled, as the repeatedly processed data are truncated. Flex based parser also achieve performance increase, since the memory copying costs are reduced for smaller data.

Parsed HTTP Header Fields Impact. This case study was designed to show the impact of a number of parsed HTTP header fields on the parser performance.

When payload packets are detected, they do not have their content parsed for additional HTTP header fields. Therefore, a test set containing only HTTP request and response packets was used. The case study starts with an empty plugin, that does not parse HTTP header fields and just labels the HTTP packets. In the next steps we cumulatively add an additional header field to parse

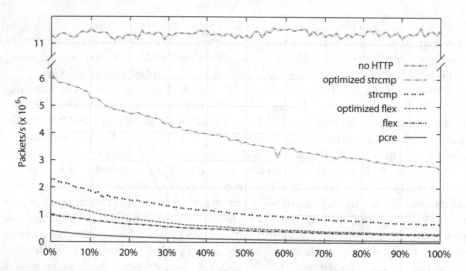

Fig. 3. Parser performance comparison with respect to HTTP proportion (0 % - no HTTP, 100 % - only HTTP headers) in the traffic - truncated packets 384 B.

until we parse all of the seven supported fields. We run the tests for both full and truncated packets. The average performance of the parsers for each of the added field is shown in Fig. 4.

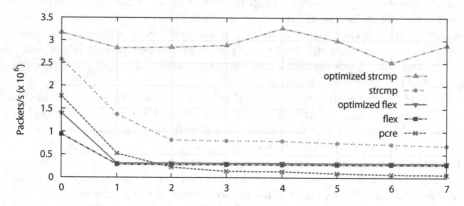

Fig. 4. An HTTP parser throughput for 1500 B packets; supported fields - (0) *none* - HTTP protocol labeling, (1) *+host*, (2) *+method*, (3) *+status code*, (4) *+request URI*, (5) *+content type*, (6) *+referer*, (7) *+user agent*.

Only the request and response packets are parsed, thus the values for the seven fields parsed in the Fig. 4 correspond to the 100 % packet/s values in the Fig. 2 and Fig. 3. For the same reason the parsed packets per second numbers are lower in comparison with the Fig. 2 and Fig. 3. The performance of *strcmp* and *pcre* parsers drops with each additional parsed HTTP header field. The *optimized strcmp* parser implementation details attentional fluctuation affect on performance shown in Fig. 4. An example is the performance increase when adding a *(4) request URI* or a *(3) status code*. It is caused by extra code snippet that extracts the URI so that this line is not processed by the more generic code designed for parsing other header fields. Due to the usage of finite automaton the data is always processed in one pass by the flex-based algorithms. Therefore, they retain the same level of performance for all additional fields. This feature could be used to automatically build powerful parsers, when the large number of parsed application fields would make it ineffective to create hand-written parsers.

Same as in the previous case study, the parsers processing truncated packets show better performance than the parsers working on full packets.

Packet Content Effect. This case study investigates the possible effects of the position of the CR and LF control characters in the packet payload on the parser performance. The mentioned ASCII characters represent the end of line in the HTTP header. Some of the proposed algorithms use these characters as the trigger to stop parsing. Therefore the position of these characters affects the parsers performance. The packets with the CRLF characters at the very *beginning* should be parsed faster than the packets having the CRLF at the *end* since the algorithm terminates as soon as it identifies the CRLF characters. The test sets with modified binary payload packets (see Section 4) enables us to compare the algorithms taking in account this perspective.

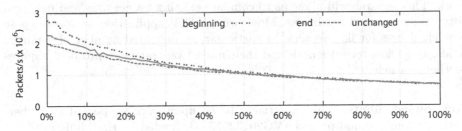

Fig. 5. Packet content effect - packet length 1500 B

We used the modified binary payload packets to test the parsers. The parsing algorithms, except the *strcmp* algorithm, show insignificant difference in their performance for all variants of the modified packets. The *pcre* and *optimized str-cmp* parsers do not search for end of line characters in order to label the packet, therefore this test does not affect them. The flex-based algorithms are not significantly affected since they stop parsing on first character that is not expected in HTTP header and therefore stop at the first character in any case. The *strcmp* parser depends on the search for end of line characters, which is confirmed by Fig. 5. The sooner the characters are found, the faster the algorithm terminates. The scenario with truncated packets is different, since the performance on *end* data set is greater than on *unchanged* data. This is caused by removing the end of packet payload together with the end of line character. When the *strcmp* algorithm cannot find the character, it terminates immediately without trying to search the data. Therefore it terminates sooner than on *unchanged* data set, where the end of line character is found and the search continues.

6 Conclusions

This paper has assessed the impacts of HTTP protocol analysis on flow monitoring performance. We implemented the state-of-the-art approaches to HTTP protocol parsing. Moreover, the new flex-based HTTP parser was designed and its performance was compared to the other approaches.

The evaluation shows that in our case the hand-written and carefully optimized parser performs significantly better than implementations with automated parsing. It also shows that the new flex-based implementations handles the increasing number of parsed HTTP fields without significant performance loss. Truncating the packets prior to HTTP protocol parsing can increase the parser throughput. The performance comparison of *no HTTP* parser with HTTP parsers shows that providing an application visibility is a demanding task. Current approaches to the application protocol parsing may not be effective enough to process a high-speed network traffic.

Although we focused on HTTP header parsing in this paper, measuring overall performance of flow meters is also essential. We will address performance evaluation and runtime requirements of entire flow meter frameworks in our future work. This research will allow us to compare existing frameworks and new prototypes under equal conditions. Monitoring HTTP application protocol expose new challenges for flow meters. In particular, an increased number of exported fields, large flow record length and their impact on transport protocol requires further research.

Acknowledgments. This material is based upon work supported by Cybernetic Proving Ground project (VG20132015103) funded by the Ministry of the Interior of the Czech Republic.

References

1. PCRE - Perl Compatible Regular Expressions (November 2012),
   http://www.pcre.org/
2. The GNU C Library (glibc) (December 2012),
   http://www.gnu.org/software/libc/
3. Bittel, J.: httpry - HTTP logging and information retrieval tool (April 2013),
   http://github.com/jbittel/httpry
4. Cisco Systems, Inc.: Application Visibility and Control (April 2013),
   http://www.cisco.com/go/avc
5. Deri, L.: nProbe: an Open Source NetFlow probe for Gigabit Networks. In: In Proc. of Terena TNC 2003 (2003)

6. Fielding, R., Gettys, J., Mogul, J., Frystyk, H., Masinter, L., Leach, P., Berners-Lee, T.: Hypertext Transfer Protocol – HTTP/1.1. RFC 2616 (Draft Standard) (June 1999), http://www.ietf.org/rfc/rfc2616.txt, updated by RFCs 2817, 5785, 6266, 6585

7. Gehlen, V., Finamore, A., Mellia, M., Munafò, M.M.: Uncovering the big players of the web. In: Pescapè, A., Salgarelli, L., Dimitropoulos, X. (eds.) TMA 2012. LNCS, vol. 7189, pp. 15–28. Springer, Heidelberg (2012), http://dx.doi.org/10.1007/978-3-642-28534-9_2

8. Inacio, C.M., Trammell, B.: YAF: Yet Another Flowmeter. In: Proceedings of the 24th International Conference on Large Installation System Administration, LISA 2010, pp. 1–16. USENIX Association, Berkeley (2010), http://dl.acm.org/citation.cfm?id=1924976.1924987

9. INVEA-TECH: FlowMon Exporter – Community Program (April 2013), http://www.invea-tech.com

10. Lesk, M.E., Schmidt, E.: Lex – a Lexical Analyzer Generator. Tech. rep., Bell Laboratories. Computing Science Technical Report No. 39 (1975)

11. Levine, J., John, L.: Flex & Bison, 1st edn. O'Reilly Media, Inc. (2009)

12. Mahanti, A., Williamson, C., Carlsson, N., Arlitt, M., Mahanti, A.: Characterizing the file hosting ecosystem: A view from the edge. Perform. Eval. 68(11), 1085–1102 (2011), http://dx.doi.org/10.1016/j.peva.2011.07.016

13. McNaughton, R., Yamada, H.: Regular Expressions and State Graphs for Automata. IRE Transactions on Electronic Computers, EC-9(1), 39–47 (1960)

14. Open Information Security Foundation: Suricata – network IDS, IPS and network security monitoring engine (April 2013), http://www.suricata-ids.org

15. Pang, R., Paxson, V., Sommer, R., Peterson, L.: Binpac: A yacc for Writing Application Protocol Parsers. In: Proceedings of the 6th ACM SIGCOMM Conference on Internet Measurement, IMC 2006, pp. 289–300. ACM, New York (2006), http://doi.acm.org/10.1145/1177080.1177119

16. Paxson, V.: Bro: A system for detecting network intruders in real-time. Comput. Netw. 31(23-24), 2435–2463 (1999), http://dx.doi.org/10.1016/S1389-1286(99)00112-7

17. Qualys, Inc.: LibHTP – security-aware parser for the HTTP protocol (April 2013), http://github.com/ironbee/libhtp

18. Roesch, M.: Snort - Lightweight Intrusion Detection for Networks. In: Proceedings of the 13th USENIX Conference on System Administration, LISA 1999, pp. 229–238. USENIX Association, Berkeley (1999), http://dl.acm.org/citation.cfm?id=1039834.1039864

19. Schneider, F., Agarwal, S., Alpcan, T., Feldmann, A.: The new web: Characterizing AJAX traffic. In: Claypool, M., Uhlig, S. (eds.) PAM 2008. LNCS, vol. 4979, pp. 31–40. Springer, Heidelberg (2008), http://dl.acm.org/citation.cfm?id=1791949.1791955

20. Šima T., Velan P., Čeleda P.: FlowMon - Plugins for HTTP Monitoring (April 2013), http://dior.ics.muni.cz/~velan/flowmon-input-http/

21. Torres, L., Magana, E., Izal, M., Morato, D.: Identifying sessions to websites as an aggregation of related flows. In: 2012 XVth International Telecommunications Network Strategy and Planning Symposium (NETWORKS), pp. 1–6 (2012)

22. Torres, L.M., Magana, E., Izal, M., Morato, D.: Strategies for automatic labelling of web traffic traces. In: 37th Annual IEEE Conference on Local Computer Networks, pp. 196–199 (2012)

IPv6 Address Obfuscation
by Intermediate Middlebox in Coordination
with Connected Devices

Florent Fourcot[1,2], Laurent Toutain[1], Stefan Köpsell[2],
Frédéric Cuppens[1], and Nora Cuppens-Boulahia[1]

[1] Institut Mines-Télécom; Télécom Bretagne
{first.last}@telecom-bretagne.eu
[2] TU Dresden; Faculty of Computer Science
stefan.koepsell@tu-dresden.de

Abstract. Privacy is a major concern on the current Internet, but transport mechanisms like IPv4 and more specifically IPv6 do not offer the necessary protection to users. However, the IPv6 address size allows designing privacy mechanisms impossible in IPv4. Nevertheless existing solutions like Privacy Extensions [20] are not optimal, still only one address is in use for several communications over time. And it does not offer control of the network by the administrator (end devices use randomly generated addresses). Our IPv6 privacy proposal uses ephemeral addresses outside the trusted network but stable addresses inside the local network, allowing the control of the local network security by the administrator. Our solution is based on new opportunities of IPv6: a large address space and a new flow label field. In combination with Cryptographically Generated Addresses, we can provide protection against spoofing on the local network and enhanced privacy for Internet communication.

Keywords: IPv6, Privacy, Security, Address Management.

1   Introduction

If IPv4 is still the most popular IP stack, IPv6 leaves the laboratory to be deployed on the Internet. For example, a lot of popular websites activated IPv6 on 6th June 2012 [1], and the French Internet provider "Free" offers IPv6 connectivity for new clients by default. This activation of IPv6 is not without privacy issues like the possibility to trace a device, thanks to the interface identifier stability [19]. Indeed, an IPv6 address is made of two parts. The first one is the routing information, read by routers across the Internet. The second part is the interface identifier, locally generated but worldwide readable. The default stateless configuration uses the MAC address to generate this interface identifier, without other parameters [17]. This means that initially the interface identifier of a device is always the same, regardless of the connected network; the device is traceable across the whole world.

T. Bauschert (Ed.): EUNICE 2013, LNCS 8115, pp. 148–160, 2013.

To obfuscate this interface identifier, there exist full fledge anonymous communication solutions, e.g. based on the ideas of mixes [11] like AN.ON [9] or Tor [13]; DC networks [10] and many similar proposals. This class of solutions offers high grade of protection even against powerful attackers but at the price of complex design and deployment. In our paper we focus on a light weight construction which offers protection only against weaker attackers. More specific we assume an attacker outside of the trusted network. A prominent example would be a web service which tries to reidentify its users.

One existing light weight solution called Privacy Extensions is defined in RFC 4941 [20]. Privacy extensions are compatible with the stateless autoconfiguration, but this solution is not really satisfactory. Usually the same address is used over a long period of time, because changing the address implies disconnection of all active connections. Thus there is a trade off between relatively stable connections versus a real privacy gain. Second, by using only one address, Privacy Extensions do not take advantage of the large IPv6 space. All applications of the connected device will use the same address, therefore an eavesdropper can easily link different communications of the same device, e.g. Instant messaging communication and the Web traffic.

From a network administrator perspective, Privacy Extensions might be unacceptable because it makes logging user's connections more cumbersome. This logging is mandated by law in some countries, i.e. administrators have to reveal who was using a given address in case of court order or police investigations. One solution is to deploy the complex DHCPv6 protocol with distribution of temporary addresses, standardized in RFC 3315 [14]. With this stateful protocol, assignments of temporary addresses can be stored and are accessible to future requests. Nevertheless, it does not solve the disconnection problem in case of address switching and still does not utilize the large address space.

Another way to manage IPv6 addresses is to use Cryptographically Generated Addresses (CGA) [8]. CGA addresses are generated by the host itself, and can be used to improve the security of communications. One example is the use of CGA in conjunction with SEcure Neighbor Discovery [6] to prevent address spoofing on the local network. The interface identifier of a CGA address is based on a cryptographic hash function, and looks like a random address for an outsider. But the computational cost of CGA generation with an adequate security level is high [3] and prevents to use it as a privacy solution with high frequency of CGA calculation.

Our solution does not change the management of IPv6 assignment, and is compatible with stateless autoconfiguration, DHCPv6 and CGA. To improve the privacy of users, we introduce a middlebox, traditionally the border router of the network or the local firewall. On an IPv4 network, the middlebox is frequently a Network Address Translator (NAT) [22], and is already more "intelligent" than a simple router. An example of middlebox on the IPv6 network is a Network Prefix Translation (NPTv6) device [24]. NPTv6 is an experimental solution to change the prefix of addresses, using a one-to-one mapping. In contrast, our middlebox is in charge of spreading addresses across all locally available addresses, typically a /64 network, this means more than 10^{20} addresses. To accomplish this spreading, the middlebox assigns a random address for each *flow* sent by local devices and rewrites the source address accordingly. This spreading divides the network in one trusted space with stable addresses and one untrusted network (the Internet) with ephemeral addresses. Moreover, this rewriting can be easily activated or deactivated for each *flow*.

This paper is organized as follow: we describe the architecture of our solution in Section 2, we describe our implementation in Section 3, we discuss impacts and consequences in Section 4. We continue in Section 5 with a solution for assigning flow labels by application. Section 6 presents a performance measurement. Finally, Section 7 and 8 conclude the paper.

2   Proposal of Architecture

2.1   Overview of New IPv6 Opportunities

Our solution is based on two new opportunities offered by IPv6, namely a large address space and flow labels.

Large Address Space: IPv6 addresses are encoded in a 128 bits field, it means that 2^{128} addresses are available, more than 10^{28} addresses for each people alive today. As shown in the introduction, each address is split into two main parts and the first part is used for the routing and identifies a network. This main part of network identifier is assigned by an Internet provider to a company or home network. The second part of the address is the interface identifier. It can be locally managed and identifies the connected device on the network. The size of the locally manageable part is not always the same, but the recommendation is to give not less than 64 bits to the end network [12]. This means that with thousands of connected computers, each with one address in use, less than 0.00000000000001% of the address space is used. Therefore, if the IPv4 address management has to minimize the number of addresses in use, we can build new paradigms based on abundance of addresses in IPv6.

The flow label is a new 20 bits field in IPv6. The usage has been experimental for a long time, but after extensive discussions [4, 18], it has been standardized in 2011 [5]. The purpose of the field is to simplify the flow classification in order to apply some policies without complex packet inspection (like the well known 5-tuple in IPv4). The flow label is added by connected devices, which are easily able to discriminate flows without additional computational overhead. The recommended usage of this field is Quality of Service oriented (for example to prioritize real time communications), but this classification can have other use cases, summarized in RFC 6294 [18].

2.2   Overview of the Solution

To increase the user's privacy, we propose to assign one external address per flow. For each independent flow of packets, the connected device assigns a new flow label[1]. Then, the middlebox assigns a new external address to each pair of (*internal IP address, flow label*) and rewrites the source addresses of the outgoing packets and the destination addresses of the incoming packets (cf. Figure 1). Because the middlebox is in position of a border router, it receives all the packets from the local network. Therefore, it does not need to send extra neighbor discovery packets. In contrast, if the rewriting happens on the end devices, this solution implies some active neighbor discovery.

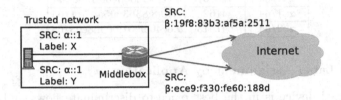

Fig. 1. Architecture of the solution: spreading by the middlebox

Since some applications can be incompatible with address rewriting (similar to the implications of NAT in IPv4 [16]), a flow label set to zero is a signal to forbid rewriting. This special label can be used if a temporary address is undesirable, for example in case of IP source address filtering on the destination device or an incompatible application layer.

To summarize, the intelligence to discriminate flows and optimize privacy is based on the end device, and all rewritings are based on the middlebox, i.e. under control of the network administrator. There is no need to change local address assignment policy. The middlebox should be located between the local firewall and the Internet; it prevents to rewrite firewall policies.

2.3   Computation on the Middlebox

Since the "intelligence" of flow classification is with in in the connected devices, the middlebox does not need to do a complex parsing of packets' headers, and to follow a TCP stream in a stateful way. But it has to maintain a context to perform rewriting (cf. Table 1). For each outgoing packet with an unknown pair (*internal IP address, flow label*) (short ($IP_{int}, label$)) the middlebox creates a context and generates a random interface identifier, which creates an address by concatenation with the prefix, named *external IP address* (short IP_{ext}). The stored context is a 3-tuple ($IP_{int}, label, IP_{ext}$), and all following packets matching the pair ($IP_{int}, label$) will be rewritten with the IP_{ext}. For all incoming

---

[1] Given the 20 bits for a flow label, the risk of exhaustion is quite low.

packets, the middlebox rewrite the destination address with IP_{int} if a context exists, or applies standard routing and firewall policies.

Note that a flow (defined by all packets sharing the same source IP and the same flow label) can be made of more than one TCP connection (or other transport protocols). For example, we recommend to use the same flow for all the elements of a given Web page. The middlebox itself does not care about upper protocol layers, because the flow assignment is done on the end device.

Table 1. Example of context on the middlebox

Internal IP	Flow label	External IP
α::1/64	120137	α:ece9:f330:fe60:188d/64
α::1/64	4162	α:19f8:83b3:af5a:2511/64
α::2/64	647513	α:6c40:9951:605f:8e03/64

2.4 Flow Label Assignment by Application

The connected device is in the best place to discriminate flows and to assign flow labels. For example, a peer-to-peer application probably needs to use the same address for more than one TCP connection, a Web browser knows if one connection is related to another, etc. In our case, the best way is to patch the application to assign flow labels efficiently.

To help a fast deployment of our solution, we propose an assignment of a flow label per application in Section 5.2.

3   Implementation of the Middlebox

To test our solution, we implemented and deployed the middlebox in a real network environment. The middlebox is based on a standard Linux Kernel, and we added a Netfilter module to spread addresses. The middlebox has to rewrite addresses for outgoing and incoming packets. The limitation of our current implementation is that it can only be load on one interface connected to the Internet and does not yet support multihoming.

3.1   Packets Processing

Outgoing Packets: for each outgoing packet, we read the flow label information. If this label is zero, we stop the work of the module and the standard policy of the kernel is applied. Otherwise, we check if a context with the pair of source address and flow label already exists.

If we do not have a context, we have to create one. The first step is to generate a random address, and to check if the address is not in collision as explained in Section 4.2. The prefix part is static and can not be rewritten, but it is possible to configure the length of the prefix (routing information), to maximize the size of the rewritable address part. We added the new external address to the pair (*source IP address, flow label*), and happen this context to the context table.

If a context exists, or after the initialization of a context, we rewrite the source address with the value stored in the fetched context. Afterwards we have to adjust the transport layer checksum. There is no standard way to rewrite this checksum, therefore we have to write code for each protocol. Currently, our implementation supports the three most popular protocols: TCP, UDP and ICMP (cf. Section 4.1). After this rewriting, we return the packet to apply standard kernel policy.

The flow label is no longer useful after the middlebox, and is set to zero.

Incoming Packets: for incoming packets, we only read the destination address. We check if a context exists for this address. If not, the packet is transmitted in the standard kernel way. Otherwise, we rewrite the destination address with the value stored in the context and we adjust the transport layer checksum.

3.2   Identification of a Context

The identification of a context has to be efficient on both directions. The identification of outgoing flows is done by matching the source address and the flow label with all existing contexts. For incoming packet, the identifier of the context is the destination address. We implement these searches with two hash tables, one for outgoing packets using "source IP address + label" as key value, and the second one for incoming packet using destination address as key value. This double hash table allows fast matching between packets and contexts.

3.3   Cleanup of Old Context

At the termination of a flow, the middlebox should remove the corresponding context to potentially reassign the address and to free the memory used. But in the IP network, there is no concept of connection and there are no communication messages to signal the end of a flow.

In IPv4 networks, RFC 4787 and 5382 [7, 15] give some recommendations to maintain a connection context for a NAT. But in your case, it is not possible (and desirable) to trace the state of a TCP connection. On the one hand, a flow can span more than a single TCP connection, on the other hand additional transport protocols can be in use. The only available solution is to introduce a timeout after an inactivity period. It should not be less than 120 seconds, according to recommendation for IPv4. A large timeout period will help to avoid breaking established connections, at cost of resource consumption. Based on our empirical tests, we recommend a value of 30 minutes, which give a good trade-off between resource consumption and connection stability. But the local administrator could overwrite this standard configuration in case of particular needs like long inactive TCP connections.

4   Impacts and Consequences

4.1   Checksum Computation

In IPv6, there is no checksum contained in the IP header but the transport layer protocols like TCP and UDP are in charge of error detections and therefore utilize a checksum. This checksum needs to be adapted if a rewriting happens. Fortunately, the flow label is not part of the checksum calculation and can be overwritten without implication. Nevertheless, the source address rewriting has an impact on the transport layer protocol checksum.

The large IPv6 address space supports some checksum neutral modifications, like in NPTv6 [24]. But in our case this solution is unacceptable. A checksum neutral modification gives a way to group all rewritten addresses of a device, with a simple checksum calculation of the source address. This removes the unlinkability between several random addresses.

But thanks to good properties of the standard Internet checksum, the cost of checksum computation is low, and an incremental update is possible [21]. We do not need to completly recompute new checksum C_{new} of a packet, since we can easily add the difference C_D between the 16-bit checksum C_{int} of the internal IP address and the 16-bit checksum C_{ext} of the external IP address to the already computed checksum C_{old}: $C_{new} = C_{old} + C_D$. During the initialization of the context, the middlebox will calculate $C_D = C_{int} - C_{ext}$ once, and caches this value.

4.2   Risk of Collision

Each generated address has to be unique behond the all local subnet, in order to not disturb the network. As a consequence, the new address should not be already used by the middlebox nor should it be assigned to any local device by any other means. The first condition can be checked easily by looking at the context table. The verification of the second condition is more complex, especially if the rewriting use the same prefix for IP_{int} and IP_{ext}. Here, there is a risk of collisions between the randomly generated addresses and addresses already assigned to end devices. One solution could be to check if the address is not already in use, using a neighbour discovery (NDP). But this is unacceptable for at least two reasons. First, it increases the latency for all connection initializations, because the middlebox has to wait until the NDP timed out before making a decision. Second, no response to a NDP request does not mean that this address is not in use, e.g. the device can currently be down. To mitigate the problem, we propose the following:

- The middlebox can be configured to not use the autoconfiguration space derived from the MAC address (this means removing results with 4th byte and 5th byte set to 0xFF and 0xFE respectively). This configuration should be enabled by default to prevent a conflict with the standard configuration;
- In case of DHCPv6 address distribution, the DHCP address space should not be included in the rewriting space configured on the middlebox;

– In case of CGA or static configured addresses, the administrator can manually forbid addresses;
– In any case, the middlebox should maintain a list of devices currently in
communication. Clearly this is not exhaustive, since devices can be connected
without established connections.

These four rules eliminate the risk of collisions in most networks, and minimize
it for some special cases. Additionally, it is important to notice that the risk of
collision is actually very low – even without applying the rules mentioned above.
The evaluation of the probability of a collision is a variant of the "birthday
paradox". Given a pool of n addresses and already j addresses assigned, the
probability $\bar{p}(n, j)$ to choose the $j + 1$ address without collision is:

$$\bar{p}(n, j) = 1 - \frac{j}{n} = \frac{n - j}{n} \tag{1}$$

This means that if we assign J addresses in a free space, we have a probability
to not have any collision of:

$$\bar{P}(n, J) = \bar{p}(n, 0).\bar{p}(n, 1)\ldots\bar{p}(n, J - 1) = \frac{n \cdot (n - 1)\ldots(n - J + 1)}{n^J} \tag{2}$$

Then, the probability to have at least one collosion is:

$$P(n, J) = 1 - \bar{P}(n, J) = 1 - \frac{n \cdot (n - 1)\ldots(n - J + 1)}{n^J} \tag{3}$$

That we can write:

$$P(n, J) = 1 - \left(1 - \frac{1}{n}\right) \cdot \left(1 - \frac{2}{n}\right)\ldots\left(1 - \frac{J - 1}{n}\right) \tag{4}$$

Since for all i in $1\ldots J$: $i \leq J$, we can give an upper bound for the probability
with:

$$P(n, J) \leq 1 - \left(1 - \frac{J - 1}{n}\right)^{J-1} \tag{5}$$

We can now perform an evaluation of this probability. In a network with only
one prefix of the minimal size for auto-configuration, the interface identifier uses
64 bits. Two bits are reserved for special purpose, so only 62 bits are actually free.
We can calculate $n = 2^{62}$. On a big network with one thousand computers, where
each of them maintains one thousand flows, we need to allocate $J = 1000 \cdot 1000 =
10^6$ addresses. A simple computation informs us than the probability of collision
is less than $2.2 \cdot 10^{-7}$.

4.3 Compatibility Analysis

In order to support wide spread deployment it is essential that our solution
integrates smoothly into existing networks. In our case, we only need to deploy
the middlebox at the border of the network and an adaptation of the end devices
to enable address rewriting. More specific the necessary changes are as follows:

Remote Routers and Servers: since our solution is based on standard IPv6 packets, it is compatible with the standard IPv6 network. There is no need to upgrade intermediate routers or remote servers. We can deploy it locally without cooperation or impact on other networks, the real source address is obfuscated but the packet is still valid.

Local Devices: for local devices, packets without flow label are not rewritten and therefore there are no compatibily implications. But to use the benefits of our solution, upgrades are usually necessary. First, not all Operating Systems (OSes) provide means to set flow labels. Second, on compatible OSes, there applications have to actually use the flow label option. We discuss assignment of flow labels in Section 5.2.

Common Address Translation Issues: Address rewriting is a kind of address translation and can have some consequences. First, some applications send the IP address to the peer within the application layer protocols, for example File Transfer Protocol (FTP) and Session Initiation Protocol (SIP). If transmitting the address at the application layer is mandatory for a given protocol, we can not easily rewrite the address.

For IMCP packets, we have to rewrite the internals addresses in quoted ICMP packet too. It makes parsing a little bit complexer but it does not break ICMP messages.

In case of IPSec, we are in the same case than NPTv6 and the conclusion is the same: peers should detect an address translator, so IPSec should work.

In all cases, our solution is better than standard address translation since it can be easily disabled. For all connections that are not compatible, the applications can set the flow label to zero, the default value.

5   Flow label Assignment at End Devices

5.1   Link between Applications and Operating System: Flow Label Management API

Unfortunately, there is no standard Application Program Interface (API) between a software package and an operating system to set or request a flow label. RFC 3542 [23] is the last standardized API for IPv6, and we can read "This API does not define access to the flow label field, because today there is no standard usage of the field". Without standardized API, each operating system has a specific approach to set and configure flow labels, and it is not easy to write portable software. This is why our work focuses only on the Linux kernel.

The Linux Flow Label API is 13 years old, and part of the Kernel since the version 2.2.7, released in April 1999. Design decisions of the implementation are explained in [2], and there is nothing really new since this time. This document is still the reference documentation for this API.

5.2 How to Patch Applications on Linux

Our proposition is simple: each application discriminates flows and sets flow labels for outgoing sockets, and if it is not done, the operating system has to set a flow label for all sockets of an application. The user can deactivate this kernel behavior (for example with the help of an environment variable).

Thanks to the GNU linker ld, it is possible to preload some libraries for dynamically linked software (the kind of linkage used by nearly all Linux distributions). We can intercept the call to the connect() function. Here we check if a flow label is already set, in this case we continue with the standard connect() function. Otherwise, we enable the flow label and set its value (derived from the process identifier PID) via the setsockopt() function.

Using this approach, we do not have to patch every application to use the spreading. At the same time, it does not interfere with a patched application since it does not overwrite an existing flow label value. Even if this is not an optimal solution, the gain is high in comparison with using just one address for all applications running on a given computer.

6 Performance Evaluation

In the following sections, we discuss various performance aspects of our solution.

6.1 Memory Consumption on the Middlebox

Within a context, we have to store:

- the real source address IP_{int} of the computer (128 bits);
- the randomized source address IP_{ext} (128 bits);
- the flow label (20 bits), stored in an integer (32 bits);
- the cached checksum difference C_D (16 bits);
- the "last seen" value, to remove old entries (same size as jiffies_64 kernel variable, i.e 64 bits);
- two node structures in the hash tables (128 bits each);

The total size is about 80 octets for each context. With the current hypothesis of 1000 computers with 1000 flows each, we need about 80MB to store all contexts. On a home network with 5 computers and 100 flows each, less than 100KB of memory is necessary.

Moroever, each context needs less space than a usual entry of the conntrack table used for NAT in IPv4. Therefore, the memory consumption of our solution will not be a problem for modern routers with NAT capacities.

6.2 Latency

Overhead of Rewriting on the Middlebox. Our implementation adds extra computation on the middlebox, before the routing of a packet. This adds some latency for packet treatment. But this computation is simple and it does not show any impact on the latency in our test networks. On a test bed with a standard latency of 300ms, it was not possible to see any impact on the latency.

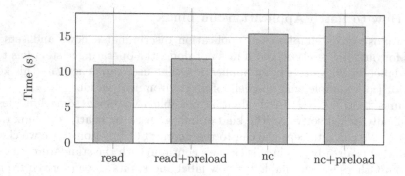

Fig. 2. Average time to run 20.000 times tests with library preload enabled/disabled

Overhead of the Library Preload. A second potential latency cost comes from the library preload, to assign a flow label to each application. Our tests were done on a virtual machine with a 2.4Ghz CPU allocated. We run 20.000 times four different tests:

- open and read a short file. The library preload is not enabled;
- the same command, but with library preload enabled;
- a short `netcat` command, this sends an UDP datagram to localhost and quits, without library preload;
- the same `netcat` command, with library preload enabled.

Figure 2 shows the measured times for the 20.000 iterations. The difference between the two file readings comes from the load of the library at the startup, even if the library does nothing. For each run, it introduces a latency of 5.10^{-5} seconds, but only at the startup of the software (we need to load the library only once). The difference between the two `netcat` tests reveals the total overhead of the library, with the time to set up the flow label included. If we subtract the time to load the library, we get a latency overhead of 9.10^{-6} seconds for each connection, Kernel time included.

As expected, our preload library does not have significant influence on the overall latency.

6.3   CPU Consumption on the Middlebox

To evaluate the CPU consumption of our solution, we made a profiling of the Kernel. We used the OProfile software, part of the standard tools of the Linux Kernel package. Our results show that our module needs about 10% of the time needed by the network card driver itself. With a bandwidth of 2.2Gb/s our module uses less than 2.5% of the CPU time of the 2.4Ghz CPU used.

Additionnaly, we install our solution in a home network on a standard router (Asus-rt16) and we do not see any CPU consumption overhead[2].

---

[2] The maximal bandwidth of the Internet connection is about 30Mb/s

7   Future Works

Currently our solution allows only to activate or deactivate the address rewriting (encoded by setting the flow label to zero). One of our ideas is to encode more data in the 20 bits of flow labels. The first bit could be used as a flag for a stateful firewall, to allow or deny incoming connections on the ephemeral address. This can be very useful in case of peer-to-peer connections.

Another possibility is to signal to disable the rewriting of the flow label to zero. This can be relevant if an upstream router uses the flow label for Quality of Service. Finally, a configuration of the timeout before erasing a context could be added too. All this flags improve the possibility of the client to adapt to specific communication context. We have enough space to provide five flags, since 32768 flows (15 bits left) should be enough to numbering all flows of a device.

Another improvement can be done in case of multihoming of the middlebox. The flow label tagging allows us to assign one outgoing interface for each flow, thus it allows us to make some load balancing on the middlebox.

8   Conclusion

Our solution provides a privacy gain, since an attacker cannot easily link differents connections of a single computer. It is compatible with all address assignment policies, and is very easy to deploy on a network. The administrator does not need to change the actual configuration and still can use CGA to prevent IP address spoofing on the local network. Our middlebox divides the network in one trusted zone under the control of an administrator and one untrusted zone, where privacy of users is protected.

The intelligence stays on the end devices, able to determine if a flow should be spread or not. On the middlebox, the resource consumption is lower than a typical IPv4 NAT setting and should not be a problem for the deployment. As for a IPv4 NAT, there is a risk of deny of service attacks from local network, by opening a lot of connections with random flow label values. It can be mitigated by limiting the number of allowed connections per devices.

Today, privacy is a hot topic for IPv6. For example, Deutsche Telekom Internet Provider uses privacy as a marketing argument for their IPv6 architecture. A patched middlebox with our solution is relevant in this context.

References

1. World IPv6 launch, http://www.worldipv6launch.org/ (Consulted the July 4, 2013)
2. Kuznetsov Alexey, N.: IPv6 flow labels in Linux-2.2, Tech. report, Institute for Nuclear Research, Moscow (April 1999)
3. Alsa'deh, A., Rafiee, H., Meinel, C.: Stopping time condition for practical. In: 2012 International Conference on IPv6 Cryptographically Generated Addresses,Information Networking (ICOIN), pp. 257–262 (February 2012)

4. Amante, S., Carpenter, B., Jiang, S.: Rationale for Update to the IPv6 Flow Label Specification, RFC 6436 (Informational) (November 2011)
5. Amante, S., Carpenter, B., Jiang, S., Rajahalme, J.: IPv6 Flow Label Specification, RFC 6437 (Proposed Standard) (November 2011)
6. Arkko, J., Kempf, J., Zill, B., Nikander, P.: SEcure Neighbor Discovery (SEND), RFC 3971 (Proposed Standard) (March 2005), Updated by RFCs 6494, 6495
7. Audet, F., Jennings, C.: Network Address Translation (NAT) Behavioral Requirements for Unicast UDP, RFC 4787 (Best Current Practice) (January 2007)
8. Aura, T.: Cryptographically Generated Addresses (CGA), RFC 3972 (Proposed Standard) (March 2005), Updated by RFCs 4581, 4982
9. Berthold, O., Federrath, H., Köpsell, S.: Web mixes: A system for anonymous and unobservable internet access. In: Federrath, H. (ed.) Anonymity 2000. LNCS, vol. 2009, pp. 115–129. Springer, Heidelberg (2001)
10. Chaum, D.: The dining cryptographers problem: Unconditional sender and recipient untraceability. Journal of Cryptology 1, 65–75 (1988)
11. Chaum, D.L.: Untraceable electronic mail, return addresses, and digital pseudonyms. Commun. ACM 24(2), 84–90 (1981)
12. Van de Velde, G., Popoviciu, C., Chown, T., Bonness, O., Hahn, C.: IPv6 Unicast Address Assignment Considerations, RFC 5375 (Informational) (December 2008)
13. Dingledine, R., Mathewson, N., Syverson, P.: Tor: The second-generation onion router. In: Proceedings of the 13 th Usenix Security Symposium (2004)
14. Droms, R., Bound, J., Volz, B., Lemon, T., Perkins, C., Carney, M.: Dynamic Host Configuration Protocol for IPv6 (DHCPv6), RFC 3315 (Proposed Standard) (July 2003), Updated by RFCs 4361, 5494, 6221, 6422
15. Guha, S., Biswas, K., Ford, B., Sivakumar, S., Srisuresh, P.: NAT Behavioral Requirements for TCP, RFC 5382 (Best Current Practice) (October 2008)
16. Hain, T.: Architectural Implications of NAT, RFC 2993 (Informational) (November 2000)
17. Hinden, R., Deering, S.: IP Version 6 Addressing Architecture, RFC 4291 (Draft Standard) (February 2006), Updated by RFCs 5952, 6052
18. Hu, Q., Carpenter, B.: Survey of Proposed Use Cases for the IPv6 Flow Label, RFC 6294 (Informational) (June 2011)
19. Lindqvist, J.: IPv6 is bad for your privacy, Defcon 15 (2007)
20. Narten, T., Draves, R., Krishnan, S.: Privacy Extensions for Stateless Address Autoconfiguration in IPv6, RFC 4941 (Draft Standard) (September 2007)
21. Rijsinghani, A.: Computation of the Internet Checksum via Incremental Update, RFC 1624 (Informational) (May 1994)
22. Srisuresh, P., Holdrege, M.: IP Network Address Translator (NAT) Terminology and Considerations, RFC 2663 (Informational) (August 1999)
23. Stevens, W., Thomas, M., Nordmark, E., Jinmei, T.: Advanced Sockets Application Program Interface (API) for IPv6, RFC 3542 (Informational) (May 2003)
24. Wasserman, M., Baker, F.: IPv6-to-IPv6 Network Prefix Translation, RFC 6296 (Experimental) (June 2011)

Balanced XOR-ed Coding

Katina Kralevska, Danilo Gligoroski, and Harald Øverby

Department of Telematics, Faculty of Information Technology,
Mathematics and Electrical Engineering,
Norwegian University of Science and Technology, Trondheim, Norway
{katinak,danilog,haraldov}@item.ntnu.no

Abstract. This paper concerns with the construction of codes over $GF(2)$ which reach the max-flow for single source multicast acyclic networks with delay. The coding is always a bitwise XOR of packets with equal lengths, and is based on highly symmetrical and balanced designs. For certain setups and parameters, our approach offers additional plausible security properties: an adversary needs to eavesdrop at least max-flow links in order to decode at least one original packet.

Keywords: XOR coding, $GF(2)$, Latin squares, Latin rectangles.

1 Introduction

Encoding and decoding over $GF(2)$ (GF stands for Galois field with 2 elements: 0 and 1) is more energy efficient than encoding and decoding in any other larger field. Recent studies concerning several new techniques in network coding [1] (Linear Network Coding (LNC) [12,10] and Random Linear Network Coding (RLNC) [6]) confirmed that encoding and decoding over $GF(2)$ are up to two orders of magnitude less energy demanding and up to one order of magnitude faster than the encoding/decoding operations in larger fields [18,14,20].

The high computational complexity of packet encoding and decoding over large finite fields and its high energy cost which makes it unsuitable for practical implementation are the main motivation to seek for coding techniques only with XOR operations. The first theoretical work was done by Riis in [16] who showed that every solvable multicast network has a linear solution over $GF(2)$. Afterwards, XOR coding in wireless networks was presented in [9], where the main rule is that a node can XOR n packets together only if the next hop has all $n - 1$ packets. A more general network coding problem which is called index coding is considered in [17,15]. In [15] the authors address the coding problem by proposing coding over $GF(2)$. The encoding scheme is based on bitwise XORing by adding redundant bits, and the decoding scheme is based on a simple but bit after bit sequential back substitution method.

The main contribution of our work is a construction of codes over $GF(2)$ by using combinatorial designs (Latin squares and Latin rectangles) [4]. Its lower computation and energy cost makes it suitable for practical implementation on devices with limited processing and energy capacity like mobile phones and wireless sensors. We will illustrate the construction of codes by the following simple example.

T. Bauschert (Ed.): EUNICE 2013, LNCS 8115, pp. 161–172, 2013.

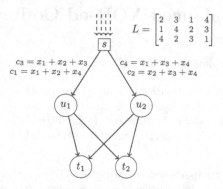

$$L = \begin{bmatrix} 2 & 3 & 1 & 4 \\ 1 & 4 & 2 & 3 \\ 4 & 2 & 3 & 1 \end{bmatrix}$$

$c_3 = x_1 + x_2 + x_3$ $c_4 = x_1 + x_3 + x_4$
$c_1 = x_1 + x_2 + x_4$ $c_2 = x_2 + x_3 + x_4$

Fig. 1. An example of balanced XOR coding where the source sends combinations of source packets (combined as the column of the Latin rectangle). The intermediate nodes just forward the data to the sink nodes.

Example 1. We use the following strategy (Fig. 1): the source s performs bitwise XOR of packets with equal length based on the incidence matrix of a Latin rectangle L. Each column of L represents a combination of source packets x_i, $i = 1, \ldots, 4$, in a coded packet c_i, $i = 1, \ldots, 4$. In the first phase, the packets c_1 and c_2 are sent, and in the second phase, the packets c_3 and c_4 are sent. The intermediate nodes u_1 and u_2 forward the coded packets to the sink nodes t_1 and t_2 which decode the packets by using the inverse matrix of the incidence matrix of L. The sink nodes need only to know the combination of source packets in each received packet. Note that the max-flow in the network is achieved.

Routinely as in other coding approaches, this information is included in the header of each coded packet. Since in this paper we use diversity coding performed just by the source nodes, there is no need for updating the coefficients in the header at each intermediate node. The length of the prepended header vector is negligible compared to the length of the packet.

The construction of our codes was not motivated by security issues, therefore the security is not the main goal in this paper. However, it turns out that for certain setups and parameters, our approach offers additional plausible security properties. The plausible security properties that accompany our approach are not based on hard mathematical problems in modern cryptology (for example factoring of large integers or discrete logarithm problems or on the Shamir's secret sharing algorithm). We show that if an eavesdropper wants to reconstruct at least one original packet, then the number of eavesdropped links should be equal to the max-flow of the network. Bhattad and al. [2] make similar observations when network coding is implemented so that a weekly secure network coding is achieved.

The rest of the paper is organized as follows: Section 2 presents the notation and the mathematical background that are used in the following sections. The construction of codes is presented in Section 3. Section 4 illustrates the security features of our approach. Sections 5 concludes the paper.

2   Notation and Mathematical Background

We define a communication network as a tuple $N = (V, E, S, T)$ that consists of:

- a finite directed acyclic multigraph $G = (V, E)$ where V is the set of vertices and E is the set of edges,
- a set $S \subset V$ of sources,
- a set $T \subset V$ of sink nodes.

Assume that vertex $s \in S$ sends n source packets to vertex $t \in T$ over disjoint paths. A minimal cut separating s and t is a cut of the smallest cardinality denoted as $\mathrm{mincut}(s, t)$. The packets are sent in several time slots, i.e., phases denoted as p. The maximum number of packets that can be sent in a phase from s to t is denoted as $\mathrm{maxflow}(t)$. The Max-Flow Min-Cut Theorem [11] indicates that $\mathrm{mincut}(s, t) = \mathrm{maxflow}(t)$. The multicast capacity, i.e., the maximum rate at which s can transfer information to the sink nodes, cannot exceed the capacity of any cut separating s from the sink nodes. A network is solvable when the sink nodes are able to deduce the original packets with decoding operations. If the network is solvable with linear operations we say that the network is linearly solvable.

2.1   XOR-ed Coding

First we recall that in [16], Riis showed that every solvable multicast network has a linear solution over $GF(2)$ in some vector dimension. The essence of his proof relies on the fact that any two finite fields with the same cardinality are isomorphic. Thus, instead of working in a finite field $GF(2^n)$ for which the conditions of the linear-code multicast (LCM) theorem [12, Th. 5.1] are met, he showed that it is possible to work in the isomorphic vector space $GF(2)^n$ that is an extension field over the prime field $GF(2)$. We formalize the work in the vector space $GF(2)^n$ with the following:

Definition 1. *A XOR-ed coding is a coding that is realized exclusively by bitwise XOR operations between packets with equal length. Hence, it is a parallel bitwise linear transformation of n source bits $x = (x_1, \ldots, x_n)$ by a $n \times n$ nonsingular matrix K, i.e., $y = K \cdot x$.*

In [16] it was also shown that there are simple network topologies where encoding in $GF(2)$ cannot reach the network capacity with the original bandwidth or by sending data in just one phase. However, it was shown that the network capacity by XOR-ed coding can be achieved either by increasing the bandwidth or the number of phases so that they match the dimension of the extended vector space $GF(2)^n$. In this paper we take the approach to send data in several phases p instead of increasing the bandwidth.

Theorem 1. *For any linearly solvable network topology with $\mathrm{maxflow}(t_1) > 1$, the sufficient condition for a single sink t_1 to reach its capacity in each of p phases by XOR-ed coding is to receive n linearly independent packets $x = (x_1, \ldots, x_n)$, where $n = p \times \mathrm{maxflow}(t_1)$.*

Proof. Assume that the network topology is linearly solvable. That means there exists a vector space $GF(2)^n$ where we can encode every n source packets with a bijective function K, i.e., $y = K \cdot x$. Having in mind that the source s succeeds to send n encoded packets to t_1 in p phases, and the max-flow in the network is maxflow(t_1) > 1, we have that $n = p \times$ maxflow(t_1) and the sink t_1 receives n packets after p phases via maxflow(t_1) disjoint paths. In order to have a successful recovery of the initial n packets, the received packets should be linearly independent.

Based on Theorem 1 we can prove the following:

Theorem 2. *For any linearly solvable network topology and for any two sinks $T = \{t_1, t_2\}$ that have maxflow(t) = maxflow(t_1) = maxflow(t_2), there always exists a XOR-ed coding for $n = p \times$ maxflow(t) packets that achieves the multicast capacity in each of p phases.*

Proof. For the sink t_1 we apply Theorem 1 and find one XOR-ed coding that achieves the capacity in each of p phases. Let us denote by $U_1 = \{u_{1,i}|$ there is an edge $(u_{1,i}, t_1) \in E\}$ the nodes that are directly connected and send packets to the sink node t_1. We have that $|U_1| =$ maxflow(t), and the set of n packets is partitioned in maxflow(t) disjoint subsets $Y_{1,1}, \ldots, Y_{1,\text{maxflow}(t)}$ each of them having p packets. The subset $Y_{1,i}$ comes from the node u_i, $i = 1, \ldots,$ maxflow(t).

The set $U_2 = \{u_{2,i}|$there is an edge$(u_{2,i}, t_2) \in E\}$ is a set of nodes that are directly connected and send packets to the sink node t_2. We denote the intersection between the sets of nodes U_1 and U_2 as $U_{1,2} = U_1 \cap U_2$. The following three situations are considered:

1. There are no mutual nodes that send packets to both sinks t_1 and t_2, i.e., $U_{1,2} = \emptyset$. In that case find one partition of the set of n packets in maxflow(t) disjoint subsets $\Gamma_1 = \{Y_{2,1} \ldots, Y_{2,\text{maxflow}(t)}\}$ each of them having p packets. The sets of packets $Y_{2,j}$ are delivered to the sink t_2 via the node $u_{2,j}$, $j = 1, \ldots,$ maxflow(t). The multicast capacity for the sink t_2 is achieved in each of p phases.

2. There are nodes that send packets to both sinks t_1 and t_2, i.e., $U_{1,2} = \{u_{(1,2)_{\nu_1}}, \ldots, u_{(1,2)_{\nu_k}}\}$. Denote the nodes that are in $U_2 \backslash U_1 = \{u_{2_{\nu_1}}, \ldots \ldots, u_{2_{\nu_{\text{maxflow}(t)-k}}}\}$. In that case, the sink t_2 receives from the nodes in $U_{1,2}$ the same packets that are delivered to the sink t_1. The number of the remaining packets that have to be delivered to t_2 is exactly $p \times$ (maxflow(t)$-k$). Find one partition of maxflow(t)$-k$ disjoint subsets $\Gamma_2 = \{Y_{2,1} \ldots, Y_{2,\text{maxflow}(t)-k}\}$ each of them having p packets. The sets of packets $Y_{2,j}$ are delivered to the sink t_2 via the node u_{2,ν_j}, $j = 1, \ldots,$ maxflow(t) $- k$. The multicast capacity for the sink t_2 is achieved in each of p phases.

3. All the nodes that send packets to the sink t_1, send packets to the sink t_2 as well, i.e., $U_{1,2} = U_1 \cap U_2 = U_1$. In that case, the sink t_2 receives from the nodes in $U_{1,2}$ the same packets that are delivered to the sink t_1. The multicast capacity for the sink t_2 is achieved in each of p phases.

Note that the proof of Theorem 2 is similar to the work by Jaggi et al. [8] where they discuss a construction of general codes using simple algorithms.

As a consequence of Theorems 1 and 2 we can post the following:

Theorem 3. *For any linearly solvable network topology and for any set of N sinks $T = \{t_1, \ldots, t_N\}$ that have $maxflow(t) = maxflow(t_1) = \ldots = maxflow(t_N)$, there always exists a XOR-ed coding for $n = p \times maxflow(t)$ packets that achieves the multicast capacity in each of p phases.*

Proof. (*Sketch*) First, we recall the construction of generic linear codes presented in the LCM theorem in [12, Th. 5.1]. Second, we use the transformation to equivalent codes over $GF(2)^n$ as it was shown in [16]. Then, the proof is a straightforward application of the mathematical induction by the number of sinks N. Let us suppose that the claim of the theorem is correct for $N-1$ sinks. By adding a new N-th sink we consider again three possible situations as in Theorem 2.

3   Construction of XOR-ed Codes

In this section we describe the construction of codes over $GF(2)$. Instead of working with completely random binary matrices, in the remaining part of this paper we work with nonsingular binary matrices that have some specific structure related to randomly generated Latin square or Latin rectangle. We do not reduce the space of possible random linear network encoding schemes, since the number of Latin squares and Latin rectangles of order n increases proportionally with factorial of n. Therefore, in our approach we have virtually an endless repository of encoding schemes that have the benefits from both worlds: they are randomly generated, but they have a certain structure and offer plausible security properties.

In order to introduce our approach, we briefly use several definitions that the reader can find in [19] and [3].

Definition 2. *A Latin square of order n with entries from an n-set X is an $n \times n$ array L in which every cell contains an element of X such that every row of L is a permutation of X and every column of L is a permutation of X.*

Definition 3. *A $k \times n$ Latin rectangle is a $k \times n$ array (where $k \leq n$) in which each cell contains a single symbol from an n-set X, such that each symbol occurs exactly once in each row and at most once in each column.*

For generating a Latin square, one can always start with a permutation of n elements that is a trivial $1 \times n$ Latin rectangle and can use the old Hall's marriage theorem [5] to construct new rows until the whole Latin square is completed. However, this approach does not guarantee that the generated Latin squares are chosen uniformly at random. In order to generate Latin squares of order n that are chosen uniformly at random we use the algorithm of Jacobsen and Matthews [7]. Further, in our approach we sometimes split the Latin square into two Latin rectangles (upper and lower), and work with the algebraic objects (matrices or block designs) that are related to either the upper or the lower Latin rectangle.

As a convention, throughout this paper, the number of packets n that are sent from the source is equal to the number of columns in the Latin square or Latin rectangle.

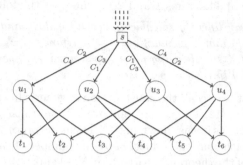

Fig. 2. A 4-dimensional binary linear multicast in a single source multicast network with delay

Example 2. As shown in Fig. 2, we assume that the source wants to send four packets $x_1, \ldots, x_4$ to the sink nodes, and that each sink node has maxflow$(t_k) = 2$, $(k = 1, \ldots, 6)$. The sink nodes receive data from different pair of intermediate nodes, u_i, $(i = 1, \ldots, 4)$. Our aim is all six sink nodes to be able to reconstruct the source packets that are exclusively coded in $GF(2)$.

Let us take the following Latin square and split it into two Latin rectangles:

$$L = \begin{bmatrix} 2 & 4 & 1 & 3 \\ 1 & 3 & 2 & 4 \\ 3 & 2 & 4 & 1 \\ 4 & 1 & 3 & 2 \end{bmatrix}.$$

Each column from the 3×4 upper Latin rectangle represents a combination of source packets in a coded packet c_i, $i = 1, \ldots, 4$. Using the incidence matrix M of the Latin rectangle the source computes the coded packets.

Definition 4. *Let* (X, A) *be a design where* $X = \{x_1, \ldots, x_v\}$ *and* $A = \{A_1, \ldots, A_b\}$. *The incidence matrix of* (X, A) *is the* $v \times b$ *0-1 matrix* $M = (m_{i,j})$ *defined by the rule* $m_{i,j} = \begin{cases} 1, & \text{if } x_i \in A_j, \\ 0, & \text{if } x_i \notin A_j. \end{cases}$

Proposition 1. *The incidence matrix* $M = (m_{i,j})$ *of any Latin rectangle with dimensions* $k \times n$ *is balanced matrix with* k *ones in each row and each column.*

Proof. From the definition of the incidence matrix it follows that the number of ones in each row is equal to the number of elements k in each column of the Latin rectangle. On the other hand, since each row of the Latin rectangle is a permutation of n elements, and there are no elements that occur twice in each column, the number of ones in each column can be neither less nor larger than k.

Note 1. The incidence matrix M of a $k \times n$ Latin rectangle is always balanced. However, the inverse matrix of the incidence matrix M^{-1} is not always balanced.

Proposition 2. *The necessary condition an incidence matrix $M = (m_{i,j})$ of a $k \times n$ Latin rectangle to be nonsingular in $GF(2)$ is k to be odd, i.e., $k = 2l + 1$.*

Proof. Assume that k is even, i.e., $k = 2l$. Recall that a matrix M is nonsingular in $GF(2)$ if and only if its determinant is 1 (or it is singular if and only if its determinant is 0). Recall further the Leibniz formula for the determinant of an $n \times n$ matrix M: $det(M) = \sum_{\sigma \in S_n} sgn(\sigma) \prod_{i=1}^{n} m_{i,\sigma_i}$, where the sum is computed over all elements of the symmetric group of n elements S_n, i.e., over all permutations $\sigma \in S_n$, and $sgn(\sigma)$ is the signature (or the parity of the permutation) whose value is $+1$ or -1. The elements m_{i,σ_i} are the elements $m_{i,j}$ of the matrix M where the value for the index $j = \sigma_i$ is determined as the i–th element of the permutation σ.

If $k = 2l$ is even, from Proposition 1 and from the fact that operations are performed in $GF(2)$, it follows that every summand in the Leibniz formula gives an even number of nonzero products, thus the final sum must be even, i.e., the determinant in $GF(2)$ is 0.

The corresponding 4×4 incidence matrix of the Latin rectangle in Example 2 is nonsingular in $GF(2)$ (Proposition 2). M is represented as

$$M = \begin{bmatrix} 1 & 1 & 1 & 0 \\ 0 & 1 & 1 & 1 \\ 1 & 1 & 0 & 1 \\ 1 & 0 & 1 & 1 \end{bmatrix}.$$

A direct consequence from Theorem 1 is the following:

Corollary 1. *A sink node $t \in T$ with $maxflow(t)$ can receive n source packets, encoded with the incidence matrix of a $k \times n$ Latin rectangle in $GF(2)$, in $p = \lceil \frac{n}{maxflow(t)} \rceil$ phases. In each phase the sink node reaches its $maxflow(t)$.*

Following Corollary 1 the number of phases in which packets are sent depends from the total number of packets and $maxflow(t_k)$.

Using M the source computes the vector of coded packets as

$$\mathbf{c} = M\mathbf{x} = [c_1, c_2, c_3, c_4]^{\top}$$

where $\mathbf{x} = [x_1, x_2, x_3, x_4]^{\top}$ is a vector of the source packets. The coded packets are XOR-ed combinations of the source packets, i.e.,

$$c_1 = x_1 \oplus x_2 \oplus x_3,$$
$$c_2 = x_2 \oplus x_3 \oplus x_4,$$
$$c_3 = x_1 \oplus x_2 \oplus x_4,$$
$$c_4 = x_1 \oplus x_3 \oplus x_4.$$

The source further prepends the information from the incidence matrix to each of the coded packets. The vector of packets that are sent becomes as follows: $\mathbf{C} = \{(1,2,3,c_1),(2,3,4,c_2),(1,2,4,c_3),(1,3,4,c_4)\} = \{C_1, C_2, C_3, C_4\}$. The sink nodes receive in each phase a pair of different packets as shown in Table 1. Their

Table 1. Description of receiving coded packets in each phase at the sink nodes

	t_1	t_2	t_3	t_4	t_5	t_6
First phase	C_4, C_1	C_4, C_3	C_4, C_3	C_1, C_2	C_1, C_2	C_3, C_2
Second phase	C_2, C_3	C_2, C_1	C_2, C_1	C_3, C_4	C_3, C_4	C_1, C_4

buffer should be large enough to store the received packets C_i, $i = 1, \ldots, 4$. The decoding at the sink nodes is performed by M^{-1}. Each sink node computes M^{-1} from the prepended indexes. The original packets x_i, $i = 1, \ldots, 4$, are reconstructed as $\mathbf{x} = M^{-1}\mathbf{c}$. Note that although our approach is similar to [16], we use a systematic selection of the encoding functions and we do not send plain packets on the disjoint paths.

4   Additional Plausible Security Properties of the Balanced XOR-ed Coding

The work with incidence matrices related to randomly generated Latin rectangles is actually a work with balanced block designs. However, as we noted in Note 1, it is not necessary both the incidence matrix and its inverse matrix to be completely balanced. If we are interested in the complexity of decoding and the security issues when an adversary can successfully decode some sniffed packets, then the easiest way to address these issues is to give equal level of security to all encoded packets. In our approach this can be easily achieved by switching the roles of the incidence matrix and its inverse matrix: the encoding of the source packets is done with the inverse matrix of the incidence matrix and decoding of the coded packets is done with the incidence matrix. By applying this approach, decoding of any of the source packets requires an equal number of coded packets.

Corollary 2. *For each value of maxflow(t) and a number of source packets n which is multiple of maxflow(t), there exists a Latin rectangle with $n-1$ or $n-2$ rows and its incidence matrix can be used for decoding.*

Due to Proposition 2, when n is even the necessary requirement for a nonsingular incidence matrix is the Latin rectangle to have $n - 1$ rows. When n is odd the necessary requirement for a nonsingular incidence matrix is the Latin rectangle to have $n - 2$ rows.

Theorem 4. *When decoding is performed with the incidence matrix from Corollary 2, any eavesdropper needs to listen at least maxflow(t) links in order to decode at least one source packet.*

Proof. Assume that an adversary eavesdrops maxflow(t) $- 1$ links. Since the incidence matrix used for decoding is related to a Latin rectangle with $n - 1$ or $n - 2$ rows, eavesdropping "just" maxflow(t) $- 1$ links is not sufficient for the adversary to receive at least one subset of $n - 1$ or $n - 2$ packets from which he/she can decode at least one original packet.

Another remark that can be given about our approach is that the number of XOR operations between different packets (both in the source and in the sink nodes) is relatively high. We can address that remark by using Latin rectangles with smaller number of rows as a trade-off between the number of encoding/decoding operations and the ability of an adversary to decode a source packet. Namely, the encoding and decoding efforts at the source and sink node are the highest when encoding and decoding requires $n-1$ or $n-2$ packets. In order to decrease the number of operations at the nodes, the Latin rectangle should have $k \leq n-2$ rows. However, we are interested to reduce the number k without reducing the number of links that have to be listened by an eavesdropper in order to decode at least one original packet. The following theorem gives the necessary and sufficient condition for that to happen:

Theorem 5. *Let the coding be done by M^{-1} obtained from a Latin rectangle $L_{k \times n}$ of size $k \times n$, where $k \leq n-2$. Further, assume that the transfer is done by sending n packets from s to t in $p = \lceil \frac{n}{maxflow(t)} \rceil$ phases on $maxflow(t)$ disjoint paths and let the sets of indexes of the packets sent via i-th disjoint path are denoted by $S_i, i = 1, \ldots, maxflow(t)$. A necessary and sufficient condition for an eavesdropper to need to listen at least $maxflow(t)$ links in order to decode at least one original packet is:*

$$\forall j \in \{1, \ldots, n\}, \forall i \in \{1, \ldots, maxflow(t)\} : L_{k,j} \cap S_i \neq \emptyset, \tag{1}$$

where $L_{k,j}, j \in \{1, \ldots, n\}$ is the set of elements in the j-th column of the Latin rectangle $L_{k \times n}$.

Proof. To show that the condition (1) is necessary assume that an eavesdropper needs $maxflow(t) - 1$ links in order to decode one original packet x_l, and let us denote by S_m the set of indexes of the packets sent via the disjoint path that was not listened by the eavesdropper. This means that for the l-th column $L_{k,l}$ of the Latin rectangle $L_{k \times n}$: $L_{k,l} \cap S_m = \emptyset$ which violates the condition (1).

To show that the condition (1) is sufficient, let us denote by $S_{i,j} = L_{k,j} \cap S_i$, $j \in \{1, \ldots, n\}, i \in \{1, \ldots, maxflow(t)\}$. It is sufficient to notice that $S_{i,j}$ are disjunctive partitions for every set $L_{k,j}$, i.e.,

$$\forall j \in \{1, \ldots, n\} : \bigcup_{i=1}^{maxflow(t)} S_{i,j} = L_{k,j}$$

and

$$\forall j_1, j_2 \in \{1, \ldots, n\} : S_{i,j_1} \cap S_{i,j_2} = \emptyset.$$

Since $|L_{k,j}| = k$, and the encoding of original n packets is done by M^{-1}, it follows that an eavesdropper can decode any original packet only by listening at least $maxflow(t)$ links.

Example 3. We present an example that illustrates the security in our approach. The goal is to achieve secrecy[1] so that a passive adversary is able to reconstruct n source packets only when at least maxflow(t) links are eavesdropped. By sending XOR-ed packets on disjoint paths (exploiting the path diversity), an adversary is unable to decode the message although several paths are eavesdropped. Let us consider the network shown in Fig.3, where a source s communicates with two sinks t_1 and t_2 with the help of intermediate nodes u_i, $i = 1, 2, 3$, and sends twelve packets to t_1 and t_2. Packets are sent in four phases since maxflow(t) = 3. Let us use the following 5×12 Latin rectangle:

$$L_{5 \times 12} = \begin{bmatrix} 4 & 2 & 11 & 8 & 12 & 1 & 9 & 5 & 10 & 7 & 6 & 3 \\ 2 & 8 & 12 & 3 & 6 & 10 & 4 & 11 & 5 & 1 & 9 & 7 \\ 3 & 4 & 2 & 9 & 11 & 12 & 5 & 6 & 7 & 8 & 10 & 1 \\ 9 & 10 & 1 & 6 & 3 & 7 & 2 & 8 & 4 & 11 & 12 & 5 \\ 6 & 5 & 7 & 10 & 1 & 11 & 8 & 3 & 12 & 4 & 2 & 9 \end{bmatrix}.$$

The colors of indexes in $L_{5 \times 12}$ correspond to the colors of the packets as they are sent in Fig 3. If the sink nodes reconstruct the source packets with M^{-1}, then not all packets have the same level of decoding complexity. That is demonstrated with relations (2) and (3). For instance, to decode x_4, x_7 and x_8 nine coded packets are needed, while to decode x_5 and x_{11} just three packets are needed. The goal is to avoid this non-balanced complexity in the decoding. Therefore, as in Theorem 5 the encoding is done by M^{-1} and the decoding by M. When s computes the vector of coded packets as $\mathbf{c} = M^{-1}\mathbf{x}$, then the coded packets c_i, $i = 1, \ldots, 12$ are XOR-ed combinations of different number of source packets. Consequently, decoding of packets is done with a balanced matrix, i.e., $\mathbf{x} = M\mathbf{c}$.

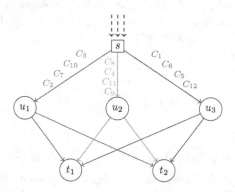

Fig. 3. Routing of 12 packets for secure coding when decoding is performed with 5 coded packets

---

[1] We use here the term *secrecy* as it is used in [13, Ch.7 pp. 185].

$$
\begin{aligned}
c_1 &= x_2 \oplus x_3 \oplus x_4 \oplus x_6 \oplus x_9, \\
c_2 &= x_2 \oplus x_4 \oplus x_5 \oplus x_8 \oplus x_{10}, \\
c_3 &= x_1 \oplus x_2 \oplus x_7 \oplus x_{11} \oplus x_{12}, \\
c_4 &= x_3 \oplus x_6 \oplus x_8 \oplus x_9 \oplus x_{10}, \\
c_5 &= x_1 \oplus x_3 \oplus x_6 \oplus x_{11} \oplus x_{12}, \\
c_6 &= x_1 \oplus x_7 \oplus x_{10} \oplus x_{11} \oplus x_{12}, \\
c_7 &= x_2 \oplus x_4 \oplus x_5 \oplus x_8 \oplus x_9, \\
c_8 &= x_3 \oplus x_5 \oplus x_6 \oplus x_8 \oplus x_{11}, \\
c_9 &= x_4 \oplus x_5 \oplus x_7 \oplus x_{10} \oplus x_{12}, \\
c_{10} &= x_1 \oplus x_4 \oplus x_7 \oplus x_8 \oplus x_{11}, \\
c_{11} &= x_2 \oplus x_6 \oplus x_9 \oplus x_{10} \oplus x_{12}, \\
c_{12} &= x_1 \oplus x_3 \oplus x_5 \oplus x_7 \oplus x_9.
\end{aligned} \quad (2)
$$

$$
\begin{aligned}
x_1 &= c_2 \oplus c_5 \oplus c_{10} \oplus c_{11} \oplus c_{12}, \\
x_2 &= c_1 \oplus c_3 \oplus c_5 \oplus c_6 \oplus c_7 \oplus c_9 \oplus c_{10}, \\
x_3 &= c_3 \oplus c_5 \oplus c_6 \oplus c_7 \oplus c_8 \oplus c_9 \oplus c_{12}, \\
x_4 &= c_4 \oplus c_5 \oplus c_6 \oplus c_7 \oplus c_8 \oplus c_9 \oplus c_{10} \oplus c_{11} \oplus c_{12}, \\
x_5 &= c_1 \oplus c_2 \oplus c_4, \\
x_6 &= c_1 \oplus c_2 \oplus c_4 \oplus c_6 \oplus c_7 \oplus c_{10} \oplus c_{11}, \\
x_7 &= c_2 \oplus c_3 \oplus c_4 \oplus c_5 \oplus c_6 \oplus c_7 \oplus c_8 \oplus c_{11} \oplus c_{12}, \\
x_8 &= c_1 \oplus c_3 \oplus c_5 \oplus c_7 \oplus c_8 \oplus c_9 \oplus c_{10} \oplus c_{11} \oplus c_{12}, \\
x_9 &= c_1 \oplus c_2 \oplus c_5 \oplus c_9 \oplus c_{10}, \\
x_{10} &= c_1 \oplus c_5 \oplus c_7 \oplus c_9 \oplus c_{10}, \\
x_{11} &= c_1 \oplus c_7 \oplus c_8, \\
x_{12} &= c_3 \oplus c_4 \oplus c_5 \oplus c_7 \oplus c_9.
\end{aligned} \quad (3)
$$

Assume that the routing is as follows: on the first path the source sends (C_3, C_{10}, C_7, C_2), on the second path (C_8, C_4, C_{11}, C_9) and (C_1, C_6, C_5, C_{12}) on the third path as it is shown in Fig.3. We use three different colors for the packets sent to three disjoint paths in order to demonstrate the essence of the proof of Theorem 5. Note that all colors are present in every column of the Latin rectangle $L_{5 \times 12}$. This corresponds to the condition (1) in Theorem 5. In order to reconstruct at least one source packet, an adversary must eavesdrop at least 3 links.

5   Conclusions

In this paper we have presented a construction of codes over $GF(2)$ which reach the max-flow for single source multicast acyclic networks with delay. The coding is exclusively performed in $GF(2)$, i.e., it is a bitwise XOR of packets with equal lengths. The encoding and decoding are based on balanced nonsingular matrices that are obtained as incidence matrices from Latin rectangles. Balanced XOR-ed coding is of particular importance for energy and processor constraint devices. Additionally, we showed that the approach offers plausible security properties, i.e., if an eavesdropper wants to reconstruct at least one original packet, then the number of eavesdropped links must be equal to the max-flow of the network.

Possible future work includes intermediate nodes to form coded packets, as well as building networks dynamically by adding more and more sink nodes that reach the max-flow when the coding is XOR-ed coding.

Acknowledgements. We would like to thank Gergely Biczók for his discussions and remarks that significantly improved the paper.

References

1. Ahlswede, R., Cai, N., Li, S.Y.R., Yeung, R.W.: Network information flow. IEEE Transactions on Information Theory 46, 1204–1216 (2000)
2. Bhattad, K., Narayanan, K.R.: Weakly secure network coding. In: Proc. First Workshop on Network Coding, Theory, and Applications, NetCod (2005)

3. Colbourn, C.J., Dinitz, J.H.: Handbook of Combinatorial Designs. Chapman, Hall/CRC (2006)
4. Colbourn, C.J., Dinitz, J.H., Stinson, D.R.: Applications of combinatorial designs to communications, cryptography, and networking (1999)
5. Hall, P.: On representatives of subsets. J. London Math. Soc. 37, 26–30 (1935)
6. Ho, T., Médard, M., Koetter, R., Karger, D.R., Effros, M., Shi, J., Leong, B.: A random linear network coding approach to multicast. IEEE Transactions on Information Theory 52, 4413–4430 (2006)
7. Jacobson, M.T., Matthews, P.: Generating uniformly distributed random latin squares. Journal of Combinatorial Designs 6, 405–437 (1996)
8. Jaggi, S., Cassuto, Y., Effros, M.: Low complexity encoding for network codes. In: IEEE International Symposium on Information Theory, pp. 40–44 (2006)
9. Katti, S., Rahul, H., Hu, W., Katabi, D., Médard, M., Crowcroft, J.: XORs in the air: Practical wireless network coding. IEEE/ACM Trans. Netw. 3, 497–510 (2008)
10. Koetter, R., Médard, M.: An algebraic approach to network coding. IEEE/ACM Trans. Netw. 5, 782–795 (2003)
11. Lawler, E.: Combinatorial Optimization: Networks and Matroids. Dover Publications (2001)
12. Li, S.Y.R., Yeung, R.W., Cai, N.: Linear network coding. IEEE Transactions on Information Theory 2, 371–381 (2003)
13. Médard, M., Sprintson, A.: Network coding. Fundamentals and Applications. Academic Press (2012)
14. Pedersen, M.V., Fitzek, F.H.P., Larsen, T.: Implementation and performance evaluation of network coding for cooperative mobile devices. In: IEEE Cognitive and Cooperative Wireless Networks Workshop (2008)
15. Qureshi, J., Foh, C.H., Cai, J.: Optimal solution for the index coding problem using network coding over gf(2). In: IEEE Communications Society Conference on Sensor, Mesh and Ad Hoc Communications and Networks (SECON), pp. 209–217 (2012)
16. Riis, S.: Linear versus nonlinear boolean functions in network flow. In: CISS (2004)
17. Rouayheb, S.Y.E., Sprintson, A., Georghiades, C.N.: On the index coding problem and its relation to network coding and matroid theory. Submitted to IEEE Transactions on Information Theory (2008)
18. Shojania, H., Li, B.: Random network coding on the iphone: fact or fiction? In: NOSSDAV (2009)
19. Stinson, D.R.: Combinatorial Designs: Constructions and Analysis. Springer (2003)
20. Vingelmann, P., Pedersen, M.V., Fitzek, F.H.P., Heide, J.: Multimedia distribution using network coding on the iphone platform. In: Proceedings of the 2010 ACM Multimedia Workshop on Mobile Cloud Media Computing (2010)

Architecture and Functional Framework for Home Energy Management Systems

Kornschnok Dittawit and Finn Arve Aagesen

Department of Telematics,
Norwegian University of Science and Technology, Norway
{kornschd,finnarve}@item.ntnu.no

Abstract. Residential consumers contribute to a substantial amount of electricity consumption. To ensure grid stability, a Home Energy Management System (EMS) that assists household inhabitants in operating home devices to achieve optimized energy usage is needed. Previous designs of Home EMS often have some issues. First, it places high implementation overhead on device vendors to manufacture devices compatible with the system. Second, it lacks the ability to scale when new device types and external variables are introduced. This paper proposes an architecture model and a functional framework for Home EMS that are simple and scalable. The framework defines functions of Home EMS components. A policy-based reasoning mechanism is proposed as part of the framework for the optimization of home energy usage. In addition, the inter-working of Home EMS components is presented. It relies on a semantic web language for data representation to provide meaningful information for reasoning and harmonization with existing standards.

Keywords: energy management system, smart home, smart grid, demand side management, policy-based reasoning.

1 Introduction

Today's power grid is the result of over hundred years of evolution [1]. At present, there is a vision to transform the present grid into what is denoted as the *Smart Grid*. In Smart Grid, distributed generation (DG) is promoted, consumers are offered more choices and real-time information, and information and communication technology is tightly integrated for better management. The market is also changing to become more deregulated with the entry of smaller power providers and the possibility of consumers to provide power. As a research area, Smart Grid is considered a multidisciplinary area that spans over multiple domains. This paper looks at the residential demand side of the power grid.

In the EU, residential electricity consumption in 2010 accounted for around one-third of the total consumption [2]. This ratio indicates the importance and the influence of households on the power grid. In other words, electricity usage by households affects grid stability as a whole. This can be seen especially during peak periods when power demand rises and causes a strain to the power grid.

T. Bauschert (Ed.): EUNICE 2013, LNCS 8115, pp. 173–184, 2013.

One way of ensuring grid stability is the adjustment of consumer energy consumption pattern. To facilitate the adjustment process, assistance to consumers will be needed to decide on how to operate home devices to achieve optimized energy usage. New commercial products are being pushed out that include some energy management functions and there have been many attempts to design a central system to manage home devices. However, the problems with most these product and system designs are 1) it does not look at the hollistic view of the system and was designed to solve a specific problem with no concern on the other components that exist on the power grid 2) it requires specially manufactured devices in order to be compatible with the system which puts a lot of implementation overhead to device vendors and prevents market entry of the system and 3) it lacks scalability when new device types and external variables are introduced. Although it is not possible in practice to design a system to handle new unknown problems, it is possible to design a framework that will serve as a solid and scalable foundation for future solutions.

This paper proposes an architecture model and a functional framework for Home Energy Management System (EMS), a system in a house that assists household inhabitants in operating home devices to achieve optimized energy usage. The architecture model looks at a hollistic view of the system and takes into account the major entities on the power grid which are the Distribution System Operators (DSOs) and Energy Service Providers (ESPs). It was designed to be simple and scalable to enable rapid deployment and also to be integratedly easily with existing standards, namely Sensor Web Enablement [3] and IEC61970-501 [4] which is suggested for use in the power industry. Home EMS components, component functions, and Home EMS inter-working framework have been defined. A policy-based reasoning mechanism is also proposed for energy management as part of the functional framework.

The remaining part of this paper is organized as follows. Section 2 discusses present technology and related works. Section 3 presents the proposed architecture and functional framework. Energy management in Home EMS is discussed in Section 4. Home EMS inter-working framework is presented in Section 5. Section 6 summarizes and concludes.

2   Present Technology and Related Works

With the increasing concerns in energy conservation and energy efficiency, device vendors are responding to this issue by developing products that facilitate energy savings in households and are more energy efficient. Most of the released products provide the basic function to control the status of home appliances. For example, a consumer may control appliance statuses from the comfort of his mobile device and PC or set a timer to turn the appliances on or off [5] [6]. Some vendors provide a way for consumers to monitor energy consumption for an individual appliance with a specific apparatus [7]. Modern washing machines have a delay start function that allows consumers to set the start time for the washing machine so as to avoid peak periods. As useful as they are, these devices were designed to solve very specific problems and the functions offered are only a small subset of functions that will be incorporated into consumer houses in the future. In addition, some functions such as the delay start function still require consumers to make difficult decisions based on various information sources with no assistance which results in most of these functions left unused. With some analysis, we would see that the value of these new appliances lies in the automation and scheduling of their basic operations, so what is needed is a decision support system that aids household inhabitants in controlling and coordinating appliances to optimize energy usage, i.e., Home EMS is needed.

There have been many research activities related to Home EMS including the effort by the European Commission which funded several research projects under the Seventh Framework Programme (FP7) such as AIM [8], Beywatch [9], and Smart House/Smart Grid (SH/SG) [10]. In AIM, the inter-working between home devices and the central system was well-designed and it is the same principle used in our proposal. The difference is our use of semantic web language for device information and message-based communication for operation and service invocation as opposed to packet-based solution in AIM. Our message-based solution provides greater flexibility and negates the need to establish standardized command codes before the manufacturing of home devices. The objective of Beywatch included the design of energy efficient white goods. As a result, the appliances that were compatible with Beywatch system had to be specifically manufactured. In SH/SG, energy management was done by algorithmic systems which means substantial effort will be required to change the logic if new device types and external variables are introduced into the picture. In terms of the system architecture, two reference models can be derived from the three projects based on the connectivity among the related systems as depicted in Fig. 1. In model A used by Beywatch, Home EMS is connected to an entity that hosts a medium which is further connected to power utilities and external service providers (SPs). The entity is called Service Provider in Beywatch which implies it can be any entity. In this case, we assume it is the DSO that takes the position of that entity and thus the utilities include only ESPs. In model B used by AIM and SH/SG, Home EMS is connected to DSO, ESPs, and external SPs directly. The comparison between the two models is presented in Table 1. The proposed architecture follows model B for the benefits described and its flexibility of consumers to switch or establish connections to other external SPs.

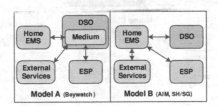

Fig. 1. Common architecture models for Home EMS

Table 1. Comparison between model A and B

Model A	Model B
Advantages: - Avoid the need to have communication infrastructure between Home EMS and ESPs - All consumers with the same DSO have equal access to external services	*Advantages:* - Promotes competition among the vendors of Home EMS to implement access to a variety of external services - Potentially less delay
Disadvantages: - There may be delay for data between Home EMS and ESPs - DSO has more responsibilities	*Disadvantages:* - Need communication infrastructure between Home EMS and ESPs

3   Home EMS Architecture and Component Functions

3.1   Overview

A Home EMS consists of various components, each responsible for different tasks and manufactured by different vendors. An overview of the architectural components and logical connections in Home EMS and external systems is illustrated in Fig. 2. There are three main component types residing in the house: Consumer Support System (CSS), home devices (e.g. energy consumer devicess, sensor devices, power producer devices, energy storage devices.), and a DSO energy meter. Home EMS is connected to external systems including DSO, ESPs, and other service providers. The connection to DSO and ESPs can be via the meter (alternative #1) or CSS (alternative #2). In the latter, the meter also sends electricity usage data to DSO for billing. Section 3.2 and 3.3 explains the functions of the two most important component types, CSS and home devices.

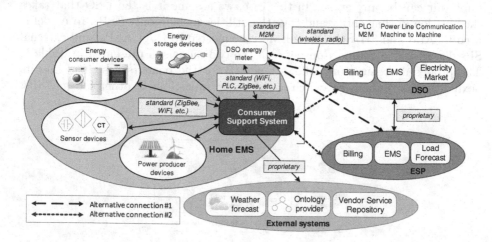

Fig. 2. Home EMS architecture

3.2   Consumer Support System Functionality

CSS is a computing device in Home EMS that is responsible for energy management, which is the monitoring, controlling, and coordinating of home devices with the help of data obtained from various external systems and home devices in order to optimized energy usage. The proposed functions required by CSS in order to perform energy management are grouped into five main function groups: basic function, policy/goal/constraint management, service and device configuration, monitoring and diagnosis, and user interface. These functions are realized by a combination of Extended Finite State Machines (EFSMs) and a policy-based reasoning machine (see Sect. 4 for more details). Each function group performs sub-functions as shown in Fig. 3. The data maintained by CSS is stored in five different repositories based on the type of data. The details of each function group and repository are given.

Basic Function (BSC). BSC performs normal operation and suspended operation. Normal operation refers to an operation mode where CSS performs actions based on the policies, goals, and constraints defined in the system. Suspended operation refers to an operation mode where energy management control actions are taken entirely by the consumer. This could occur from system failure or from deactivation by the consumer.

Policy/Goal/Constraint Management (PGC). PGC maintains policies, goals, and constraints in the system. This includes the specification, update, and (re-)validation actions. (Re-)validation applies only to policies. The actions of specifying and updating policies, goals, and constraints could be initiated by the consumer through the CSS user interface or by CSS itself.

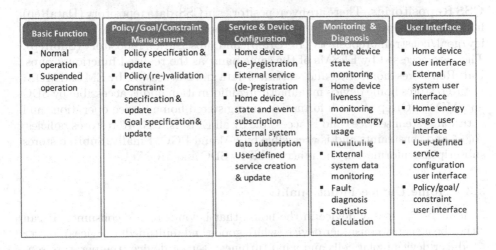

Basic Function	Policy/Goal/Constraint Management	Service & Device Configuration	Monitoring & Diagnosis	User Interface
• Normal operation • Suspended operation	• Policy specification & update • Policy (re-)validation • Constraint specification & update • Goal specification & update	• Home device (de-)registration • External service (de-)registration • Home device state and event subscription • External system data subscription • User-defined service creation & update	• Home device state monitoring • Home device liveness monitoring • Home energy usage monitoring • External system data monitoring • Fault diagnosis • Statistics calculation	• Home device user interface • External system user interface • Home energy usage user interface • User-defined service configuration user interface • Policy/goal/constraint user interface

Fig. 3. CSS functions

Service and Device Configuration (SDC). SDC mainly handles the registration and deregistration of home devices and external services. It also maintains subscription of data and event from home devices and external systems. In addition, it creates and updates consumer-defined services from the consumer inputs given through the user interface.

Monitoring and Diagnosis (MON). MON performs home device state monitoring, home device liveness monitoring, home energy usage monitoring, external system data monitoring, fault diagnosis, and statistics calculation. Home device state monitoring monitors the states of home devices. Home device liveness monitoring monitors the operating status of the device, which could at one time be normal mode, standby mode, or off mode. Home energy usage monitoring monitors energy consumption, production, and storage for the entire household and for individual home devices. External system data monitoring monitors data provided by external systems. Fault diagnosis is the analysis of faults found in Home EMS components. Statistics calculation is the collection and calculation of historical data such as electricity cost and energy consumption heuristics.

User Interface (UI). UI is responsible for providing graphical user interfaces for the consumer to manage home devices, external system services, consumer-defined services, and policies/goals/constraints. It also displays results from consumer requests, feedbacks from executed actions, and subscribed data and event notifications. CSS must be able to render any device's and system's generic user interface based on the information of the device and system provided in the common agreed format. It may render a vendor-customized user interface if a custom template is provided. The user interface is web-based and is rendered by XSLT (http://www.w3.org/TR/xslt) technique.

CSS Repositories. There are five repositories in CSS: data repository (DataRep), home device repository (DevRep), service and operation repository (SORep), policy/goal/constraint repository (PGCRep), and subscription repository (SubRep). They are accessed by EFSMs of the same name as the realized function groups. DataRep stores monitoring and statistical data and is accessible by EM and MON. DevRep stores home device manufacturing information and is accessible by SDC and MON. SORep stores information on registered home device operations and external system services and is accessible by all EFSMs. PGCRep stores policies, goals, and constraints and is accessible by EM and PGC. Finally, SubRep stores subscription information and is accessible by SDC and MON.

3.3   Home Device Functionality

A home device is any device in the house that belongs to the consumer. It can either be a energy consumer device (white goods and multimedia devices), power producer device (solar cells and wind turbines), sensor device (temperature sensor and motion sensor), or energy storage device (electric vehicles). In most cases,

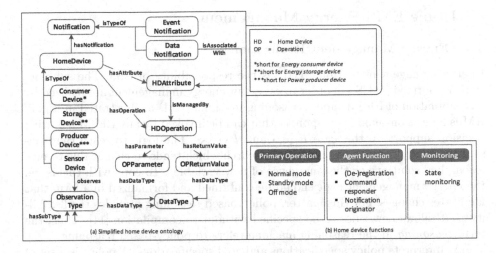

Fig. 4. Home component ontology and functions

a home device has attributes (e.g. temperature and status) and performs operations (e.g. get/set temperature, get/set status). This could be slightly different in case of a sensor. A sensor normally provides measurements on its observed environmental property. Some sensors only publish measurements to CSS hence no operations. Others might be capable of returning measurements upon request. See Fig. 4(a) for a home device ontology. The functionalities of a home device are grouped into three function groups: primary operation, agent function, and monitoring. Each function group is comprised of subfunctions as shown in Fig. 4(b). Note that for a simple device such as a sensor, some functions may not be implemented. For example, there could be only one operation mode for a sensor. In addition, a home device needs a functional component for both communicating with CSS and with itself via electrical signals to perform Primary Operation and Monitoring functions as instructed by CSS. This component is denoted as a CSS Agent and it is the entity performing Agent Function.

Primary operation handles home device operations in different operating modes. A device can be in normal mode where it is able to receive commands and send responses and notifications to CSS, standby mode where it is able to receive wakeup signal, or off mode. In off mode, the device is still a part of Home EMS but cannot interact with the system. It has to be turned on manually by the consumer.

Agent function responds to commands, and sends out subscribed notifications. It also handles the (de-)registration of the device to CSS.

Monitoring monitors the inherent attributes of itself, i.e. the state, and may store the state data in its internal datastore.

4   Home EMS Energy Management

4.1   Energy Management Realization

Energy management in Home EMS is the responsibility of CSS. The subfunctions performed by CSS in order to carry out energy management are realized by a combination of EFSMs and a reasoning machine (RM) as illustrated in Fig. 5. RM is a decision-making component that can be invoked by any EFSM requiring decision support, in this case E_{BSC} and E_{MON}. The logic to reach the decisions normally comes from extensive research which tends to change due to new researched solutions or the emergence of new variables. To cope with this issue, the energy management logic should be contained and formalized in a form that facilitates changes. For this matter, policy-based reasoning provides the flexibility that allows new rules to be specified without re-compilation [11]. Thus, the term *reasoning* in the reasoning machine refers to policy-based reasoning.

RM interprets policy specifications and goal specifications. A policy is a set of rules and actions. Rules are defined by variables and constraints. Variables are relevant data required in order to select actions. There are two types of variables: decision variable and dynamic variable. A decision variable is what needs to be determined by RM, e.g. the start time of a device. A dynamic variable is data that changes as a function of time and may be beyond the control scope of RM, e.g. energy and grid prices. Dynamic variables influence the values of decision variables. For example, grid price (dynamic) during certain time of day is high so the start time (decision) could be delayed to reduce cost. Constraints are imposed on decision variables which, consequently, restrict the possible actions. Each action has a cost. Goals are associated with policies and define the targets to achieve. The goal specification and costs of actions determine the selection

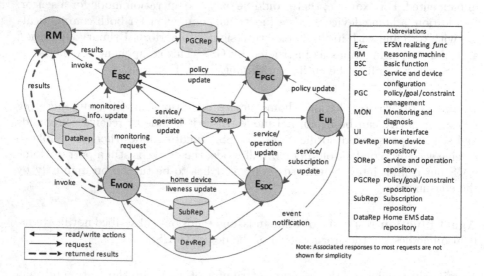

Fig. 5. ESFM and RM interaction diagram

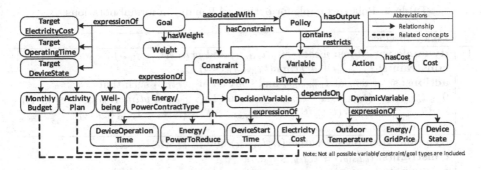

Fig. 6. Policy and goal ontology model

of actions when more than one action set is applicable. The decided actions, which are mainly operating instructions, will be executed on home devices. Fig. 6 depicts an ontology model for all related concepts. For readability, the example constraints are high-level concepts that can be formulated by decision variables.

Policies are ideally created and updated by the CSS vendor. The constraint values are set by the consumer. Apart from the policies themselves, statistics related to energy consumption heuristics of home devices can be used to adjust some estimates that will improve the decision making by RM.

4.2 Policy Example: Optimized Laundry

One policy example that operates a washing machine (wm) at the optimal time and further suggests the method and time to dry clothes (electric dryer (ed) or outdoor drying (od)) is described. The maximum delay between activities is one hour. The goal is to minimize the electricity cost. The constraint is the latest finish time. Two policies are described in Table 2. Dynamic variables are specified explicitly. Decision variables are the start time, dry time, and cost. The first policy describes a case when od is selected while the second policy describes a case when ed is selected. For both cases, the optimal times to start wm, od, and ed are selected based on the weather conditions retrieved from an external weather service and electricity prices retrieved from DSO and ESP which are used to calculate the end time and the electricity cost.

Let:

t_c	represents	currrent hour
$t_{[device],start}$	represents	start time of the *device*
$t_{[device],end}$	represents	end time of the *device*
t_{latest}	represents	latest finish time
t_{wash}	represents	washing duration (hour)
t_{edry}	represents	drying duration by electric dryer (hour)
$w_{[device]}$	represents	power consumption by *device* (kW)
$weather(t_1, t_2)$	represents	a set of weather conditions from t_1 to t_2
$prices(t_1, t_2)$	represents	a set of electricity prices from t_1 to t_2
$p(t_1, t_2)$	represents	average electricity price from t_1 to t_2

Table 2. Policy example for optimized laundry in formal notations

#	Policy specifications
1	**dynamic variables:** $weather(t_c, t_{latest})$ and $prices(t_c, t_{latest})$ **constraints:** $t_{od,start} + drytime(t_{od,start}) \leq t_{latest}$ **actions:** start wm at $t_{wm,start}$ and start od at $t_{od,start}$ such that $0 \leq t_{od,start} - (t_{wm,start} + t_{wash}) \leq 1h$ and $t_{od,start} + drytime(t_{od,start}) \leq t_{latest}$ and $c(t_{wm,start}) < c(t) \quad \forall t \in T - t_{wm,start}, T = \{t_c, t_c + 1, ..., t_{latest}\}$ **cost:** $c(t) = w_{wm} \times t_{wash} \times p(t, t + t_{wash})$
2	**dynamic variables:** $weather(t_c, t_{latest})$ and $prices(t_c, t_{latest})$ **constraints:** $t_{ed,start} + t_{edry} \leq t_{latest}$ **actions:** start wm at $t_{wm,start}$ and start ed at $t_{ed,start}$ such that $0 \leq t_{ed,start} - (t_{wm,start} + t_{wash}) \leq 1h$ and $t_{ed,start} + t_{edry} \leq t_{latest}$ and $c(t_{wm,start}, t_{ed,start}) < c(t_1, t_2) \quad \forall (t_1 \in T - t_{wm,start}, t_2 \in T - t_{ed,start}), T = \{t_c, t_c + 1, ..., t_{latest}\}$ **cost:** $c(t_1, t_2) = (w_{wm} \times t_{wash} \times p(t_1, t_1 + t_{wash})) + (w_{ed} \times t_{edry} \times p(t_2, t_2 + t_{edry}))$

And $drytime(t)$ is the estimated outdoor drying duration in hours which is calculated as a function of the weather conditions from time t to t_{latest} (see (1)). The estimation is based on the heuristics related to the temperature, wind, and humidity. Infinite duration means outdoor drying is not possible.

$$drytime(t) = f(weather(t, t_{latest})) \in \{1, 2, ..., \infty\} \tag{1}$$

5 Home EMS Inter-working Framework

An inter-working framework is here defined as an application layer framework that governs how CSS, home devices, and external systems communicate with one another. Two things are defined: 1) a common and formal format for operation and service description and 2) operation and service invocation.

Operations and services provided by home devices and external systems need to be defined in a common agreed format to be accessible and executable by CSS. The required elements to be defined are ID, name, and description, with the optional addition of parameters and return values. We propose the use of RDF/XML as a language for operation and service definitions as well as home device and external system information. Resource Description Framework (RDF) [12] is a semantic web language for describing resources on the web. There are four reasons for choosing RDF: 1) it can be expected that full ontology models for appliances will be standardized 2) RDF is good at modeling relationships in a meaningful way which can be used by CSS to make decisions 3) RDF is suggested as a data exchange format to be used by power utilities in IEC61970-501 [4] hence simpler integration with DSO and ESPs. 4) Semantic Sensor Network Ontology [13] coupled with Sensor Web Enablement [3] can be used for the description and measurement data of sensors. Fig. 7(a) shows a simplified device information file of a washing machine. RDF terms used are

```
<rdf:Description rdf :about="washing-TS169">
   <rdf:type rdf :resource ="&hems;WashingMachine "/>
   <hems:hasVoltageLevel >230</hems:hasVoltageLevel >
   <hems:hasOperation rdf :resource ="SetProgram "/>
   <hems:hasOperation rdf :resource ="StartLaundry "/>
   <hems:hasNotification
      rdf:resource ="FilterNeedsReplacing "/>
</rdf:Description >

<rdf:Description rdf :about="SetProgram ">
   <owl:sameAs
      rdf:resource ="&hems;SetWashingProgram "/>
   <hems:opName >setProgram </hems:opName >
   <hems:hasParameter
      rdf:resource ="SetProgramParam _watertemp />
</rdf:Descripton >

<rdf:Description
   rdf:about="SetProgramParam _watertemp ">
   <hems:hasDataType
      rdf:dataType ="&hems;Integer "/>
</rdf:Description >
```

(a) Simplified device information description in RDF/XML

```
M-POST / HTTP/1.1                          HTTP header
HOST : 192.168.1.20
Content-Type: application /json; charset =utf-8
Content-Length : xxxx
hems : http://sg.item.ntnu.no/homeems /
terms #;ns=66
66-HEMSOperation : RequestMessage
```

```
{                                              Payload
   "msgID": "CSS201220504170000 ",
   "type": "http://sg.item.ntnu.no/homeems /
                      terms #RequestMessage ",
   "source": "http://homeems -aagesen .net/
                      CSS",
   "destination ": "http://g-appliance .com/
                      devices /washing-TS169",
   "operation ": "SetProgram ",
   "parameters ": {
      "SetProgramParam _watertemp ": 30,
      "SetProgramParam _spinspeed ": 1400 }
}
```

(b) Example request message in JSON

Fig. 7. Device information description and request message

in accordance to the ontology depicted in Fig. 4. The highlighted line shows how a standardized operation name can be specified. This line can be added at any time and the vendor only needs to provide the updated information file which may be pushed to CSS. What this really means is device vendors and CSS vendors can manufacture their products separately without being concerned on naming protocols because declaring that one operation is the same as the other only requires one line. This device information file contains operation descriptions along with other device information. It must be provided by a home device to CSS upon registration. Services exposed by external systems are defined in the same way but the registration is often a manual process by the vendor of the CSS at manufacture time. This is because existing web services use different methods for service execution and thus have to be handled differently. In this regard, service descriptions for external services exist only to enable consistent processing and semantic classification of available services.

Operation and service invocation between CSS and home devices or CSS and external systems is done through message exchange. There are three types of messages: request, response, and notification. All messages are included as HTTP payloads. The format of the message is JavaScript Object Notation (JSON) (http://www.json.org). JSON was chosen as opposed to XML-based languages because the processing needs for production is low and thus can be constructed by most devices including microcontrollers. However, any reference to device or system in a JSON-encoded message needs to be the same URI as defined in the RDF/XML device or system information file. See Fig. 7(b) for an example request message in JSON. Note that this inter-working framework only specifies the interface for the communication between Home EMS components. The translation and conversion of the received messages into electrical signals for the actual control of home devices is a necessary and inevitable process that must be done by the device vendors.

6   Summary and Conclusion

Residential consumers contribute to a substantial amount of electricity consumption. Energy consumption pattern can affect the stability of the grid. Home Energy Management System (EMS) can assist household inhabitants in operating home devices to optimize energy usage. This paper proposes an architecture model and a functional framework for Home EMS with focus on simplicity and scalability to enable the system's rapid deployment. Energy management is carried out by a central system whose functions are realized by a combination of EFSMs and a policy-based reasoning machine. Our proposal to use policy-based reasoning offers an advantage to cope with changes in variables and simplifies incorporation of new energy management solutions as new policies. In addition, a Home EMS inter-working framework based on RDF and JSON was also proposed. Data representation with RDF provides the necessary semantics and enables harmonization with existing standards while JSON messages can be constructed by most microcontrollers. We are currently working on the construction of more energy management policies to cover broader aspects including indoor temperature adjustment and load scheduling involving more devices. A prototype system based on the proposed functional and inter-working frameworks will be implemented. The prototype will also be used as a platform to evaluate the effectiveness of the constructed policies with respect to electricity cost saved by consumers and the reduction of peak loads.

References

1. Li, F., Qiao, W., Sun, H., Wan, H., Wang, J., Xig, Y., Xu, Z., Zhang, P.: Smart transmission grid: Vision and framework. IEEE Transactions on Smart Grid 1(2), 168–177 (2010)
2. European Commission: Energy efficiency status report 2012 EUR 25405 EN (2012)
3. Open Geospatial Consortium: Sensor Web Enablement,
   http://www.opengeospatial.org/projects/groups/sensorwebdwg
4. International Electrotechnical Committee: IEC 61970-501 ed. 1 Energy Management System Application Program Interface (EMS-API) - part 501: Common Information Model Resource Description Framework (CIM RDF) Schema (2006)
5. Belkin International, Inc.: Belkin WeMo Home,
   http://www.belkin.com/uk/c/WSWH
6. X10: Home automation solutions, http://www.x10.com/automation/
7. eGauge Systems LLC: eGauge overview, http://www.egauge.net/overview.php
8. AIM: A novel architecture for modelling, virtualizing and managing the energy consumption of household appliances, http://www.ict-aim.eu/home.html
9. Beywatch: Beywatch Home, http://www.beywatch.eu/index.php
10. SmartHouse-SmartGrid Consortium: Smart House/Smart Grid,
    http://www.smarthouse-smartgrid.eu
11. Aagesen, F.A., Thongtra, P.: On Capability-related Adaptation in Networked Service Systems. Int. Journal of Computer Networks and Communications 4(4) (2012)
12. World Wide Web Consortium: Resource Description Framework (RDF),
    http://www.w3.org/RDF/
13. W3C Incubator Group: Semantic Sensor Network XG Final Report,
    http://www.w3.org/2005/Incubator/ssn/XGR-ssn-20110628

Interdependency Modeling in Smart Grid and the Influence of ICT on Dependability

Jonas Wäfler and Poul E. Heegaard

Norwegian University of Science and Technology
7491 Trondheim, Norway
{Jonas.Waefler,Poul.Heegaard}@item.ntnu.no

Abstract. The smart grid is a complex system consisting of interdependent power grid and information and communication (ICT) components. Complex systems have different properties than simple networks and give raise to new risks and failure types. In this paper, we study the dependencies in smart grid and the influence ICT may have on the dependability. We start with giving a categorization of the smart grid components and define state machines for these categories and for smart grid services. Then we investigate their interactions and interdependencies from a dependability perspective. Further, we investigate the positive and negative effects ICT can have on the dependability of the system. Finally, we introduce a meta-model which incorporates the information about the states of the components and services to create a state estimator for the smart grid considering ICT and power components.

1 Introduction

The reliability analysis of power grids has traditionally not included the state of supporting information and communication technology (ICT) infrastructure [1–3]. However, in the last ten years several authors pointed out the need of studying the power grid as complex network by including the cyber or ICT part in the analysis [1, 4, 5]. This complex network is called *cyber-physical* system or more general *system of systems.*

Theoretical results indicate the importance of analyzing the power grid (PG) and its supporting ICT together in one common model as a *system of systems.* It has been shown for interdependent random graphs that *system of systems* have different properties than simple systems [6]. Additionally, with an increasing number of interconnections and therefore a higher interdependency between the systems the vulnerability to random failures increases also [7].

A classification of particular types of failures which are caused by the interdependency of systems is put forward by [8]. Failures are classified as *cascading*, *escalating* and *common cause* failures depending on the interaction of the systems. Studies of major power grid incidents show that these interdependency effects between the PG and the ICT already exist in the current power grid [6, 9, 10]. A chain of cascading failures, i.e. failures in one system that trigger failures in another system, was a major reason for the large blackout in Italy in 2003 [6].

T. Bauschert (Ed.): EUNICE 2013, LNCS 8115, pp. 185–196, 2013.

And an escalating failure, i.e. independent failures in the systems that amplify each other, was an important reason why the blackout in the US in 2003 could become so large [9]. Another analysis of the disturbances in the US power grid from 1979 to 1995 found that *"problems in real-time monitoring and operating control system, communication system, and delayed restoration contribute to a very high percentage of large failures"* [10]. The smart grid will rely even stronger on ICT than the legacy power grid, therefore, it can be expected that these effects will become even stronger.

The smart grid has the potential to increase the reliability of the power supply with new services like self-healing and demand response, which may reduce downtime and increase dependability [11]. However, misbehaving ICT and interdependency effects between ICT and PG have to be analyzed carefully and included into the dependability analysis, otherwise the results may be inaccurate and could lead to false conclusions about the system.

An interdependency model for the electricity and information infrastructure was presented in [12]. Using four to five different states for both infrastructures the model accommodates the three new failure types of *system of systems* as described in [8]. The model contains interesting features like passive and active latent errors; however, it is very high-level and the repair is not covered in details. Both power grid and ICT components are repaired in one step at the same time.

In 2009 an interdependency model for the power grid was put forward to illustrate the effect ICT can have on the reliability of the whole power grid [1]. In this model, both ICT and PG have a binary state variable and can either be in a normal or abnormal state leading to a four state model. The model is very conceptual and concentrates mostly on the transitions. Because of the high abstraction level most details are hidden within the states.

A more detailed approach is taken by [13] by introducing a three-level assessment hierarchical architecture consisting of a device, network and service level. Each level has its own properties and is modeled individually.

In this paper, we start bottom-up with the components constituting the smart grid and give a categorization based on their use of ICT. We then give state machines for the components and services and explain their interactions from a dependability perspective. Further, we discuss the positive and negative effects ICT can have on the dependability of the system. Finally, we introduce a meta-model which incorporates the information about the states of the components and services to create a state estimator for the smart grid considering ICT and power components.

2   Components and Services in the Smart Grid

The power grid consists of the power infrastructure on the one hand and of intelligent devices and a communication infrastructure to control and monitor it on the other hand. We categorize all components of the power grid into five categories as shown in Fig. 1. Category A contains power components with no communication means and no software like power lines and mechanical power

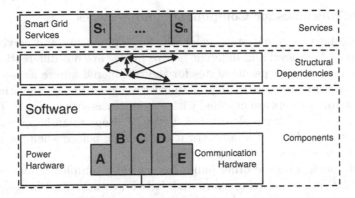

Fig. 1. Services and components of smart grids

devices. Category B contains power components that are configurable but run autonomous and have no communication means like certain distributed energy resources. Category C contains software controlled power components with communication means like intelligent electronic devices used for monitoring and controlling the power grid. Category D contains software controlled communication components like routers. Category E contains communication components with no software like communication cables. It is important to note that some devices can be in several categories like a power cable which is also used as carrier of a PLC (power line communication) signal. Such structural dependencies can be the cause for common cause failures.

Devices in the categories B, C and D are in the following called intelligent devices. Components in A and E are called hardware (HW) components. Power HW components like power lines and transformers build the physical connections in the power grid between production sites and loads. The intelligent devices and the communication HW components are needed to operate the whole grid.

Smart grid services run on top of these components and they need a certain subset of components and other smart grid services to work. This partial dependency is called in the following *structural dependency*. The services are used to operate the power grid and include power delivery, monitoring, control, protection and more advanced services like demand response.

The biggest change in the transition from the legacy power grid to the smart grid will lie in the increase of software capabilities of B and C components and the quantitative increase of C components. In other words, the components become more intelligent and there will be more intelligent electronic devices to increase the system awareness and control, especially in the distribution grid. The latter will also lead to an increase of D and E devices in the smart grid. Additionally, the transition to the smart grid will change the power grid services. On the one hand, they are extensions to existing services like an increased monitoring and controlling in the distribution grid. On the other hand, they introduce new functionalities like smart metering or demand response.

2.1   State Machines for Components and Services

In the following we present state machines for components and services. The states are on a high level and different failure modes are not differentiated. For a quantitative analysis separate states for the considered failure modes have to be created and transition rates or probabilities assigned to the transitions.

Hardware components are modeled with two states as seen in Fig. 2. They can either be in a working state *ok* or a failed state F. Repair can happen after the monitoring system detected a failure or it can happen before when the failure is only temporary and disappears on its own.

Intelligent devices on the other hand, have a more complex failure behavior. First, we differentiate between *errors* and *failures*, as described in [14]. A fault can trigger an error in a device but only when the provided service is incorrect it becomes a failure. Differentiating errors and failures allows for example to model intermittent failures. While the failure disappears for some time, the responsible error does not. Second, a failure may be either passive (F_p) or active (F_a), depending on their behavior. We use the following definition similar to [12]:

passive failure: The device works incorrectly in a passive way, i.e. it does not respond when needed (e.g. not sending monitoring data, not responding to a control signal, not triggering a breaker when needed).
active failure: The device works incorrectly in an active way, i.e. it functions but not as intended (e.g. sending wrong monitoring data, executing the wrong control command, triggering self-healing when not necessary).

The corresponding errors are accordingly termed *passive errors (E_p)* and *active errors (E_a)*. A device may also directly change its state from *ok* to F_p for example if parts of the hardware fail.

The devices are controlled by highly capable software which may cause harm to the system if working incorrectly. Due to the potential complexity of designing, configuring and updating such devices, faults are likely and errors may reside undiscovered in a device for a long time. Faults can be unintentional like design and configuration faults but also intentional like viruses/worms, intrusions and sabotage. Design, configuration or maintenance errors like software bugs, erroneous configuration/reconfiguration or the distribution of a faulty software update will affect potentially many devices at the same time. Failures may propagate on their own like in the case of a virus or a worm. The degree of the spreading depends on the detection and repair time.

The state of smart grid services may depend on the working and operational state of certain components, their structural dependencies, other services and on the input or the situation the system is in. The working states of a component are the states described above, the operational states are states in normal operation which can have an influence on a service. For example an open breaker which was opened by an undetected failure in an IED may cause the disconnection of parts of the grid and a state change for a service. The reason for the state change is the operational state of the breaker and only indirectly a failure. A service is said to be in the failed state F if the service produces incorrect output.

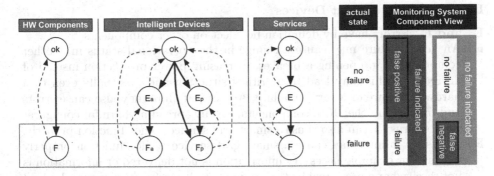

Fig. 2. State machines for components and services and the perception of their state in the monitoring system

If components fail which are necessary to create correct output but the output itself is not yet incorrect, then the service is in the error state E. For example, consider a protection service which is responsible for opening breakers in a high overload situation. This service relies on protection devices installed throughout the power grid. The failure of one of these devices is already critical if there are no redundant devices. However, as long as there is no overload in which this specific device is needed to operate the service does not produce wrong output, hence the service is in the error state E while the device itself is in a failed state. In the error state the failure probability is much higher than in the working state. It is not the same as a failed state because for dependability analysis this state is considered as *not failed*. The monitoring system may detect the device failure and initiate the repair before the service fails.

2.2 Interactions

The components and services are highly depending on each other. The transitions between the states depend theoretically on the state of all the other components and services at a given time. For practical analysis of large systems the states may be modeled as depending only on the state of a subset of all components and services which are either geographically or logically close. In the following, we discuss the influence components can have on other components or services depending on their states.

Influence of HW Components

F A failure may increase the load on other HW components and the probability for them to fail. This is especially the case for power HW components. Intelligent components may fail if a power HW component fails and there is no other power source (transition into F_p).

Influence of Intelligent Devices

$\mathbf{E}_a$ **and** $\mathbf{E}_p$ Errors have by definition no effect on other components.

$\mathbf{F}_a$ An active failure may cause a change in the operational status in another component, e.g. opening a breaker, increasing power production instead of decreasing. This may lead to a critical situation and eventually even to a hardware failure or a service failure. An active failure may also cause errors and failures in other ICT components, e.g. by spreading harmful configuration or virus. It can also cause a smart grid service to not function properly.

$\mathbf{F}_p$ A passive failure may cause a smart grid service to not function properly because for example necessary information is not delivered or information is not received and processed by the component. A passive failure may also lead to a failure in a power grid HW component, e.g. by not alarming the control center about a critical situation which could lead to an overload failure.

Influence of Services

E An error has by definition no effect on other components or services.

F A failure can cause problems for the components or services relying on the output of this service. It may provoke a critical situation end eventually even to a failure in a component. For example, if the service *demand response* is increasing the loads instead of decreasing. If this happens in a distribution grid with a high number of charging electrical vehicles it could lead to an overload in that particular area and eventually even to a blackout, i.e. a failure of the power delivery service.

2.3 Perception of Components and Services

The monitoring system has its own perception of the system which is not the same as the actual state of the system. This is because the monitoring system is also just a service which can fail. The monitoring system can either indicate *failure* or *no failure*. The error states are considered as *no failure* as the delivered service is per definition still correct. As shown in Fig. 2 the indication can be wrong, i.e. be a *false positive* if a failure is indicated when there is none or be a *false negative* if no failure is indicated when there is indeed one.

The deviation of the indication in the monitoring system from the actual state is critical. If false positives are frequent it may cause high costs for the clarification of the cause and eventually to a loss of trust. False negatives may prolong the time a component or service stays in the failed state which decreases the dependability of the system. The longer a component is in the failed state the longer the negative interactions described above take place and more state changes in other components may happen.

2.4 Techniques for Quantitative Analysis

A difficulty when modeling the smart grid for quantitative analysis is that it consists of dynamic parts, i.e. the components with their state machines, and structural parts, i.e. the structural dependencies between services and components. This becomes clearer when considering the smart grid services. The working and failed state of a given service may be described by a fault tree, where the events are failures of components or other services. This fault tree represents the structural dependency of the given service. The dynamic parts are the different failure modes leading to the events, i.e. failure of components or services.

A straight forward way of quantitatively analyzing a service is by creating markov models for each individual component and computing with them the dependability parameters needed for the fault tree. In this way, both availability and reliability of a service can be computed. However, this method assumes all events or state changes to be independent which is a very strong assumption and usually not true in real systems.

A way of including dependencies between components in an analytical model has been proposed in [15]. It starts with a reliability block diagram, i.e. a structural model which is equivalent to a fault tree and has the same independence assumption. The dependencies are then included by either isolating them or by using a combination of pivotal decomposition and markov chain. This method is most useful if the number of dependent components is small.

Another solution is to use a stochastic reward net (SRN) [16] which is an extension of a stochastic Petri net. The state machines from Fig. 2 can be used as a basis for the SRN in which the individual components and services are modeled as tokens. The transitions in SRN may be enabled by boolean functions on the markings of states and the transition rates may also depend on the marking of states. This allows to create a small model for a complex problem. However, this holds only if the components or services are treated as anonymous. If the identity of the different components and services become important, the model becomes more complex as well.

If the two mentioned methods are unpractical then a simulation may also be used for quantitative analysis.

3 Role of ICT in the Smart Grid

ICT components and services have a large potential for supporting the operation of a smart grid and increasing its dependability. The software part allows for smarter decision making processes and the communication allows for sharing information. Both are important for the most fundamental services: monitoring and controlling. An optimal monitoring system shows the actual state of the system with as little delay as possible and minimizes the discrepancy between perceived and real state. Precise data can help to operate the system in an optimal state and reduce errors and failures in the first place. For example, exact monitoring data in the distribution grid may optimize its use, maintenance and replacement, i.e. not wasting capacity or wearing the infrastructure unnecessarily out and preventively initiate repair or replacement before an incident happens. In case of a failure the monitoring service helps to detect and localize the failure. The reparation time may also be shortened by finding an optimal repair strategy, by self-healing or by enabling the repair or mitigation by remote control, e.g. by isolating a line failure and possibly reconnect disconnected loads by an alternative route to reduce the impact of the failure.

By aggregating the data from the components new insights can be gained. For example, by finding patterns for failures which might improve error and failure prevention or failure detection. With a wide-area monitoring and control, enabled by communication, the optimal strategy for operation can be found for a certain area or the whole grid and not only for the local component. In case of an incident a coordinated protection or isolation scheme may prevent a propagation of the failure in the system.

While ICT can help to improve dependability, it can also have a negative effect. Passive failures in monitoring lead to a mismatch between perception and reality. A critical situation or failure may not be detected due to the missing data. In a controlling service a passive failure in a component leads to the disregard of the control signal. If no acknowledgment message is used this stays undetected and a mismatch between the assumed state of the component and the real state arises.

Passive failures reduce the potential improvement of ICT. The total failure of an ICT service nullifies its effect and intuitively one may conclude that additional ICT services will either improve the dependability of the whole system or at least keep the status quo. However, this is a dangerous conclusion because of two reasons. First, if services or controllers blindly rely on the service a passive failure may have a worse effect as not having the service at all. In the former case there is a strong assumption that the service works correct, in the latter case there is no correctness assumption and nobody is left with a false sense of security. Second, active failures may trigger new failures which would not exist without the specific service or ICT component.

Active failures in monitoring lead to a mismatch between perception and actual state and eventually even to undesired decisions and actions. For example, wrong information about the status of a breaker or the load of a line can trigger the isolation of a power grid part and lead to an unnecessary outage. Active failures in controlling lead also to a mismatch of perception and actual state but have in addition a direct effect on some components. Examples are protection devices initiating a protection process, breakers opening or closing, or the sending of wrong control signals. Frequent active failures of ICT components may negate the positive effect ICT can have and lead to an overall negative effect.

Last but not least, ICT plays a big enough role in the smart grid to qualify it as *system of systems*, which have particular interdependency effects and failure types, i.e. *Cascading Failure*, *Escalating Failure*, and *Common Cause Failure* [8].

4   Aggregated view for the Control Center

In the legacy power grid the control centers for the power grid and the communication system are usually separated. However, as new failure paths emerge in the smart grid which originate in or include ICT components, it becomes crucial to incorporate the information of both into the state estimation of the whole

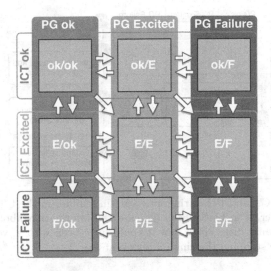

Fig. 3. Meta-model for smart grid

smart grid. This allows an early detection of possible failures coming from the ICT components.

In the following, we propose a meta-model to describe the state of the whole system for the control center. The meta-model is an aggregation and interpretation of the information from the monitoring system to determine the criticality level of the system. It has two axis using the states of the power grid (PG) and the ICT, see Fig. 3. The most important service in the power grid is the power delivery to the customers. The state of this service plus the state of supporting components are used to determine the power grid (PG) state. On the other hand, the states of ICT components and services are used together with a logic which indicates which services are critical to determine the state of the ICT system.

The model follows a service-centric approach. *Failure* means a service is not delivered correctly and action has to be taken immediately. *Excited* means that the service may run soon into a critical situation. More detailed, the states of the two axis are defined as:

PG ok: The system operates normally.
PG Excited: All customers are powered but the system is excited (N-1 redundancy is harmed, the load is critical, etc.)
PG Failure: At least one customer is disconnected from the power supply.

ICT ok: The ICT system operates normally.
ICT Excited: All critical ICT services are delivered correctly but the system is excited (non-critical components failed, congestion in the system)
ICT Failure: Some critical ICT services are incorrectly delivered.

The nine states are then created by the intersections of this two axis. Both excited states denote states of the system where the corresponding system is still

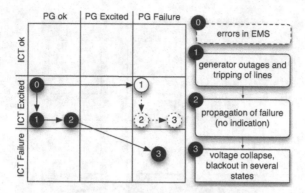

Fig. 4. Events in ICT and PG during an escalating failure in the US in 2003 as seen by the control center. The black disks indicate the information about the events as it happened. The white disks show how it could have been with a working detection mechanism, may be stopping the chain after event 1 or 2.

working correctly but the stability and robustness is decreased. They are a key factor in the meta-model because the system may be much weaker than in the failure-free state and failures may propagate.

The states are as perceived by the control center and can be wrong as discussed above. These monitored states should be as close to the real states as possible. The fast detection of failures reduces the risk that the failure can propagate or cascade to other components. Monitoring should also be reliable to reduce the risk of having false positives and false negatives.

The meta-model is a highly condensed view of the whole grid to create a clear and easy understandable warning system. Due to the aggregation it is highly scalable. In large systems or in presence of autonomous structures like micro grids it may be useful to use several meta-models.

4.1   Applications

The primary application for the proposed meta-model is the state indication of the smart grid for the control center as explained above. However, there are additional applications.

In ex post incident analysis the meta-model can be used to show the basic cause and effect chains in a clear way and study alternative scenarios. In Fig. 4 we give an example of such an analysis by showing the events of an escalating failure in the US in 2003 [9]. In short, several generators had an outage, which led to a tripping of several lines. When that happened, the energy management systems (EMS) of the two responsible network operators were not fully functional and the failure could propagate in the PG and ended in a voltage collapse and a blackout spanning several federal states. In the figure, the black disks indicate the information the control center had during the events. The control center knew about the reduced functionality of the EMS but did not learn about the outage in the power grid until it was too late. The white disks indicate the information the control center would have had if the monitoring system had worked. The first outage could have been detected and the failure perhaps isolated which could have stopped the chain of events.

As an extension of the ex post incident analysis the meta-model can also serve as a tool to visualize and illustrate interdependencies in two systems. The new failure types propagation, escalation and common cause failures can be explained in an intuitive way and new failure paths are revealed.

5   Conclusion

The wide introduction of ICT changes the way the smart grid may fail. It is necessary to consider the states of both the ICT and the PG in the dependability analysis due to the following reasons:

- Dependability analysis for smart grid services yield inaccurate results if the possible non-functioning or malfunctioning of ICT is not included. ICT can have special dynamics like failure propagation within the system and active latent errors, which can have a strong effect on the smart grid.
- ICT plays a big enough role in the smart grid to qualify it as *system of systems*, which introduces particular interdependency effects and failure types. In individual models it is difficult to include those.

In this paper we categorized the smart grid components and services and showed the interactions between them. We motivated that their state and especially the state of the ICT components and services will play an important role in the dependability analysis of smart grids. We proposed a meta-model which takes this into account and combines the states of ICT and power grid components and services. It can be used as a tool for the control center to estimate the state of the smart grid. The proposed meta-model facilitates the understanding of the mechanisms of previous incidents by tracing their trajectories in the model. The simple structure creates an intuitive model that allows explaining the interdependencies and new failure types that are created by connecting systems. Understanding the risks is the first step to make a system more dependable and secure.

This work is meant to generally describe dependencies in the smart grid and to create a basis for future work. Future work will focus on specific interactions and interdependencies of components and services. We are especially interested in studying the new failure modes and evaluating and quantifying the dependability effects of new smart grid services.

References

1. Kirschen, D., Bouffard, F.: Keeping the lights on and the information flowing. IEEE Power and Energy Magazine 7(1), 50–60 (2009)
2. Bose, A.: Models and techniques for the reliability analysis of the smart grid. In: Proc. IEEE PES General Meeting, Minneapolis, USA, pp. 1–5 (July 2010)
3. Singh, C., Sprintson, A.: Reliability assurance of cyber-physical power systems. In: 2010 IEEE PES General Meeting, Minneapolis, USA, pp. 1–6 (July 2010)
4. Amin, M.: National infrastructure as complex interactive networks. In: Samad, T., Weyrauch, J. (eds.) Automation, Control and Complexity, pp. 263–286. Wiley, New York (2000)
5. Little, R.G.: Toward more robust infrastructure: Observations on improving the resilience and reliability of critical systems. In: Proc. of 36th Annual Hawaii International Conference on System Sciences (HICSS 2003)- Track 2, vol. 2, pp. 58–66 (2003)
6. Buldyrev, S.V., Parshani, R., Paul, G., Stanley, H.E., Havlin, S.: Catastrophic cascade of failures in interdependent networks. Nature 464(7291), 1025–1028 (2010)
7. Parshani, R., Buldyrev, S.V., Havlin, S.: Critical effect of dependency groups on the function of networks. Proc. National Academy of Sciences of the United States of America 108(3), 1007–1010 (2011)
8. Rinaldi, S., Peerenboom, J., Kelly, T.: Identifying, understanding, and analyzing critical infrastructure interdependencies. IEEE Control Systems 21(6), 11–25 (2001)
9. Andersson, G., et al.: Causes of the 2003 major grid blackouts in north America and europe, and recommended means to improve system dynamic performance. IEEE Trans. Power Syst. 20(4), 1922–1928 (2005)
10. Xie, Z., Manimaran, G., Vittal, V., Phadke, A.G., Centeno, V.: An information architecture for future power systems and its reliability analysis. IEEE Trans. Power Syst. 17(3), 857–863 (2002)
11. Vadlamudi, V.V., Karki, R., Kjølle, G.H., Sand, K.: Challenges in smart grid reliability studies. In: Proc. 12th Int. Conf. on Probabilistic Methods Applied to Power Systems (PMAPS), Istanbul, Turkey (June 2012)
12. Laprie, J.-C., Kanoun, K., Kaâniche, M.: Modelling interdependencies between the electricity and information infrastructures. In: Saglietti, F., Oster, N. (eds.) SAFECOMP 2007. LNCS, vol. 4680, pp. 54–67. Springer, Heidelberg (2007)
13. Zhang, R., Zhao, Z., Chen, X.: An overall reliability and security assessment architecture for electric power communication network in smart grid. In: 2010 International Conference on Power System Technology (POWERCON), pp. 1–6 (October 2010)
14. Avizienis, A., Laprie, J.C., Randell, B., Landwehr, C.: Basic concepts and taxonomy of dependable and secure computing. IEEE Trans. Dependable and Secure Computing 1(1), 11–33 (2004)
15. Wäfler, J., Heegaard, P.E.: A combined structural and dynamic modelling approach for dependability analysis in smart grid. In: Proceedings 28th ACM Symposium on Applied Computing (SAC), Coimbra, Portuga, pp. 660–665 (March 2013)
16. Muppala, J.K., Ciardo, G., Trivedi, K.S.: Stochastic reward nets for reliability prediction. In: Communications in Reliability, Maintainability and Serviceability, pp. 9–20 (1994)

Development and Calibration of a PLC Simulation Model for UPA-Compliant Networks

Ievgenii Anatolijovuch Tsokalo, Stanislav Mudriievskyi, and Ralf J. Lehnert

Chair for Telecommunications,
Technische Universtität Dresden, 01062 Dresden, Germany
{ievgenii.tsokalo,stanislav.mudriievskyi,ralf.lehnert}@tu-dresden.de
http://ifn.et.tu-dresden.de/tk

Abstract. Communication network of the Smart Grid is intended to serve a numerous amount of applications of different types. Its complicated structure often requires a utilization of several communication technologies: wireless, cable, etc. Power line communication (PLC) also remains a challenging solution for usage in this area. The present paper is targeted to explore the communication protocol of UPA (Universal Powerline Association) technology - one of Broadband PLC (BB-PLC) solutions, which are used today in the Smart Grid. In the paper the test field measurements of this technology are summarized and the development of the UPA simulation model is described. Among this description one of the most important stages of the simulation model design, i.e. calibration with the measurement results, is explained. The obtained simulation model is intended be used as a part of the PLC network planning tool.

Keywords: Broadband Power line communication, UPA, TDMA, simulation model, test-field, ns3.

1 Introduction

This paper presents the measurement results and the simulation model, which were obtained and built within the PLC4SG project [1]. This project is targeted to investigate two powerline technologies: UPA [2] and G.hn [4] for Smart Grid applications in access networks. The former one, UPA, is considered in this paper. It was developed within the OPERA 1, 2 projects [3]. It is a broadband PLC solution with up to 200 Mbps data rate on physical layer. It maintains TCP/UDP IPv4 data transmissions and has a master-slave structure. The architecture of the measurement system is depicted in fig. 1. Hereinafter a master is referred to as a Measurement Computer (MC) and a slave − Terminal Device (TD). The PLC network can be managed either with the remote computer or with the remote desktop, connected though internet with the remote computer. The MC uses UMTS to get connected with the remote computer. Each device in the PLC network, MC and TDs, consist mainly of two parts: the actual PLC modem and the device, which runs the measurement software. We have selected GuruPlug computer for this purpose, which runs Debian as operating system [11].

T. Bauschert (Ed.): EUNICE 2013, LNCS 8115, pp. 197–208, 2013.

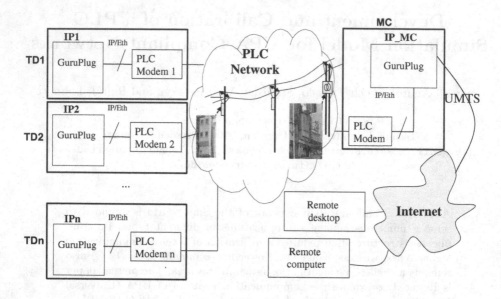

Fig. 1. Architecture of the measurement system

The paper is based on already published measurement results and description of the measurement tool in [6,7]. The test field measurement consists of three test sites: urban, rural and industrial, located in Hanoi, Vietnam. Each of the test sites has up to 15 TDs and one MC. The network performance is estimated with the measurement of the network goodput under greedy traffic and the round trip time with a tool, described in [7]. The measurement of the traffic is executed with several routines: uplink and downlink point-to-multipoint and point-to-point measurements. In each point-to-point measurement the traffic between MC and one selected TD is transferred. The parallel measurement corresponds to starting the point-to-point ones with all TDs at a time. The packet length on TCP layer is kept constant throughout one measurement with one routine. The traffic with two packet lengths was tested: 100 and 1000 bytes. The developed tool calculates one data rate measurement value each second. The duration of each routine for each length of packet comprised several weeks. Alongside with the data rate measurement on the TCP layer, the physical layer data rates were measured with a special tool of the UPA chip manufacturer Marvell.

The conclusions on the obtained information from the measurement results are given in sect. 2. The description of the UPA simulation model is presented in sect. 3. The steps for the simulation model calibration with the measurement results are introduced in sect. 4. The last section describes the possibility of the available flexible channel model usage within the developed UPA simulation model.

2   Measurement Results

In the PLC4SG project the execution of the test field measurements had two main targets: estimation of the possible data rates in a real scenario and also the use of the statistical data for the calibration of the simulation model. Afterwards such model can be used within a network planning tool, helping to predict the network behavior in realistic scenarios. The measurements to allow investigate the following factors that can help in the analysis of the UPA protocol behavior:

- ☐ dependence of the data rate on the number of repeating hops between MC and TD;

- ☐ dependence of the data rate on the distance between MC and TD;

- ☐ point-to-point link quality with varying channel conditions;

- ☐ sharing the channel resources;

- ☐ system warm-up time;

- ☐ routing strategy.

We observed that the data rates of the point-to-point connections varied with the time of the day. This variation is caused by the channel conditions changing. It is clear that the PLC signal transfer function is not static and depends on impedances and noise of all electrical appliances, connected to the power grid. Our tests confirm the significant influence of electricity consumers on the PLC signal quality. The tool of the UPA chip manufacture Marvell for physical data rates measurement also allows read-out of the logical network structure, i.e. identification of the repeaters in the network. This structure was also changing depending on the time of the day.

The most noticeable time variation concerns the urban test field scenario.

Also the measurements have shown that the PLC channel is highly asymmetric, so that the logical network structures in downlink and uplink are often different.

The accuracy of the measurement results is given by calculating the confidence intervals.

The detailed description of the test fields and measurement results can be found in [7].

3   Simulation Model

The ns-3 simulator [9] has been selected for implementation of the UPA simulation model, which layer structure is described in fig. 2.

Each layer implementation specialitites one can find in the following subsections.

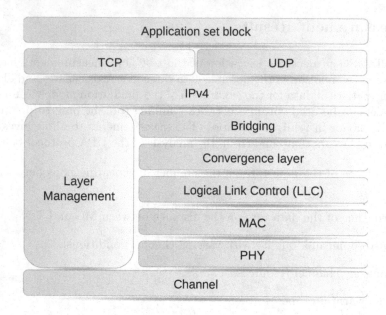

Fig. 2. Structure of the UPA simulation model

3.1   Physical Layer

Usually physical layer and channel simulation models consume much computing capacity. Therefore in the present work the detailed modeling of this simulation blocks is not introduced, but the physical layer and the channel are denoted with the empirically derived statistical model. For this purpose the measurement results of the physical data rates are transformed into the physical data rate table of point-to-point connections, which entries vary over time. Here we have introduced two levels of time variation: hours long and minutes long variation periods. Each hour long period is characterized with a table of statistical values: mean and standard deviation of the point-to-point data rates for each connection in down- and uplink. The example of one point-to-point test field measurement is shown in fig. 3. It explains the calculation of the time variant point-to-point data rate for one pair of nodes. We can distinctly observe the periodic variation of the data rate.

From this result we choose 6 intervals:
$[23 : 30 - 04 : 30], [04 : 30 - 11 : 45], [11 : 45 - 16 : 30],$
$[16 : 30 - 18 : 30], [18 : 30 - 21 : 00], [21 : 00 - 23 : 30],$
where the mean value of the data rate remains approximately constant without regard of that we take the values from all interval or from the half of it. It enables us to calculate the confidence interval for each period. We perform such division into period for each point-to-point connection separately for up- and downlink. The periods for different connections do not coincide.

The number of the measured values in a selected period depends on its length. The measured values of the physical data rates are gathered each 15 minutes.

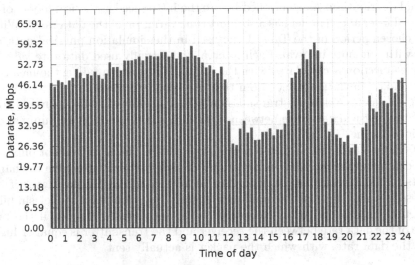

Fig. 3. Physical data rate of one point-to-point connection in one direction for 9 days of measurement

Table 1. Table example of the statistical values for the physical layer and channel modeling

Source ID	Destination ID	Mean data rate	Standard deviation
⟨value⟩	⟨value⟩	⟨value⟩	⟨value⟩

Each period can include up to $(N \cdot T_P \cdot /15)$ values, where N is the number of days, when the measurement was executed and T_P - length of the period in minutes. The presented in fig. 3 measurement lasted 9 days.

Each bunch of the measurement points in the selected time intervals we additionally divide into 20 groups with equal number of points. The groups are chosen in such a way that each one contains the points of the different time subintervals. These groups are called subruns, which we use for confidence interval calculation. The mean value and the standard deviation of the subrun mean values we save in the table for corresponding source and destination ID entry (Table 1[1]).

Such table is created for each of the selected periods, covering all the time of the day. The simulation model uses different tables one after another. How the actual point-to-point data rate values are calculated is described in the following.

In accordance to the definition of the confidence interval the mean values of each subrun are independent random variables and can be described with the

---

[1] Source and Destination ID values run through all possible combinations.

normal distribution. As mentioned before the introduced statistical model of the physical layer and channel has also short time variation of the data rates. Within each chosen period of the Table 1 the used in the simulation physical data rate vary with 1 minute interval. Each interval the actually used data rate value for every connection is calculated with the normal distribution taking the mean and the standard deviation values from the corresponding table.

We also assume that the transmission between a pair of nodes is always possible if the physical data rate between these nodes is more than the minimal one, provided by the UPA specification.

Of course the data transmission in real systems is characterized not only with a special data rate but also with the level of signal deterioration due to channel effects and the packet is considered to be received from physical layer if it is successfully decoded with redundancy codes. The simulation model simplifies this effect and the packet is considered to be successfully decoded if the table value of the data rate between the receiver and the transmitter is equal or higher than the data rate, with which the packet is actually sent.

3.2   MAC Layer

The scheduling algorithm defines the channel share depending on available information of demands - the values of data amount to transmit downlink to each destination and of each priority and uplink from each slave and of each priority. The master is the only modem that can initiate any transmission. It periodically asks the slaves to send the information about the length of their queues on all layers to all destinations and of all priorities. Keeping such information in memory the master runs a special algorithm to schedule the channel resources. OPERA simulation model uses fair share algorithm for traffic scheduling [8] and therefore this one is implemented in UPA model.

3.3   Logical Link Layer (LLC)

The data unit of the LLC level is called the burst. It is measured in a number of OFDM symbols and the symbols have constant time duration. The number of bits that can be packed in one symbol depends on the PLC channel quality.

LLC layer calculates the routing tables, which is also based on the current speed of physical connections. The UPA specification uses Spanning Tree Protocol for detection of the best routes. This protocol is described in the IEEE 802.1D standard. The best route selection is done first of all depending on data rates of physical connections, then on modems' IDs and other options, that define the privileges of one modems over others. We regard all modems "equal in rights" and concern only the first criteria. The calculation of the best route we explain with the example in fig. 4. This test scenario is not based on the measurement rsults and we have used it just to check the LLC layer functionality.

The picture describes the test scenario with 3 TDs. TD3 has different route in down- and uplink:

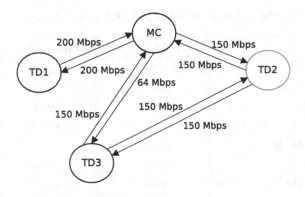

Fig. 4. Test simulation scenario

☐ Link MC → TD3 (downlink): $150 > 1/(1/150 + 1/150)) \Rightarrow$ Choosing direct route: MC → TD3.

☐ Link TD3 → MC (uplink): $64 < 1(1/150 + 1/150) \Rightarrow$ Choosing route with repeating: TD3 → TD2 → MC.

3.4   Layer Management Block

On MAC layer a special queue is created to store the MAC packet data units, that contain information from this block. This queue is served at the first priority level. Layer Management Block contains a number of services:

☐ Adaptive bit loading;

☐ Access Protocol;

☐ Polling Protocol;

☐ Port Solver Protocol;

☐ Cluster Discovery Protocol;

☐ Connection Admission Control Protocol;

☐ Spanning tree protocol.

All these services work to exchange the information between the modems about the neighbors, about the PLC connections quality and so on. The simulation model is constructed in such a way that all such information is already known by all the network members. It was not the aim to investigate the performance of these services. Therefore there is no necessity to implement them with their full functionality. Nevertheless such services are used by real modems and consume certain amount of the channel capacity. This amount can be calculated basing on OPERA specifications. Most of the services are periodic and the services' data

Table 2. The overhead of the UPA protocol layers

Layer	Overhead Downlink	Overhead Uplink
IPv4	1,2%	1,48%
Convergence	1,5%	1,9%
LLC	0,3%	0,26%
MAC access time	20,53%	21,31%
MAC headers	0,05%	0,05%
PHY	21,5%	22,0%
Layer Management	0,3%	0,3%
Total	**45,42%**	**47,29%**

units have almost not changeable size. Therefore it is possible to implement each service as a traffic consumer only, which sends packet of certain length with a certain period. The total amount of the channel utilization by the management block is estimated in the section 3.6.

3.5 Application Block

This block contains the source of simple and the greedy traffic. A simple traffic generator creates a fixed amount of packets at the simulation start-up. Greedy traffic generator cares about new packets generation each time, when the length of the convergence layer queues reach certain threshold value. The possibility to add other traffic generators is forseen.

3.6 Analysis of the Channel Resource Consumption

On the example of the test scenario fig. 4 we analyzed the overhead that is created by each protocol layer, when running the Parallel Down- and Uplink routines with a packet size of 1000 bytes. The summary is given in the Table 2.

Hereafter one can see that the Layer Management Block creates very little part of the total network traffic. MAC layer overhead consists of two parts: additional headers and the time, which is used to transfer the channel sharing information. The comparable with MAC part of capacity is consumed by physical layer. Therefore the total overhead takes about a half of the channel capacity.

4   Calibration of the Simulation Model

We have also designed the simulation scenario, which is analog to the real urban test case. Table 3 gives a characteristic of hop distances between the slaves and the master. The total number of modems in the test site is 15. From this table one can see how many slaves locate at distance of 1, 2, ... 6 hops from the master.

Table 3. Hop distances in the real test case scenario

Number of hops	Number of modems in Downlink	Number of modems in Uplink
1	4	4
2	5	3
3	1	4
4	2	1
5	2	1
6	0	1

The distance between directly (one hop) connected modems varies from 30 to 80 meters.

As mentioned above during the test field two types of measurement data was gathered: data rates on physical and application layers. The calibration of the simulation model is done with the following principle: using the created statistical model of the physical layer model we should adapt the mechanisms of the Datalink layer in such a way, that on application layer we receive the data rates, which were received during the testfield measurements.

The calibration is proposed to be done in several steps, which are described below. This sequence of steps is chosen in such a way, that different protocol constants and algorithms can be calibrated independently from each other. For example, first of all we decided to compare the measurement and simulation results for a case, when the logical mechanisms of the communication protocol create the least overhead. In such a way we can consider only the calibration of the constants in the simulation (Subsections 4.1 and 4.2).

4.1 Round Trip Time without Traffic

The MAC scheduler updates periodically the information about the length of the slaves' queues. For this purpose it sends the special service MAC data units (SMPDUs). If there is no traffic present, the update period is constant. This constant is not provided by specification but we can estimate it with this routine. It should be directly proportional to the round trip time.

With presence of other traffic this period can be extended because of two effects. At first, when the slaves send the MAC data units (MPDUs), they also write to the MPDU header the information, which is normally requested by SMPDUs. Therefore the master does not need to send SMPDUs itself so often as without uplink traffic. At second, when the time for the SMPUD sending comes the channel can be busy. In such case the SMPDU sending is delayed till the end of current transmissions. The extended value of the update period can be measured with round trip time during the network full load with traffic. This extended value of the period defines the maximal time that can be granted for one point-to-point transmission. This routine is described in subsection 4.6.

4.2   Point-to-Point in Downlink with 1 Hop Distance

With this routine we check the amount of headers of all protocol layers. We can do it only with this routines as far as with others the protocol creates much MAC overhead, that changes very dynamically. It originates because of the channel resource scheduling. For the selected routine it is also present but it does not change much and can be approximately calculated.

4.3   Point-to-Point for Multiple Hop Transmissions

During this routine it should be possible to see what is the priority of packets in repeating queues[2] in comparison to the application queues [3].

4.4   Point-to-Point Up- and Downlink Routines

In comparison of up- and downlink routines it is possible to discover the algorithm with which the channel resources are shared between these types of traffic.

4.5   Point-to-Multipoint Routines

These routines reveal the information about the sharing the channel resources between different users. The relation between the queues of all types[4] can be estimated.

4.6   Duplex Routines

This routine mainly serves as a verification of the previously obtained conclusions, i.e. the verification of the scheduling algorithm. Additionally as mentioned in subsection 4.1 this routine can be used for setting up the maximal time, which can be reserved for each point-to-point transmission.

5   Accurate Channel Model

As it was mentioned before we have used the statistical model of the physical layer and the channel, which is based on the measurement results. We considered it as the most accurate physical layer and channel model for the simulation model calibration. But its usage also has a significant drawback. We cannot simulate other scenarios, but only the ones, that were used during the test field

---

[2] Repeater queue contains the packets, that are received by the modem from other modems and have to be repeated.

[3] Application queue contains the packet that were generated by the modem itself.

[4] In the convergence layer of each node there are two kinds of queues: repeaters and application. This layer has queues for all destinations and all priorities separately for both queue kinds.

measurements. Therefore after the calibration we replace this statistical model with another one, which allows the setup-up of arbitrary scenarios. This model was implemented in the network simulator 3 (ns-3) by the group [10]. It uses another way to model the PLC channel - the deterministic approach with the usage of transmission line theory. For details, please, refer to [10].

In order to use the channel model provided by this ns-3 module it is necessary to set up the parameters of the transmission medium. For this the impedances of the point (called outlet) where the PLC modems are connected to the line should be given. Furthermore the nodes in the network must be fixed with the coordinates and the connection cable type must be specified. In the provided module authors already included several types of cable. Afterwards the transmit power spectral density and noise floor is set and the channel transfer functions are calculated. Now the physical and higher layers can be connected to the channel and complete network can be simulated. With the given module it is also possible to change the impedances during the simulation what will cause the immediate recalculation of the transfer functions for the channel. Therefore the influence of the time-varying channel on the network performance can be produced. The test results with arbitrary simulation scenarios, which can be realized with a help of this channel model, are left for further study.

Conclusions

During the test field measurements the UPA technology has proved its stability in the work conditions of strong and fast PLC channel variation. All the PLC modems were reachable all the time, while the network logical structure was considerably changing.

The observation of the physical data rates of the point-to-point connections allowed the design of the simulation test scenario, which can be considered analog to the real test case. The obtained results of mutliple measurement routines on application layer give a possibility for accurate calibration of the developed UPA simulation model.

After the calibration phase the model can be connected with the accurate PLC channel model and can be used as a part of the network planning tool.

Acknowledgments. The authors thank the following people: Marco Dietrich and Hendrik Schwuchow, Elcon Systemtechnik for providing the PLC modems.

References

1. PLC4SG project, http://www.pt-it.pt-dlr.de/de/2711.php
2. UPA model description, http://www.ipcf.org/company/upa/
3. OPERA Technology Specification. Part 1 and Part 2
4. G.hn. physical layer specification, http://www.itu.int/rec/T-REC-G.9960/en
5. G.hn. Datalink layer specification, http://www.itu.int/rec/T-REC-G.9961/en

6. Tsokalo, I.A., Bernstein, R., Lehnert, R.: Investigation of Powerline Communication Modems for Energy Management Systems. In: Workshop on Powerline Communication 2012, Italy, Rome (2012)
7. Tsokalo, I.A., Bernstein, R., Lehnert, R.: Measurement Software For Power Line Communication Network Traffic Analysis. In: Workshop on Powerline Communication 2012, Italy, Rome (2012)
8. Do, L.P., Lehnert, R.: Scheduling Strategies for Adaptive Resource Sharing System-Application to the OPERA System. In: Workshop on Network Design and Protocol Engineering for Powerline Communications Dresden, Germany, Dresden (2007)
9. ns-3 simulator, `http://www.nsnam.org/`
10. Model of the PLC channel,
    `http://www.ece.ubc.ca/~faribaa/ns3_plc_software.htm`
11. GuruPlug product,
    `http://www.globalscaletechnologies.com/t-guruplugdetails.aspx`

Efficient Data Aggregation with CCNx
in Wireless Sensor Networks

Torsten Teubler, Mohamed Ahmed M. Hail, and Horst Hellbrück

Lübeck University of Applied Sciences, Electrical Engineering and Computer Science,
Mönkhofer Weg 239, 23562 Lübeck, Germany
{teubler,hail,hellbrueck}@fh-luebeck.de
http://www.cosa.fh-luebeck.de

Abstract. CCNx is the reference implementation for a content centric
networking (CCN) protocol developed by the Palo Alto Research Center CCNx group. It serves also as reference for our CCN-WSN, a CCNx
implementation for wireless sensor networks (WSN). Efficient data aggregation with CCN-WSN is a challenge. In order to collect data from
source in the network data sinks have to poll data sources with interests and exclude fields in interests are necessary bloating the interest
messages. We solve the problem by introducing three building blocks in
CCN-WSN: unicast faces for packet filtering and "link" abstraction, a
forwarding service for creating network overlay structures used by applications and an intra-node protocol providing an API for applications
to interact with the forwarding service. For evaluation purpose we implement an application using a forwarding service implementing a tree
topology to collect data in the WSN.

Keywords: Content Centric Networking, Aggregation, Wireless Sensor
Networks, Internet Integration, Future Internet.

1 Introduction

Wireless Sensor Networks (WSN) and Content Centric Networking (CCN) are
two emerging technologies. WSN consist of spatially distributed often battery-
driven autonomous sensors to monitor physical or environmental conditions.
They gather real world data in applications like habitat or industrial monitoring, or agriculture. Data is processed in the network and aggregated information
is provided to a gateway or a data sink within the network. Several WSN approaches use specialized routing and processing protocols which are different
from today's protocols in the Internet. Recent approaches foresee even the use
of IPv6 stacks [8] on sensor nodes.

The Internet Protocol IP addresses nodes via hierarchical addresses based on
location. However, users are interested in content and information instead of
the location of data. To overcome this issue content centric networking (CCN)
approaches have been developed in the recent past. CCN addresses data itself
instead of the location where data is stored.

T. Bauschert (Ed.): EUNICE 2013, LNCS 8115, pp. 209–220, 2013.

Users of WSN are also interested in content instead of the nodes that retrieve this content. Consequently, a content centric approach fits well in the WSN domain.

One emerging and advanced implementation in content centric networking is the CCNx protocol [4]. We have recently implemented CCN-WSN [12] a CCNx derivate which covers a subset of CCNx functionality.

In this paper we add the following contributions:

- We suggest unicast faces for wireless broadcast networks that enable packet filtering and provide a "link" abstraction.
- We propose a forwarding service for creation of overlay structures, that offers efficient forwarding.
- We develop an intra-node protocol as an API for applications to interact with forwarding services.

Section 2 discusses related work. Section 3 introduces fundamentals of CCNx. A problem statement for different request types is given in Section 4. Section 5 describes the concept followed by implementation details in Section 6. An example in Section 7 implements a forwarding service and an application. Section 8 concludes this work and discusses further topics of research.

2   Related Work

In this section we discuss related work in the area of routing, data exchange, and data aggregation in content centric networking (CCN) and wireless ad-hoc networks.

The goal of research of routing in CCN is efficient data delivery to requesters based on content names. The goal of [5] and [9] is to reduce the overhead of interest routing in CCN by adding different information to the interest message like frequency of node usage. Interest routing needs extra mechanisms to route interests to certain nodes (unicast), otherwise interests are flooded. Our approach uses a forwarding service and unicast faces to route the content efficiently.

[11] argue that Named Data Networking (NDN) forwarding is complicated and challenging. The main concept of this approach is to reach large scale flows for efficient forwarding in NDN. The authors do not consider data traffic and network load for the total network using this approach.

Neighborhood-Aware Interest Forwarding (NAIF) [10] achieves bandwidth reduction of interest flooding by forwarding only fractions of interest packets at eligible relays. A similar approach is introduced in [6] and [7]. The authors discuss the forwarding of Interest messages based on the hop distance from the previous forwarder to the destination. [10], [6] and [7] virtually forward interests, whereas our approach forwards content objects.

The authors in [2] propose an approach to support content search and content retrieve as a native process of the network. The authors indicate that only end user has the possibility to aggregate data in the network. In contrast to our approach, intermediate nodes can aggregate data. Additionally, this approach is

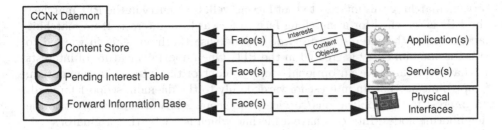

Fig. 1. CCNx Node Model

designed for PCs running Linux OS. Our approach is implemented on resource constraint devices in WSN like sensor nodes.

To the best of our knowledge, we are the first to propose a concept for data aggregation in WSN using CCNx implementation. Our approach is compatible to CCNx and therefore interoperable with existing CCNx implementations.

3   CCNx Overview

This section introduces to CCNx and highlights some features we use in this work. More detailed information is available on CCNx technical documentation web page [1] and [12].

Figure 1 illustrates the CCNx node model with the daemon and its main data structures *Content Store* (CS), *Pending Interest Table* (PIT), and *Forward Information Base* (FIB) on the left hand side. Applications, services, and physical interfaces (e.g. network interface cards) communicate via the CCNx daemon using *faces*. Faces in CCNx are a generalization of an interface comparable to TCP/IP sockets. In CCN-WSN the radio is a broadcast face that allows forwarding of interests and content within the network.

Message types in CCNx are *interests* and *content objects*. Interests request content objects by name.

CCNx follows a hierarchical naming scheme using the slash ("/") as name component delimiter. It is recommended that the first component is a registered unique DNS name to avoid name clashes among different content providing authorities. CCNx content names contain ASCII characters and bytes coded as two hexadecimal digits with a preceding percent character ("%"). A valid CCNx content name for example is: /th-luebeck.de/forward/%C1.de.fhl.tree~1~17~0.

Interests are sent by applications or services. At interest reception, the daemon looks up the CS if it contains a content object matching the interest name. An interest name matches a content name, if the interest name equals the prefix of the content name and the prefix is the longest prefix among all compared content names. If no content object matches in the CS, the PIT is searched. If the PIT contains a matching interest, the incoming face of the recent interest is added to the list in this PIT entry. This allows forwarding incoming content objects matching this interest to that face as well. If no entry in the PIT matches, the FIB is searched for a matching face to forward the interest. If no matching face is found the interest is discarded. Otherwise the interest is forwarded to this face and an entry is created in the PIT. One important feature of interests is that they can have an optional scope to control the interest dissemination. Scope 0 means that an interest forwarded only to the daemon, scope 1 forwards an interest to the applications/services, and scope 2 forwards an interest to the neighboring nodes. Interests have a lifetime which is set by the originator.

Content objects are sent only as a response to an interest. They are stored in a CS and arrive through faces generated by applications or services. On reception of a content object the CS is searched and if a matching content object is found the new content object is discarded to avoid unnecessary copies of duplicated content. If no entry in the CS matches, the PIT is searched. If a matching interest is found in the PIT the content object is forwarded to the list of faces of that interest and stored in the CS for the lifetime of the content object. As the interest is satisfied the corresponding entry is removed from the PIT.

4   Problem Statement

This section discusses the problem of data aggregation with standard CCNx and CCN-WSN forwarding mechanisms for two request types. We distinguish between *any* and *all* requests.

Any Requests. An *any request* is the standard request type in CCNx. A node requesting some content sends an interest and receives exactly one matching content object from any node providing this content.

This situation is depicted in Figure 2. Node 17 is interested in some content. Nodes holding content objects matching the interests name are depicted in black. In the first step node 11, 15 and 19 have the available content. Node 17 sends an interest through the network along the communication links (dashed arrows in Figure 2(a)). However, node 19 does not forward the interest because it is able satisfy it.

The nodes forward the content objects back to the face the interest arrived. E.g. content object from node 19 reaches node 13 (Figure 2(b)) and is forwarded to node 17 (Figure 2(c)). Content object providers add additional information e.g. node id as name suffix which allows the originator of the request to learn about the content provider.

As node 13 already stored and forwarded the content object, the content object from node 11 is either stored but not forwarded because there is no matching interest or discarded if it is a duplicate. This behavior of CCNx is intentional by design and reasonable if the content of the matching content objects is identical.

However, if we consider that sensor nodes observe e.g. temperatures and an application sends an interest for temperature this application retrieve a temperature value from any node. In standard CCNx behavior, one node "wins". For

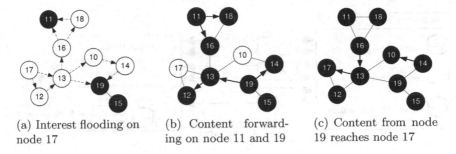

(a) Interest flooding on node 17

(b) Content forwarding on node 11 and 19

(c) Content from node 19 reaches node 17

Fig. 2. Any Request: Nodes with matching Content are marked in black

many applications any requests are not satisfying e.g. when an average temperature is requested. For this case we need another type of request.

All Request. In contrast to the previously described *any request* the result of an *all request* is data provided from all nodes that originate this data under a specific name. Examples of all requests may include a list of all measurements or aggregated values like *average*, *min* or *max* values.

Standard CCNx supports only any requests but it is possible to build all requests with CCNx *exclude* mechanism. Excludes are content names added as field to an interest to avoid these content names from matching this interest. To make content objects unique the CCNx daemon adds a digest (SHA-256 digest of the encoded content object) as last component of the content objects name when provided by an application. In our CCN-WSN application the daemon adds the node identifier as a name component. By this mechanism every content name is unique.

Invoking an *all request* using excludes works as follows: an *any request* is sent and a content object is received. Using the name of the received content object in an exclude in a further any request, a second content object is delivered different from the first one. All content objects can be fetched from the network with that name prefix by iterative sending of any requests using excludes.

This approach works well but has some obvious drawbacks. For every content object an interest has to be sent. Even if some content objects got stored in nearby nodes as a result of the first interest—like the content object from node 11 stored in node 13 in Figure 2(c)—this is a significant overhead. Furthermore, not all content objects come closer to the requester by iteratively sending interests, see content object from node 15 Figure 2(c)

Excludes occupy significant space in the message. This approach does not scale with the number of nodes in the network because messages have a limited length determined by the maximum transfer unit (MTU) of the physical layer.

These issues limit the use of CCNx with wireless resource constrained (especial energy constrained) devices. Sending takes a lot of energy and the MTU is very limited (e.g. 127 Byte with IEEE 802.15.4) in WSN.

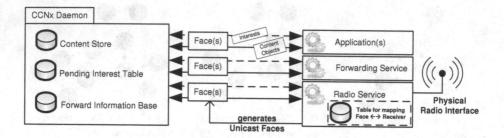

Fig. 3. Conceptual overview of our node model

5   Concept

Our concept adds three main components to the CCNx-Model: *forwarding service, unicast faces, intra node protocol* as illustrated in Figure 3. This section introduces these components and their functionality. -

Forwarding Service. The forwarding service builds an overlay network on top of the wireless broadcast network. This forwarding service provides efficient forwarding mechanisms for applications on top of existing CCNx forwarding mechanisms like the forwarding information base of the daemon. To save resources the overlay is constructed on demand of the application like a reactive routing protocol in ad-hoc networks. Furthermore, the forwarding service hands data to applications to allow aggregation of the data. Aggregated data from the application will be forwarded to the next node in the network by the forwarding service.

Unicast Faces. For WSN devices explicit faces based on TCP or UDP sockets across a network are not available like in the CCNx reference implementation. In wireless broadcast networks the radio is a broadcast face sending all interests and content objects to the neighborhood. Figure 4 illustrates this behavior for a single interest and content message exchange. In this scenario links between all nodes exist. In Figure 4(a) an interest with scope 2 is sent from node 1 to the neighbors node 2 and 3 (see dashed line) matching the content object stored on node 2. With the radio as broadcast face like illustrated in Figure 4(b) the content object is stored at node 3 as well because the content object matches the previously received interest from node 1. Node 3 will forward the content again to node 1.

With unicast faces in Figure 4(c) the content object is only stored and cached on node 1. Node 3 rejects the message because the destination address of the message of the content object is node 1. WSN benefit from reduced number of messages and less processing. Unicast faces are a basis for our forwarding service as inter node communication is now well under control and predictable.

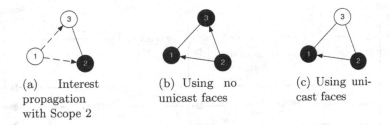

(a)   Interest propagation with Scope 2

(b) Using no unicast faces

(c) Using unicast faces

Fig. 4. Need of unicast faces with wireless ad-hoc links

Intra Node Protocol. The intra node protocol allows an inter process communication between services and applications using CCNx command marker technique. Interests with command marker (so called commands) of an intra node protocol have scopes smaller or equal to one to avoid interest propagation beyond the node and use a special name component *intra_node*.

Summarizing the concept, we foresee support for several applications e.g. one for each sensor and our approach is fully compatible with CCNx using only standard CCNx features. Therefore, it can be applied to all existing CCNx implementations. Implementation details are presented in the next section.

6   Implementation

In this section we describe the implementation of the unicast faces and the intra node protocol of our approach using CCNx. An example implementation of a forwarding service is given in Section 7.

Unicast Faces. Unicast faces are implemented as a part of the radio service depicted in Figure 3. The requirement is that the radio layer uses some node addressing scheme and radio packets include destination and source addresses. The service establishes a new unicast face automatically if a broadcast interest (destination is the broadcast address) from a neighboring node is received. The radio service maintains a mapping between this new face and the neighbor address. Unicast faces have a limited lifetime. When links break the resources on the node are released.

Intra Node Protocol. Communication between applications and services is performed via faces and the daemon. For our approach we suggest an intra-node protocol for communication with the forwarding service. Figure 5 shows a message exchange between *forwarding service*, *CCNx daemon*, and *aggregation application(s)* in a path time diagram. The intra-node communication is identified by the name component *intra_node*. In the example presented here the aggregation application communicates with the forwarding service. Dashed arrows depict interests, solid arrows depict content objects. Interests with scope 0 are sent to the daemon only, whereas interests with scope 1 are forwarded to applications or services on the local node. The first interest is sent with scope 1 and the second interest with scope 0 just to the daemon.

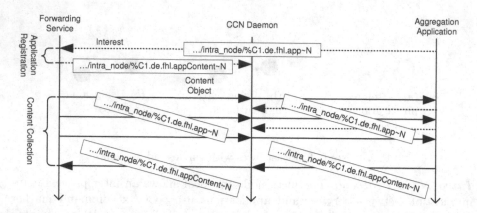

Fig. 5. Path Time Diagram of the Intra-node Protocol

At node startup the application registers at the forwarding service. This interest (.../intra_node/%C1.de.fhl.app~N) is implemented as a command denoted by the command marker %C1 with one parameter N (delimited by a tilde character ("~")) identifying the application. Application identifiers need to be globally unique and the same for all applications in the network. When a forwarding service receives this interest it sends an interest (.../intra_node/%C1.de.fhl.appContent~N) also implemented as command with one argument (application identifier) and with scope 0 to receive content from the application. With the application identifier the forwarding service distinguishes between multiple applications running on a node. The lifetime of the two initial interests is as long as the predicted application lifetime.

If a content object is received from a neighboring node the forwarding service changes the name of this content object to same name of the interest sent from the application during the application registration to match even this interest. When the application receives a content object, it sends an interest with scope 0 to be able to receive further content objects from the forwarding service. This is necessary in the case where data from several nodes has to be collected for aggregation.

The application receives content objects from the forwarding service and processes the data. When the application finishes processing the data, it sends a content object matching the name of the interest sent during application registration by the forwarding service. An example for interaction of intra and inter node communication is provided in Section 7.

When the forwarding service receives a content object from the application it will then forward the content object with a new name on the network. As the interests from the application registration are satisfied the application registration has to be performed again.

7   Example of Data Aggregation

This section describes an implementation of a forwarding service as a proof of concept. The forwarding service named *tree forwarding* in this example constructs a directed tree. Along this tree data is forwarded by the service to the sink while it is collected and aggregated by the application. The application we implemented is a simple WSN node discovery which concatenates received lists (maybe empty) of node id's and adds its own node id.

Our example implementation has three phases. In phase zero the application registers as already described in Section 6. In phase one the tree is constructed. In phase two data is forwarded along the tree, collected and aggregated on the nodes. We describe phase one and two in detail in the following.

Phase One: Tree Construction. Figure 6 illustrates the steps for creating a tree graph according to [3]. Rectangles in Figure 6 aside the nodes show received interests. These interests are additionally stored in the tree forwarding service to make forwarding decisions later. In Figure 6(a) a *tree construction interest* (`.../%C1.de.fhl.tree~1~17~0`) is sent from node 17 because it is the sink in our example. The name follows the CCNx command message format with command name *tree* from namespace *de.fhl*. The first parameter is the application id ("1" in this example), the second parameter is the sender id and the third is a hop count. All tree construction interests are sent with scope 2 to reach the neighboring nodes only.

When the forwarding service receives a tree construction interest with a hop count smaller than its own interest it sends a new tree construction interest by adding its node id as second parameter and incrementing the hop count (Figure 6(b)). Newly received interests are highlighted in bold face in Figure 6. For simplicity we show only the parameters instead of the whole interests beginning from Figure 6(b). As the network in our example has three hops from the sink tree construction takes four steps. Step three is illustrated in Figure 6(c). Figure 6(d) shows the final result of the tree construction process before phase two starts.

Phase Two: Forwarding. The end of phase one is detected if no more interests are received by the nodes for a certain time.

In phase two, the forwarding service of a *leaf node* starts to send data. Leaf nodes can be identified as the forwarding service has not received any tree construction interest from neighbors with a higher hop count.

The tree forwarding service sends a content object without data via the intranode protocol (see Section 6) to the application. The application itself sends a content object back to the forwarding service containing the current data (node id) using the intra node protocol.

Figure 7(b) shows an example where node 14 forwards data. At node 14, the forwarding service sends a content object named `.../intra_node/%C1.de.fhl.app~1` with empty data. The application sends back a content object named `.../intra_node/%C1.de.fhl.appContent~1`

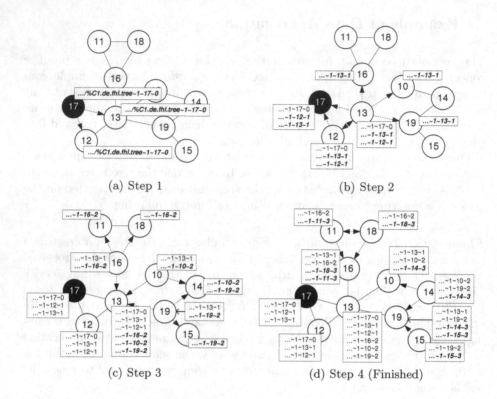

(a) Step 1   (b) Step 2

(c) Step 3   (d) Step 4 (Finished)

Fig. 6. Phase 1: Tree construction

containing data, in our example the node id 14. Content received from the application is forwarded by the forwarding service along the tree.

The forwarding service changes the name of the content object received by the application to `.../forward/%C1.de.fhl.tree~1~10~2` to forward the content to node 10. Node 10 is chosen because the interest from node 10 has a hop count less than the own hop count. The content object is forwarded on the unicast face the interest arrived. If several interests with a smaller hop count are available one of them is chosen.

The tree forwarding service on node 10 receives the content object. The received content objects name is changed to `.../intra_node/%C1.de.fhl.app~1` and handed to the application the same way as in node 14. At node 10 the aggregation application waits for content objects from all neighbors upwards the tree, aggregates the data and sends it to the tree forwarding service.

A special case occurs at node 19. Node 19 waits for data from node 14 and node 15. However node 14 forwarded data already to node 10. Therefore, intermediate nodes send their content object after a timeout even though they have not received the content object from all neighbors upwards the tree. Data is continuously forwarded until the sink is reached as shown in Figure 7(a).

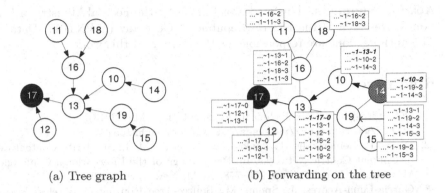

(a) Tree graph   (b) Forwarding on the tree

Fig. 7. Phase 2: Forwarding

When a content object is received the interest with the matching name is removed from the PIT. Therefore, the forwarding service resends the interest with scope 0 to be able to receive further content objects matching the interest. Resending these interests is important e.g. in Figure 7(b) node 13 will receive content objects from node 16 and 19 as well. As all interests have a certain lifetime the tree discontinues if no more content objects are sent.

In this section we presented tree forwarding as an example implementation of a forwarding service. As an example application we implemented a node discovery providing a list of all nodes available in the WSN.

8 Summary and Outlook

In this paper we have motivated the need for a further development of CCN-WSN to achieve efficient data aggregation in wireless sensor networks. Our approach extends CCN-WSN by three major components: unicast faces to reduce the number of message in a broadcast medium, forwarding service to create overlay structures on a given physical topology, and an intra-node protocol for communication between applications and the forwarding service. The daemon as the main component and the interfaces of CCN-WSN (and CCNx respectively) are unchanged in this approach. The communication between the components follows the basic mechanisms of CCNx. We have shown in an example implementation that a tree routing can be easily integrated with this approach.

In the future we will perform an evaluation against 6LoWPAN and CoAP. We foresee that using CCN straight away on top of IEEE 802.15.4 will provide an efficient solution with less overhead. Furthermore, we will add applications and semantic functionality to query wireless sensor networks. To improve the performance we will provide a compression scheme for the content names and implement persistent memory for content. Furthermore, we will add lightweight security measures in the implementation to prevent passive and active attacks against CCN and design and implement a gateway for seamless integration of CCN-WSN into CCNx implementation.

Acknowledgments. This work was funded by the Federal Ministry of Education & Research of the Federal Republic of Germany (17PNT017, DataCast). The authors alone are responsible for the content of this work.

References

1. CCNx Project: CCNx Technical Documentation (May 2013),
   http://www.ccnx.org/releases/latest/doc/technical/
2. Daras, P., Semertzidis, T., Makris, L., Strintzis, M.G.: Similarity Content Search in Content Centric Networks. In: Proceedings of the International Conference on Multimedia, MM 2010, pp. 775–778. ACM, New York (2010)
3. Garcia-Luna-Aceves, J., Spohn, M.: Source-Tree Routing in Wireless Networks. In: Proceedings of Seventh International Conference on Network Protocols, ICNP 1999, pp. 273–282 (1999)
4. Jacobson, V., Smetters, D.K., Thornton, J.D., Plass, M.F., Briggs, N.H., Braynard, R.L.: Networking Named Content. In: Proceedings of the 5th International Conference on Emerging Networking Experiments and Technologies, CoNEXT 2009, pp. 1–12. ACM, New York (2009)
5. Lee, G., Han, L., Park, Y., Lee, J.B., Kim, J., In, H.P.: An Energy-Efficient Routing Protocol for CCN-based MANETs. International Journal of Smart Home, 143–151 (2013)
6. Meisel, M., Pappas, V., Zhang, L.: Ad Hoc Networking via Named Data. In: Proceedings of the Fifth ACM International Workshop on Mobility in the Evolving Internet Architecture, MobiArch 2010, pp. 3–8. ACM, New York (2010)
7. Meisel, M., Pappas, V., Zhang, L.: Listen First, Broadcast Later: Topology-Agnostic Forwarding under High Dynamics. In: Annual Conference of International Technology Alliance in Network and Information Science (September 2010)
8. Montenegro, G., Kushalnagar, N., Hui, J., Culler, D.: Transmission of IPv6 Packets over IEEE 802.15.4 Networks (RFC 4944) (September 2007)
9. Sun, L., Song, F., Yang, D., Qin, Y.: DHR-CCN, Distributed Hierarchical Routing for Content Centric Network. Journal of Internet Services and Information Security (JISIS) 3(1/2), 71–82 (2013)
10. Yu, Y.T., Dilmaghani, R.B., Calo, S., Sanadidi, M., Gerla, M.: Interest Propagation In Named Data MANETs. In: 2013 International Conference on Computing, Networking and Communications (ICNC), pp. 1118–1122 (2013)
11. Yuan, H., Song, T., Crowley, P.: Scalable NDN Forwarding: Concepts, Issues and Principles. In: 2012 21st International Conference on Computer Communications and Networks (ICCCN). pp. 1–9 (2012)
12. Zhong, R., Hail, M.A., Hellbrück, H.: CCN-WSN - a lightweight, flexible Content-Centric Networking Protocol for Wireless Sensor Networks. In: 2013 IEEE Eighth International Conference on Intelligent Sensors, Sensor Networks and Information Processing (IEEE ISSNIP 2013), Melbourne, Australia (April 2013)

EpiDOL: Epidemic Density Adaptive Data Dissemination Exploiting Opposite Lane in VANETs

Irem Nizamoglu[1], Sinem Coleri Ergen[2], and Oznur Ozkasap[1]

[1] Department of Computer Engineering
[2] Department of Electrical Engineering
Koc University, Turkey
{inizamoglu,sergen,oozkasap}@ku.edu.tr

Abstract. Vehicular ad-hoc networks (VANETs) aim to increase the safety of passengers by making information available beyond the driver's knowledge. The challenging properties of VANETs such as their dynamic behavior and intermittently connected feature need to be considered when designing a reliable communication protocol in a VANET. In this study, we propose an epidemic and density adaptive protocol for data dissemination in vehicular networks, namely EpiDOL, which utilizes the opposite lane capacity with novel probability functions. We evaluate the performance in terms of end-to-end delay, throughput, overhead and usage ratio of the opposite lane under different vehicular traffic densities via realistic simulations based on SUMO traces in ns-3 simulator. We found out that EpiDOL achieves more than 90% throughput in low densities, and without any additional load to the network 75% throughput in high densities. In terms of throughput EpiDOL outperforms the Edge-Aware and DV-CAST protocols 10% and 40% respectively.

1 Introduction

For improving safety of the roads, vehicular ad-hoc networks (VANETs) has become popular both in industry and academia. Efficient usage of vehicular networks has significant potential considering the fact that the amount of traffic accidents is massive. For instance, every year just in the United States almost six million traffic accidents, ten thousands of deaths and millions of injuries occur [1]. Certainly, VANETs are expected to significantly improve the safety of our transportation systems by making information available beyond the drivers' knowledge. In ad-hoc networks, routing protocols are crucial to maintain reliable and efficient communication. Despite this importance, most of the protocols offered for VANET are reinterpretations of the well known mobile ad-hoc network (MANET) routing protocols. However, VANETs behave in fundamentally different ways than the models that predominate in MANET researches. Unlike traditional MANETs, they have high but more predictable mobility models with rapid changes due to high speed and frequent fragmentation in network topology [2]. Geographic position information is available through Global Positioning

T. Bauschert (Ed.): EUNICE 2013, LNCS 8115, pp. 221–232, 2013.

System (GPS) with no power or hard delay constraints. Therefore, communication methods developed for VANETs must consider various dimensions including delay and reliability requirements, protocol specifications, vehicle mobility, topology characteristics and physical constraints. Thus, instead of using existing protocols proposed for MANETs, design of protocols specifically for VANETs to mitigate its disadvantages and utilize GPS information is needed.

In this study, we propose and develop a novel data dissemination protocol for VANETs. In contrast to prior studies, our protocol EpiDOL uses epidemic routing by using the advantage of opposite lane as relaying with novel probability functions among vehicles. Epidemic technique introduces intelligence into data dissemination by reducing contentions and collisions while not requiring infrastructure support. Our probability functions are simple but effective in providing adaptivity to density. Therefore, the comparison of our approach with state of the art protocols DV-CAST [3] and Edge-Aware [4] in realistic traces, proved the efficiency of EpiDOL in terms of lower delay, higher throughput rates and better utilization of opposite lane relaying. The novelties of this work as following.

- We propose and develop a density adaptive epidemic data dissemination protocol, EpiDOL which uses only limited network information and control flags that indicate packet dissemination direction and vehicles' movement direction.
- In EpiDOL, we propose a new probabilistic approach to utilize opposite lane nodes as relay node to solve disconnected networks problem.

The original contribution is to propose probabilistic density adaptive epidemic data dissemination protocol, EpiDOL. Also, we analyze the dependence of optimal parameters of epidemic routing on the density and the direction of vehicles. In addition, we evaluate the performance of EpiDOL compared with the current routing algorithms with simulations that use realistic traffic traces.

The rest of this paper is organized as follows. Section 2 describes related works. Section 3 discusses the system model. Section 4 describes the details of EpiDOL with performance metrics that we used during the simulations. Section 5 provides scenarios used in simulations and performance criteria. Section 6 presents simulation results and Section 7 concludes the paper.

2   Related Works

Distributing Internet on roads [5] or using mobile phones and in-car embedded devices for collecting and processing data [6] are possible applications of VANET. To realize these applications, we have to disseminate the data throughout a network. While thinking ad-hoc networks, the simplest and the most common way of data dissemination is flooding. However, as a result of the redundant broadcasts there may be contentions and collisions in the shared wireless medium. VANET routing protocols mainly deal with two problems, broadcast storm and disconnected networks [4]. When high number of nodes start to disseminate their packets at the same time, it is highly probable that the collisions will occur. The loss of data packets due to these collisions are defined as broadcast storm problem. [7] and [8] try to solve this problem in MAC layer level by including some new ideas such as disseminating packets with probability functions. [9] develops a scheme to distribute packets fairly to the network by using the local knowledge. We have further improved these approaches by introducing probability functions adaptive to density. EpiDOL uses epidemic approach with different probability functions succeeded to decrease the packet loss and overhead while increasing the throughput significantly.

According to [10] other challenges in VANET i.e. vehicle movements and driver's behavior cause rapid topology changes and frequent fragmentation on the network. Possible link breakages are predicted using the velocity of the nodes in [11] and [12]. We deal these problems by using periodically updated neighborhood info. Additionally the dynamic behaviors of the vehicles and the sparsely connected networks introduce new problems. However it is already shown that Gossip-based (Epidemic) protocols are effective to solve these problems and provide reliable and efficient communication [13].

Reactive and proactive protocols have different behaviors under different traffic regimes [2], they should be robust to different density levels. [14] presents a zone-based forwarding scheme to deal with density problems. At low density networks the disconnected network problem is a severe issue. It can be defined as the case when there are not sufficiently enough nodes for data transmission in the network. It is proposed that by choosing the best packet structure this problem can be solved [11]. To deal with this problem, the proposal and successful implementation of the intelligible use of the vehicles in the opposite lane for relaying packets between disconnected networks in the original lane is another novel contribution of this work.

[15] and [16] reinterpret well-known protocols AODV, GPSR and OLSR instead of proposing specialized approaches for VANET. Addition to this different techniques, Edge-aware Epidemic Protocol [3] is the most relevant study to this work. Edge-aware detects edge nodes and assigns high probabilities to these nodes. However, EpiDOL extends this approach with its opposite lane usage and simple but effective probabilistic forwarding technique.

3   System Model

We consider an ad-hoc network with randomly distributed vehicles on a multilane bidirectional highway. Each vehicle is equipped with GPS and has the communication capability with 802.11p protocol [17]. We assumed that the nodes are only interested in the packets that are generated by nodes that lead them within less than a certain region of interest (ROI). All packets are generated by a leading node with the same priority and the same dissemination distance. Any packet can be lost due to collisions, however, if a packet is received successfully, then there are no bit errors that lead to the misinformation of the node.

Since there is no central control or clustering mechanism, all nodes in the network act independently. They are only aware of their neighbors' locations and directions by periodical updates which will be discussed in Section 4. It is assumed that any further information about the network topology or density are not available to the vehicles.

Algorithm 1 Flag Value Decision

algorithm executed after each data packet arrives

```
1:  if df = 1 then
2:     while myDir = sourceDir do
3:        if neighSame > 0 then
4:           set of = 1 and df = 1
5:        else if neighOpp > 0 then
6:           set of = 0 and df = 0
7:        end if
8:     end while
9:  else if df = 0 then
10:    while myDir ≠ sourceDir do
11:       if neighSame > 0 then
12:          keep flag values same
13:       else if neighOpp > 0 then
14:          set of = 1 and df = 0
15:       end if
16:    end while
17: end if
```

Abbreviation	Explanation
df	Direction flag
of	Original flag
neighSame	Number of same directional neighbors
neighOpp	Number of opposite directional neighbors
myDir	Direction of the current node
sourceDir	Direction of the source node

Table 1: Abbreviations used in algorithm

4   Algorithm Description

In this section, we describe principles of EpiDOL with its system architecture and probability functions.

4.1   System Architecture

In our approach, we aim to create an intelligent packet dissemination system by using flags on application layer. We use two binary flags: *of* shows the actual dissemination direction of the data packet, and *df* shows the vehicles riding direction with respect to the direction of the source node. With the help of the information that we gathered from these flags, the opposite lane is used effectively to provide the data connectivity and propagation.

Unnecessary packet dissemination is obstructed by using density adaptive probability functions p_{same}, p_{opp} and $p_{sameToOpp}$ which are the probabilities of forwarding packets in the same direction, in the opposite direction and transmitting packets from original direction to the opposite direction, respectively. This approach solves the broadcast storm problem by decreasing the collision rate. We have information about neighbors of each node by sending hello packets periodically. The neighbor number provides a simple but effective density adaptation in the algorithm.

In our system, there exist two types of packets. One of them is the periodic hello packet that includes source id, x-y coordinates of the source and its traveling direction. When hello packets are received, the receiver node creates its neighborhood list which includes information about its neighbors. Hello packets are like control packets. By using this method, we can easily manipulate the number of neighbors and their locations. The second type is data packet which includes the senders' id, x-y coordinates, the packet dissemination distance, the direction flag and the original flag. The dissemination distance shows how far the data packet should be propagated.

Algorithm 1 shows the decision phases of flag values in EpiDOL. While the vehicle is moving in the packets' dissemination direction (Line 1-2), if there are any same directional neighbors (Line 3), it means that packet will propagate in the original side, of is 1 (Line 4). Additionally, for providing the continuity of the packet dissemination, EpiDOL sends this packet to the opposite directional vehicles (Line 5) by setting the of and df to 0 (Line 6). Another case is when the value of df is 0 (Line 9-10). This shows that vehicle is moving in the opposite direction of the packets' dissemination. If there are any same directional neighbors (Line 11), packet is sending to them with the same flag values (Line 12). If there are any opposite directional neighbors (Line 13), which are actually in the original side, of value is set to 1 (Line 14), showing that the packet returns its original directional side.

4.2 Probability Functions

The decision of forwarding a packet or not is taken by a probabilistic manner at each node independently. Prior to the each packet transmission, a probability that estimates the necessity of the transmission of a packet from a particular node is calculated with the help of the number of total neighbors. We assumed that the more the neighborhood number is, the higher the chance of nodes receiving the data packet. With this assumption in mind the most trivial probability function is $p = 1/N$, where N is the number of neighbors, however it can easily be proven that this function will not perform good in dense networks. Within a neighborhood with N nodes, the probability of a packet which is not transmitted by a particular node is $p^c = 1 - 1/N$. In homogeneously distributed dense network, we can safely assume that there are no clustering, so each node will approximately have the same number of neighbors. Since each node decides independently with the assumption of a packet is received by N nodes the probability of a packet not forwarded by any nodes is;

Let $N = \#of Neighbors$. Then,

$$p_N^c = \left(1 - \frac{1}{N}\right)^N \qquad (1)$$

If we take the limit of this probability as N goes to infinity, to see the probability of a packet being not forwarded by any nodes in a dense network,

$$\lim_{N \to \infty} p_N^c = \lim_{N \to \infty} \left(1 - \frac{1}{N}\right)^N$$
$$= \lim_{N \to \infty} \left(\frac{1}{e} - \frac{1}{2eN} - \frac{5}{24eN^2} + ...\right) = \frac{1}{e} \approx 0.37 \qquad (2)$$

This shows that, in dense networks since p is so small, the dissemination of the packet will be stopped with approximately 0.37 probability. In real life, due to collisions in a dense network, the number of nodes that receive a packet is much less than N. Consequently the probability of a packet not forwarded by any nodes is even higher than 0.37. For avoiding these situations, we multiply our value with α parameter. So we choose $p = \frac{\alpha}{N}$ which decreases the p_N^c to $\frac{1}{e^\alpha}$ for large N. Note that the case of $p > 1$ is treated as if $p = 1$. Both p_{same} and p_{opp} are calculated with this function. However, according to our simulations, we detected that the best α values are different for propagating packets in the original and in the opposite directions. Thereon we use 2 different α values; α_{same} and $\alpha_{opposite}$ which are optimized by evaluating the different α values on various scenarios.

The decision of using opposite lane nodes as relay nodes not only depends on the number of neighbors but also depends on the spatial distribution of the nodes around. The extreme case is the vehicles at the rear end of a cluster. Basically they will have large number of neighbors due to number of vehicles that lead them, however these neighbors are not helpful for propagating packets to backward direction. With this intuition we proposed the following Algorithm 2 to decide on usage of opposite lane nodes. Therefore, the corresponding $p_{sameToOpp}$ is equivalent to $P\{\#BackwardNeighbors \leq backwardValue\}$. This function helps to solve the disconnected networks problem by continuing the packet dissemination using opposite sided vehicles as relaying nodes. Backward functions use Algorithm 2. In this function, only vehicles in the rear end of a connected cluster are sending packets to the opposite lane.

Algorithm 2. Backward Function
---
algorithm executed after each data packet arrives
if $NumberOfBackwardNeighbors \leq backwardValue$ then
   send with $p = 1$
else
   $p = 0$
end if
---

5 Implementation

In our simulations, we use SUMO [18] for generating realistic low and high density traces. The simulation environment is ns-3 [19]. According to [20], the typical transmission range is 400 meters. We consider a network with randomly distributed vehicles over a 6-lane bidirectional highway. Our region of interest (ROI) has a length of 5km. Since we assumed that there are not any intersections in our ROI, neither death nor birth of a node are allowed. To imitate the dynamic behavior of a highway, the speeds of the vehicles are uniformly distributed from 80km/h to 120km/h.

5.1 Performance Metrics

EpiDOL is designed for merging epidemic approach with highly mobile ad-hoc networks. In order to evaluate its reliability and efficiency, we use the following performance metrics versus node density which is vehicles/square meter. Moreover, these metrics also enable an objective comparison of our proposed algorithm with other approaches.

- **End-to-End Delay:** Time taken for packet transmission from source to nodes which are in the range of dissemination distance. For each packet received by every node, it is given by; $End\text{-}to\text{-}End\ Delay = t_{receive} - t_{firstSending}$.
- **Throughput:** This parameter shows the rate of successfully received packets by all nodes which are in the dissemination distance. Calculation is as follows: $Throughput = \frac{\#received\ packets\ for\ each\ node}{\#\ all\ transmitted\ packets} \times 100$.
- **Opposite Lane:** This parameter measures how many times opposite lane nodes resend the packets that are taken from the original side. Calculation is as follows: $Opposite\ Lane = \frac{\#packets\ sent\ by\ opposite\ directional\ nodes}{\#\ all\ packets} \times 100$.
- **Overhead:** The number of duplicate packets received during the simulation. The overhead is simply equal to the number of received duplicate packets at each node.

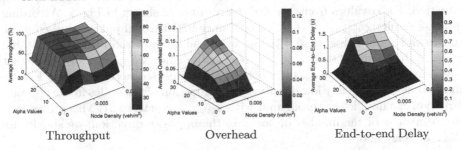

Throughput   Overhead   End-to-end Delay

Fig. 1. Choosing optimal α_{same}

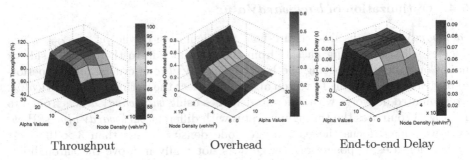

Throughput   Overhead   End-to-end Delay

Fig. 2. Choosing optimal $\alpha_{opposite}$

5.2   Optimization of α_{same}

For optimization of the α_{same} value, we generated SUMO traces which include 10 to 500 vehicles ride in the same direction. Changing α values from 3 to the 30, we produced 3D graphs in Fig. 1. According to these results, α_{same} is chosen as 15, since 90% throughput is achieved while the end-to-end delay is less than 0.06s and the overhead is lower than 0.07. α_{same} being equal to 15 ensures if we have less than 15 vehicles within the coverage area, all nodes will try to forward packets. This is desirable in a sparse network, since at low density our main concern is the survival of the packet rather than the packet collisions. Besides, as the neighbor numbers increase and p_{same} decreases the expected number of retransmissions in a certain area will remain around 15. As seen in Fig. 1b, after a certain node density the overhead does not increase at all for $\alpha_{same} = 15$. This supports our claim about our p_{same} being sensitive to node density in the network. It is obvious that the performance can be increased with the perfect knowledge of the network density. However, due to excessive control packets, acquiring this information will increase the network overhead significantly, that might even decrease the overall throughput.

5.3   Optimization of $\alpha_{opposite}$

For optimization of the $\alpha_{opposite}$ value, we generated SUMO traces which include 10 to 300 vehicles in the opposite direction and 60 vehicles in the original (same) direction. For α values from 3 to 30, the results are shown in Fig. 2. According to these results, $\alpha_{opposite}$ is chosen as 21, since 97% throughput is achieved while end-to-end delay is less than 0.1s and overhead is lower than 0.1. The optimal $\alpha_{opposite}$ being more than α_{same} is reasonable since we need more persistent transmissions to carry packets in between disconnected networks. Also Fig. 2a shows that even in really low densities, the utilization of the nodes in the opposite direction can double the throughput with $\alpha_{opposite}$ equals to 21. This proves that the regardless of the number of nodes in the opposite direction, we should use them as relay nodes.

5.4   Optimization of $backwardValue$

$backwardValue$ is used as a threshold in calculation of the $p_{sameToOpp}$ which decides whether sending packets from the original side to the opposite side or not. Consequently, choosing the best $backwardValue$ is crucial for the performance of the algorithm. To reason about and select the optimal $backwardValue$, we simulated networks with different densities using $backwardValue$'s from 0 to 17. Fig. 3 compares the throughput rates with different $backwardValue$'s. However we should focus the part where node density is less than 3×10^{-3}. At higher densities, opposite lane usage does not really improve the throughput, since we do not observe disconnected networks problem anymore, consequently all $backwardValue$'s converge to same throughput levels. However, the average overhead for densities higher than 3×10^{-3} does not significantly differ for different $backwardValue$'s as shown in Fig. 4. At high density conditions, the necessity of using opposite lane decreases. According to our function, the number of eligible vehicles which send packets to opposite lane also decreases while the density increases. In summary, by using the appropriate $backwardValue$ we can double the throughput in low densities in return of higher overhead, however our main concern is to maintain connectivity rather than overhead in low densities. On top of this for higher densities, even though backward function can not improve the throughput, it also does not significantly increase the overhead which is the limiting factor. This proves the density adaptivity of our approach. To decide the optimal value of $backwardValue$, we have to consider Fig. 3 and Fig.

4 simultaneously. According to Fig. 3, to achieve 90% throughput in lower densities, *backwardValue* should be higher than 9. However, for *backwardValue*'s greater than 9, the throughput does not increase at all. Furthermore, considering overhead values of Fig. 4 for several different vehicle densities, the optimum *backwardValue* is determined as 11. As shown in Fig. 5, an evaluation of this *backwardValue* along with two others has been performed and these results indicate the density adaptive nature of opposite lane usage ratio with the probability function making use of number of backward neighbors.

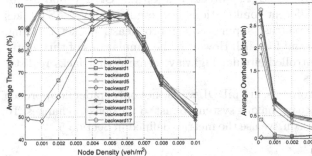 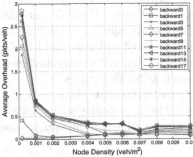

Fig. 3. Throughput for Backward Functions

Fig. 4. Overhead for Backward Functions

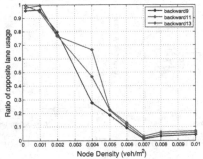

Fig. 5. Opposite Lane Usage Ratio

5.5   Compared Protocols

To prove the efficiency of EpiDOL, we compared it with state of the art data dissemination protocols designed for VANET, namely Edge-Aware [3] and DV-CAST [4]. Edge-Aware is also an epidemic protocol that utilizes the GPS information. Basically it calculates the probability of rebroadcasting P as

$$P = \begin{cases} 1, & \text{if } N_f \text{ or } N_b = 0 \\ 1 - exp\left(-\alpha\frac{|N_f - N_b|}{N_f + N_b}\right), & \text{otherwise} \end{cases} \tag{3}$$

where N_f and N_b are the number of times the car has received that particular message from front and from back respectively. With this approach, they have managed to give higher probabilities to vehicles near the head or tail of a cluster.

However, they have not proposed a specialized function to use opposite lane that can increase the connectivity and the throughput considerably for disconnected networks as we proved in this work. Also, the proposed protocol is only compared with simple flooding protocol in a controlled scenario rather than realistic traces.

DV-CAST [4] is a distributed broadcast protocol that utilizes opposite lane vehicles. By exchanging GPS information, every vehicle classifies its network as a well connected, sparsely connected or totally disconnected network. Then depending on this classification, vehicles set the values for three flags, MDC (message direction connectivity), DFlg (direction flag) and ODC (opposite direction connectivity). For different combinations of these flags, DV-CAST takes different actions such as broadcast suppression, rebroadcast, packet relaying, carry and forward and wait and forward. However, the simulations of this protocol is only limited with controlled circular highway scenario that lacks realistic traces such as SUMO traces.

Compared to these two protocols, in EpiDOL we use not only epidemic approach but also add some intelligence by making system robust to the density changes. To achieve an objective comparison, we use the metrics defined in Section 5.

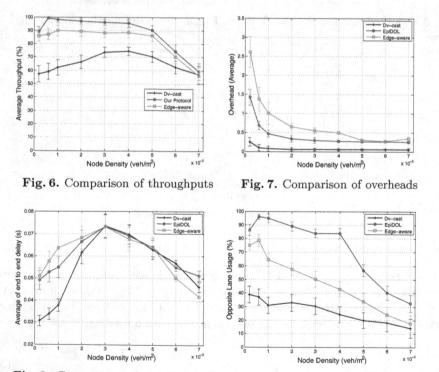

Fig. 6. Comparison of throughputs

Fig. 7. Comparison of overheads

Fig. 8. Comparison of end-to-end delays

Fig. 9. Comparison of opposite lane usage

6 Results

We have compared the selected protocols in ns-3 with realistic SUMO traces by using 10 random runs. Our results are shown in Figures.6-9.

Fig. 6 shows the ratio of successfully received packets by all same directional nodes in terms of percentage. Error bars in the figure show standard deviations around averages. In low densities, only EpiDOL achieves more than 90% throughput. Higher opposite lane usage shown in Fig. 9 ensures higher throughput. This proves that our protocol handles the disconnected network problem more effectively than the other protocols. According to Fig. 8, end-to-end delays of all protocols are comparable. Since DV-CAST can not distribute packets to the whole network, it is expected to see lower end-to-end delays. Like Overhead of EpiDOL is lower than Edge-aware but higher than DV-CAST as shown in Fig. 7. However, in these densities our main concern is maintaining connection between disconnected networks rather than overhead.

In high densities, as seen in Fig. 6 throughput is slightly better than the other protocols. Fig. 7 shows that this improvement is realized without introducing additional overhead to the network. EpiDOL has managed to deliver packets to higher number of nodes with comparable end-to-end delays as seen in Fig. 8. Achieving higher throughputs with low overheads in high densities shows that EpiDOL was able to deal with broadcast storm problem.

7 Conclusion

We proposed EpiDOL which is an epidemic and density adaptive protocol for data dissemination in VANETs that utilizes the opposite lane capacity with novel probability functions. We have optimized parameters of the algorithm based on analysis by using traffic traces from SUMO. We compared the performance of the proposed algorithm with the existing algorithms in terms of end-to-end delay, overhead, throughput and opposite lane usage.

According to results in low densities we achieved more than the 90% throughput with comparable end-to-end delay, overhead and opposite lane usage. This showed that EpiDOL handled the disconnected network problem. In high densities, without excessive values in end-to-end delay and overhead, throughput achieved by EpiDOL is better than the others. This also indicates that broadcast storm problem did not effect our protocol due to its probabilistic density adaptive functions.

As a future work, we aim to focus on the analysis of the performance of EpiDOL for different data dissemination scenarios.

Acknowledgement. This work has been conducted as part of Turk Telekom Research project under Grant Number 11315-07.

References

1. Biswas, S., Tatchikou, R., Dion, F.: Vehicle-to-vehicle wireless communication protocols for enhancing highway traffic safety. IEEE Communications Magazine 44(1), 74–82 (2006)

2. Li, F., Wang, Y.: Routing in vehicular ad hoc networks: A survey. Vehicular Technology Magazine 2(2), 12–22 (2007)
3. Nekovee, M.: Epidemic algorithms for reliable and efficient information dissemination in vehicular. Intelligent Transport Systems, IET 3(2), 104–110 (2009)
4. Tonguz, O., Wisitpongphan, N., Bai, F.: Dv-cast: A distributed vehicular broad- cast protocol for vehicular ad hoc networks. IEEE Wireless Communications 17(2), 47–57 (2010)
5. Fleetnet project (2003), http://www.neclab.eu/Projects/eetnet.htm
6. Cartel project, http://cartel.csail.mit.edu/doku.php
7. Tonguz, O., Wisitpongphan, N., Bai, F., Mudalige, P., Sadekar, V.: Broadcasting in vanet. In: 2007 Mobile Networking for Vehicular Environments, pp. 7–12 (May 2007)
8. Wisitpongphan, N., Tonguz, O., Parikh, J., Mudalige, P., Bai, F., Sadekar, V.: Broadcast storm mitigation techniques in vehicular ad hoc networks. IEEE Wireless Communications 14(6), 84–94 (2007)
9. Schwartz, R., Ohazulike, A., Sommer, C., Scholten, H., Dressler, F., Havinga, P.: Fair and adaptive data dissemination for traffic information systems. In: 2012 IEEE Vehicular Networking Conference (VNC), pp. 1–8 (2012)
10. Blum, J., Eskandarian, A., Hoffman, L.: Challenges of intervehicle ad hoc networks. IEEE Transactions on Intelligent Transportation Systems 5(4), 347–351 (2004)
11. Taleb, T., Ochi, M., Jamalipour, A., Kato, N., Nemoto, Y.: An efficient vehicle-heading based routing protocol for vanet networks. In: Wireless Communications and Networking Conference, WCNC 2006, vol. 4, pp. 2199–2204. IEEE (April 2006)
12. Taleb, T., Sakhaee, E., Jamalipour, A., Hashimoto, K., Kato, N., Nemoto, Y.: A stable routing protocol to support its services in vanet networks. IEEE Transactions on Vehicular Technology 56(6), 3337–3347 (2007)
13. Costa, P., Gavidia, D., Koldehofe, B., Miranda, H., Musolesi, M., Riva, O.: When cars start gossiping. In: Proceedings of the 6th Workshop on Middleware for Network Eccentric and Mobile Applications, MiNEMA 2008, pp. 1–4 (2008)
14. Meireles, R., Steenkiste, P., Barros, J.: Dazl: Density-aware zone-based packet forwarding in vehicular networks. In: 2012 IEEE Vehicular Networking Conference (VNC), pp. 234–241 (2012)
15. Naumov, V., Baumann, R., Gross, T.: An evaluation of inter-vehicle ad hoc networks based on realistic vehicular traces. In: Proceedings of the 7th ACM International Symposium on Mobile Ad Hoc Networking and Computing, MobiHoc 2006, pp. 108–119 (2006)
16. Zuo, J., Wang, Y., Liu, Y., Zhang, Y.: Performance evaluation of routing protocol in vanet with vehicle-node density. In: 2010 6th International Conference on Wireless Communications Networking and Mobile Computing (WiCOM), pp. 1–4 (September 2010)
17. Ieee standard for information technology- local and metropolitan area networks specific requirements- part 11: Wireless lan medium access control (mac) and physical layer (phy) specifications amendment 6: Wireless access in vehicular environments, IEEE Std 802.11p-2010 (Amendment to IEEE Std 802.11-2007 as amended by IEEE Std 802.11k-2008, IEEE Std 802.11r-2008, IEEE Std 802.11y- 2008, IEEE Std 802.11n-2009, and IEEE Std 802.11w-2009), pp. 1-51, 15
18. Sumo - simulation of urban mobility, http://sumo.sourceforge.net
19. Network simulator, ns-3, http://www.nsnam.org/
20. Zhang, M., Wolff, R.: Routing protocols for vehicular ad hoc networks in rural areas. IEEE Communications Magazine 46(11), 126–131 (2008)

Advanced Approach to Future Service Development

Tetiana Kot[1], Larisa Globa[1], and Alexander Schill[2]

[1] National Technical University of Ukriane «Kyiv Polytechnic Institute», Ukraine
[2] Technische Universitat Dresden, Fakultat Informatik, Deutschland

Abstract. Modern companies, including telecommunication ones and mobile operators, working in the global environment, need to guarantee technological effectiveness and innovation, renewing their technologies and services. Communication technologies and variety of services are to be improved and developed extremely fast. This results in the need for constant adaptation and reconfiguration of complex software systems, used in global environment to provide and monitor deployed services. For instance, OSS/BSS is used in the domain of telecommunication companies. Reconfiguration of complex software systems covers application development for service provisioning, their dynamic monitoring and reconfiguration. Currently, system adaptation and service design strategies are poorly formalized and validated. In current state-of-the-art approaches, several iterations involving analysts and system architects are necessary, resulting in time and money consuming service development. The approach proposed in this paper fills this gap. It employs a well-defined workflow and analysis model for developing and adapting complex software systems. The applicability of this novel approach is confirmed by an implemented software tool. The proposed approach and tool provide automation of service development, focusing on planning and design stages, considering both functional and non-functional requirements and realizing computational independent workflow transformation into its execution model.

Keywords: service development, OSS/BSS, non-functional requirements, workflow design and transformation, Dia editor.

1 Introduction

Today, companies, working in global environment, constantly renovate and improve their technologies, providing services by web-oriented applications [1]. This is realized via service development and re-engineering. Companies tend to minimize time of service provision, constantly improving communication technologies and applications. Thus, means and tools for fast workflow design and reengineering during system runtime and for providing services within a minimal time are in high demand.

The lifecycle of service development is an iterative process, consisting of the following stages:

1. workflow design: development and description of computation independent and computational workflows, including service planning, applications prototyping;

T. Bauschert (Ed.): EUNICE 2013, LNCS 8115, pp. 233–244, 2013.
© IFIP International Federation for Information Processing 2013

2. workflow analysis and simulation, considering several system parameters;
3. workflow enactment, providing deployment models, considering both hardware and software service deployment alternatives;
4. service/workflows monitoring, leading to services re-configuration.

Currently, the service planning stage is performed manually. This does not result in optimal solutions because a lot of factors have to be considered when planning differentiated services [2]. Furthermore, in the current state-of-the-art computational independent workflow design, being performed using existing notations and tools, on one hand all required parameters, necessary on the service planning stage, such as numerical values of execution time and resources, and also document and information flows, supporting service provision, are not considered and on the other hand poor connection to system functionality, realizing these workflows are provide.

When service design and deployment, an important aspect concerns NFR[1] to service provision. It is extremely important to meet NFR on design stage, otherwise provided service may be useless in practice.

Currently, NFR are not considered with perspective of provided services list as legacy methods can design service according to NFR, but cannot model an influence of concurrent services on particular NFR because of collaboration between services. There are also no tools allowing flexible balancing between services.

Transformation processes between workflow modeling stages is still an open question, though there are transformation standards and languages [3], but this issue is not fully automated and has to be investigated to make service design correct.

This paper describes an advanced approach to future service development, including novel computational independent workflow design method, NFR balancing method and modified service workflows transformation method.

The paper is structured as follows: Section 2 contains state of the art analysis of workflow design notations and tools. State of the art analysis of methods and approaches to considering NFR. NFR analysis methods and service implementation technologies are described. BPMN to BPEL transformation strategies are also considered.

Section 3 introduces advanced approach to service development. It includes workflow design method, focusing on two core aspects: a computational independent workflow model and workflow analysis method, providing service provisioning time minimization; NFR balancing method, focusing on functional and non-functional requirements collaboration; modified service workflows transformation method.

Section 4 presents a prototypical realization of the advanced approach, including design and transformation tools and highlights evaluation results of the developed tools. The evaluation has been applied using a real-world scenario within a telecommunication company.

Section 5 concludes the work with a summary and outlook on future work.

---

[1] Non-functional requirements.

2   State of the Art and Background

2.1   Workflow Design Notations and Tools

Service planning is defined by finding a good way to create service provision at minimal time, having specific resource values as a limitation. In the following a summary of the state of the art of the central areas of this overall field will be discussed. A state of the art analysis of workflow design notations and tools, workflow analysis methods and systems, parameters, which should be taken into account at the planning stage and NRF design methods are presented.

Computational Independent Workflow Design

Computational independent workflows are designed using graphical standards, allowing their formalization in a diagrammatic way. Analysis has shown that in practice computational independent workflows are usually designed using graphical notations such as BPMN 2.0^2, UML AD^3, $USDL^4$ and tools such as CA ERwin Process Modeler[5] and Enterprise Architect[6].

The main criteria, used when analyzing current state-of-the-art notations and tools for computational independent workflow design, are possibility to consider and analyze several parameters, necessary on the service planning stage, such as service provision time and resources, and on the other hand provide connection to system functionality, which should realize these workflows.

USDL doesn't meet all the requirements of workflows analysis and design, its usage is difficult due to its complexity, in spite of its comprehensiveness.

The main argument against using regular BPMN is that management of resources can be expressed only via lanes (actors, roles, etc.) or performers of user or manual tasks [4], when execution time parameters are not considered. All further existing workflow modeling notations have this core criticism in common.

Nevertheless, BPMN, providing computational independent to computing workflows transformation (BPEL[7] diagrams), was applied as a basic notation for computational independent workflow design, being extended with added missing concepts [5].

Workflow Analysis

The overview of the workflow analysis methods and tools has shown, that there exist two types of analysis, both considering computational workflow [6]:

1. Design time analysis (simulation and verification);
2. Runtime analysis (i.e., process mining, based on the execution logs).

---

2   http://www.omg.org/spec/BPMN/2.0/
3   UML Activity Diagram.
4   http://www.internet-of-services.com/index.php?id=264
5   http://erwin.com/products/detail/ca_erwin_process_modeler/
6   http://www.sparxsystems.com/products/index.html
7   Business Process Execution Language.

Software tools such as Cactus, ASKALON, GLUE, etc. [7] are used for these analysis fields. Mentioned and analyzed current possibilities for this task stage are very limited. Shortcomings of workflow analysis methods and tools are clearly described in [8]. The central criticism is that the requirements analysis stage is applied mainly in a manual manner.

2.2 Methods and Approaches to Considering NFR

Early-phase requirements engineering should address organizational and NFR, while later-phase engineering focuses on completeness, consistency and automated verification of requirements. Not proper dealing with NFR leads to considerable delays in the project and consequently to significant increase of the final costs [9].

NFR are considered on design stage and there are several approaches to model NFR within the scope of developed service. NFR framework [10] is a methodology that guides system to accommodate change with replaceable components. Such NFR as security, accuracy, performance and cost are used to drive the overall design process and choosing design alternatives.

KAOS [11] is another methodology, considering NFR. It allows requirements engineering, enabling analysts to build requirements models and derive requirements documents from KAOS models.

There are some other approached and methods to NFR modeling [12, 13], but all of them don't consider collaboration between FR[8] and NFR. The legacy software tools, such as NFR-Assistant CASE[9], ARIS[10], don't provide functionality to model NFR and consider their influence on system functionality.

2.3 BPMN to BPEL Transformation Strategies

There are various BPMN to BPEL transformation strategies, such as Element-Preservation, Element-Minimization, Structure-Maximization and Structure-Identification [14], Event-Condition-Action-Rules [15] and others. A basic idea of mapping which is used in most algorithms of translating BPMN or any other WF-net into BPEL code uses a mix of mentioned strategies.

Two categories of tools are applied in practice:

1. BPMN graph is serialized to an XML document. Then the last one is automatically translated into an abstract BPEL document. The abstract BPEL is enriched with the pieces of information, necessary to make it executable.
2. BPMN graph is translated directly into executable BPEL code. This is only possible when input/output files of the future Web Service (WSDL files) are created in advance.

---

[8] Functional requirements.
[9] Quan Tran "NFR-Assistant: tool support for achieving quality", Application-Specific Systems and Software Engineering and Technology, 1999. ASSET '99. Proceedings. 1999 IEEE Symposium.
[10] http://www.softwareag.com/corporate/products/aris_platform/default.asp

There are three main problems of BPMN-BPEL translation:

— fundamental mismatch between these two languages: BPMN is graph-structured notation while BPEL is block-structured language;
— readability of the resulting BPEL code is very low;
— translation of extended notations with additional workflow parameters is not possible.

Hence, development of the method providing automated translation of extended BPMN elements is an important aspect in service development process.

3   Advanced Approach to Service Development

Proposed advanced approach to future service development includes:

1. novel computational independent workflow design method, focusing on the workflow model and its analysis, allowing to automate service planning stages;
2. NFR balancing method, focusing on collaboration between functional and non-functional requirements, allowing to automate service planning stages;
3. modified service workflows transformation method, providing abstract to execution workflows transformation, considering workflows required parameters.

Each of the proposed method is briefly described below.

3.1   Workflow Design Method

Workflow design includes workflow modeling and simulation. The novel method of workflow design presented in this section is focused on computational independent workflow and consists of the following stages:

1. extended modeling of computational independent workflow;
2. computational independent workflow analysis, including:
   2.1   forming workflow graph and verifying its connectivity;
   2.2   workflow execution time minimization;
   2.3   transformation of workflow to realization diagram.

The suggested method modifies MDA[11] on the business logic level [6].

Workflow Model
The workflow model is one of the core aspects of the proposed method, allowing its formal description and thus its in-depth analysis and transformation to more fine-grained representations. In the following, the workflow formalization variant used within our approach is presented.

The mathematical formalization of a workflow can be done by using:

$$BP = (E, I, P) \tag{1}$$

---

[11]   Model Driven Architecture.

where E is the set of workflow identification objects; I is the set of workflow informational objects and P is the set of workflow parameters of service provisioning.

The identification objects $\{E_{id,\ id=1,4}\}$ include: E_1 = name, E_2 = description, E_3 = executor, $E_4 = O$ – set of works.

The set of workflow informational objects includes income and outcome document and data objects:

$$I = \{I_{doc}^{in}\} U \{I_{dat}^{in}\}\ U\ \{I_{doc}^{out}\} U \{I_{dat}^{out}\} \tag{2}$$

The workflow parameters $\{P_{i,\ i=1,6}\}$ cover: $P_1 = T_{ex}$ – execution time; $P_2 = R$ – resource, required for execution; $P_3 = A$ – ability to be automatically executed; $P_4 = S$ – set of subsystems, used for workflow execution; $P_5 = F^S$ — set of separate subsystem functions, realizing task execution; $P_6 = P_{ad}$ – set of additional workflow parameters.

Separate work models can be represented in a formal manner as:

$$O = (O, I^O, P) \tag{3}$$

where O is the set of identification objects; I^O is the set of informational objects; P is the set of service provision parameters.

Identification objects $\{O_{id,\ id=1,3}\}$ include: $O_1 = N_o$ – name; $O_2 = d$ – description; $O_3 = E$ – executor. Task informational objects include income and outcome informational objects (document and data). Set of work parameters $\{P^O_{i,\ i=1,7}\}$ include: $P^O_1 = \xi_{kl}\ (r_{kl})$ — execution time of work l of stage k; $P^O_2 = r_{kl}$ – resource, required for execution work l of stage k; $P^O_3 = a$ – the ability to be automatically executed; $P^O_4 = S$ – set of OSS/BSS[12] subsystems, used for workflow execution; $P^O_5 = F^S$ – set of OSS/BSS subsystem functions, realizing works execution; $P^O_6 = R_O^n$ – work realization alternatives, defining execution time and resource values:

$$R_O^n = (N_R, \xi_{kl}^n\ (r_{kl}), r_{kl}^n) \tag{4}$$

$P^O_7 = P_{ad}$ – set of additional work parameters.

The proposed model allows to perform workflow analysis at a planning stage, applying graph theory and optimization algorithm, represented below.

Workflow Analysis

The workflow analysis method, providing workflow model verification, execution time minimization and automating its transformation, is briefly described below.

The workflow graph model can be represented as sequential stages, containing a few parallel executed tasks, enabling the definition of execution time as follows:

$$T_{ex} = \sum_k \max_l \xi_{kl} (r_{kl}) \tag{5}$$

The suggested method of workflow analysis is represented mathematically as:

$$M = (G_f, G_V, M_{min}, M_{tr}) \tag{6}$$

---

[12] Operation Support System/Business Support System.

where G_f is the graph generating procedure; G_V is the graph connectivity verification; M_{min} is the execution time minimization and M_{tr} is the diagram into realization model transformation. Each of the procedure is described in details in [6].

Each work of the workflow has one to three implementation variants, defining execution time and resources, the task is to find such implementation variant for each task to minimize the total workflow execution time, when the total resource is limited and known. The objective function of the task is represented below:

$$F(r) = \min_{\sum_{kl} r_{kl} = r} M \sum_k \max_l \xi_{kl}(r_{kl}) \tag{7}$$

It is also necessary to find the implementation variant for each task, i.e. $\{r_{kl}, k = 1, ..., n, \; l = 1, ..., m\}$, where the required minimum of time (7) is reached. Solution for function (7), applying dynamic programming, is described in [6].

3.2   NFR Balancing Method

The proposed NFR balancing method is based on creating FR and NFR collaboration model. Implementation of functional requirements is presented by listed FB[13]. Each of FB is responsible for particular logical function. The proposed method includes NFR Catalogue development, FR decomposition, NFR mapping, FB distribution and Balancing stages. NFR balancing method uses NFR Catalogue and FR and create collaboration model between them. The main stages of the concept are described in [16] and briefly represented below.

Catalogue of NFR. It is proposed to operate with catalogues for performance and serviceability. Catalogues are updated with further operationalizations to keep own NFR catalogues updated, which facilitates reuse of acquired knowledge on NFR.

FR decomposition. It describes influence of services features on NFR. Services and features are depicted for each FB (Table 1).

Table 1. FR decomposition

Service	Functional Block	Functional Requirement
Service1	FB1.1 or FB1.2	FR1, FR2
Service1	FB2.1 and FB2.2	FR3, FR1
Service2	FB1.1	FR5, FR6
Service2	FB3	FR1, FR7

NFR mapping. Each call of FB requests a defined amount of system resources (memory, processor time, etc.) and has list of characteristics: response time, availability, etc. These characteristics are mapped to NFR from catalogue with values, specifying how exact FB meets particular NFR (it is graded from 0 to 100, Table 2). One FB can provide the same functionality with different NFR (FB1.1, FB1.2). From functional point of view there is no difference between these two blocks. The difference is

---

[13] Functional block.

how each FB meets the NFR. NFR mapping requires considering every service and connecting it to required FB, covering requested functionality.

Table 2. NFR mapping

Functional block/ NFR	Availability	Performance	Security
FB1.1	90	80	10
FB1.2	80	70	20
FB2.1	50	10	10
FB2.2	5	20	30

FB distribution. Using NFR catalogues and FR decomposition, FB distribution can be realized. Fig.1 shows that FR 1 and FR 2 from Table 1 can be implemented either by FB1.1 or FB1.2. The implementation way depends on NFR specification for particular case.

Balancing and target models. The target model is obtained by using balancing between NFR and approaches to implementation of a particular functionality with FB. For instance, there is the Customer's demand for service supporting the highest availability and there is no specified requirement for security and performance. Such case can be realized by the model, represented on Fig.2. A priority is assigned to the requirements, considered during target model development.

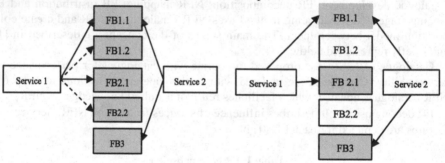

Fig. 1. Functional blocks distribution   **Fig. 2.** Target deployment model

3.3   Modified Service Workflows Transformation Method

The modified method is based on BPD2BPEL translation algorithm [17] which can translate arbitrary diagrams into BPEL code. BPMN extension (BPNE) [5] has been taken as an input extended business process diagram.

Key feature of proposed method is modified analysis process. When the element is analyzed, its additional parameters are also checked. If new parameters are found, information about them is saved for their subsequent transformation into BPEL elements. Proposed method considers each BPNE element.

4   Service Design Tool

BPMA. The proposed workflow design method is implemented in a new developed tool BPMA[14] (fig.3). It uses standard GTK+, Dia diagram editor, PyDia interface, Python Interpreter, PyGTK[15] and developed module BPEA, implementing workflow modeling and analysis algorithms. Main BPMA components functions are described further. "Init" realizes Dia and user intercommunication and launches modules functions. "Props" provides setting, changing and saving of workflows and its objects parameters. "Bplyzer" implements time minimization algorithms. "Transform" implements the transformation logic to create a realization diagram from workflow requirements. "Reports" generates reports on workflow modeling and analysis.

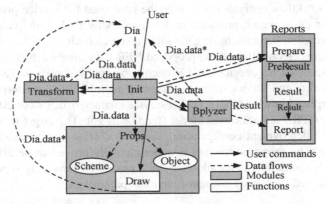

Fig. 3. BPMA functioning scheme

BPNE-BPEL transformation tool implements presented BPNE-BPEL transformation method (fig.4) [18].

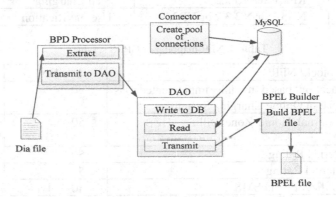

Fig. 4. Structural scheme of the BPNE-BPEL transformation tool

---

[14] Business Process Modeling & Analysis.
[15] Set of Python wrappers for the GTK+ GUI library.

The tool performs transformation of data, extracted from BPNE file, into representation form, convenient for the subsequent work; translation of BPNE elements into BPEL code, using its object-oriented model; gathering all translated elements and components in a single BPEL file.

4.1   Case-Study

Workflow design. BPMA has been tested during the planning and design of several services, such as «Bonus program», «Selling Electronic Voucher», «Tariff Plan Change» [6], in the SITRONICS Telecom Solutions company. Testing results have shown that for services, having 1-1.5 months of development time, it can be reduced by 3-5 days and development costs can be decreased by 5-7 man-days for one service; the proposed workflow analysis can reduce the time used for service provision up to 20 seconds for the services, provided in 3-5 minutes by finding the combination of tasks implementation variants, having the same resource limit.

NFR balancing. Evaluation of the proposed NFR balancing method is demonstrated on charging of GPRS service. Its FR decomposition is shown in Table 3. GPRS service availability and service delay are taken as main NFRs. Considering statistical data and enterprise knowledgebase, GPRS service characteristics were estimated (Table 4) and the GPRS service target model (fig.5) was got. The target model provides service optimal deployment configuration, ensuring service highest availability with minimal delay. The proposed method is experimentally proved to be efficient when services design and deployment, allowing NFR modeling, providing service functionality with required functional and non-functional parameters.

Table 3. FR decomposition of GPRS service

Service	Functional Block	Functional Requirement
GPRS	LBS1.1 or LBS1.2	Location Base Charging
GPRS	RF2.1 and RF2.2	Step Charging
GPRS	NB3.1 or NB 3.2 or NB3.3.	User notification

Table 4. NFR mapping of GPRS service

Functional block/ NFR	Availability	Delay
LBS1.1- location based module implemented as internal cache in Online Charging System	90	80
LBS1.2 –external Home Zone Billing -HZB platform	50	10
RF2.1 – internal Rating	50	20
RF2.2 – external Rating	5	15
NB3.1 – notification via SMS	40	50
NB3.2 –online notification via USSD	50	40
NB3.3 – offline notification via email	50	10

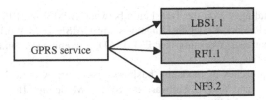

Fig. 5. Target model for GPRS service

5   Summary and Outlook

A novel approach for analyzing and developing modern services, provided by web-oriented applications, has been proposed. The discussion is focused on the development of a computational independent workflow model, its analysis, transformation of abstract into executional workflows, and also aspect of NFR balancing when service development. The proposed workflow model provides formalization of service provision parameters, required for the planning stage. The analysis methods allow automating service planning and minimizing service provision time. The workflow design method reduces the time of service re-engineering up to 10% by improving and automating the service planning stage.

The proposed NFR balancing method provides NFR description, considering collaboration between services and meeting NFR by system FB. The method increases efficiency of service development on design and deployment stages and allows fast system reconfiguration on customer demand.

Modified BPMN-BPEL transformation method and tool provide automation of abstract workflows transformation into execution ones, allowing to consider workflow required parameters.

Future work will focus on analysis of computing workflows and their enactment, services monitoring and re-configuration, which are strongly connected to the design and analysis stages. NFR balancing method will be extended with possibility to consider possible change of NFR list and their priorities during different time periods (e.g. periods with high load) and also take into account changing priority between services.

Key aspects of the proposed approach to future service development can be applied to extend ISO/IEC/IEEE 29148:2011 Standard, dealing with the processes and products related to the engineering of requirements for systems and software products and services throughout the life cycle, to raise the overall efficiency of service development and re-engineering.

References

1. Terplan, K.: OSS Essentials: Support System Solutions for Service Providers, 610 p. John Wiley, New York (2001)
2. RFC 2474: Definition of the Differentiated Services Field (DS Field) in the IPv4 and IPv6 Headers, http://tools.ietf.org/html/rfc2474

3. Recker, J., Mendling, J.: On the Translation between BPMN and BPEL: Conceptual Mismatch between Process Modeling Languages. In: CAiSE 2006 Workshop Proceedings - Eleventh International Workshop on EMMSAD, Luxembourg, June 5-6, pp. 521–532 (2006)

4. Börger, E.: Approaches to modeling business processes: A critical analysis of BPMN, workflow patterns and YAWL. Software and System Modeling 11(3), 305–318 (2011)

5. Kot, T., Globa, L., Schill, A.: Applying business process modeling method when telecommunication services development. In: Proceedings of International Conference on Microwave and Telecommunication Technology (CriMiCo), Sevastopol, vol. 1, pp. 457–458 (2011)

6. Kot, T., Reverchuk, A., Globa, L., Schill, A.: A novel approach to increase efficiency of OSS/BSS workflow planning and design. In: Abramowicz, W., Kriksciuniene, D., Sakalauskas, V. (eds.) BIS 2012. LNBIP, vol. 117, pp. 142–152. Springer, Heidelberg (2012)

7. Taylor, I.J., Deelman, E., Gannon, D.B., Shields, M.: Workflows for e-Science. Scientific Workflows for Grids, 523 p. Springer (2007)

8. van der Aalst, W.: BPM and Workflow Analysis. BPTrends 5(4), 1–2 (2007)

9. Software Errors Cost U.S. Economy $59.5 Billion Annually. NIST Assesses Technical Needs of Industry to Improve Software-Testing (2002),
http://www.cse.buffalo.edu/~mikeb/Billions.pdf

10. Chung, L., Nixon, B.A., Yu, E., Mylopoulos, J.: Non-Functional Requirements in Software Engineering, 472 p. Kluwer Academic Publishers, Boston (2000)

11. A KAOS Tutorial (2007),
http://www.objectiver.com/fileadmin/download/documents/
KaosTutorial.pdf

12. Yu, E., Giorgini, P., Maiden, N., Mylopoulos, J.: Social Modeling for Requirements Engineering, 752 p. MIT Press, Cambridge (2011)

13. van Lamsweerde, A.: Requirements Engineering: From System Goals to UML Models to Software Specifications, 650 p. John Wiley and Sons (2009)

14. Mendling, J., Lassen, K., Zdun, U.: Transformation Strategies between Block-Oriented and Graph-Oriented Process Modelling Languages. In: MKWI 2006, Band 2, XML4BPM Track, pp. 297–312. GITO-Verlag, Berlin (2006) ISBN 3-936771-62-6

15. Mendling, J., Lassen, K., Zdun, U.: On the Transformation of Control Flow between Block-Oriented and Graph-Oriented Process Modeling Languages. IJBPIM. Special Issue on Model-Driven Engineering of Executable Business Process Models 3(2), 96–108 (2008)

16. Kot, T., Reverchuk, A., Globa, L., Schill, A.: Method of non-functional requirements balancing when service development. In: Proceedings of the International Multi-Conference ACS-AISBIS 2012 (May-June 2012), Szczecin: Journal of Theoretical and Applied Computer Science 6(3), 50–57 (2012)

17. Ouyang, C., van der Aalst, W.M.P., Dumas, M., ter Hofstede, A.H.M., Mendling, J.: From Business Process Models to Process-Oriented Software Systems. ACM Transactions on Software Engineering and Methodology 19, 1–37 (2006)

18. Pukhkaiev, D., Kot, T., Globa, L.: Translating BPMN/BPNE into BPEL. In: Proceedings of 11th International Conference TCSET 2012, Lviv-Slavske, Ukraine, vol. 1, p. 386 (2012)

A Transversal Alignment between Measurements and Enterprise Architecture for Early Verification of Telecom Service Design

Iyas Alloush[1,2], Yvon Kermarrec[1,2], and Siegfried Rouvrais[1,3]

[1] Telecom Bretagne, Institut Mines-Telecom, Université européenne de Bretagne
Technopole Brest Iroise, CS 83818 29238, Brest Cedex 3, France
[2] UMR CNRS 6285 Lab-STICC
[3] IRISA
firstname.lastname@telecom-bretagne.eu

Abstract. Early verification of Telecom Services (TS) at the design time helps an enterprise to avoid wasting of implementation cost and time. Simulation provides the designer with helpful feedbacks on TS design leaving the implementation and installation costs behind. Our objective in this paper is to present our approach to obtain valuable feedbacks from network simulators and relate them to the information from high abstract scenario of a TS. Relying on Model Driven Engineering discipline and Enterprise Architecture standard, we propose to associate measurement elements with the design ones of different abstraction levels. We implement a model transformation to generate automatically the configurations for NS-3 simulator as a test-bed for our case studies. We illustrate our approach with a video conference example, presenting the different abstract levels and their relationship with measurements.

Keywords: Telecommunication Service, Enterprise Architecture, Model Driven Engineering, Tool Chains, Simulators, Measurements, NS-3, OPNET, Early Verification, Model Transformation, Code Generation.

1 Introduction

The production of Telecommunication Services (TS) is a long term process and consumes many resources. A mistake in the TS design may result in serious consequences to the rest of the life cycle activities. It is difficult and cost expensive to fix errors and flaws in the design after the implementation activity, especially if there are hardware elements to be installed. Therefore, we will take into consideration two points: the TS characteristics, and the TS creation activity.

The TS have several characteristics that make them different from other software systems. The platforms that a TS relies on are large scaled [19] and used by enormous number of customers. The TSs themselves are pervasive [4] and context aware [5] in many cases. A TS may rely on software and hardware elements to perform its tasks. Normally, the TS is composed of numerous number of applications that interact with each other, this results in a complex TS design

T. Bauschert (Ed.): EUNICE 2013, LNCS 8115, pp. 245–256, 2013.

[9]. Describing TS designs using Enterprise Architecture (EA) helps in managing the complexity problem [14].

The contribution of this paper is in the scope of TS creation activity (TSC) [13] and relies on a recent dissertation [11]. We address the early verification activity right after the design one, and before the implementation phase. The aim of the verification activity is to "check that the software meets its stated functional and non-functional requirements" [21]. The Service Creation Environment (SCE) [6] is a collection of software tools that rely on reuse infrastructure used according to the service development methodology, to assist the service developer(s) by automating and simplifying the Service Creation process.

In our research we face the challenges: (1) improving Quality of Service (QoS) that meets the customer satisfaction, and some performance non-functional requirements (NFRs) that concern the service and network providers such as CPU and memory loads; (2) the time to market that should be as short as possible; (3) improving the cost efficiency.

Our aim is to assist the different stakeholders that are involved in the TS specification activity, taking into consideration the three factors mentioned recently. In this paper, we will answer to the following research question: **How to enable the estimation of the Quality of Service (QoS) violations and other possible performance non-functional requirements in the TS design using network simulators, and relying on the different abstraction levels of a TS architecture?**

Our objective in this paper is to propose a centric solution that enables the TS designer and developer to obtain valuable feedbacks on the design. This will help the TS designer/developer to improve the quality and to detect the errors or flaws of the design.

Our approach is to bring the measurement element from the operation activity and insert it into the design activity, so to enable the observation of the TS virtual execution through network simulators. Our first contribution is to propose a transversal alignment between the measurement and design elements by extending the design meta-model that was proposed in [11] to include measurement and probe elements. The second contribution is to map between the design and both of simulation Technical SPace (TSP) and Java Virtual Machine (JVM) taking a case study of NS-3 as a network simulator, where we intend to aggregate the measurements from the different architectural elements related to the upper layers of ArchiMate [22].

We illustrate our approach with an example of a TS: video conference, presenting the generated code according to the design and measurement configurations. This example relies on a previous work done in [11,7].

In section 2, we highlight the Enterprise Architecture (EA) with its architecture, and show the benefits from applying its structure to our approach. In section 3, we will provide an explanation about Model Driven Engineering (MDE) and its role in our approach, and we explain model transformations as we rely on code generations to generate the code. Section 4 presents in details our approach to answer to the mentioned research question. In Section 5, we present a short explanation about network simulators, and show how do we map between design and simulation technical spaces. Thus, we show our work to create a reliable test bed for our current and future experiments. In Section 6, we present an example of obtaining data that are related to different layers of EA using to different technical spaces (simulation and JVM). In section 7,we present some of the related work, highlighting the points of interest to our objective. Then we conclude in section 8 and discuss our future work.

2   Enterprise Architecture and ArchiMate

An **Enterprise Architecture (EA)** [14] "is an instrument to articulate an enterprise's future direction, while also serving as a coordination and steering mechanism toward the actual transformation of the enterprise".

EA framework facilitates dealing with complex architectures, as it applies the different viewpoints of the different stakeholders [20] (e.g. service designer, service developer, customer, etc) in order to capture all the aspects of the enterprise objectives.

Thus, we are interested in the underlying platform and business viewpoints. When the TS design is to be implemented, there are two types of models that compose the TS: Platform Independent Model (PIM) and the Platform Specific Model (PSM). PIM contains the components that are independent from the execution platform, while the PSM contains elements of the execution platform and their functions.

We apply ArchiMate [22] which is an EA modeling language. It decomposes the system as the EA does according to different viewpoints. Additionally, its profile contains means that help the TS designer, as they are suitable for the IT domain. They define behavioral and structural elements connected to each other by wide range of relationships. This layered architecture allows changes on the design to be independent from other layers [21], and makes finding an error or design flaw much more easier.

In [11,7], ArchiMate profile is extended to define the Domain Specific Modeling Language (DSML), where different elements that are related to TS domain are included in the extended profile. For the verification activity (Fig. 3), we extend ArchiMate abstract syntax to include measurements, simulation and analysis tools with their relationships that are inherited from ArchiMate definition [22].

A TS designer should verify the TS through its architecture that is composed of layers of different levels of abstraction (PIMs and PSMs). In this paper, we present our approach to connect measurement elements to these different layers.

3   Model Driven Engineering and Model Transformations

System modeling [17]: "refers to an act of representing an actual system in a simple way". With modeling, the parameters of the system can be modified, experimented, and analyzed. In our approach (Fig.3), models plays a central role to represent systems of different technical spaces: Design, and Simulation. MDE is well supported by Eclipse IDE [1]. Eclipse contains powerful tools for MDE

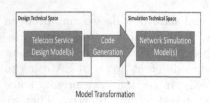

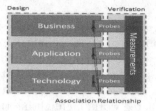

Fig. 1. Applying MDE to bridge between Design and Simulation modeling

Fig. 2. A transversal Alignment Approach between Measurements and Design

such Eclipse Modeling Framework (EMF) which forms the core of our modeling environment in the design Technical SPace (TSP).

Model transformation (MT) is one of the key concepts in MDE, and in our approach. MTs offer automated way to create new models from given ones according to the mapping rules that controls them.

XPAND [2] is a model-to-text transformation language that makes it possible to iterate over input model instances to generate text files. This enables us to generate executable and simulation codes for Platform Independent Models (PIMs) [11] and Platform Specific Models (PSMs) [7].

4   Measurement and Design Transversal Alignment Approach

The TS designer needs to get feedbacks for his design related to errors/flaws or quality violations. We have recently associated the measurement model to the elements of the technology layer that represents the underlying platform in our approach, and its model is a PSM. We have selected the IMS core network platform to be represented in this layer [7,12]. Such association will provide a TS designer feedbacks that are related to the network level, which is very low in abstraction. This leads us to a question: *How can we perform measurements on elements of higher level of abstraction?*

We use ArchiMate language (section 2). It contains the business layer that provides the ability to relate the business actors from an enterprise (e.g. user) with the different types of behavioral elements (such as business interactions, events, functions, etc) in the system and in high level of abstraction [22]. Thus, ArchiMate business layer can cover both of the (Use Case and Scenario [21]) representation fundamentals. ArchiMate language provides relationship between every two neighboring layers [22] in abstraction (e.g. Business and Application layers), which makes it possible to exchange events and interactions between the 3 layers of ArchiMate.

We propose to enable the association between the measurement element (the Probe) and all behavioral and structural elements (Fig. 2) of ArchiMate on the Meta-Model. The measurements are aligned transversally with ArchiMate layers and their probes are following the layering concept of ArchiMate (Fig. 2), thanks to the one-to-many aggregation relationship between the Measurement and Probe(s) in the Meta-Model (Fig. 4). Respecting the ISO-Square standard

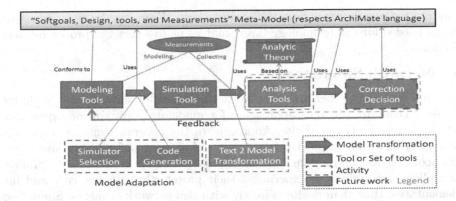

Fig. 3. Verification of Telecom Services relying on tool chains

[8], we propose the measurement meta-model as composed in the following structure (Fig. 4): (1) Measure: Represents the output value of the measurement; (2) Probe: Represents an entity that captures the data when an event is triggered (e.g. a packet is dropped), an action is performed, or during all of the simulation time. The probe concept is inspired from OPNET [1] structure [10]. The probe element is associated with structural and behavioral entities from ArchiMate profile. This provides the ability of collecting measurements from elements of the different layers of EA. Probes have different types due to the nature of the data type that they can obtain (e.g. numerical, time). In the verification activity, one may use all the probes that are related to one measurement in one layer of EA, or distribute them between different layers. In this paper, we will consider the probes per layer case, leaving the other one to future work; (3) Probe Function: The probe function defines the procedure (how) to capture the data; (4) Measurement Function: Represents the function (how) to aggregate the data collected by the different probes.

The measurement meta-model (MM) that we propose (Fig. 4) makes it possible to use the measurement per layer or as a multi-layer measurement, where the probes may be associated with the elements of one layer or distributed between the different layers. In this MM, the layer and data type attributes are clear in the probe element. Thus, the probes are aligned with the design elements in the same layers, while the measurement elements are aligned with the EA architecture transversally (Fig. 2) as they collect the data from the different probes thanks to the aggregation relationship between them (Fig. 4).

This meta-model (Fig. 4): (1) Makes it possible to tune the granularity level of the data collection during the verification of the TS design; (2) Classifies the measurements according to the viewpoint of the stakeholder and to the different domains that are used in an enterprise. So we can have business, application, and technology classes of measurements. This can help in managing the classification of QoS requirements [18]; (3) Enables earlier selection of the measurements

---

[1] OPNET is a wide-used network simulator, it can handle different network elements of both hardware and software nature. www.opnet.com

knowing the requirements from the business layer. Knowing the set of measurements needed for the technology layer, enables us to select the proper network simulator.

5   Network Simulators

We need to find a proper approach to execute virtually and analyze the design models. There are different approaches for modeling a system for experimentation purposes: (1) Simulation Approach: In the network simulation domain, Discrete-Event Simulation (DES) is a powerful research technique to investigate protocol designs, interactions, and large-scale performance issues [16]. Simulation allows researchers to experiment their prototypes with low cost and implementation time than dealing directly with real network elements. Simulators provide a TS designer with valuable observations and measures that helps in detecting design errors/flaws and quality violations; (2) Analytic Approach: Analytical modeling approach is to model the system mathematically using applied mathematical theories (e.g. Queuing and Probability theories).

In our approach, we rely on simulation approach. Modeling using EMF in eclipse (section 3) differs from modeling the same design using the simulation program language. We can map each element from the design TSP to the corresponding one in the simulation TSP using model transformations (section 3).

The objective from any network DES program is to run a scenario that contains structural (e.g. nodes) and behavioral (e.g. send message function) elements for a previously-set simulation period, in order to obtain traces and logs at the end of the simulation run. These logs can be then analyzed later to find the possible errors/flaws or quality violations in the design.

Our approach takes into consideration the structural and behavioral elements of the TS design. The challenge here is to find the simulator elements that correspond correctly to the design elements, and to implement the simulation program

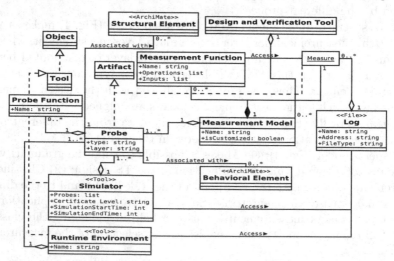

Fig. 4. Measurement view of the meta-model

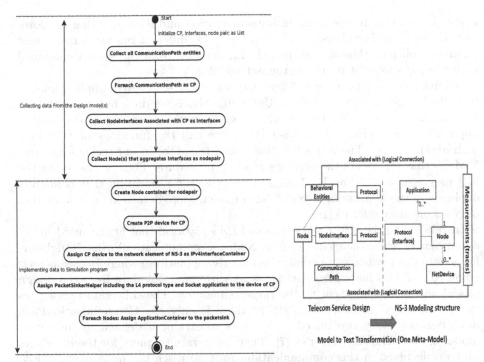

Fig. 5. The activities to map design structural entities to NS-3 simulation program

Fig. 6. Mapping between Design model and NS-3 simulation program

in the right way. Every element from the design model should be mapped to the simulation program. Such a mapping needs experience in both areas: TS design, and simulator specifications, this can be considered as a limitation in our approach. Because implementing the mapping rules in the model transformation template (e.g. XPAND template, section 3) needs the mentioned expertise and a considerable time to be sure that no design elements were missed, also to insure that the language rules of the simulation program were respected.

5.1 NS-3 Simulator: A Test Bed for Experiments

Network simulators help to estimate the TS performance and QoS metrics. But they differ from each other in their capabilities, certificate level, graphical interfaces, granularity levels, and built-in integrated tools (e.g. animators, report generators, analyzers, etc).

Regarding to the capabilities, we are interested in the measurement capability to differentiate between the different network simulators. There is an important point in NS-3 [3] is that the whole simulation program can be implemented in one C++ file in NS-3, where all of the simulation parameters can be configured including generation of traces and logs [3]. This feature in NS-3 enables us to generate code automatically (according to section 3) for measurements aggregation in addition to the scenario implementation and its underlying platform (e.g. IP Multimedia Subsystem (IMS)). C++ has different functions that assist plain-text output, thus we can include information from the design combined with the measurement results in the output files.

Additionally, NS-3 supports different types of easy-configured applications [3] (e.g. Socket using TCP or UDP). Unfortunately, NS-3 does not support IMS core network model yet. Taking advantage from the advanced models of the application layer provided in NS-3 [16,3], we call the functions of IMS in a high abstract level. There is a function called (SendTo) in our technology layer MM [7] that represents the message sending procedure. Thus, we generate the SIP messages as UDP or TCP packets using socket application that is already deployed in the application layer of NS-3 model. More details about the models of NS-3 one may refer to [16].

In relation to the structural entities of IMS platform that is presented in [7], a mapping between these entities (e.g. Nodes, CommunicationPaths, NodeInterfaces, etc) was performed to create the underlying platform where the scenario is going to run. Our mapping activities start with collecting data from the design model and then map them to the target simulator. The collection procedures start from the CommunicationPath as there is only one CommunicationPath links between every two linked nodes, this constraint is defined in the meta-model of the technology layer of [7]. Then we iterate to query for the interfaces that are involved in this communication until we reach the node pairs... (Fig. 5). The steps to implement code in NS-3 appears in the same figure. Figure 6 presents the architecture of both technical spaces: Design and NS-3 simulator. The activities in (Fig. 5) show that we rely on collections and iterations without any exceptions and respecting the types and constraints of the meta-model. This should confirm that every design element is covered when mapping to the simulation TSP.

6   Example on Measurements Associated with Video Conference TS: NS-3 and JVM Case Study

There is a major difference between the technical spaces of network simulation such as NS-3/OPNET and general purpose languages (GPLs) such as Java. Our example in this paper illustrates the measurement correspondence to the different layers of the design architecture described in ArchiMate language. We will give an example of two layers: the business and technology. We generate Java code from the business layer, and simulation code from the technology one following the description in section 5. The Java code generation relies on the model transformation rules that were defined in our previous work in [11].

We rely on a scenario (Fig. 7) for video conference which is modeled using a Domain Specific Modeling Language (DSML) [11]. This scenario is represented in the business layer of ArchiMate, and shows the correspondence of business actors with the different activities that compose it.

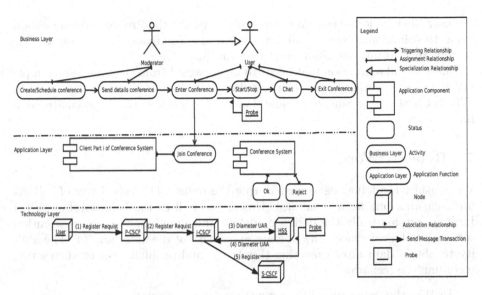

Fig. 7. Video Conference models inspired (with modifications) from [11]

6.1   Associating Probes with the Elements of the Business Layer

Associating probes with the business layer elements gives the ability of obtaining data from the business domain such as user-related information. Figure (7) shows that when the user enters to the conference system joining the group, a function in the application layer called join conference is triggered (called) by the (Enter Conference) activity. This application function triggers a registration procedure in the technology layer, to register the user into the conference service in the simulation technical space.

Figure (9) presents the Java code that is generated by the MT rules for the business layer elements. It shows how the probe function (getName) is called inside the method (enterconference), where this function is not modeled to be triggered by the activity (Enter Conference) in (Fig. 7). This illustrates an example for our method in obtaining the data from different elements of Business Layer relying on our approach. One can also find in (Fig. 9) that there is a method named (setName) which is used to set the name of the customer during the runtime execution, and it should be called by the running system such as a mobile device.

6.2   Associating Probes to the Elements of the Technology Layer

Associating the probes with elements from technology layer gives the ability to obtain different type of measurement data from the elements of the underlying platform (IMS in our research [7]). For the example (Fig. 7), we generate the simulation code that is used to configure NS-3 as a case study. We rely on the video conference example presented in [7] to generate the configuration script. The association relationship between the probe (named (RegistrationTime) of type (Time) and layer (technology)) is used to capture the registration time of the user when he joins the conference system. We set the ProbeFunction method value to (Simulator::Now()) (Fig. 8), which is a command used to obtain the current time during the NS-3 simulation runtime.

There is still a question that needs to be answered from the previous example about the aggregation between the results of the probes, which are attached to different TSPs (e.g. Simulation and JVM). We consider this problematic as a future work.

7   Related Work

We consider the following aspects during the review: (1) The ability of collecting measurements from structural elements as well as the behavioral ones; (2) Linking automatically the design modeling and Simulation or other execution software technical spaces; (3) Domain Specificity of the approach; (4) The ability to obtain data after executing the design and on high level of abstraction including the scenarios.

- In [15], the paper describes a model-based approach to create telecom services. They implement the service relying on IP Multimedia Subsystem (IMS) infrastructure and using code generation techniques from the MDE discipline. Using Eclipse software, they could close the abstraction gap between the design and the execution environment, by hiding the low level protocol and architecture details. Although their approach considers the domain specificity and high abstraction level of the design models, but no measurement capture method appears in their approach;
- The paper [23] presents work that is very close to the formalism which we use. The authors apply MDE and rely on DEVS (Discrete EVent Systems Specification) formalism to smooth the modeling and simulation cycle and facilitate the coupling of models using heterogeneous formalisms. They provide the SimStudio software which aims at providing modeling and simulation tool chain. Their approach and ours depend on meta-models that contains different views to the different activities of the tool chain (modeling, simulation). Their approach doesn't have support for structural elements representation while limited to the behavioral ones. Their approach seems to depend on one abstraction level of measuring capability, while we use probes to obtain data from different layers of EA;
- The work presented in [6] addresses the same scope of service creation activity. They propose a methodology that takes into consideration the customer and service provider requirements. They apply code generation to produce Java and C++ codes directly from these PIMs, with no mention to simulation tools;
- In [5], the authors work on context aware services creation process. Not far from our approach, they link between the knowledge modeling and implementation activities, relying on model transformations. Their approach doesn't seem to rely on simulators but on runtime environments such as JVM. Their approach takes the end-user only into consideration, where we

```
void f_RegistrationTime_64274c95 (Time oldval, Time newval){
    std::cout << "Traced" << oldval
        << "to" << newval << std::endl;
    std::cout << "Traced:"
        << Simulator::Now()<<std::endl;
    NS_LOG_INFO ("The probe RegistrationTime_64274c95 is set from the value "
        << oldval << " to the value " << newval);
}
void f_DevQueueDrop_64274c93 (uint64_t oldval, uint64_t newval){
    std::cout << "Traced" << oldval
        << "to" << newval << std::endl;
    NS_LOG_INFO ("The probe DevQueueDrop_64274c93 is set from the value "
        << oldval << " to the value " << newval);
}
```

```
public String getName() {
    return name;
}
public void setName(String newName) {
    this.name = newName;
}
public void exitconference() {
}
public void enterconference() {
    Clientpartiofconferencesystem clientpartiofconferencesystem
        = new Clientpartiofconferencesystem();
    clientpartiofconferencesystem.joinConference();
    this.startStop();
    this.getName(); <=
}
```

Fig. 8. Probe function implemented in NS-3 to capture the registration time of a user

Fig. 9. User Class Java code-Business Layer

take service designer and user models into account thanks to the EA standard. Their approach respects domain specificity and data capturing during and after the execution, but it is only from high abstract models.

8 Conclusion and Future Work

In this paper, we have presented our work in the activity of TS verification, by defining a new meta-model that links measurements to the design. We have implemented a test-bed based on NS-3 network simulator to rely on for case studies. Our approach is to link the measurements to the different elements of the TS design as aligned transversally with the EA framework. We have illustrated our approach with example on the video conference service, presenting the code that is generated from models of different abstraction levels. This provides a centric solution that enables the TS designer to obtain valuable feedbacks on the design so to improve the qualities and detect possible design errors or flaws.

Our approach, as presented, assists the different stakeholders during the design activity thanks to EA and ArchiMate. It is capable to implement structural and behavioral entities of the design in the simulation technical space, while implementing the required measurements automatically as well. Raising the measurements' association to the layers higher than technology (PSM) one in the abstraction level makes it possible to obtain data from the PIMs directly. This enables us to link goals, design, and verification elements together.

On the other side, the number of inputs of the measurement function is limited to two in our implementation. The implementation of code generation templates is a time consuming activity and needs experience in both simulation and modeling domains.

For the future, we intend to answer to the problematic that we raise in section 6, where aggregating the data obtained from different design layers is important but still challenging. Additionally, we intend to analyze automatically the measurements resulted from the simulation activity to check the goals' satisfaction.

References

1. Eclipse IDE, http://www.eclipse.org/
2. Eclipse modeling, http://www.eclipse.org/modeling/

3. NS-3 Manual-Release ns-3 (November 30, 2012)
4. Achilleos, A., Yang, K., Georgalas, N., Azmoodech, M.: Pervasive service creation using a model driven petri net based approach. In: International Wireless Communications and Mobile Computing Conference, IWCMC 2008, pp. 309–314 (2008)
5. Achilleos, A., Yang, K., Georgalas, N.: Context modelling and a context-aware framework for pervasive service creation: A model-driven approach. Pervasive and Mobile Computing 6(2), 281–296 (2010)
6. Adamopoulos, D., Pavlou, G., Papandreou, C.: Advanced service creation using distributed object technology. IEEE Communications Magazine 40(3), 146–154 (2002)
7. Alloush, I., Chiprianov, V., Kermarrec, Y., Rouvrais, S.: Linking telecom service high-level abstract models to simulators based on model transformations: The IMS case study. In: Szabó, R., Vidács, A. (eds.) EUNICE 2012. LNCS, vol. 7479, pp. 100–111. Springer, Heidelberg (2012)
8. Azuma, P.M.: Iso/iec cd 25000.2 - software and systems engineering – software product quality requirements and evaluation (square) (2003)
9. Bowen, T., Dworack, F., Chow, C., Griffeth, N., Herman, G., Lin, Y.: The feature interaction problem in telecommunications systems. In: SETSS (1989)
10. Chang, X.: Network simulations with opnet. In: Simulation Conference Proceedings, vol. 1, pp. 307–314 (Winter 1999)
11. Chiprianov, V.: Collaborative Construction of Telecommunications Services. An Enterprise Architecture and Model Driven Engineering Method. Ph.D. thesis, Telecom Bretagne, France (2012)
12. Chiprianov, V., Kermarrec, Y., Rouvrais, S.: Extending enterprise architecture modeling languages: Application to telecommunications service creation. In: The 27th Symposium on Applied Computing, pp. 21–24. ACM, Trento (2012)
13. Combes, P., Renard, B.: Service validation. Computer Networks 31(17), 1817–1834 (1999)
14. Greefhorst, D., Proper, E.: Architecture Principles. The Enterprise Engineering series, vol. 4. Springer (2011)
15. Hartman, A., Keren, M., Kremer-Davidson, S., Pikus, D.: Model-based design and generation of telecom services (2007)
16. Henderson, T.R., Roy, S., Floyd, S., Riley, G.F.: ns-3 project goals. In: Proceeding from the 2006 Workshop on NS-2: The IP Network Simulator, WNS2 2006. ACM, New York (2006)
17. Issariyakul, T., Hossain, E.: Introduction to Network Simulator NS2 (2009)
18. Lee, C., Lehoczky, J., Siewiorek, D., Rajkumar, R., Hansen, J.: A scalable solution to the multi-resource qos problem. In: Proceedings of the 20th IEEE Real-Time Systems Symposium, pp. 315–326 (1999)
19. Nicol, D.M., Liljenstam, M., Liu, J.: Advanced concepts in large-scale network simulation. In: Proceedings of the 37th Conference on Winter Simulation, WSC 2005, pp. 153–166 (2005)
20. Simonin, J., Le Traon, Y., Jezequel, J.M.: An enterprise architecture alignment measure for telecom service development. In: Proceedings of 11th IEEE International Enterprise Distributed Object Computing Conference, pp. 476–483 (2007)
21. Sommerville, I.: Software Engineering, 9th edn. Pearson (2011)
22. The Open Group: ArchiMate 1.0 Specification (2009)
23. Touraille, L., Traoré, M.K., Hill, D.R.C.: A model-driven software environment for modeling, simulation and analysis of complex systems. In: Proceedings of the Symposium on Theory of Modeling & Simulation, pp. 229–237 (2011)

DOMINO – An Efficient Algorithm for Policy Definition and Processing in Distributed Environments Based on Atomic Data Structures

Joachim Zeiß[1,2], Peter Reichl[2,3], Jean-Marie Bonnin[2], and Jürgen Dorn[4]

[1] FTW Forschungszentrum Wien, Donaucitystr. 1, 1220 Vienna, Austria
[2] Télécom Bretagne, 2 Rue de la Châtaigneraie, 35510 Cesson-Sévigné, France
[3] University of Vienna, Währingerstr. 29, 1090 Vienna, Austria
[4] Vienna University of Technology, Favoritenstraße 9-11, 1040 Vienna, Austria
zeiss@ftw.at, {peter.reichl,jm.bonnin}@telecom-bretagne.eu,
juergen.dorn@ec.tuwien.ac.at

Abstract. While two decades of semantic web research so far have failed to fulfill the high initial promises and expectations, and the underlying quest for categorizing the world has led to increasing complexity and new levels of bureaucracy instead, in this paper we introduce a new concept for distributed reasoning aiming at simplicity, consistency and computational efficiency. To this end, we propose the DOMINO algorithm, which is based on term logic for realizing an efficient syllogism reasoner. This novel concept is illustrated and evaluated for a context experience sharing system and can be applied in distributed reasoning use cases integrating mobile devices.

Keywords: semantic policies, semantic data abstraction, rule definition, distributed reasoning, mobile reasoning, artificial intelligence.

1 Introduction and Motivation

Following Tim Berners-Lee's vision that "a new form of Web content that is meaningful to computers will unleash a revolution of new possibilities" [5], significant research efforts have been undertaken to realize his idea of a "Semantic Web", focusing on converting raw data into information and turning search queries into question-answer use cases between human and machine. At the same time, Web service architects have integrated semantic web technologies into their API definitions, e.g. WSDL files for finding and collaborating automatically with Web services inside the cloud.

However, after two decades of semantic web research, we have to observe that the initial dreams have not come true so far, and have rather turned into increasing complexity and creating yet another level of bureaucracy instead, eventually causing more problems than they intended to solve. Indeed, the somewhat exaggerated desire for categorizing the world has led to a dictatorship of ontologies versus the democracy of folksonomies (currently blooming in Web 2.0), leaving key concepts of artificial intelligence, formal semantics and logic programming unexploited.

T. Bauschert (Ed.): EUNICE 2013, LNCS 8115, pp. 257–269, 2013.
© IFIP International Federation for Information Processing 2013

In this paper, we argue that, instead of e.g. introducing yet another (graphical) tool or a novel method or procedure for complexity reduction, we better use the powerful rich set of features in a simple way by introducing machine-readable rules which allow devices to act autonomously on behalf of their users. This enables a new way of distributed reasoning with software executing decisions based on user defined policies.

More precisely, we aim at simplicity and intuitiveness by allowing users to verbally define their intents with (almost) no predefined vocabulary, only minimal semantic and syntactic requirements, and without the need to explicitly distinguish between conditions and conclusions. At the same time, detecting contradictions and contraries becomes part of the reasoning process and is performed directly while defining policies. Finally, for a given set of policy definitions, the reasoner should be able to run in a browser with reasonable response time, thus guaranteeing sufficient performance.

In order to achieve these goals, we have designed and implemented a reasoning system and language based on (Aristotelian) term logic [6] which has experienced a revival since the 1970s, mainly due to the constant criticism that predicate logic is unnatural as its syntax does not follow the one used in people's everyday reasoning. Also in the field of artificial intelligence it has gained momentum, e.g. as probabilistic term logic, "Non-Axiomatic Reasoning System" (NARS) or "OpenCog" [7][8].

The remainder of this paper is structured as follows: in Section 2, we provide essential background on term logic and discuss related work. Section 3 presents the DOMINO algorithm for semantic reasoning. Section 4 discusses the application of this approach for a specific use case, i.e. the context experience sharing system KRAMER [1]. Section 5 concludes the paper with a brief summary and outlook on future work.

2   Background and Related Work

2.1   Syllogisms and Term-Based Logic

The DOMINO reasoning system as described later is based on Aristotelian logic which is composed of the three doctrines of categorical terms, propositions and syllogisms. Here, (categorical) terms are universal concepts like "man", "mammal", "human", "animal", etc. In the following description we will denote these terms with small letters x, y, z etc. (Categorical) propositions are formal sentences combining two different terms, e.g. x and y. There exist four different types of propositions:

- $A(x,y)$: All x are y; e.g.: All man are mammal.
- $E(x,y)$: No x are y; e.g.: No mammal are birds.
- $I(x,y)$: Some x are y; e.g.: Some Austrians are musicians.
- $O(x,y)$: Some x are not y; e.g.: Some mammal are not vegetarians

According to the above propositions, we call the x term "subject" and the y term "predicate". A proposition is called "premise" when it is applied to a syllogism for concluding a new proposition. Finally, "(categorical) syllogisms" are rules which allow inferring from a set of propositions (premises) additional propositions (conclusions). For instance, from the premises "All swan are white: $A(s,w)$" and "No white are raven: $E(w,r)$", the Aristotelian system will conclude "No swan are raven: $E(s,r)$".

The corresponding rule is denoted as "$A(x,y), E(y,z) \rightarrow E(x,z)$". Aristotle has defined 14 different such rules (the "συλλογισμοι"), see [10] for comments on the proofs.

2.2 Computational Syllogism

For implementing these rules, when comparing any two premises, first their terms x, y, z are compared. If any of the terms in one premise matches with a term in the other premise, concluding a new proposition is possible. To this end, it is checked whether the types of the premises match one of the mentioned rules; if yes, the rule is executed to produce a new proposition, which itself can serve as an additional premise, and so on. If a new proposition is already included in the set of existing premises, it is not added as a new premise; the iteration process ends if no new propositions are found.

While [6] describes a computational syllogism web page implemented on a php server, we have implemented our own DOMINO reasoner in pure Javascript. The implementation has a small footprint, does not depend on server side computing and can be run in any browser (even as local html file) or used as a library for W3C or other HTML widgets or apps for the WAC [9] runtime, the Firefox OS or Google Chrome. Our Javascript code allows detecting contradictions, contraries and sub-contraries to identify misleading ambiguities in premise definitions or conclusions. For the usage of our reasoner, triggers and their namespaces are defined as Javascript functions which are executed if namespace and trigger name match the terms in a concluded proposition.

3 DOMINO

3.1 Basic Idea of the DOMINO Algorithm

We now introduce a novel method for reasoning over data for automated decision making. We call it DOMINO as its basic functionality reminds of the well-known social game where bricks with two numbers on each side are connected to a chain where bricks with equal numbers lay side by side (see Fig. 1). In our DOMINO system, the bricks correspond to term logic premises, where each premise is composed of two terms (subject and predicate). Like with the domino game, bricks are linked according to syllogistic rules [10], which can be computed by software [6].

In principle, DOMINO may use the full set of syllogism rules. However, just like with Horn clauses [12], for decision-making based on positive affirmation using a single rule is sufficient, and we therefore restrict ourselves to a well-known rule which is traditionally called "Barbara" and chains propositions which are of type "all" and have the term x in common: $A(p,x),A(x,q) \rightarrow A(p,q)$.

For computation purposes, the terms are represented as strings, and DOMINO checks whether they are matching. Note that matching of two expressions can be defined in different ways, e.g numbers checked for equality or matching strings (as used in [6]). In DOMINO, we opt for flexibility and allow numbers to be compared, or being matched with intervals or "<" and ">" relations, while strings could be matched using regular expressions. This also allows pattern matching, a feature no other reasoner of this kind provides as of today. Other matching strategies are conceivable, e.g. for matching date/time expressions and periods. DOMINO also allows executions on conclusion results validating the subject and predicate of a concluded proposition for an existing function to be invoked. The subject of a proposition would hold for the namespace in which a function with the name of the predicate would be executed. Such a function may even inject arbitrarily created new propositions for further computation of conclusions. As no duplication of premises is possible, each trigger function routine would be called exactly once. By linking DOMINO bricks all of which include execution triggers, a sequence of function executions can be defined.

Alternatively, one does not need to trigger functionality during the computation: instead, once as all possible conclusions have been obtained, one could search for particular expressions and take decisions based on the filtering results. The reasoning process would be performed only once and its results are kept in a cache. The conclusion process is finished if no new (unknown) proposition can be deduced, and the list of all given and conducted proposition is the result set of the reasoning.

Summarizing, DOMINO is a computational syllogism system using a subset of term logic figures and conditions to reason over data represented as term logic premises. The basic exercise of concluding new information out of existing premises is performed by linking the term of one premise with a term of another premise. Two premises may be linked if they have a common term, which computationally is verified by checking if the terms in string format are equal. DOMINO extends this notion of identity also to checking number range and regular expressions, as basically any kind of rule or procedure could be used to declare two terms as being equal. Also multistep comparison is possible, where initially high accuracy strict checking is applied, and if this does not bring the desired result, in a second run comparison checks can be relaxed, to produce a match according to the "Barbara" rule. Another novelty added to DOMINO is the possibility to trigger execution of software routines if new premises are concluded. Note that, while Aristotelian syllogisms are concluding on categories, not on individuals, for pragmatic reasons we do not distinguish between categories and individuals, classes or instances in DOMINO. Thus, the syllogistic terms may lose their philosophical meaning, the validity of conclusions, however, remains.

3.2 Formal Description

As we only use premises of type $A(p,q)$ in the sense of "all p are q", we abbreviate this statement to be a simple data tuple t made of the two values p and q as follows:

$$A(p,q) \quad \Leftrightarrow \quad t = (p,q) \tag{1}$$

Next, we define the conjunction operator " $\oplus$ " for the "Barbara" syllogism:

$$A(p,x), A(x,q) \to A(p,q) \quad \Leftrightarrow \quad (p,x) \oplus (x,q) = (p,q) \tag{2}$$

Then, let K_0 define the initial set of all predefined tuples where none of the tuples in the set has identical p and q values (to avoid indicating mere tautologies which are useless for producing new tuples). This initial set of tuples represents the entire data (facts and rules) of our knowledge base, i.e. all data or information which is already known before starting the reasoning process:

$$K_0 = \{(p_x, q_x) | p_x \neq q_x; x \in X\} \tag{3}$$

where X is the set of indices related to the tuples.

Finally, we define the cardinality of a tuple as being 1 for elements of K_0:

$$|t| = |(p, q)| = 1 \quad \text{if} \quad (p, q) \in K_0 \tag{4}$$

$$|t_j \oplus t_k| = |t_j| + |t_k| \quad \text{for all} \quad t_j, t_k \in K_{i-1}; \quad i = 1, 2, \ldots \tag{5}$$

The cardinality of a derived tuple equals the sum of the cardinality of the two tuples on which the derivation is based. As no tuple can be represented twice, always the shortest way to produce tuple t_k applies, and the cardinality is thus uniquely defined.

We now define formally the DOMINO algorithm. Starting with K_0 as described in (3), step i of the algorithm uses the elements of K_{i-1} to produce a new set of tuples:

$$B_i = \{(p_y, q_y) | \exists q_x : (p_y, q_x) \in K_{i-1} \wedge (q_x, q_y) \in K_{i-1} \wedge (p_y, q_y) \notin K_{i-1}; x, y \in X\} \tag{6}$$

Hence, B_i represents all the new information inferred based on set K_{i-1}, therefore

$$K_i = K_{i-1} \cup B_i \tag{7}$$

and so on for $i = 1, 2, 3, \ldots$, until $B_i = \varnothing$. The algorithm converges as K_0 is a finite set and no tuple can be represented twice. Note that the cardinality of a tuple represents its importance in terms of the new information, i.e. newly inferred tuples are considered more important as already existing information. In general, the cardinality n of a tuple is rooted in chaining n-1 other tuples, hence the larger n the more previous information has been condensed to this new piece of information, indicating as well a higher computational effort.

3.3   Evaluation against Triple-Based Reasoning

Defining Horn Clauses with DOMINO

With traditional inferring systems, Horn clauses are used to define rules or formulae for computing conclusions. A definite clause has exactly one positive literal, while a clause with no negative literal is called a fact and in propositional logic is expressed as $\neg p \vee \neg q \vee \ldots \vee \neg t \vee u$, which can also be written in the form of an implication, i.e. $(p \wedge q \wedge \ldots \wedge t) \rightarrow u$ (meaning: if p, q, ..., t are all true then u must be true as well).

Declaration of those rules, e.g. for policy definitions, is based on implications, i.e. "IF-THEN" declarations, quantification and variables. Decision-making is declared by means of logic programming in conjunction with semantic web ontologies. With DOMINO, it is not necessary to define quantifications, and IF-THEN statements become obsolete, as declaring a decision as well as executing a decision process by the reasoner is entirely based on linking DOMINO bricks (like with the social game).

While DOMINO is not capable of quantifying variables, it is possible to define rules the same way it is done for Horn clauses in propositional logic, and any Horn clause construct can be expressed as a DOMINO sequence, see Fig. 1. Basically, DOMINO expresses implications by splitting conditions when they are defined, and recombining them when they are evaluated with actual data.

For example, a single condition for buying a product when the price matches 99.90 ("*price = 99.9 ⇒ buy*") reads with DOMINO as "{(*trigger, price*), (*99.9,buy*)}". When only these tuples are present, no conclusions can be drawn, but if another tuple is added (e.g. by browsing through a database or checking the annotated web page of an online shop) which says "(*price, 99.9*)", applying the conjunction results in (*price, 99.9*) ⊕ (*99.9, buy*) = (*price, buy*), and we can conclude (*trigger, price*) ⊕ (*price, buy*) = (*trigger, buy*). Hence, upon conclusion of a new tuple, DOMINO checks the namespace *"trigger"* for a function called *"buy"* and, if present, will execute it.

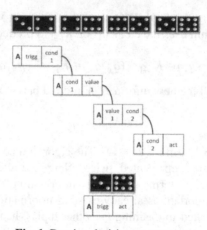

Fig. 1. Domino decision sequence

The same principle works for an arbitrary number of conditions. Consider for instance the Horn clause "$p = x \wedge q = y \wedge r = z \rightarrow action1, action2$". This rule will be represented as the following set of DOMINO tuples:

$$R = \{(\text{trigger}, p), (x, q), (y, r), (z, \text{action1}), (\text{action1,action2})\} \quad (8)$$

Upon retrieval of the data set $D = \{(p, x), (q, y), (r, z)\}$, we will apply $R \cup D$ in order to produce the result set

$$\{(\text{trigger}, \text{action1}), (\text{trigger}, \text{action2})\}, \quad (9)$$

which will execute the functions "action1" and "action2" in namespace "trigger".

Finally, we would also like to demonstrate how to model Horn clauses for a rule like *"if p and q have the same value then do action"*. The Horn clause reads

$$p = ?val \wedge q = ?val \Rightarrow action \tag{10}$$

The corresponding DOMINO tuples look like

$$\{(\text{trigger}, p), (p, p\_val), (q\_val, q), (q, \text{action})\} \tag{11}$$

Eventually, the tuples specified in (11) would conclude to (trigger, action) for the data tuples $\{(x, q\_val), (p\_val, x)\}$.

Declaring Decision Trees with DOMINO

Although separated in the examples so far, in DOMINO there is no difference between data declarations and defining conditions or implications – it is all about declaring pairs of terms. This generalization or abstraction of facts and rules into a common format allows declaring also complex decision patterns, for example decision trees.

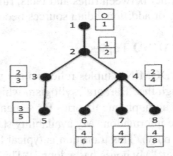

Fig. 2. Domino decision tree

The example given in Figure 2 maps to the following DOMINO sequences and can be proved by recursively applying the conjunction operator:

$$(0,1) \oplus (1,2) = (0,2), (0,2) \oplus (2,3) = (0,3), (0,3) \oplus (3,5) = (0,5).$$
$$(0,1) \oplus (1,2) = (0,2), (0,2) \oplus (2,4) = (0,4), (0,4) \oplus (4,6) = (0,6).$$
$$(0,1) \oplus (1,2) = (0,2), (0,2) \oplus (2,4) = (0,4), (0,4) \oplus (4,7) = (0,7).$$
$$(0,1) \oplus (1,2) = (0,2), (0,2) \oplus (2,4) = (0,4), (0,4) \oplus (4,8) = (0,8).$$

In fact, not only trees but any kind of graph topology can be described. If, e.g. by accident, a graph is created which contains loops, the reasoning process will still come to an end, as each derived tuple is added to the set of existing tuples for reiteration if and only if it does not already exist.

3.4   Advantages over Conventional Semantic Reasoning

The advantages of DOMINO over existing reasoning systems based on propositional or first order logic are manifold. As it does rely on term based calculation for its reasoning instead of logical operations, it allows for

- human readable data and rule definitions;
- easy integration with tag based systems and hence relating messages and media of different topics down the conclusion chain and defining their in-

formational distance using cardinalities (for example, given T1 containing tags #x and #y, T2 containing tags #y and #z and T3 containing #z and #w, T1 on topic #x would be associated to T3 about topic #w because of T2);

- easy integration of pattern matching or any other equality concept (e.g. range checks, probability or similarity statements) into the reasoning algorithm.

Furthermore, DOMINO allows for closing knowledge gaps by asking the user simple yes/no questions: tuples that might be worth being combined, as they have a certain cardinality value, can be presented to the user asking if the second value of one tuple can be related to the first value of another tuple. In contrast to reasoners based on predicate logic, DOMINO avoids running into loops, which is especially important when it comes to allowing user-defined rules and reasoning on mobile devices. Finally, DOMINO does not require any special set up or topology descriptions for distributed evaluation of rules. Instead, distributed reasoning becomes as simple as putting tuples together from any data sources. As DOMINO's knowledge base solely consists of tuples and does not distinct between rules and facts, rules may change dynamically based on new data arriving or additional data sources tied in the reasoning process.

3.5   Readability of DOMINO Tuples

The human readability of DOMINO tuples relies on the usage of terms and the linking of pairs of terms through the "Barbara" syllogism which is closely related to natural thinking (cf. G. Evan's homophonic theories for semantic investigations [17]).

Consider for instance the information "My availability status *is* busy" which translates to (my_availability_status, busy). This transition is typical for patterns à la "all a are b", "this is that" or "c has d", e.g. "My house has a door.", "The door is green.", etc.

Verbally expressed rules in DOMINO are defined as follows: "Check the eyes. Are they blue? Check hair. Is it blonde? Ask for a date. Check humor. Is it good? Marry this person!" will become (check, eyes), (blue, hair), (blonde, ask_for_date), (ask_for_date, humor) (good, marry!). With data tuples (hair, blonde) and (eyes, blue) the check would result in asking for a date, and with an additional tuple (humor, good), the happy end becomes almost inevitable.

Hence, a tuple (1) can be a name-value pair, (2) when inferred/produced it can be a question and answer, and (3) for a rule the left side entry is the expected value of a previous parameter and the right side entry the name of the next parameter to evaluate.

Alternatively, hashing the terms of a sentence can produce tuples, e.g.: "Today #Peter was very #happy and the #weather was #nice" leads to (peter, happy), (weather, nice). When interested in special properties, this can be filtered and combined to new tuples.

Finally, in formal logic, the word "not" is an operator, while DOMINO does not imply the concept of negation. The semantic relevance of "not" is assigned to the person using it: "Should I buy the house? The wall is green, the roof is pink, do not buy it" is modeled as (should_I_buy_the_house, wall), (green, roof), (pink, do_not_buy_it). With (wall, green) and (roof, pink), DOMINO suggests (should_I_buy_the_house, do_not_buy_the_house), where the way the word "not" is interpreted is up to the user.

4   Application Example: KRAMER

In [11] a phonebook application has been introduced that provides users with context information about their contacts and notifies them in important situations. This application deploys the so-called KRAMER system, which uses an abstraction process to derive situations where to perform the afore-mentioned notifications by identifying semantic generalizations of user-defined situations that are similar to each another [1].

In this chapter we describe how DOMINO can be used to perfectly describe semantic information for decision making in such an environment.

Semantic similarity is defined by two conditions [1]: (1) the conceptual graphs of similar situations have to match, and (2) there needs to be a close semantic distance between each other. Both can be easily evaluated with DOMINO by first checking if tuples exist where start nodes and end nodes are comparable for all the graphs. Secondly, due to the substitution process during DOMINO reasoning, these (start-node, end-node) tuples will also be generated if sub-graphs are added or if nodes are linked to each other via several paths. The cardinality of those tuples is used to compare the similarity of these paths.

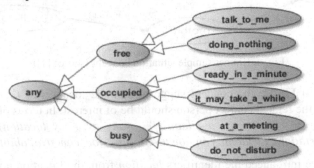

Fig. 3. KRAMER availability taxonomy (source [1])

Fig. 3 depicts the KRAMER availability taxonomy. With DOMINO, the is-a relationship taxonomy is described in the form of A-type propositions, such that the relationship *"x is-a y"* is expressed by the proposition *"all y are x"*, giving the DOMINO tuple (y,x). Hence, the relationships denoted in Fig. 3 result in the DOMINO sets:

A_1 = {*(any_av, availability), (free, any_av), (occupied, any_av), (busy, any_av),*
(talk_to_me, free), (doing_nothing, free), (ready_in_a_minute, occupied),
(it_may_take_a_while, occupied), (at_a_meeting, busy), (do_not_disturb, busy)}

Applying the DOMINO algorithm produces the following tuples with cardinality 2:

A_2 = {*(at_a_meeting, any_av), (do_not_disturb, any_av),(ready_in_a_minute,*
any_av), (it_may_take_a_while, any_av), (talk_to_me, any_av), (doing_nothing,
any_av), (free, availability), (occupied, availability), (busy, availability)}

After one more iteration, the following tuples with cardinality of 3 are produced:

A_3 = {*(at_a_meeting, availability), (do_not_disturb, availability),*
(ready_in_a_minute, availability), (it_may_take_a_while, availability),
(talk_to_me, availability), (doing_nothing, availability)}

For the location taxonomy, the following tuples exist:

L_1 = {*(any_loc, location), (bistro, any_loc), (bar, any_loc), (office, any_loc), (downtown, any_loc)*}

We now apply the DOMINO algorithm and get

L_2 = {*(bistro, location),(bar, location),(office, location),(downtown, location)*}

The third taxonomy is about relations:

R_1 = {*(any_rel, relation), (mother, any_rel), (parent, any_rel),(boss, any_rel)*}

After applying DOMINO yet for another time, we end up with

R_2 = {*(mother, relation), (parent, relation),(boss, relation)*}

Eventually, we have derived the three taxonomy sets:

$$A = A_1 \cup A_2 \cup A_3; \quad L = L_1 \cup L_2; \quad R = R_1 \cup R_2$$

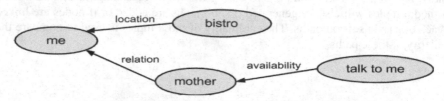

Fig. 4. Kramer sample situation concept (source [1])

According to Fig. 4, the concept suggests that the location of the user and the availability of the related contact person should be of interest. In terms of DOMINO:

C = *{(me, my_availability), (any_av, my_location), (location, my_relation), (relation, con_location), (any_loc, con_availability)}*

Note that we introduced the identifiers *location* from the Location taxonomy set L and *relation* from the Relation taxonomy set R. This allows for any value under *location* and *relation* in their related taxonomy trees to be valid.

Expected tuples to be produced are: (me, *location*) and (me, *availability*). If these tuples are produced, the sample situations below can be considered to be similar to the concept. These two tuples also express that for the given situation: "I am at location: *location* and my contact is available for: *availability*".

Table 1. Example contact situations (source [1])

	me		contact		
	location	availability	relation	location	availability
1	bistro	any	mother	any	talk to me
2	bistro	any	parent	any	free
3	bar	any	mother	any	doing nothing
4	bistro	any	mother	downtown	free
5	office	any	boss	any	busy
6	bar	any	mother	any	it may take a while

Taking the exemplary contact situations listed in table 1 [1] gives the DOMINO sets:

S_1 = {(my_availability, *any_av*), (my_location, *bistro*) (my_relation, *mother*), (con_location, *any_loc*), (con_availability, *talk_to_me*)}

S_2 = {(my_availability, *any_av*), (my_location, *bistro*) (my_relation, *parent*), (con_location, *any_loc*),(con_availability, *free*)}

S_3 = {(my_availability, any_av), (my_location, bar) (my_relation, mother), (con_location, any_loc), (con_availability, doing_nth)}

S_4 = {(my_availability, *any_av*), (my_location, *bistro*) (my_relation, *mother*), (con_location, *downtown*), (con_availability, *free*)}

S_5 = {(my_availability, *any_av*), (my_location, *office*) (my_relation, *boss*), (con_location, *any_loc*), (con_availability, *busy*)}

S_6 = {(my_availability, *any_av*), (my_location, *bar*) (my_relation, *mother*), (con_location, *any_loc*),(con_availability, *it_may_take_a_while*)}

Now we apply: $S_i \cup C \cup L \cup R$ for all the samples, which adds following start-node, stop-node tuples mentioned above to the following situation sample sets:

S_1 : (me, bistro), (me, talk_to_me)
S_2 : (me, bistro), (me, free)
S_3 : (me, bar), (me, doing nothing)
S_4 : (me, bistro), (me, downtown)
S_5 : (me, office), (me, busy)
S_6 : (me, bar), (me, it_may_take_a_while)

Observe that S1, S2, S3, S5 and S6 match the concept, whereas S4 does not. The difference becomes more obvious when we also add the availability set A to all S:

S_1 : (me, location), (me, availability)   // also (me, free)
S_2 : (me, location), (me, availability)
S_3 : (me, location), (me, availability)   // also (me, free)
S_4 : (me, location)
S_5 : (me, location), (me, availability)
S_6 : (me, location), (me, availability)   // also (me, occupied)

With this final evaluation we come to the same and potentially more granular grouping of situation as the KRAMER system shown in table 2.

Table 2. Kramer semantic grouping (source [1])

Gr.	#	me	contact	availability	
I	1	bistro	mother	talk to me	
	2	bistro	parent	free	
	3	bar	mother	doing nothing	
	5	office	boss	busy	
	6	bar	mother	it may take a while	
II	4	bistro	mother	free	downtown

5   Conclusions and Outlook

In this paper we have introduced a new concept for distributed reasoning in mobile networks. Based on term logic, we aim at simplicity, consistency, and computing efficiency. For easy adaptation by users in mobile networks we intend to achieve simplicity and intuitiveness by allowing them to verbally define their intents. We provided a formal description of the algorithm and demonstrated its capability by re-modeling standard proposition logic and decision graph concepts. We finally illustrated and evaluated this concept for a context experience sharing system targeted for mobile applications.

Summarizing, the DOMINO concept is a novel approach for automated decision making in a distributed mobile environment. The advantages over traditional semantic web or first order logic programming approaches are its simplicity, flexibility and adaptability for verbal human reasoning. As the system is designed for end users, as part of our future work we plan to perform a user study and compare the results with related work in [4, 14-16] to show the advantages over predicate logic based systems. We will investigate a simplified modeling of conditional variables and the interpretation of tuple cardinalities as semantic similarity indicators and quantification of information quality. Beyond that, current and future work uses the DOMINO algorithm for various other applications (like, e.g., Location-Aware Campaigning).

References

1. Szczcerbak, M., Bouabdallah, A., Toutain, F., Bonnin, J.-M.: Generalizing Contextual Situations. In: Proc. IEEE ICSC 2012, Palermo, Italy, pp. 293–301 (2012)
2. Bouabdallah, A., Toutain, F., Szczerbak, M., Bonnin, J.: On the benefits of a network-centric implementation for context-aware telecom services. In: Proc. ICIN 2011 (2011)
3. Zeiß, J., Zhdanova, A.V., Gabner, R., Bessler, S.: Semantic Policy Aware System Description. FTW Technical Report, FTW-TR-2007-010 (September 2007)
4. Zhdanova, A.V., Zeiß, J., Dantcheva, A., Gabner, R., Bessler, S.: A Semantic Policy Management Environment for End-Users and its Empirical Study. In: Pellegrini, T., Auer, S., Tochtermann, K., Schaffert, S. (eds.) Networked Knowledge - Networked Media. SCI, vol. 221, pp. 249–267. Springer, Heidelberg (2009)
5. Berners-Lee, T., Hendler, J., Lassila, O.: The Semantic Web. Feature Article, Scientific American (May 2001)
6. Glashoff, K.: Computational Aristotelian Term Logic: Introduction, http://webapp5.rrz.uni-hamburg.de/syllogism/aristotelianlogic/introduction.html
7. Wang, P.: Non-Axiomatic Reasoning System - Exploring the essence of intelligence. PhD thesis, Indiana University (1995), http://www.cogsci.indiana.edu/farg/peiwang/papers.html
8. Opencog: General Intelligence via Cognitive Synergy, http://opencog.org/theory/
9. Zeiß, J., Günther, P., Davies, M.: The Role of WAC in the Mobile Apps Ecosystem. InTech (2012)

10. Cohen, M.: Aristotle's Syllogistic,
    http://faculty.washington.edu/smchen/433/Syllogistic.pdf
11. Szczerbak, M., Toutain, L., Bouabdallah, A., Bonnin, J.-M.: Collaborative context experience in a phonebook. In: Inter-Clouds and Collective Intelligence Workshop at IEEE AINA 2012, pp. 1275–1281 (2012)
12. Horn, A.: On sentences which are true of direct unions of algebras. Journal of Symbolic Logic 16, 14–21 (1951)
13. Zeiß, J., Zhdanova, A.V., Gabner, R., Bessler, S.: Semantic Policy Aware System Description. FTW Technical Report, FTW-TR-2007-010 (September 2007)
14. Zeiß, J., Gabner, R., Zhdanova, A.V., Bessler, S.: A Semantic Policy Management Environment for End-Users. In: Proc. I-Semantics 2008, Graz, Austria (2008)
15. Bessler, S., Zeiß, J.: Semantic Modeling of Policies for Context-aware Services. In: 17th Meeting World Wireless Research Forum (WWRF), Heidelberg (November 2006)
16. Zeiß, J., Sanchez, L., Bessler, S.: Policy-driven Formation of Federations between Personal Networks. In: 16th IST Mobile and Wireless Communications Summit, Budapest (July 2007)
17. Evans, G.: Pronouns, Quantifiers, and Relative Clauses (I). Canadian Journal of Philosophy vii, 467–536 (1977)

Poster Abstract: Performance Evaluation of Machine-to-Machine Communication on Future Mobile Networks in Disaster Scenarios

Thomas Pötsch[1], Safdar Nawaz Khan Marwat[1],
Yasir Zaki[2], and Carmelita Görg[1]

[1] Communication Networks, TZI, University of Bremen, Germany
{thp,safdar,cg}@comnets.uni-bremen.de
[2] Computer Science Department, New York University Abu Dhabi (NYUAD),
Abu Dhabi, United Arab Emirates
yz48@nyu.edu

Long Term Evolution (LTE) is the recent standard of wireless communication developed by the Third Generation Partnership Project (3GPP). As the future mobile network, it is currently being rolled out to numerous areas world-wide. Besides other objectives such as enhancing the spectral efficiency and reducing latency for broadband services, LTE has been designed as a pure packet switched system. Hence, it targets the data volume requirements of cellular mobile users by increasing the peak-user data throughput to up to 100 Mbit/s [1]. However, legacy circuit switched services are no longer supported by this technology. Contrary to the existing, wide-spread GSM network, this implies that the support of voice calls and Short Message Service (SMS) have to be realized by voice and SMS via the IP Multimedia Subsystem (IMS). In other words, voice calls are no longer separated from pure data traffic and hence influence each other.

Along with the "Internet of Things" as a new paradigm for connected devices, Machine-to-Machine (M2M) communication is a world-wide, fast growing field of application. According to [3], the mobile traffic of the variety and number of connected devices will grow significantly within the next decade. Therefore, the multitude of remotely monitored equipment is growing and includes buildings, vending machines, vehicles and other physical equipment. The application fields incorporate for example health monitoring, logistics and shipping, environmental monitoring, or asset tracking. Besides that, the overall mobile network is expected to grow 24-fold from 2012 to 2017 and the number of mobile connected devices will exceed the world's population by the end of 2013 [3].

Looking at the increasing number of mobile connected devices and on one particular scenario where mobile communication is very beneficial in terms of life-saving measures, the capacities of future mobile networks are becoming more and more important. Over the past decades, natural disaster and emergency events have been increasing significantly all over the world [4][2]. Although the capabilities of predicting natural disasters have been become more precise and reliable, certain natural disasters are unpredictable. Besides that, other emergency events such as terror attacks or multiple accidents are not predictable at all, and when occurring, mostly numerous people are affected. However, throughout almost any emergency event, mobile communication plays an important role

T. Bauschert (Ed.): EUNICE 2013, LNCS 8115, pp. 270–273, 2013.

for both, involved persons and rescue activities. Besides the regular and existing network traffic, additional traffic emerges and is indirectly caused by the emergency event itself. However, taking such a scenario as a rather rare and unlikely event, but where mobile communication plays a tremendous and important role, M2M operators have to cope with severe challenges, like for example, how does M2M communication perform in an emergency event when numerous people instantaneously begin to use IP-based services. Although a possible off-time of M2M communicating devices does not play a severe role, an off-time of devices facilitating e-healthcare, etc. might be critical.

Figure 1 shows an example of the traffic load in a mobile network during an event of disaster. Shortly after an event of disaster, the traffic load of the mobile network increases significantly by emergency calls. Right after emergency calls, people usually start sending out messages to notify others about their current situation and condition. Those messages could be regular phone calls, text messages and/or status updates in social networks. Nowadays, SMS services have been widely replaced by Instant Messaging (e.g. Whatsapp, iMessage, etc.) and social networking (e.g. Facebook, Google+, etc.) have been become very popular. Therefore, it is very likely that people start sending out numerous messages, pictures and videos to inform others about their current situation and to spread the scale of the disaster to others.

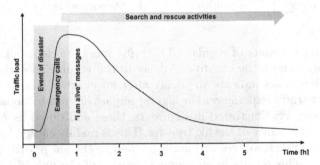

Fig. 1. Example of Traffic Load in Event of Disaster (adapted from [5])

To investigate the influence of such a situation, a simulation model was developed using the OPNET simulator [6] with the main focus on end-to-end performance evaluations on the user plane. All nodes in the network contain the full protocol stack implementation that was done following the 3GPP release 8 specification. Further details of the simulation model can be found in [7] and [8].

During the first 1000 seconds of the simulation, the scenario consists of 10 VoIP users, 10 file transfer users and 100 M2M devices. M2M devices and file transfer users share the same QoS class. These terminals are operating continuously with the parameters shown in Table 1. After 1000 seconds, an emergency event occurs where additionally 60 emergency VoIP users and 30 Instant Messaging (IM) users start to operate. The emergency VoIP users behave like regular VoIP users whereas the IM user start sending messages, videos and pictures.

Table 1. Simulation Parameters

Parameter	Setting	Parameter	Setting
Cell layout	1 eNodeB, 3 Cells	**File transfer traffic model**	
System bandwidth	5 MHz (~25 PRBs)	Quantity	10
Frequency reuse factor	1	File size	2 MB
		File inter-request time	Uniform (15s, 25s)
Cell radius	375 m		
UE velocity	3 km/h	**M2M traffic model**	
Max UE power	23 dBm	Quantity	100
Path loss	$128.1+37.6 \log_{10}(R)$, R in km	Message size	6 kB
Slow fading	Log-normal shadowing, 8 dB standard deviation, correlation 1	Message inter-transmission time	30 s
		Instant messaging traffic model	
		Quantity	30
Fast fading	Jakes-like method	Message size	Uniform (0.2 kB, 2MB)
Mobility model	Random Way Point		
UE buffer size	∞	Message inter-request time	Uniform (10s, 20s)
Power control	Fractional PC, $\alpha = 0.6$, $P_0 = $ -58 dBm	**Voice traffic model**	
Traffic environment	Loaded	Quantity	10 + 60 emergency
LTE uplink scheduler	BQA [8]	Silence/talk spurt length	Exponential (3 s)
Simulation time	2000s		
Time of disaster	1000s	Encoder scheme	GSM EFR

The simulation results of regular LTE traffic users are depicted in Figure 2. The green bars denote the end-to-end delay in the regular scenario (t<1000s), whereas the blue bars indicate the delay after an event of disaster (t>1000s). The best effort traffic experiences the highest impact of the additional users in an emergency event. As illustrated in Figure 2a, these additional users drastically degrade the performance of the file transfer. This is mainly caused by the limited amount of remaining resources within the cell and by the low priority given by the LTE scheduler. This results in an average increase of the upload response time by the factor of 19.6. The simulation results of the M2M users are represented in Figure 2b as a subset of 10 users. These 10 users are randomly chosen and reflect the overall performance of all 100 M2M users. It can be seen, that all user experience a 4.8 fold increase of the upload response time. The voice user results (cf. Figure 2c) do not reveal a considerable effect of the increasing traffic load within the LTE cell. Since voice traffic is delay sensitive traffic, the LTE scheduler gives strict priority to this traffic. Resulting from this, the packet end-to-end delay is increased on average by the factor 1.1.

Even though the performance of voice user remains unaffected by the additional users during an emergency event, file upload and M2M traffic experience a considerable delay. In comparison to M2M traffic, file upload traffic experience a ~4 times higher delay. However, time sensitive M2M application, like e-healthcare, could suffer from this increase.

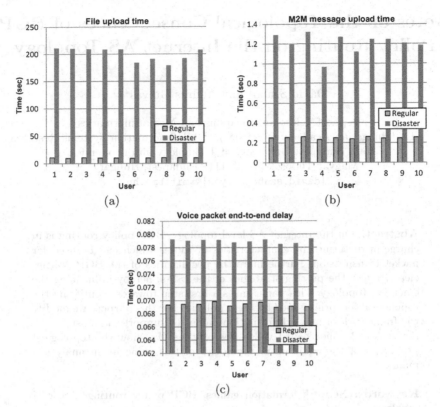

Fig. 2. (a) Average File Upload Time of File Transfer User (b) Average File Upload Time of M2M User (c) Average Voice User Packet End-to-End Delay

References

1. 3GPP Technical Report TR 25.913: Requirements for Evolved UTRA and UTRAN. v 2.1.0 (June 2005)
2. Cavallo, E., Noy, I.: The Economics of Natural Disasters: A Survey (2009)
3. Cisco Systems Inc.: Cisco Visual Networking Index: Global Mobile Data Traffic Forecast Update, 2012-2017. Digital Publication (February 2013)
4. Guha-Sapir, D., Hargitt, D., Hoyois, P.: Thirty Years of Natural Disasters 1974-2003: The Numbers. Presses univ. de Louvain (2004)
5. Hofmann, R.D.: Smart Operation of a Mobile Network in Event of Disaster. In: Proc. of 30th International Telecommunications Conference, SanDiego, USA (September 2008)
6. OPNET Modeler, http://www.opnet.com
7. Zaki, Y., Weerawardane, T., Görg, C., Timm-Giel, A.: Long Term Evolution (LTE) Model development within OPNET Simulation Environment. In: OPNET Workshop 2011, Washington D.C., USA, August 29 - September 1 (2011)
8. Zaki, Y., Zahariev, N., Weerawardane, T., Görg, C., Timm-Giel, A.: Optimized Service Aware LTE MAC Scheduler: Design, Implementation and Performance Evaluation. In: OPNET Workshop 2011, Washington D.C., USA, August 29 - September 1 (2011)

Notes on the Topological Consequences of BGP Policy Routing on the Internet AS Topology

Dávid Szabó[1] and András Gulyás[2]

[1] Dept. of Telecommunications and Media Informatics
[2] MTA (Hungarian Academy of Science) - BME Information Systems Research
Group Budapest University of Technology and Economics,
Magyar Tudósok krt. 2, 1117 Budapest, Hungary
{david.szabo,gulyas}@tmit.bme.hu

Abstract. On the Internet AS level topology, BGP policy routing is in charge of dictating the characteristics of routes which can be used for packet transmission. Furthermore the peculiarities of the BGP policies clearly affect the peering strategies of the ISP-s, hereby influencing the emerging topology. This paper takes a first step towards identifying the topological footprint issued by these policies. For this purpose we modify the framework of network formation games to support the most fundamental BGP policy called valley-free routing. We show the topological properties of the equilibrium topologies of this game in an analytical manner.

Keywords: Network formation games, BGP policy routing, AS level topology.

1 Introduction

Resembling many of real world networks (e.g. social networks, biological networks etc.), the Internet AS level topology is a complex network exhibiting similar macroscopic features such as power-law degree distribution, high clustering coefficient and logarithmic diameter [1]. Exploiting this amazing structural resemblance, general complex network models are widely used for generating Internet-like topologies as an input for evaluating Internet related architectures, business models, protocols etc. For obtaining more realistic AS topology models one should incorporate also some microscopic features, which cannot be captured by high level statistics but contribute fundamentally to the final shape of the network.

In this paper we try to grab some of the microscopic features of the AS level topology. First we notice that there is a mutual correspondence between the network topology and the used routing policy. Topology trivially affects routing since one cannot choose routes having edges not contained in the topology. On the other side of the coin, the routing policy can fundamentally influence the topology of the network. For the illustration of this idea consider the simple example on Fig. 1.

T. Bauschert (Ed.): EUNICE 2013, LNCS 8115, pp. 274–281, 2013.
© IFIP International Federation for Information Processing 2013

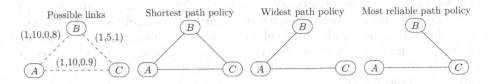

Possible links   Shortest path policy   Widest path policy   Most reliable path policy

Fig. 1. Policy drives topology: We have three nodes (A, B, C) among which we decide to build a network. The characteristics of the possible edges (A, B), (A, C), (B, C) are defined by a triplet: latency, bandwidth and reliability (l, b, r) (rightmost). Now we have to decide what topology we should build. Clearly if the routing policy is the shortest path policy, then we have to use all the links. If the policy is the "widest path" meaning that we are shooting for the highest bandwidth between the nodes, then the third topology from the left is the appropriate choice. Finally if the policy is the "most reliable path" policy then the corresponding network will be the leftmost topology.

According to our best knowledge, the topological footprint[1] of the Internet's routing policy, called the BGP [5] policy routing, are not fully understood and hence not incorporated in the current structural models of the AS level topology[2]. Our goal in this paper is therefore to take a first step towards characterizing the topological artifacts imposed by the BGP policies. We show the footprint of the most fundamental BGP policy called *valley-free routing* on the AS topology in an analytical manner. Since the AS level the topology of the Internet is formed by the business interactions between the ISP-s, such an analysis should be highly incentive-oriented. For this purpose we generalize the concept of Network Formation Games (NFG) and define a network game accommodating the valley-free routing policy. We study the Nash equilibrium topology of this game and characterize its features.

The rest of the paper is organized as follows. In Section 2 we give a brief overview on network formation games and the valley-free routing policy. In Section 3 after modifying the NFG framework to incorporate the valley-free policy, we examine the topological consequences of valley-free routing in an analytical manner. Section 4 discusses our findings and describes future work.

2 Background

Network Formation Games – Network Formation Games constitute a game theoretic framework which provides considerable insight into the mechanisms

---

[1] Several other aspects (e.g. stability [2], memory requirement [3], path diversity [4] etc.) of BGP policy routing have been analyzed so far.

[2] There are "computational" models [6,7] which can generate very realistic AS level topologies based on fully emulating the business decisions of the AS-s fed by complex datasets. Although these models generate considerably realistic networks they can scale only for around a few hundred nodes.

that forms the topology of networks [13]. In the NFG the players are identified
as the nodes of the network, while the strategies of the players is to create some
set of links towards an arbitrary subset of the other players. The goal of the
players is to minimize their cost function which consists of two parts: link costs
and communication costs. The cost function for some player u was originally
defined by Fabrikant [13] as:

$$c_u = \underbrace{\sum_{\forall u \neq v} d_{G(s)}^{\text{sh}}(u, v)}_{\text{communication costs}} + \underbrace{\alpha|s_u|}_{\text{link costs}} , \quad u, v \in \mathcal{P}, \tag{1}$$

where $d_{G(s)}^{\text{sh}}(u, v)$ denotes the length of the shortest path between players u and
v on the graph $G(s)$ characterized by the union the strategies of the players,
s_u stands for the set of nodes towards which u creates links, while α represents
the cost of building one edge. Thus the NFG effectively analyzes the trade-off
between link costs and communication costs for rational (selfish) players, as the
key incentives of building specific topologies. As defined in (1), distance is usually
measured as the average length of shortest·path from the given node to all other
nodes. An important state of the game is called as *Nash equilibrium* in which no
player (node) has anything to gain by unilaterally changing it's strategy.

The Valley-Free Routing Policy – BGP is the core inter-domain routing
protocol of the Internet. It is responsible for distributing available forwarding
paths between Autonomous Systems (ASes) and lets each one to choose the path
it prefers according to its own special interests. The business relationships of different ASes can be diverse, based on exclusive contracts, service-level agreements
and other policy issues. Still we can classify most AS-AS links into basically just
two major groups [14]: in a *customer-provider* relationship one AS pays another
for forwarding its traffic, while in a *peering* relationship neighboring ASes vol-
untarily exchange traffic with each other in a settlement-free manner[3]. In this
paper we focus on the topological consequences of the most fundamental policy
called valley-free routing [15] [16]. This policy encompasses the basic economic
fact that the flow of traffic must obey the flow of cash. The policy dictates that
AS A can use a link to a neighboring AS B to route traffic if and only if either
the incoming traffic is from a customer or B is a customer of A. All paths that
induce valley-free routing have the same preference; the only concern this policy
addresses is not violating elemental business rules.

3   Topological Consequences of Valley-Free Routing

For the analysis of the topological footprint generated by valley-free routing we
modify the framework of network formation games as follows:

Players and Valley-Free Routing – Let $\mathcal{P}$ be the a set of players (identified
as network nodes) with cardinality N. Recall that the rules of the valley-free

---

[3] For the sake of simplicity, we omit sibling and backup relationships in this paper.

policy dictate that a player u can forward traffic originated from player w to a neighboring player v if and only if: (i) the incoming traffic of u is from a customer (in this case the relationship between u and v is indifferent and can be both provider-customer or peering), or (ii) v is customer of u (in this case the type of relationship between w and u becomes indifferent). In other words: *after a provider-customer edge or a peer edge, the path can not traverse customer-provider edge or another peer edge.[17]*

Strategies and Topology – The strategy space of player $u \in \mathcal{P}$ is to create some set of undirected edges to other players in the network. The created edges can be of types customer-to-provider (p) and peer (r) edges in accordance with the relationships of the valley-free routing. The r edges are paid at both sides, however p edges are paid by the customer. Note that in some of the following arguments, according to the direction of traversing customer-to-provider links, we may write provider-to-customer link but these terms are referring to the same edge. Thus the complete strategy space of player u is $S_u = 3^{\mathcal{P}\setminus\{u\}}$, where the number 3 covers the third choice of node u: creating no edge. Let s be a strategy vector containing the strategies of all players hereby representing the current state of the game: $s = (s_0, s_1, ..., s_{N-1}) \in (S_0, S_1, ..., S_{N-1})$. Then the graph $G(s) = \cup_{i=0}^{N-1}(i \times s_i)$ represents the topology between the players.

Payoff – The goal of the players is to minimize their costs. The cost of player u is defined as:

$$C_u = \sum_{\forall v \neq u} d_{G(s)}(u, v) + \varphi_p u_p + \varphi_r u_r, \quad u, v \in \mathcal{P} \tag{2}$$

where φ_x is the cost an edge of type x, u_x is the number edges of type x and $d_{G(s)}(u, v)$ is the communication cost between u and v over $G(s)$ given by:

$$d_{G(s)}(u, v) = \begin{cases} 0 & \text{if valley free path exists between } u \text{ and } v \\ \infty & \text{otherwise.} \end{cases} \tag{3}$$

In what follows we identify the Nash equilibrium of the game in different settings of the parameters. The Nash equilibrium is one of the most fundamental states of a game, because it shows a stable state in which none of the nodes would alter its strategy, though they are rational (selfish) players being interested in their own utility.

Definition 1 (Valley-free footprint (VFF)). *A graph is a valley-free footprint if consists of (i) a clique K_r comprising peer (r) links only, and (ii) trees rooted at some subset of $V(K_r)$ having customer-to-provider links (p) only, such that the provider in the relationship is always closer to the root than the customer (see Fig. 2).*

Theorem 1. *Every Nash equilibrium of the game is a VFF having $|V(K_r)| = \left\lfloor \frac{\varphi_p}{\varphi_r} \right\rfloor + 1$.*

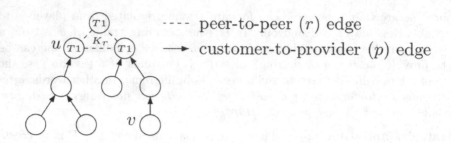

Fig. 2. Example for a VFF topology. In such a topology there could be two type of nodes, T1 and none T1. T1s are connected by r edges, which are counted on both sides in the cost function, however p edges are paid only by the customer, who requested it. The flow of cash is visualized by arcs. Conversely there are two possible cost functions: (i) $C_u = \varphi_r u_r = \varphi_r(|V(K_r)| - 1)$ and (ii) $C_v = \varphi_p$.

Proof. The proof consists of three parts: first we show that a VFF with $|V(K_r)| = \left\lfloor \frac{\varphi_p}{\varphi_r} \right\rfloor + 1$ is a Nash equilibrium, secondly that a VFF with $|V(K_r)| \neq \left\lfloor \frac{\varphi_p}{\varphi_r} \right\rfloor + 1$ is not and finally that a non-VFF topology is also not a Nash equilibrium.

1. The VFF topology with $|V(K_r)| = \left\lfloor \frac{\varphi_p}{\varphi_r} \right\rfloor + 1$ is a Nash equilibrium: We show that no player has anything to gain by changing his own strategy if others don't change theirs. Let C_u represent the cost of player u residing in the VFF. It is clear that in a VFF every player can reach others through valley-free paths, hence in the cost functions the communication cost is always zero $(\sum_{\forall v \neq u} d_{G(s)}(u, v) = 0)$. Moreover it is clear that any meaningful state of the game permits valley-free paths between arbitrary pairs of players (otherwise the cost of some player would be infinite), so we will omit writing this tag hereafter.

   (a) if $u \in K_r$:

$$C_u = \varphi_r u_r = \varphi_r(|V(K_r)| - 1) = \varphi_r \left\lfloor \frac{\varphi_p}{\varphi_r} \right\rfloor \qquad (4)$$

   If u wants to deviate then it will use some other strategy. In this case the corresponding cost is given by $C_u' = \varphi_r u_{r'} + \varphi_p u_{p'}$. If $u_{p'} \geq 1$ then $C_u \leq C_u'$ since:

$$C_u = \varphi_r \left\lfloor \frac{\varphi_p}{\varphi_r} \right\rfloor \leq \varphi_r \frac{\varphi_p}{\varphi_r} = \varphi_p \leq C_u'. \qquad (5)$$

   If $u_{p'} = 0$ then again $C_u \leq C_u'$ since $u_r \leq u_{r'}$ must hold to ensure valley-free connectivity to all other nodes. This is because if $u_r > u_{r'}$ then there is at least one node $v \in K_r$ to whom u is not connected thus cannot be reached from u via valley-free path.

   (b) if $u \notin K_r$:

$$C_u = \varphi_p \qquad (6)$$

$u_{p'} \geq 1$ is trivially not an option for u since that case immediately implies $C_u \leq C_u{}'$. What remains is the case $u_p' = 0$. In this case to ensure valley-free connectivity u has to create r edges to all other nodes residing in K_r. This would mean $C_u{}' = \varphi_r(\lfloor \frac{\varphi_p}{\varphi_r} \rfloor + 1)$, but even then $C_u < C_u{}'$:

$$C_u = \varphi_p = \varphi_r \frac{\varphi_p}{\varphi_r} \leq \varphi_r \left\lceil \frac{\varphi_p}{\varphi_r} \right\rceil \leq \varphi_r(\lfloor \frac{\varphi_p}{\varphi_r} \rfloor + 1) = C_u{}' \qquad (7)$$

2. The VFF topology with $|V(K_r)| \neq \lfloor \frac{\varphi_p}{\varphi_r} \rfloor + 1$ is NOT a Nash equilibrium:

Easily if $|V(K_r)| < \lfloor \frac{\varphi_p}{\varphi_r} \rfloor + 1$, then any leaf node u from a rooted tree can lower its cost by joining K_r as:

$$C_u{}' = \varphi_r(|V(K_r)| - 1) < \varphi_r \left\lfloor \frac{\varphi_p}{\varphi_r} \right\rfloor \leq \varphi_r \frac{\varphi_p}{\varphi_r} = \varphi_p = C_u \qquad (8)$$

Similarly if $|V(K_r)| > \lfloor \frac{\varphi_p}{\varphi_r} \rfloor + 1$ then some node $u \in K_r$ can lower its cost by leaving K_r and connect to some other $w \in K_r, w \neq u$ with a p edge.

$$C_u{}' = \varphi_p = \varphi_r \frac{\varphi_p}{\varphi_r} \leq \varphi_r \left\lfloor \frac{\varphi_p}{\varphi_r} \right\rfloor < \varphi_r(|V(K_r)| - 1) = C_u \qquad (9)$$

3. Finally we show that graphs differing from VFF can't constitute Nash equilibria. Let G be an arbitrary graph on which the valley-free connectivity is satisfied, i.e., $\forall u \in G : C_u \neq \infty$. It's obvious that without this property G can't constitute a Nash equilibrium. In such graph let u be a node whose strategy differs from the nodes in a VFF. The possible cases are:

(a) u has p edge: The strategy of the nodes in the VFF having p edges is to pay for only a single p edge and nothing more (They can have other p edges attached to them but these are paid by their customers, see Fig. 2). Since u differs from this, the corresponding cost function is characterized as:

$$C_u = \varphi_p u_p + \varphi_r u_r, \quad u_p \geq 1, u_r \geq 0 : (u_p, u_r) \neq (1, 0). \qquad (10)$$

Now let the edge (u, w) be a p edge of u. Since w can reach every other player via valley-free path, u also has valley-free paths to all others through w. This means that u can delete its edges except the (u, w) edge, giving $C_u > C_u{}' = \varphi_p$.

(b) u doesn't have a p edge: The cost function of u is:

$$C_u = \varphi_r u_r. \qquad (11)$$

The valley-free connectivity implies that every path from u to others starts with one r edge which can be followed only by *provider-to-customer* edges. Let t be the number of nodes having no p edges. Such nodes must be the neighbors of u otherwise u cannot reach them. This imposes $u_r \geq t$. Furthermore for differing from VFF $u_r \neq t$ must also hold. In summary we get $u_r > t$. In this case u has edges (u, w) where

w has a provider. Now these edges can be deleted since u can reach w through its provider too. This gives:

$$C_u = \varphi_r u_r > \varphi_r t = C_u' \tag{12}$$

According to Theorem 1 aside from two trivial cases – (i) $\varphi_p \geq (n-1)\varphi_r$, when the Nash equilibria is a tree, and (ii) $\varphi_r > \varphi_p$, when the Nash equilibria is a complete graph – the Nash equilibria of our very simple game exhibits some level of structural resemblance with the Internet AS level topology. It is well known, that on the AS level topology there are only a few nodes in the whole network which can reach every other node without purchasing service (i.e. without having a customer-to-provider edge), we call such node a tier-1 (T1). T1s are in a clique having peering agreements with each other, this is the top of the hierarchy. The rest of the nodes are customers of T1s either in a direct or in an indirect way. These topological features are clearly reflected by our results and now we can understand them as a clear consequence of the valley-free policy.

4   Discussion and Future Work

In this paper we have taken a first step towards identifying which topological features of the AS level Internet follow from BGP routing policy. We modified the framework of network formation games for support the valley-free routing, which is the most fundamental BGP policy, and defined a new game. We've given a mathematical analysis for the Nash equilibria. For positioning our work we recall that our main motivation is to gain deeper insight into the driving forces forming the topology of the Internet. Since BGP is the core inter-domain routing protocol of the Internet our long-term goal is to identify what topological features this protocol implies. As the first step we have analyzed the topological footprint of its core building block, the valley-free policy, and identified the VFF as its consequence. Meanwhile the topologies produced by our simple model seems promising they are far from being realistic. In the future we plan to broaden the spectrum of BGP policies and investigate the topological consequences of the *local preference rule* and the effect of the *AS pathlength*. The in depth analysis of these policies may eventually lead us to more realistic AS level topology generators which may worth the comparison with the existing models as well.

Acknowledgement. This work was partially supported by the European Union and the European Social Fund through project FuturICT.hu (grant no.: TAMOP-4.2.2.C-11/1/KONV-2012-0013).

References

1. Wang, X.F., Chen, G.: Complex networks: small-world, scale-free and beyond. IEEE Circuits and Systems Magazine 3(1), 6–20 (2003)
2. Gao, L., Griffin, T.G., Rexford, J.: Inherently safe backup routing with bgp. In: Proceedings of the IEEE Twentieth Annual Joint Conference of the IEEE Computer and Communications Societies, INFOCOM 2001, vol. 1, pp. 547–556. IEEE (2001)

3. Rétvári, G., Gulyás, A., Heszberger, Z., Csernai, M., Bíró, J.J.: Compact policy routing. In: Proceedings of the 30th Annual ACM SIGACT- SIGOPS Symposium on Principles of Distributed Computing, pp. 149–158. ACM (2011)

4. Arjona-Villicana, P., Constantinou, C., Stepanenko, A.: The internet's unexploited path diversity. IEEE Communications Letters 14(5), 474–476 (2010)

5. Rekhter, Y., Li, T.: A border gateway protocol 4 (bgp-4). RFC 1771, Draft Standard (March 1995), Obsoleted by RFC 4271

6. Lodhi, A., Dhamdhere, A., Dovrolis, C.: Genesis: An agent-based model of interdomain network formation, traffic ow and economics. In: 2012 Proceedings IEEE, INFOCOM, pp. 1197–1205 (2012)

7. Dhamdhere, A., Dovrolis, C.: An agent-based model for the evolution of the internet ecosystem. In: First International Communication Systems and Networks and Workshops, COMSNETS 2009, pp. 1–10 (2009)

8. Papadopoulos, F., Krioukov, D., Bogua, M., Vahdat, A.: Greedy forwarding in dynamic scale-free networks embedded in hyperbolic metric spaces. In: 2010 Proceedings IEEE, INFOCOM, pp. 1–9 (2010)

9. Krioukov, D., Papadopoulos, F., Kitsak, M., Vahdat, A., Boguñá, M.: Hyperbolic geometry of complex networks. Phys. Rev. E 82, 036106 (2010)

10. Krioukov, D., Papadopoulos, F., Kitsak, M., Serrano, M., Boguna, M.: Popularity versus similarity in growing networks. Bulletin of the American Physical Society (2012)

11. Boguná, M., Papadopoulos, F., Krioukov, D.: Sustaining the internet with hyperbolic mapping. Nature Communications 1, 62 (2010)

12. CAIDA AS Ranking webpage, http://as-rank.caida.org/

13. Fabrikant, E.M.A., Luthra, A.: On a network creation game. In: PODC, pp. 347–351 (2003)

14. Huston, G.: Interconnection, peering and settlements: Part I. Internet Protocol Journal 2(1) (June 1999)

15. Gao, L., Rexford, J.: Stable internet routing without global coordination. ACM/IEEE Transactions on Networking 9(6), 681–692 (2001)

16. Yang, X., Clark, D., Berger, A.: NIRA: A new inter-domain routing architecture. IEEE/ACM Transactions on Networking 15(4), 775–788 (2007)

17. Gao, L.: On inferring autonomous system relationships in the internet. IEEE/ACM Trans. Netw. 9(6), 733–745 (2001)

Graph-Theoretic Roots of Value Network Quantification

Patrick Zwickl[1] and Peter Reichl[2,3]

[1] FTW Forschungszentrum Wien, Donaucitystr. 1, 1220 Vienna, Austria
[2] Télécom Bretagne, 2 Rue de la Châtaigneraie, 35510 Cesson-Sévigné, France
[3] University of Vienna, Währingerstr. 29, 1090 Vienna, Austria
zwickl@ftw.at, peter.reichl@telecom-bretagne.eu

Abstract. Value Networks (VN) are gaining increasing importance for the analysis of highly complex business ecosystems. While most of the related work focuses on qualitative aspects, we are mainly interested in developing tools for a quantitative VN analysis. In this paper, we discuss the fundamental relationship between graph theory and VN analysis and outline some of the consequences for the specific use case of network interconnection services.

Keywords: Network Economics, Value Networks, Network Interconnection.

1   Introduction

While in the telecommunications industry, tremendous network IP traffic growth rates [1] are opposed by fading revenues[1], a proper understanding of inter-firm business relationships has become critical for Network Service Providers (NSPs), especially in the interconnection (IC) business. Tough, the traditionally prevailing sequential description of production activities as value chains is not sufficient for the strategic assessment of such complex business ecosystems anymore. Instead, we aim at capturing the inter-firm perspective through Value Network (VN) analysis [2][3] which focuses on interactions between business entities in networks rather than sequential chains.

Orthogonally, the broadly applied intra-firm concept of Business Models has emerged about a decade ago [4], and recently has been interlinked with VN concepts [5]. In this paper, we thus focus on strategic inter-firm aspects playing a key role in networking IC, while providing proper links to Business Model Design aspects known from literature. While the relatively limited amount of related work on VN analysis [2][6] strongly emphasizes a qualitative approach, we are mainly interested in tools supporting the quantitative analysis of inter-actor value creation. More specifically, this paper outlines the fundamental relationship between graph theory and VN analysis and thus aims at a very general perspective on VN quantification.

The remainder of the paper is structured as follows: in Section 2, we briefly review recent advances in quantitative VN analysis, before we describe in Section 3 the concept of Value Network Graphs (VNG) and atomic operations on them. Section 4 outlines resulting extensions to the basic model, before Section 5 concludes with a brief summary and outlook on future work.

---

[1] Tellabs: http://www.tellabs.com/markets/
tlab_end-of-profit_study.pdf, last accessed: June 26, 2013.

T. Bauschert (Ed.): EUNICE 2013, LNCS 8115, pp. 282–286, 2013.

2   Value Network Quantification

Our general approach for quantifying VN dependencies is depicted in Fig. 1, with three main building blocks: (i) competitive information as input for VN quantification, mainly based on a VN dependency model [7], (ii) the computation phase which calculates actual dependencies, and (iii) the resulting dependency indicators. In contrast to [7] which is based on six relevant factors strongly inspired by Porter's "five forces" [8] and putting them to an inter-firm context, in the present model we aim at an aggregation into two dependency indicators only which are synthesized from and revised over [9]. They are derived separately from the bargaining power of suppliers and customers and joined into a final dependency metric afterwards.

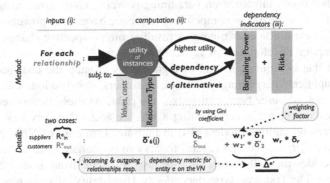

Fig. 1. Framework for VN Dependency Quantification

Computation starts from the utility assessment of potential relationship alternatives, e.g. due to industry rivalry, potential market entrance or substitution. The utility is subject to the fungibility of exchanged resources, which equals the fraction of entities to which a resource could be supplied or sold. Then, the utility for the j-th best alternative for a given relationship of an entity is calculated using exponential spreading factors, which ensures that alternatives with high utility (low j) are picked with higher probability. The revised utilities then feed a Gini-based value distribution coefficient – widely applied in economics – for each entity. In this way, we determine a dependency indicator relative to the maximum Gini coefficient for any outgoing/incoming (to customers/suppliers) relationship. Thus, the dependency quantification shifts towards fine-granular relationship instances, which together reflect an entity's bargaining power of suppliers/customers [9]. Furthermore, whenever an entity strongly depends on a single customer/supplier, its relative dependency rises w.r.t. the VN.

While the idea of dependency indicators is built on well-known concepts, it still lacks formal validation of its adequacy. Therefore, in the rest of the paper we provide first steps into this direction, leveraging on graph-theoretic foundations, defining the concept of VN Graphs and discussing their properties as starting point for an axiomatic derivation of basic forces which impact dependency indicators for VN quantification.

3   Value Network Graphs

In order to be able to create and manipulate graphs representing VNs, we define a Value Network Graph (VNG) as a directed, labeled consistent graph where each node represents an entity of the VN, and each edge corresponds to a business relationship between two entities, whose properties are described by corresponding labels. The following atomic modifications of VNG are considered relevant:

- Addition and deletion of edges or nodes: this is caused by product development and/or stakeholder substitution (→ influence on bargaining powers).
- Modification of edges or nodes: this may be caused by the exchange of different resources   (→ fungibility), redirection e.g. due to diversification (→ substitution, influence on bargaining powers), entity size changes and market entrance/exit (→ competition, influence bargaining powers, risks).
- VNG evolution over time: this results from perspective changes, e.g. due to temporal development of vertical integration.

Based on that, we obtain a total of eight forces causing the changes: bargaining power of suppliers, bargaining power of customers, substitution, industry rivalry, market entrance, resource type, entity size, and risks. As these factors seem to have a high influence on the graph representing a VN, we argue that they have to be considered as forces on entities (nodes) also in the inter-firm case of VNs. Nevertheless, following up on [9] we see that several forces can be merged to form the mechanism in Fig. 1. Besides that, all factors (not exclusively) arise from atomic edge or node modifications. The resource type dependency (fungibility of resources) may result from modifying the type (e.g., to money) of the edge, as already targeted in [7][9] based on [10].

However, the size of entities has not been sufficiently targeted so far: in the context of economies of scale of Internet services, the size of companies may have considerable influence on their dependency on a VN. Furthermore, risks like e.g. customer ownership, large-scale substitutions, and product evolutions of other entities represent more complex special cases and may have relevant influence on the nature of the graph. Moreover, unmentioned risks like financial risks or unstable business partners may pose dis-utilities for a firm's long-term strategic positioning, while being hardly captured by graph manipulations. The following section will give an outlook on how these missing components can be added to the quantification concept of [7][9].

4   Revised Dependency Quantification

So far, our graph-theoretic analysis supports the relevance of the six factors identified in [7] as well as the need for risk and size of entity forces as additional forces. In this chapter we briefly discuss the consequences for the model in [9].

As demand-side and supply-side bargaining powers need to be independently assessed, two independent dependency factors are created whose weights may vary from industry to industry, depending on the role of economies of scale. The dependency resulting from entity sizes may best be captured by the worth/volume of resources exchanged with suppliers and customers, i.e., shifts in bargaining powers. Risk forces are more complex to be treated. While low profitability may lead to drop outs or defaults and thus creates risks for business partners, comparable risks may originate from many intrafirm sources and are hardly to be controlled exogenously. Moreover, entities at larger distances to customers or (raw) materials may especially be prone to spreading risks, i.e., customer ownership is critical. However, such factors spanning multiple nodes may be difficult to be captured by graph modifications, and thus we propose to additionally resort to context-independent risk analysis methods.

There exists a wide range of risk analysis concepts in literature [11], however no approach dedicated to network services is available, and thus we have to adapt more generic frameworks like the Composite Risk Index (CRI) for our purpose. Our aim is to construct such an adaptation for the networking industry on the basis of feasible VN crossings with Business Model (BM) design parameters. Likewise to [5], we distinguish *control parameters* (VN parameters, functional architecture parameters) and *value parameters* (financial model parameters, value proposition parameters), which amongst others cover customer ownership in the VN parameters. From this we derive corresponding risk categories, which are eventually quantified or estimated.

5   Conclusions and Outlook

Our graph theoretic analysis has largely confirmed VN dependency indicators introduced by [7][9]. By a top-down reorganization originating from the bargaining powers of entities and an integration of context-optimal risk assessment techniques as well as entity sizes as scaling factors, an enhanced and modular quantification system has been derived. The determination of corresponding weighting factors together with the revision of quantification details and practical applications remain for further work.

References

[1] Cisco Visual Networking Index: Forecast and Methodology, 2012–2017. White Paper (2013)
[2] Gulati, R., Nohria, N., Zaheer, A.: Strategic Networks. Strat. Mgmt. J. 21, 203–215 (2000)
[3] Peppard, J., Rylander, A.: From Value Chain to Value Network: Insight for Mobile Operators. European Management Journal 24(2-3), 128–141 (2006)
[4] Teece, D.: Business Models, Business Strategy and Innovation. Long Range Planning 43(2-3), 172–194 (2010)
[5] Ballon, P.: Business models revisited: the configuration of control and value. Info 9(5), 6–19 (2007)
[6] Allee, V.: Reconfiguring the value network. J. Busin. Strat. 21(4), 36–39 (2000)
[7] Zwickl, P., Reichl, P., Ghezzi, A.: On the Quantification of Value Networks: A Dependency Model for Interconnection Scenarios. In: Cohen, J., Maillé, P., Stiller, B. (eds.) ICQT 2011. LNCS, vol. 6995, pp. 63–74. Springer, Heidelberg (2011)
[8] Porter, M.: How Competitive Forces Shape Strategy. Harvard Bus. Rev. 102 (1979)

[9] Zwickl, P., Reichl, P.: An Instance-based Approach for the Quantitative Assessment of Key Value Network Dependencies. In: Becvar, Z., Bestak, R., Kencl, L. (eds.) NETWORKING 2012 Workshops. LNCS, vol. 7291, pp. 97–104. Springer, Heidelberg (2012)

[10] Biem, A., Caswell, N.: A Value Network Model for Strategic Analysis. In: Proc. HICSS-41, pp. 361–367 (2008)

[11] White, D.: Application of system thinking to risk management: A review of the literature. Management Decision 3(10), 35–45 (1995)

A Publish-Subscribe Scheme
Based Open Architecture for Crowd-Sourcing

Róbert L. Szabó[1,2] and Károly Farkas[1,3]

[1] Inter-University Centre for Telecomm. and Informatics, Debrecen, Hungary
[2] HSNLab, Dept. of Telecommunications and Media Informatics,
[3] Dept. of Networked Systems and Services,
Budapest University of Technology and Economics, Budapest, Hungary
szabo.robert@etik.hu, farkask@hit.bme.hu

Abstract. Participatory sensing, when a crowd of users collaborate to collect useful information, based applications are getting popular these days thanks to the proliferation of powerful mobile devices. The built-in sensors of smartphones offer an easy and handy way to monitor the environment and collect data which can serve as the basis of smart applications. However, the quick and flexible development and deployment of these applications call for a unifying open architecture. In this paper we propose a publish-subscribe based open participatory sensing architecture.

1 Introduction

The vision of collecting information by the assistance of the crowd and exploiting its voluntary work has been boosted recently thanks to the emergence of the web and mobile technologies. This is called participatory sensing whose power is that basically everybody has the possibility to contribute on a voluntary basis. In essence, a participatory sensing system enlists and utilizes a crowd of users to collaborate in building a system that is beneficial to the whole community.

The form of participatory sensing has been influenced by the development of technologies. Smart mobile devices open the way for mobile participatory sensing. They do not only serve as the key computing and communication platforms of choice, but also come with a rich set of embedded sensors, such as accelerometer, digital compass, gyroscope, GPS, microphone and camera. Collectively, these sensors are enabling new applications across a wide variety of domains, such as healthcare, social networks, safety, environmental monitoring and transportation [1]. Thus, mobile smartphones are possible bridges of everyday objects to our enriched world and a plethora of Internet of Things (IoT) applications can be envisioned that will be available in the future through community based sensing and monitoring [2].

Today the development of a participatory sensing application follows the Silo approach. These applications are developed in a stand-alone manner recreating all the necessary building blocks from scratch on both the client and the server/cloud side. This makes the development slow, cumbersome, error-prone

T. Bauschert (Ed.): EUNICE 2013, LNCS 8115, pp. 287–291, 2013.

and inflexible. On the contrary, instead of the vertically integrated Silo approach our goal is to design a horizontally layered application framework and an open architecture enabling rapid prototyping to experiment with participatory sensing based innovative use-case scenarios. In such a situation, an architecture based on the publish-subscribe (pubsub) communication scheme is well suited where information sources publish events autonomously to the pubsub service whenever something happens. Users can subscribe to event contents and the pubsub service delivers the events to all the interested parties.

In the next section, we propose an XMPP publish subscribe based architecture for mobile participatory sensing.

2   Open Participatory Sensing Architecture

2.1   Requirements

Unifying Open Architecture: A typical participatory sensing application today has two *application specific* components: *i*) one at the user's device and *ii*) another one in the cloud [2]. This results in many parallelism, unnecessary developments and slow application innovation cycle.

We envision that the separation of application logics and some core communication, privacy and trust functions could result in a *unifying open architecture* where innovation can be done at the end systems focusing on the application and presentation layers. This could boost the developments similarly to the innovation at the application front enabled by IP. Such unifying open architecture shall not only allow independent application development but also the independent development of application support services.

Extensible Information Model: We want to allow independent application innovation. This can only be done if the middleware can transparently pass extra information which applications may attach to the basic messages.

Decoupling between Producers and Consumers: If we accept the fact that by participatory sensing we aim at monitoring a larger-scale phenomena that cannot be easily monitored by individuals, then we need to decouple producers and consumers efficiently in space, time and synchronization.

2.2   System Model

We propose a generic publish-subscribe interaction scheme with an extensible event language as our system model. The roles in this model are *Producers, Service Providers* and *Consumers*. They communicate through event based pubsub nodes as the core service. The model must be easily extensible and support the needs of the basic pubsub operations.

Producers: They are original *participatory* information sources in our model and are central to a participatory sensing setup. These individuals are actively involved in contributing their sensor data related to a larger-scale phenomena. They produce the raw data to the system.

Service Providers: They would like to introduce *extra* value to the raw data collected by participatory sensing. Thus, Service Providers *add extra value* to the information flow from participatory Producers to the Consumers. They might collect (Consumer role), store and analyze Producers' information to produce (Service Provider role) new information. Therefore they might, but not necessarily must, act at the same time as both Service Provider and Consumer. For example, data can be introduced into the participatory application from external systems/sources. If this data is larger in scope what an individual can possibly provide, then we call the associated role as Service Provider.

Consumers: They are the beneficiaries of the information flow. In general, participatory sensing is considered to be an open call for anybody to participate typically on-line in a task. This task can either belong to an owner (e.g., a company seeking solutions to its problem) or to a community or group of users. Nevertheless, the task (collection, analysis and dissemination of data) aims to give value to some beneficiaries or Consumers. Sometimes, these Consumers also act as Producers. When users act on both the Producer and the Consumer side of the process we call them as *Prosumers*.

Event Service: It realizes the *publish-subscribe* communication scheme, whereby decoupling Producers (publishers) and Consumers (subscribers) in time, space and synchronization.

Producers create original information by sensing their environment. They publish (marked with empty arrowheads) their information to event nodes (raw information nodes marked with blue). Service Providers subscribe (black arrowheads) to raw event nodes and receive information asynchronously. They combine their information with the participatory sensed data to publish value added information to Consumers. The information they produce are published to different content nodes. Consumers subscribe to content nodes according to their topics of interest and receive information from these nodes asynchronously.

2.3   Architecture

Our model can be directly mapped to the Extensible Messaging and Presence Protocol's (XMPP) [3] publish-subscribe service as follows (see Fig. 1):

A Service Provider creates a raw pubsub data node to collect Producers' data for their services. Producers must have at least *publisher-only* affiliation to be able to publish into these nodes. This requires either a pre-authorization or an extended access right management at the XMPP side.Similarly to the *open* node access mode, an *open-publish-only* node access can be introduced, whereby Consumers can openly publish to the corresponding nodes, but only affiliated Consumers and the owner can retrieve events. Producers with proper access rights can publish (stream) their sensors' data or annotations to these raw data nodes at the XMPP server. Service Providers collect these data by the pubsub

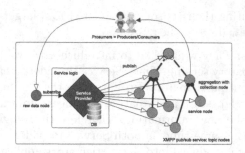

Fig. 1. XMPP Based Publish-Subscribe Architecture

subscription service and map their value added services to a structure, which allows reasonable content filtering for their Consumers. Prosumers participate in sensing and publish their sensor data or annotations into some raw XMPP pubsub nodes. Service Providers subscribed to these raw pubsub nodes collect, store and analyze data and derive new information realizing value added services (related to a larger scale phenomena). This information is published into a structured collection of pubsub nodes, to which Consumers (Prosumers) can subscribe. The structure of pubsub service nodes can utilize XMPP's aggregation feature through collection nodes, where a collection node simply receives all events of its child nodes. Note however, that XMPP's collection node cannot filter events throughout the aggregation mechanism, therefore scalable content aggregation can only be realized through the Service Provider role. Such use-case is shown in the figure, where XMPP's aggregations are depicted with dark circles at the container node while empty circles represent only logical containment and intelligent aggregation through the service logic.

3   Summary

We proposed a horizontally layered, open, participatory sensing architecture based on XMPP's publish-subscribe interaction scheme. We described players and their roles related to the architecture. Use cases and implementation experiments will be shown in the accompanying poster.

Acknowledgments: The publication was supported by the TÁMOP-4.2.2.C-11/1/KONV-2012-0001 project. The project has been supported by the European Union, co-financed by the European Social Fund. This work has been partially supported by the KIC ICTLabs under the activity 13064 CityCrowdSource of the action line Digital Cities. Károly Farkas has been partially supported by the János Bolyai Research Scholarship of the Hungarian Academy of Sciences.

References

1. Lane, N., Miluzzo, E., Lu, H., Peebles, D., Choudhury, T., Campbell, A.: A survey of mobile phone sensing. IEEE Communications Magazine 48(9), 140–150 (2010)
2. Ganti, R., Ye, F., Lei, H.: Mobile Crowdsensing: Current State and Future Challenges. IEEE Communications Magazine, 32–39 (November 2011)
3. Saint-Andre, P.: Extensible Messaging and Presence Protocol (XMPP): Core. RFC 6120 (Proposed Standard) (March 2011)

A Testbed Evaluation of the Scalability
of IEEE 802.11s Light Sleep Mode

Marco Porsch and Thomas Bauschert

Chemnitz University of Technology,
Reichenhainer Str. 70, 09126 Chemnitz, Germany
{marco.porsch,thomas.bauschert}@etit.tu-chemnitz.de

Abstract. Wireless mesh networks have not yet made their breakthrough in consumer electronics, although they are well suited for use in home or on-the-go environments. Especially IEEE 802.11s is ideal for multimedia sharing on handheld devices as it uses regular Wi-Fi hardware, but provides connectivity without requiring an access point. To maintain proper battery runtime on mobile devices 802.11s introduces new power save schemes. Despite the increased complexity due to the meshed connectivity, these schemes allow efficient energy saving for the mesh nodes. In this paper we present a testbed implementation of the IEEE 802.11s power save schemes on off-the-shelf hardware and assess their effects on current consumption for the idle network case in detail.

Keywords: wireless mesh networks, IEEE 802.11s, power save, green networking, energy efficiency.

1   Introduction

Today's smartphone users are struggling with the low battery runtime of their devices, as standby times of just one day average have become quite common. As groundbreaking new battery technologies are yet to be found, increasing the energy efficiency is the task at hand. Concerning the power consumption for connectivity, Wi-Fi is already a better choice than cellular for its higher rate and overall better energy-efficiency under network load [1]. In the next generation of smartphones the Wi-Fi functionalities may be extended with the wireless mesh network amendment IEEE 802.11s, which—among other features—allows sharing multimedia contents without requiring the presence of an access point. 802.11s is a standard for wireless mesh networks based on regular Wi-Fi hardware as commonly found in today's laptops and mobile phones. It allows simple connectivity of user devices, similar to Wi-Fi Direct, but also allows meshed multi-hop connectivity when partaking in bigger networks. In IEEE 802.11s networks all mesh nodes are true peers and share the same behavioral rules. Concerning power save, this allows employing equally sophisticated power save schemes on all nodes. Of course there are also new issues; while in managed mode the client has to schedule only the access point's periodic beacon transmissions, in the meshed connectivity of 802.11s the power save scheme has to take all peers into account for its sleep schedule. In this paper we focus on the case of an idle

T. Bauschert (Ed.): EUNICE 2013, LNCS 8115, pp. 292–297, 2013.

network with no user data being sent or received. For typical user devices this case is very relevant: a smartphone rests in standby state in the user's pocket most of the time and just periodically checks for incoming mails; a laptop or tablet does not send or receive data while the user is reading a web page. Conserving energy in these situations is most crucial for proper battery runtime.

Key contributions of this paper are testbed measurements of the IEEE 802.11s power save algorithm's effects on current consumption and an analysis of its scalability with respect to an increasing number of peers. The paper is structured as follows: section 2 gives an introduction on the main concepts of IEEE 802.11s power save before section 3 shows and interprets measurements done in our mesh testbed. Subsequently, section 4 concludes and summarizes this paper.

2   IEEE 802.11s Power Save

The 802.11s power save schemes are defined in the IEEE 802.11 standard for wireless LAN [2] which, in its 2012 revision, incorporates the 802.11s amendment of 2011. All 802.11 family protocols have a common approach to power save; for saving energy the radio is suspended in times of no activity. With the complex receiver baseband processing disabled the device power consumption is reduced drastically. This makes it more useful than transmission power control as it especially allows idle nodes to conserve energy. Also, without any receiver interrupts, the CPU may spend more time in low power sleep states. The radio will be reactivated for sending a packet or for a scheduled receipt, e.g. of a neighbor beacon.

To reliably schedule doze and wakeups in any of the 802.11 family power save schemes, a tight synchronization is required. The time reference is given by maintaining a local clock and transmitting beacon frames periodically at the TBTT (target beacon transmission time). Dissimilar to wireless LAN ad-hoc and managed mode, mesh mode does not shift the TBTT to a common time; instead, it focuses on keeping the arbitrary offsets between the TSF and TBTT of neighboring nodes constant in the presence of imperfect reference clocks. With the time references synchronized, a power save schedule may be set up to doze and wakeup according to the neighbor TBTTs. Again, the IEEE 802.11s schemes differ from those of managed and ad-hoc mode. Other than waking up at the singular IBSS or access point TBTT in mesh mode there are multiple wakeup events given by multiple peer TBTTs and the own beacon transmission. Also while infrastructure and ad-hoc WLAN employ just a singular power mode towards all neighbors, in IEEE 802.11s the power mode is set for each peer link individually by both parties. This power mode is not a binary representation of power save being on or off; instead three power modes are defined: active, light sleep and deep sleep mode. A link in active mode may receive packets anytime and therefore the radio cannot be suspended at all. A peer link in light sleep mode will only receive packets at certain times. This allows suspending the radio while there are no receipts scheduled on any link. A link in deep sleep mode behaves similarly but the amount of wakeups—and also the possible performance—is further reduced.

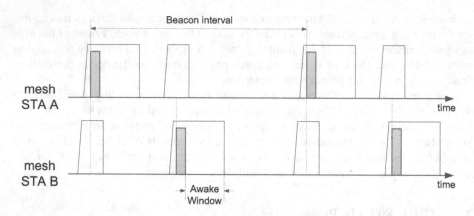

Fig. 1. Wakeup scheduling of two peers in light sleep mode towards each other

Links operating in deep sleep mode require special routines for synchronization and frame forwarding which are left undefined in the 802.11 standard. Therefore, we will focus solely on light sleep mode in the remainder of this paper. The link-specific power mode currently used is announced in unicast frames towards the corresponding peer. If any of a node's links is in power save mode, this is also indicated in broadcast frames. The standard leaves the rules defining which power mode to choose for a link up to the implementation.

Fig. 1 illustrates the behavior of a peer link in light sleep mode; here both peers A and B are in light sleep mode towards each other. In this example no further links are established and the sleep/doze schedule is solely determined by the own and the single peer's TBTT. After waking up to transmit its own beacon, node A stays awake for the awake window duration, which is advertised in an information element within the beacon. During this time interval peer B may transmit frames to A. After the awake window passed, node A resumes its doze. B wakes up just before the TBTT of its light sleep peer A to receive its beacon frame. Equally, peer A will later wake up before B's TBTT to receive its beacon. This process repeats periodically with the beacon interval. Beacon frames may contain a TIM (traffic indication map) information element with information about buffered frames, which may be polled during the awake window as part of a subsequent Peer Service Period. For more information on traffic forwarding on mesh links in light sleep mode we would like to refer the interested reader to [3] where we examine this topic using testbed measurements or to [4] where similar research has been conducted by Alam et al. using ns-2 simulations.

An issue of the IEEE 802.11s power save algorithm is its scalability concerning the number of peers; with more peers more wakeups are necessary when links are in light sleep mode. Theoretically, this should not be much of an issue, as the time needed to receive a mesh beacon is typically very low compared to the beacon interval. But to the actual receive time there are additional delays due to CSMA channel access and the delays for powering up the receiver's radio, processing the beacon and resuming doze.

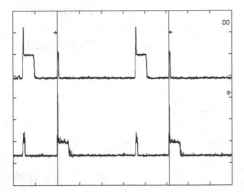

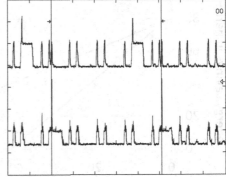

Fig. 2. Doze/wakeup cycle of nodes with one peer link in light sleep mode

Fig. 3. Doze/wakeup cycle of nodes with seven peer links in light sleep mode

3   Testbed Implementation and Results

In order to evaluate the power save algorithm of IEEE 802.11s we chose to test it under real-life conditions in a testbed. In cooperation with cozybit Inc. [5] we implemented the routines necessary in the Linux kernel's Wi-Fi stack [6]. Most of these are made open source and are available in current Linux distributions. Given suitable hardware, the full range of the 802.11s power save schemes can be implemented in software. In our testbed we used two types of off-the-shelf Wi-Fi routers using the "ath9k" device driver: Netgear WNDR3800 and TP-Link TL-MR3020. In our test setup we measured the overall device power consumption which also includes unrelated power sinks like CPU, Ethernet controller and others. We used a 1Ω shunt resistor in line with a lab voltage supply of 12V for the WNDR3800 and 5V for the TL-MR3020. The measurements are plotted with a Tektronix TLS-216 digital oscilloscope and logic analyzer. Unless defined differently all plots use a sampling rate of 1kS/s and a scale of 50mV/div vertical and 200ms/div horizontal. To reduce transients and noise effects all plots shown use an averaging factor of 10.

Fig. 2 shows the doze and wakeup cycle during one beacon interval for a single peer link with both nodes in light sleep mode. Clearly visible is the sharp spike in power consumption when the beacon frame is transmitted followed by the awake window. The spike of the lower plot serves as trigger source for the oscilloscope. Both nodes are configured with an awake window duration of 100TU and a beacon interval of 1000TU. It can be seen that just before one node transmits its beacon, the peer node wakes up to receive it and goes back to doze just afterwards. When compared to Fig. 1 it is visible that the testbed implementation precisely follows the standard's mandate. The upper plot is the WNDR3800 with current levels of 337mA in doze and 390mA in awake state, the lower plot corresponds to the TL-MR3020 with 108mA and 139mA readings. The area under the graphs between the drawn reference bars corresponds to the current consumption per beacon interval of both devices. Given that the network is idle, this curve will periodically repeat for each beacon interval. The oscilloscope readings show that the WNDR3800 consumes 352,81mAs per

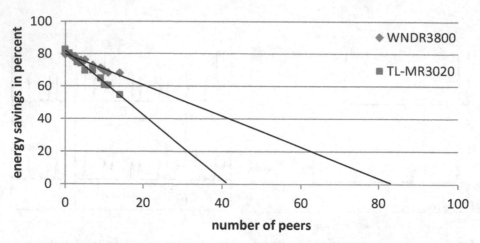

Fig. 4. Energy savings for increasing number of peers with common beacon interval

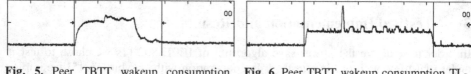

Fig. 5. Peer TBTT wakeup consumption WNDR3800

Fig. 6. Peer TBTT wakeup consumption TL-MR3020

beacon interval, the TL-MR3020 112,59mAs respectively. The generally higher energy consumption of the WNDR3800 is due to the more complex design of this router model with its additional hardware and our measurement setup where we measure the overall device power consumption. Fig. 3 shows a similar setup as Fig. 2 but here both routers each have seven mesh peer links established. It is obvious that the current consumption is increased due to the further wakeups necessary; now the current consumption per beacon interval is 358,04mAs for the WNDR3800 and 118,16mAs for the TL-MR3020. In case the wakeups do not overlap, it can be expected that the energy savings will decrease linearly with increasing number of light sleep peers as each peer adds another wakeup per beacon interval. We can also expect that with a sufficient number of peers the doze ratio will decrease until the device is practically active full-time. It should be noted that wakeups may randomly overlap, thus reducing the overall awake time. We will subsequently assume the worst case scenario for power save which corresponds to the case of no overlapping wakeups.

Fig. 4 shows the calculated effectiveness of the power save algorithm in relation to the number of established peer links. In the diagram the energy savings due to the power save algorithm are shown as percent value of the difference between the active mode consumption and the consumption with the Wi-Fi device off. The lower limit of 0% energy savings is given by the consumption in active state when the radio is never put to doze, while 100% energy savings would mean that the Wi-Fi functionality draws no power at all. In the graph a situation with zero peers achieves the maximum energy savings of around 80% for both devices. Here no additional wakeups are performed except for transmitting the own beacon every 1000TU and the subsequent awake window of 100TU in our setup. The remaining consumption of the Wi-Fi chipset is due to the mentioned beacon transmission and awake window, but also due to the now activated MAC coprocessor and host interface. One interesting observation is that the power save effectiveness decreases more rapidly for the TL-MR3020 router. The linear interpolation shows that the WNDR3800 would be effectively awake full-time with approximately 84 peers, the TL-MR3020 with 42 peers respectively. The reason for this effect may already be seen in Fig. 3 where the TL-MR3020 in the lower plot showed wider consumption spikes for its wakeups. Fig. 5 and Fig. 6 analyze the characteristics of a peer TBTT wakeup in more detail using a higher sampling rate of 50kS/s and a horizontal scale of 4ms/div. Here we measure about 12ms from waking up until resuming doze for the WNDR3800 and 23ms for the TL-MR3020. This is due to the different hardware of both router models with different revisions of the built-in Wi-Fi chipset and different processing power of the CPU.

4   Conclusion

In this paper we have analyzed and evaluated the IEEE 802.11s power saving schemes in terms of scalability. By implementing these schemes in the Linux kernel's Wi-Fi stack, we provide energy consumption measurements of off-the-shelf hardware. Our results show that, even for the not power-optimized router hardware, considerable energy savings are achieved. We analyzed that—unless TBTTs randomly overlap—the efficiency of the power save algorithm decreases linearly with the number of light sleep peers. The reason for this decrease is that the power-saving node has to wake up from doze for each light sleep peer link individually. The slope of the efficiency decrease depends on the hardware employed. In future work will aim to solve these scalability issues while staying in compliance with the 802.11 standard. Furthermore, we will address open implementation issues of links in deep sleep mode and intend to perform measurements with respect to energy-efficiency in bigger networks.

References

1. Castignani, G., Montavont, N., Lampropulos, A.: Energy Considerations for a Wireless Multihomed Environment. In: Lehnert, R. (ed.) EUNICE 2011. LNCS, vol. 6955, pp. 181–192. Springer, Heidelberg (2011)
2. IEEE Std. 802.11™-2012, Wireless LAN Medium Access Control (MAC) and Physical Layer (PHY) Specifications. IEEE Computer Society (May 2012)
3. Porsch, M., Bauschert, T.: A Testbed Analysis of the Effects of IEEE 802.11s Power Save on Mesh Link Performance. In: Szabó, R., Vidács, A. (eds.) EUNICE 2012. LNCS, vol. 7479, pp. 1–11. Springer, Heidelberg (2012)
4. Alam, M.N., Jäntti, R., Kneckt, J., Nieminen, J.: Performance Study of IEEE 802.11s PSM in FTP-TCP. In: 2012 IEEE Vehicular Technology Conference (VTC Fall), pp. 1–5 (2012)
5. cozybit inc., http://www.cozybit.com
6. Linux Kernel wireless driver API for SoftMAC devices, mac80211 kernel module source code, http://git.kernel.org/cgit/linux/kernel/git/torvalds/linux.git/tree/net/mac80211

HTTP Traffic Offload in Cellular Networks via WLAN Mesh Enabled Device to Device Communication and Distributed Caching

Chris Drechsler, Marco Porsch, and Gerd Windisch

Chemnitz University of Technology
Chemnitz, Germany
{chris.drechsler,marco.porsch,gerd.windisch}@etit.tu-chemnitz

Abstract. Mobile network operators are currently observing a tremendous increase of mobile data traffic due to the increased usage of smartphones or other Internet-enabled devices (e.g. tablets, laptops). A natural solution for reducing the transmission costs and for improving the QoE is caching of frequently requested content. In this contribution we propose a distributed caching architecture where the clients perform the caching of frequently requested HTTP content by allowing a partial use of the user equipments memory for local caching. Furthermore we engage clients to exchange content via WLAN mesh enabled device-to-device communication in order to offload traffic from the 3GPP radio access network.

Keywords: HTTP caching, device-to-device communication, cooperative caching.

1 Introduction

Internet usage has significantly evolved in the last few years and the growing data traffic contributes substantially to risings costs for network operators. Especially cellular network operators observe a tremendous increase of mobile data traffic due to increased usage of smartphones or other Internet-enabled devices (e.g. tablets, laptops). According to a recent study of Cisco [2] the global mobile data traffic grew by 70 % in 2012. To cope with the increasing data traffic in mobile networks and to reduce transmission costs, caching of frequently requested content within operator networks is a natural solution. Recent studies have shown that HTTP traffic accounts for up to 82 % of the average downstream traffic in mobile networks [5] and that the potential of HTTP caching is quite high. Between 28 % - 68 % of all bytes transferred via HTTP are basically cacheable [6], [3].

In this context we investigate the question of applying caching in mobile networks. An obvious approach would be to deploy classic HTTP cache systems like Squid [1] at different locations within the core network of the mobile operator, e.g. at S-/P-GW sites. In contrast to that we propose a distributed caching approach where the clients perform the caching of frequently requested HTTP

T. Bauschert (Ed.): EUNICE 2013, LNCS 8115, pp. 298–303, 2013.

content. By allowing a partial use of the user equipments (UEs) memory for local caching (which is free of charge from the operators perspective), clients are engaged to share their already downloaded HTTP content with other clients. Besides the 3GPP air interface for default Internet access, we assume that the clients in parallel participate in an open WLAN mesh network via their WLAN interface. Thus, by device-to-device communication over the WLAN mesh network they can directly support each other in retrieving frequently requested HTTP content.

The paper is organized as follows: Section 2 provides an overview of related work in the context of caching in cellular networks close to UEs (e.g. at eNodeB sites) and of device-to-device communication. In Section 3 the new distributed cooperative caching approach is described and detailed information about its operation is provided. Section 4 concludes the paper.

2 Related Work

Ahlehagh et al. introduced in [4] new ideas for caching video content at base stations. They propose to provide a large number of micro-caches (with up to 50 GByte capacity) basically one micro-cache for each base station. Together with new replacement strategies they demonstrate the feasibility and effectiveness of caching at the edge of the RAN. However contrary to our work they do not consider a distributed and cooperative caching approach with caching performed in the UEs.

Most contributions related to device-to-device communication in cellular networks (like, e.g. [7]) contrary to our work assume that 3GPP radio resources are used for the device-to-device communication. Thus the main research question is on how to opti-mally allocate radio resources for device to device communication and how to minimize interference.

Other contributions consider traffic offload in mobile networks via WLAN hotspots [8]. In contrast to our work the focus is on offloading delay tolerant traffic to the Internet. WLAN is used in infrastructure mode and not for device to device com-munication.

3 Distributed Cooperative HTTP Caching

Our distributed and cooperative caching approach is based on three main concepts:

- HTTP header field extension
- distributed caching architecture
- distributed cache operation

In the following, these main concepts are explained in more detail.

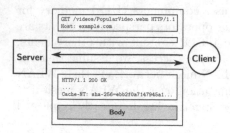

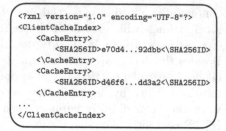

Fig. 1. HTTP header field extension   **Fig. 2.** ClientCacheIndex.xml

3.1   HTTP Header Field Extension

One reason for the partly unused caching potential is that todays HTTP cache systems like Squid [1] mainly rely on the URL to detect duplicate transfers. But mechanisms like server load balancing and the placement of content on several servers within CDNs often lead to different URLs for one specific resource (URL aliasing). Another reason is the personalization of HTTP messages (e.g. via cookies or parameters in the query string).

To overcome this issues we propose to use a hash key for identifying the HTTP content more precisely than with URLs. The hash value is computed over the specific representation of a requested resource and is added to the header of the HTTP response messages (see figure 1).

3.2   Distributed Caching Architecture

The distributed caching architecture consists of two main entities (see figure 3):

- **Origin HTTP Server:** The origin HTTP server is located in the domain of the content producer and acts like a normal HTTP server but with one difference: it adds the above explained header attribute with the hash value of the requested resource to the header of the transferred HTTP message (for details see chapter 3.1).
- **Sharing Clients:** Sharing clients are the UEs in the domain of the mobile operator. On the one hand they are connected to the Internet via the 3GPP air interface and on the other hand they participate in an open WLAN mesh network via their Wi-Fi interface in order to directly share resources with nearby UEs. The sharing clients consist of the following three sub-entities:
  - **User Agent:** Sharing clients can act like normal clients by retrieving web content with an ordinary user agent (web browser) like e.g. Firefox. The only change in our architecture is that the user agent forwards the HTTP traffic to the smart proxy (see below).
  - **HTTP Server:** The sharing clients are running a normal HTTP server which acts like a simple file server with a flat hierarchy. Shared resources can be identified and accessed by their hash value (see chapter 3.1). To announce which resources are shared, the client offers an index.

In our approach a simple xml file (called ClientCacheIndex.xml) is made available on the HTTP server of each sharing client (see figure 2).

- **Smart Proxy:** The smart proxy is located in the data path between the origin server and the user agent (web browser), see figure 3. It serves as a central element and manages the data exchange of web content. By default the 3GPP interface is used. In case that at least one sharing client participating in the WLAN mesh network has a copy of the requested content, the WLAN interface is used. For a detailed explanation of the cache operation see chapter 3.3. The smart proxy fulfills the following two basic functions:
  - ∗ Indexing: The smart proxy builds an index of all resources that are shared by nearby sharing clients. For that it periodically (e.g. every 5-10 minutes) scans the mesh network for available sharing clients/UEs and queries each of them for the index of its shared HTTP resources.
  - ∗ Analyzing HTTP traffic: To enable the distributed cache operation the smart proxy analyzes all incoming HTTP traffic on the 3GPP interface wrt. the HTTP header attributes (that includes the hash value of the transferred content). In case a copy of the requested resource is available by at least one nearby sharing client/UE the smart proxy intercepts the HTTP transfer from the origin HTTP server and retrieves the content from the nearby sharing client.

3.3 Distributed Cache Operation

To explain the distributed cache operation in more detail we provide the following example which is based on the scenario depicted in figure 3.

The user agent of client A sends a HTTP request message (method GET) for a desired resource to its smart proxy (1), which forwards it directly to the origin HTTP server (2). The origin HTTP server answers with a HTTP response message (3) and adds the header attribute with the computed hash value of the requested resource to the header of the transferred HTTP message. The smart proxy of client A analyzes the incoming HTTP response message and looks for the header attribute (4). In the example it is assumed that the smart proxy recognizes that a nearby sharing client B in the WLAN mesh network has an object with the same hash value. Therefore the smart proxy sends a HTTP request message (method GET) for the resource to the HTTP server of client B (5) and the client returns a HTTP response message with the resource contained in the body (6). Thus, the smart proxy receives the resource from both, the origin HTTP server via the 3GPP interface and the client B via device to device communication over the WLAN mesh network. It concatenates the HTTP header received by the origin HTTP server with the HTTP body received by client B and forwards the message to the user agent of client A (7). As soon as the transfer is successful established the smart proxy aborts the connection to the origin HTTP server (8).

There are frequent concerns regarding the sharing of copyright protected content in the Internet. With our caching architecture this concerns are repealed.

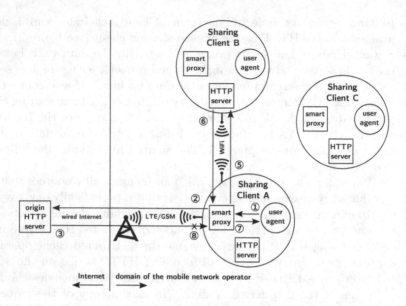

Fig. 3. HTTP data flow in the distributed caching architecture (example)

As explained above, the origin server is always requested. If it responds with a 2xx HTTP response code (and if the header field extension is applied) then the smart proxy can intercept the transmission and the content might be retrieved from a nearby sharing client. On the other hand this means that no content can be retrieved from sharing clients if the content isnt available on the origin server.

4   Conclusion

In this contribution we present a distributed caching approach where the clients (UEs) perform the caching and support each other in retrieving frequently requested HTTP content via device-to-device communication in a WLAN mesh network. We already implemented the concepts of our approach in a testbed where notebooks are used instead of UEs. Currently we are replacing the notebooks with real smartphones and are porting the software to Android OS. For future work we plan to perform a comprehensive performance evaluation of our approach

References

[1] Homepage squid project, http://www.squid-cache.org/
[2] Cisco visual networking index: Global mobile data traffic forecast update, 2012-2017 (February 6, 2013), http://www.cisco.com/en/US/solutions/collateral/ns341/ns525/ns537/ns705/ns827/white_paper_c11-520862.html
[3] Ager, B., Schneider, F., Kim, J., Feldmann, A.: Revisiting cacheability in times of user generated content. In: INFOCOM IEEE Conference on Computer Communications Workshops, pp. 1–6 (March 2010)

[4] Ahlehagh, H., Dey, S.: Video caching in radio access network: Impact on delay and capacity. In: 2012 IEEE Wireless Communications and Networking Conference (WCNC), pp. 2276–2281 (2012)

[5] Erman, J., Gerber, A., Hajiaghayi, M., Pei, D., Sen, S., Spatscheck, O.: To cache or not to cache: The 3g case. IEEE Internet Computing 15(2), 27–34 (2011)

[6] Erman, J., Gerber, A., Hajiaghayi, M.T., Pei, D., Spatscheck, O.: Network-aware forward caching. In: Proceedings of the 18th International Conference on World Wide Web, WWW 2009, pp. 291–300. ACM, New York (2009)

[7] Fodor, G., Dahlman, E., Mildh, G., Parkvall, S., Reider, N., Miklos, G., Turanyi, Z.: Design aspects of network assisted device-to-device communications. IEEE Communications Magazine 50(3), 170–177 (2012)

[8] Ristanovic, N., Le Boudec, J.Y., Chaintreau, A., Erramilli, V.: Energy efficient offloading of 3g networks. In: 2011 IEEE 8th International Conference on Mobile Adhoc and Sensor Systems (MASS), pp. 202–211 (2011)

Protocol-Independent Detection
of Dictionary Attacks

Martin Drašar

Masaryk University
Institute of Computer Science
Botanická 68a, Brno, Czech Republic
drasar@ics.muni.cz

Abstract. Data throughput of current high-speed networks makes it prohibitively expensive to detect attacks using conventional means of deep packet inspection. The network behavior analysis seemed to be a solution, but it lacks in several aspects. The academic research focuses on sophisticated and advanced detection schemes that are, however, often problematic to deploy into the production. In this paper we try different approach and take inspiration from industry practice of using relatively simple but effective solutions. We introduce a model of malicious traffic based on practical experience that can be used to create simple and effective detection methods. This model was used to develop a successful proof-of-concept method for protocol-independent detection of dictionary attacks that is validated with empirical data in this paper.

Keywords: traffic classes, anomaly detection, network behavior analysis.

1 Introduction

Conventional methods of deep packet inspection (DPI) are being replaced with methods of network behavior analysis (NBA). The ordinary traffic volume often exceeds units and tens of gigabits per second. This is a problem for classic methods of DPI and signature matching that start to demand more processing power than the current hardware can supply. NBA methods are seen as a potential remedy, because of their ability to work with aggregated data and to detect unknown threats [8].

The development of NBA methods diverged into two branches that pursue different goals using different means. On the one hand, there is the academic research with a lot of theoretical work and application of sophisticated concepts. On the other hand, there is the industry practice of using relatively simple, but effective methods to protect from current threats.

In this paper we try to bring these two branches together by introducing a model of an attack traffic based on practical experiences with network protection in the University's CSIRT[1]. This model can be used to design anomaly detection

---

[1] Computer Security Incident Response Team – organizational unit responsible for maintaining security of the University's network.

T. Bauschert (Ed.): EUNICE 2013, LNCS 8115, pp. 304–309, 2013.
© IFIP International Federation for Information Processing 2013

schemes that are effective and relatively easy to implement as is demonstrated by creating a proof-of-concept method for detection of dictionary attacks.

This paper is divided into six sections. Section 2 describes dictionary attacks. It also presents current advancements in dictionary attack detection and evaluates their detection schemes. Section 3 introduces the concept of traffic classes to describe attacking traffic. Section 4 is focused on a connection between traffic classes and different types of attacks. Section 5 presents the detection method based on properties of one traffic class and also evaluates its effectiveness. Section 6 concludes the paper.

2   Dictionary Attacks

Dictionary attacks exploit valid authentication mechanism, abusing the fact that users tend to choose weak credentials [6]. It is complicated to detect such attacks, especially low-profile ones, because an isolated attack attempt differs from a legitimate one only by intention and not any measurable properties. That is why they are so prevalent [3], [7], [9]. However, they do not receive enough academic attention as most research is focused on DoS attacks, botnet activity and other disturbant behavior [8].

There is a large variety of industry-provided tools to detect dictionary attacks. They are often tied to one particular service and detection is done on a machine or an application level. Such tools, however, often lack knowledge of network context and can be bypassed by distributed low-profile attacks. Agent-based [2] and SIEM systems partially solve this problem by matching anomalies from end computers in one central point. They require specific software to be configured in end computers and thus fail with BYOD paradigm, though. Network-level monitoring gives a context and does not require any alteration in end computers.

We present four tools for network-level detection of dictionary attacks. *SSH-Monitor* detects SSH attacks by matching attack signatures [11]. It also comes with an observation that an attack is always preceded with a port scan and that most often two or more machines are targeted. *SSHCure* is based on an observation that an SSH attack is divided into three phases with distinct flow properties: the scanning phase, the brute-force phase and the die-off phase [4]. *RdpMonitor* is an extension of previous tools that is focused on a detection of RDP attacks [10]. *Honeyscan* uses synergy of honeypots and network monitoring to detect various dictionary attacks [5].

These tools, although each taking a different approach, share similar properties. They use thresholds, focus on statistical properties, and do not take into account the character of a traffic, i. e. variations in attack. Attackers could easily subvert these tools by changing their behavior, but practical experience shows they are not likely to. One reason is the supply of bruteforcing tools that in general operate on the same principle. They attack as much as a network or a user lets them and do not alter traffic character. Their attacks are then very similar and therefore detectable. In the terminology described further, they all belong to one traffic class.

3   Traffic Classes

A *traffic class* is a concept that tries to formally describe the character of an attack traffic by focusing on markers of automated action without special-casing for networks of different sizes. It is tailored for NetFlow, but it can be modified to work with e. g. packets. A basic primitive in this concept is a *slice* – a set of flows from one source IP address in a given time interval. This *slice* is characterized by four traffic dimensions.

The first traffic dimension is *visibility* that describes traffic in terms of newly created flows. It is quantized into two values that are functions of current defense capabilities of given network. Traffic in a *slice* is *visible* if there is at least one detection mechanism in a network that will mark it as anomalous/suspicious based on flow analysis. Traffic in a *slice* is *stealthy* otherwise. As a result the dimension is relevant for networks of different sizes and detection capabilities.

The second dimension is *periodicity* that describes temporal relations between flows in a *slice*. It has three possible values. *Aperiodic* traffic has no discernible pattern in flow occurrence. *Periodic* traffic has a pattern in flow occurrence. *Constant* traffic has roughly the same number of flows in all *slices* of the same length.

The third dimension is *similarity* that deals with flow similitude. Flows in a *slice* can be *similar* or *different* based on arbitrary criteria. In this paper we use overall byte count and duration as a discriminant.

The fourth dimension is the *target count* that has two possible values: *one target* and *many targets*.

Dimensions that we introduced are orthogonal, so one value for each dimension can be chosen for every traffic sample. Therefore, any traffic can be described as a combination of these dimensions. Let any such combination of traffic dimensions be called the *traffic class*.

4   Relation between Traffic Classes and Attacks

By combining all dimensions we get 24 traffic classes in total. However, they can be categorized into several groups depending on a dominant detectable dimension.

The first group is *noisy traffic* that consist of all *visible* combinations. Because traffic is considered *visible* if it was marked as an attack by at least one mechanism, this entire group of traffic classes is marked as an anomaly or an attack. Although this group covers one half of traffic classes, it does not necessarily cover half of attacks a network is facing. For example, a network with only a port scan detection based on thresholding would be able to detect periodic, aperiodic and distributed scanners, but would fail to detect dictionary attacks, DoS or massive spamming.

The second group is *flat traffic* that consist of *stealthy* and *constant* combinations. This group covers traffic generated by bruteforcing tools as described in Section 2. Traffic with constant pattern that is disrupted only by network conditions and eventual proxy delays. However, not all flat traffic can be considered anomalous or harmful as there are valid use cases for such pattern, e. g. keep-alive. It is important to be aware that *constant* traffic is defined in terms of constant creation of new flows in given slice and not e. g. constant byte rate. Such constant appearance of new flows in case of authenticated protocols like SSH or RDP is always suspicious.

The third group is *spiked traffic* that consist of *stealthy* and *periodic* combinations. This group is a superset of *flat traffic* and it contains anomalies like beaconing [1], but also a lot of traffic that looks anomalous but in fact is not.

The fourth group is *episodic traffic* that consist of *stealthy* and *aperiodic* combinations. This group is interesting because there is no discernible pattern in flow occurrence. Virtually nothing in the character of traffic points to whether it is an attack or not. Unless an attacker crosses some threshold, such attacks are undetectable on a network level.

5 Detecting Dictionary Attacks by Detecting Flat Network Traffic

In this section we present a proof-of-concept method that is built upon the assertion that *flat traffic* to authenticated services is always suspicious. We then analyze results of this method and compare it with other detection mechanisms running in the same network.

This method was developed and tested in the campus network of Masaryk University (about 15.000 devices online every day) in the course of two months from February 24, 2013 to April 24, 2013.

When designing the detection method, we have directly applied the definition of *constant* traffic that says that traffic is constant if all *slices* of the same length have roughly the same number of flows. However, we had to decide on three key characteristics – length of *slices*, their relative temporal position, and measure of their equal flow count. For the sake of brevity, we omit analyses behind our choices and present here only the final decisions. These analyses, however, are available upon request.

The method works with 60 second slices of 5-minute batches of NetFlow data. These slices are adjacent and non-overlapping, i. e. there are at most 5 slices for one source IP address in a batch. *Slice* flow count equality is given by a function that measures the relative difference between flow count in adjacent non-zero *slices*. The method was successfully used with following protocols: FTP(S), SSH, Telnet, LDAP, HTTP(S), AFP, RDP and SMTP. *Flat traffic* detection for HTTP(S) was found to be ineffective, because valid AJAX updates common on Web 2.0 tend to produce flat traffic pattern.

5.1   Identification of Attackers

Figure 1 presents the number of identified instances of flat traffic in 5-minute traffic windows and unique source IP addresses for various thresholds of relative difference. Only differences up to 100 % were taken into account. Anything higher was automatically considered non-flat traffic. As was expected, series of identified source IP addresses grow faster than the graphs of attacks. In case of SSH and RDP services that are often targets of attacks, even the 50 % threshold was enough to identify more than 90 % of potential attackers.

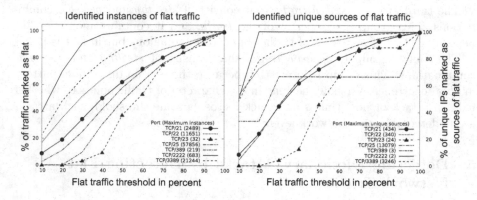

Fig. 1. Amount of flat traffic and its sources based on a relative difference threshold

Ground-truth evaluation of data is complicated because the detection was carried out on an unannotated data, therefore, we decided to compare our results with three other detection mechanisms deployed in the same network. We chose 60 % as a relative difference threshold and identified 3139 unique IP addresses targeting port TCP/3389. *RdpMonitor* [10] that detects attacks on this port found at the same time 852 attackers of which our method detected 410. Our method also identified 320 unique IP addresses targeting port TCP/22. *SSHMonitor* [11] found 29 attackers on this port of which we found 5, and *honeyscan* [5] found 57 attackers of which we found 15. Manual inspection of a sample of remaining addresses undetected by other tools concluded that they were likely to be actual attacks. However, conclusive proof is not available because the data on targeted end hosts is not available. The likely reason why the proof-of-concept method detects order of magnitude more attackers than deployed methods is their high threshold to avoid false positives.

6 Conclusion

In this paper we have presented a model of attack traffic that puts emphasis on a distinction between artificial and human-initiated traffic. Based on this model, we created the proof-of-concept method that successfully detects one type of attacks against various services. By applying concepts of this model, other methods can be devised that will detect other previously overlooked attacks that currently hide below detection thresholds. Relative simplicity of this model and its application also lowers bars for industry adoption.

Detection of malicious traffic based on a character of traffic proved to be a promising approach. In our future work, we will explore other detection schemes based on a character of traffic that can be used as a stand-alone or complementary detection mechanisms. We will also research other possible traffic classes and their respective groupings.

Acknowledgment. This paper is based on a work supported by the Czech Ministry of Interior under Identification code VF2013201531.

References

1. Balland, P.: An Analysis of Network Beaconing Activity for Incident Response (2008), http://www.cert.org/flocon/2008/presentations/balland_flocon2008.pdf (retrieved online March 27, 2013)
2. Dasgupta, D., et al.: CIDS: An agent-based intrusion detection system. Computers & Security 24(5), 387–398 (2005)
3. Dragon Research Group: SSH Password Authentication Report (2013), http://www.dragonresearchgroup.org/insight/sshpwauth.txt (retrieved online February 22, 2013)
4. Hellemons, L., Hendriks, L., Hofstede, R., Sperotto, A., Sadre, R., Pras, A.: SSHCure: A Flow-Based SSH Intrusion Detection System. In: Sadre, R., Novotný, J., Čeleda, P., Waldburger, M., Stiller, B. (eds.) AIMS 2012. LNCS, vol. 7279, pp. 86–97. Springer, Heidelberg (2012)
5. Husák, M., Drašar, M.: Flow-based Monitoring of Honeypots. To Appear in: Proceedings of 7th International Conference on Security and Protection of Information (SPI 2013) (2013)
6. Menezes, A.J., Van Oorschot, P.C., Vanstone, S.A., Rivest, R.L.: Identification and Entity Authentication. In: Handbook of Applied Cryptography. CRC Press, Boca Raton (1997)
7. Seifert, C.: Analyzing Malicious SSH Login Attempts (2006), http://www.securityfocus.com/infocus/1876 (retrieved online March 27, 2013)
8. Sperotto, A., Schaffrath, G., Sadre, R., Morariu, C., Pras, A., Stiller, B.: An Overview of IP Flow-Based Intrusion Detection. Communications Surveys Tutorials 12(3), 343–356 (2010)
9. Thames, J.L., Abler, R., Keeling, D.: A Distributed Active Response Architecture for Preventing SSH Dictionary Attacks. In: IEEE Southeastcon 2008, pp. 84–89 (2008)
10. Vizváry, M., Vykopal, J.: Flow-based Detection of RDP Brute-force Attacks. To Appear in: Proceedings of 7th International Conference on Security and Protection of Information (SPI 2013) (2013)
11. Vykopal, J.: A Flow-Level Taxonomy and Prevalence of Brute Force Attacks. In: Abraham, A., Lloret Mauri, J., Buford, J.F., Suzuki, J., Thampi, S.M. (eds.) ACC 2011, Part II. CCIS, vol. 191, pp. 666–675. Springer, Heidelberg (2011)

Distributing Key Revocation Status in Named Data Networking

Giulia Mauri and Giacomo Verticale

Department of Electronics, Information, and Bioengineering, Politecnico di Milano
{gmauri,vertical}@elet.polimi.it

1 Introduction

Content Centric Networking (CCN) [1] is a new network paradigm designed to satisfy user needs considering the growth of data demand. Named Data Networking (NDN) [2] is a research project that is developing the future Internet architecture using the principles behind CCN. In this novel architecture, the contents are addressed by their name and not by their location. Thus, the attention is shifted from user to content, resulting in a caching network that is more efficient and flexible than an IP network for content distribution and management with beneficial effects on timely delivery. In NDN, the content objects are divided into chunks, each digitally signed by its producer, and most papers assume that verification is made only by the content consumer. In order to perform signature verification, a node needs the signer's key, which can be easily retrieved by issuing a standard interest message. Although content verification at the end node prevents disruptive attacks in which false data is delivered to applications, the verification of key validity is also necessary. Otherwise, false data would be cached and forwarded instead of correct data resulting in a denial of service and paving the way for more sophisticated attacks.

Indeed, content signed with a compromised key may remain in caches for an indeterminate amount of time, and possibly be served to end users. Even if caches implement a freshness mechanism that deletes content that has been in the cache longer than a given threshold, a compromised node could resend data making it extremely difficult to remove from the network the objects signed with a compromised key. In the standard PKIX (Public Key Infrastructure Certificate X.509) [3], the issue of delivering key revocation status to the end nodes is solved by using the OCSP (Online Certificate Status Protocol) protocol [4].

This paper proposes a way to implement similar functionality of OCSP protocol in the NDN scenario. In particular, we suggest three alternative ways to guarantee key freshness proposing two reactive methods and comparing them with a proactive method that is based on the ccnx-repository synchronization protocol. Finally, we use the open-source ndnSIM [5] package to run simulations for different network scenarios. We evaluate the performance in terms of latency, throughput and hit ratio gained by the proposed methods.

T. Bauschert (Ed.): EUNICE 2013, LNCS 8115, pp. 310–313, 2013.

2 Distributing Key Revocation Status

Attacker Model

Our attacker model assumes an active eavesdropper, a *malicious non-intrusive* attacker, with the following properties:

- It behaves as a legitimate node of the network and communicates with any other node. In particular, it can send interests for contents and receiver the corresponding data packets;
- In response to an interest message it can deliver content packets created on the fly and signed with any signature for which it knows the corresponding signing key or with an invalid signature;
- In response to an interest message it can reply any content it knows even if the corresponding signing key is known to be compromised.

We observe that the attacker cannot (1) modify other nodes' routing tables and (2) break any cryptographic algorithm.

The attacker purpose is to inject bad contents into the end-node caches. Particularly, the saboteur could reach his goal in two ways:

1. responding to Interests with corrupted Data packets;
2. signing false packet with a revoked key.

We consider a packet *corrupted* if its signature is invalid, while *false* if its signature is valid but generated with a compromised key.

We state that the protocol is **secure** if it is not possible that a honest end-node (we call it consumer or leaf node) accepts a corrupted or false packet in its cache or delivers it to its neighbors.

Our Proposal

Since the attacker has the ability to retrieve and use old keys to sign messages, in this section we provide three methods to guarantee that in a predefined time interval the key has not been revoked.

In the following paragraph, first we present two reactive modes based on a CCNx approach and then we report a proactive mode based on CCNx synchronization protocol.

Nonce-Based. In this method, we guarantee the up-to-date status of the key assuring that the key would be sent directly by the possessor. Particularly, the requesting node sends an Interest for the key specifying the `AnswerOriginKind`, that is 0, and it means "do-not-answer-from-content-store". The node expects to receive a Data packet containing the key and signed with the root key.

TimeStamp-Based. In this case, the node sends an Interest for the key to all its neighbors specifying in the name a timestamp that indicates a threshold validity. When a node receives the Interest, it checks if it has the key and if its key TimeStamp is more recent than the Interest TimeStamp, i.e. $TS_I < TS_D$. If the condition is satisfied, the node sends the corresponding Data packet containing the key. Otherwise, the node forwards the Interest to the following node. If no node has the fresh key, the Interest is forwarded till the original key possessor.

Proactive Mode. As comparison, we consider the proposal of [6] and we adapt it for our purpose. All the key names have the conventional prefix "/keys" in order to facilitate the key management. The keys stored in ccnx-repositories are revoked, that is all the keys that are no longer valid to sign a packet. The repositories are synchronized using ccnx-sync protocol. Particularly, the root node defines the *Revoked Key Collection* where it can store the keys, then a SyncAgent is responsible for keeping Repository up to date as some changes happen. Every Δt seconds, where Δt is a time interval longer than the timestamp of the previous section, the synchronization between root and router repositories is performed using a RootAdvise message.

Security Evaluation. We suppose indispensable in the content-centric scenario that each end-node should follow the signature verification process for each data packet and that it should check the key freshness. Moreover, we hypothesize that an attacker can only obtain or find invalid keys. In other words, we guarantee that a node doesn't accept a corrupted or false packet in its cache or delivers it to its neighbors within a time interval longer than Δt, that depends on freshness method used. Thus, we can say that the network is **secure** under these assumptions.

2.1   Numerical Results

In this subsection, we present simulative results to evaluate which is the impact on network performance for implementing key retrieval. Especially, we report only data concerning delay, due to space constraints, considering the different choices that a node can make for the freshness method.

In Figure 1 are depicted the mean round trip times to obtain data and key as a function of content class (the lower is the class, the higher is the popularity). Results are reported for the first 20 classes of popularity. The round trip time is the interval of time that incurs from the first interest sent for a data till the corresponding key reception. The delay is highly correlated to the distance between user and content and also to the content popularity. Moreover, the latency depends on the freshness method used: the Nonce-based method requires more time than the others because the key is asked more frequently and it comes from the root, that is the farthest node; the proactive mode is the faster method, since the revoked key repositories are synchronized off-line; while the TimeStamp-based approach stays in the middle and it depends also on time interval length of key validity. We note that increasing the key validity interval, the delays of proactive mode and timestamp methods coincide.

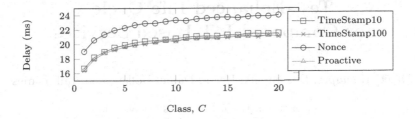

Fig. 1. Mean latency related to popularity classes in tree topology considering alternative freshness methods

Observing the results, we think that the timestamp-method not only prevents nodes accepting a corrupted or false packet in their cache but also achieves the better compromise in terms of delay, throughput and hit ratio. Moreover, we believe that the proactive mode can be used when the channel capacity is limited, since the revoked key update is done off-line. While, the nonce-based method guarantees that the keys have a shorter interval of uncertainty but we have to introduce more traffic on the network and also wait more time for each content.

3   Conclusion

Whenever a cryptographic key is revokated, the nodes should reject all the contents signed with that key and these packets should be removed from the network. This paper compares three possible methods to achieve this result. In the reactive methods, the consumer nodes request status certificates for the keys they need. The freshness of these certificates can be verified by using nonces or timestamps. In the proactive method revocation lists are broadcast using the ccnx synchronization protocol. We compare the performance of content retrieval in terms of delay, throughput and hit ratio. We conclude that the solution based on timestamps provides the best compromise between delay and key status distribution overhead. This research represents also a first step into the problem of authenticity and integrity of contents.

References

1. Jacobson, V., et al.: Networking named content. In: Proceedings of the 5th CoNEXT 2009, pp 1–12. ACM, New York (2009)
2. Zhang, L., et al.: Named data networking (ndn) project. University of California and Arizona, Palo Alto Research Center and others, Tech. Rep. (October 2010)
3. Cooper, D., et al.: Internet x.509 public key infrastructure certificate and certificate revocation list (crl) profile. RFC 5280 (May 2008)
4. Myers, M., et al.: X.509 internet public key infrastructure,online certificate status protocol - ocsp. RFC 2560 (June 1999)
5. Afanasyev, A., et al.: ndnsim: Ndn simulator for ns-3. UCLA, Tech. Rep. (2012)
6. Bian, C., et al.: Deploying key management on ndn testbed. UCLA, Peking University and PARC, Tech. Rep. (February 2013)

Test-Enhanced Life Cycle
for Composed IoT-Based Services

Daniel Kuemper, Eike Steffen Reetz, Daniel Hölker, and Ralf Tönjes

University of Applied Sciences Osnabrück,
P.O. Box 1940, 49009 Osnabrück, Germany
{d.kuemper,e.reetz,d.hoelker,r.toenjes}@hs-osnabrueck.de

Abstract. Major challenges in developing services for the Internet of Things (IoT) are based on heterogeneous interfaces and radio technologies. This paper proposes a knowledge driven service life cycle, which enables a structured utilisation of semantic descriptions for re-usability and testing. Furthermore the approach facilitates the process of encapsulating IoT resources into services.

Keywords: SOA, IoT, Test, Life Cycle, Composition, Deployment.

1 Introduction

Scalability and interoperability are key challenges in the composition of Internet of Things (IoT) applications by reusing existing IoT resources like sensors and actuators. The IoT.est project aims at surmounting available silo architectures with varying, partly proprietary interfaces by re-using Service-Oriented Architecture (SOA) approaches to ensure compliance, scalability and the ability to test and monitor IoT services. The main approach is to encapsulate the communication with heterogeneous IoT resources into Representational State Transfer based (RESTful)[1] services that are linked to an extensive, formal description of their functional and non-functional capabilities. The encapsulation prevents the need of re-implementing proprietary IoT resource interfaces for every invocation and enables the usage of widespread clients, proxies and analysis tools. The service descriptions, stored in a semantic knowledge management, ensure re-usability and the ability to find services for composition by providing extensive information about their in- and outputs as well as their Quality of Service (QoS) and Quality of Information (QoI). The service descriptions are also used to facilitate the (semi-) automated derivation of test cases[2] to ensure service reliability.

This work assumes that a common understanding of the service life cycle is crucial in order to build successful IoT-based services [3][4]. To ensure a knowledge driven service composition and testing approach the annotation process of the service becomes eminent. While previous life cycle approaches like the classical V-Model or agile programming such as Extreme Programming have already considered techniques like test-first [5] and test-driven development they did not

T. Bauschert (Ed.): EUNICE 2013, LNCS 8115, pp. 314–319, 2013.

explicitly describe the process of knowledge annotation. The proposed life cycle approach overcomes these limitations by adding a clear view of knowledge representation, annotation and the process of test derivation from this knowledge.

In this project the creation and composition of new services is guided by a service life cycle framework that is aligned to support a consistent workflow[6]. The service life cycle employed in the IoT.est project is outlined in the following sections towards a brief definition of the utilised service model.

1.1 IoT.est Service Model

This work utilises RESTful interfaces to encapsulate IoT services for enhanced reusability. It defines two types of services to ensure direct usage and composition of IoT services without dealing with heterogeneous interfaces:

The **Atomic Service (AS)** is a RESTful web service, accessing $0 - n$ IoT resources via their own individual interfaces and radio technologies. It enables access to these resources via standardised `Get, Post, Put, Delete` request methods, whose invocation is defined in a dedicated Web Application Description Language (WADL) document[7]. Input parameters as well as response documents of these methods are extensively described in the semantic knowledge management, to e.g. identify a specific service parameter not just as a *double* but rather as a *temperature/Celsius* value. The implemented AS can be deployed to a run time environment for web services and is registered in the knowledge management.

The **Composite Service (CS)** enables a business process-based composition of various AS and CS. It also provides a RESTful interface for service invocation and does not directly connect to IoT resources using their proprietary interfaces. It only uses AS and CS interfaces to acquire sensor information and to control actuators. The interfaces are also described by WADL and a semantic description to enable reusability.

2 Life Cycle Phases

The documentation of life cycle iterations is stored in the projects knowledge management component. The following sections describe the different phases and stages of the life cycle that can be followed in Fig. 1. Stages are represented by circles. Short arrows show typical stage succession. Larger curved arrows show shortcuts, which occur if needed amendments are identified.

2.1 Modelling Phase

Stage A: Identification / Adaptation of the Business Process

Description: Initial stage to identify the goal of a new service from a business perspective. Adaptation during further iterations of the life cycle due to enhanced requirements or technical restrictions. Business process adaptation leads to a new version of the service where older versions can independently be developed further.

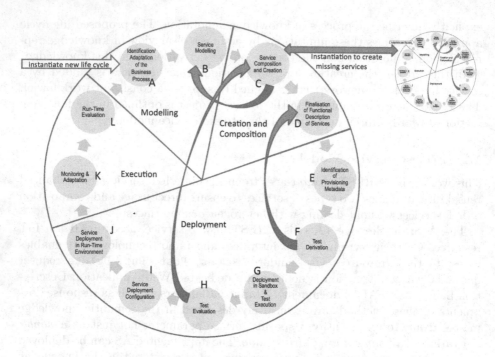

Fig. 1. Phases and Stages of the Service Life Cycle

Outcomes: A human readable description of the functionality/goal of the service (e.g. for an atomic service: providing the heart rate of patients; for a composite service: providing monitoring and alarm functionality for patients with cardio-vascular issues). This description also includes non-functional capabilities like QoS requirements derived from the desired user experience and estimated usage.

Stage B: Service Modelling

Description: Identification of a technical realisation to achieve the goal of stage A.
Outcomes: Abstract view of an engineer on how to solve the problem using services (Block diagram, data flow, event-based behaviour, process description).

2.2   Creation and Composition Phase

Stage C: Service Composition and Creation

Description: Lookup for services that provide the required functionality to achieve the goal defined in Stage A/B. Composition of available services to create a composite service (described in Business Process Model and Notation (BPMN)). Initiation of the creation of a non-available atomic or composed service by instancing a new life cycle.

Decision: Is the proposed service model feasible with available resources and can missing services be created or composed? Not possible: stage B; If new atomic services are needed and new life cycle instance for them is created: stage A (of new life cycle). After new creation or if the creation/composition is possible: stage C.

Outcomes: If an AS is created: an implemented service that can be deployed to a run time environment. If a CS is composed: the available services required for the composition and the BPMN implementation of the service logic exists an is executable for testing.

Stage D: Finalisation of Functional Description of Services

Description: After the description of raw interfaces and data types, included during development via annotations, a semantic description of in- and output parameters and the stateful description of the service behaviour has to be added. The semantic description enables the developer to explicitly specify used parameters that can be reused for composition and test derivation.

Outcomes: The full semantic description of the service (functional features and expected QoS) and the service interface description (WADL).

2.3 Deployment Phase

Stage E: Identification of Provisioning Metadata

Description: Based on the service description the resources for deployment ensuring functionality, connection to the IoT resources and QoS have to be determined to select a sufficiently equipped runtime environment.

Outcomes: Provisioning metadata - agreed by the service developer and the service provider. Platform independent deployment descriptor.

Stage F: Test Derivation

Description: The derivation of a System Under Test (SUT) and test cases is generated. Semantic information is used to narrow down the variety of test cases. E.g. the parameters of a service accepting latitude/longitude coordinates as input to deliver data are not simply modelled as two `float`-values. They will be described with an upper ontology as geo-coordinates each with possible value range $\{-90.0°, 90.0°\}/\{-180.0°, 180.0°\}$. With this information valid values for tests are clearly specified.

Decision: If service description is conflicting or insufficient the service life cycle will return to stage D.

Outcomes: Set of all executable test cases as Testing and Test Control Notation Version 3 (TTCN-3)[8] code.

Stage G: Deployment in Sandbox and Test Execution

Description: Based on stage E a sandbox environment is selected to execute a set of test cases created in stage F. The IoT resources are emulated during testing[9].
Outcomes: Test results (TTCN-3 log files) are stored in the knowledge management to ensure detailed evaluation of failed test cases.

Stage H: Test Evaluation

Description: A test developer analyses the results of the test case execution.
Decision: If errors occur: report to stage C to redevelop the service. If service behaves like expected, go on to stage I.
Outcomes: Go/No-go decision made by the test developer based on the resulting log files.

Stage I: Service Deployment Configuration

Description: After the service has been tested, one or more run time platforms are selected for service provisioning.
Outcomes: Final form of the provisioning metadata and deployment descriptor (platform dependent - manifest file).

Stage J: Service Deployment in Runtime Environment

Description: The deployment on the final run time platform is made.
Outcomes: Deployable package (platform dependent e.g. `war`) deployed in runtime. Configured and instantiated service. The service is running and available for monitoring.

2.4   Run Time Phase

Stage K: Monitoring and Adaptation

Description: While the service is running it is an on-going process to monitor service availability and functionality. In the IoT.est Framework CSs are not implicitly bound to specific service endpoints of ASs. If an alternative AS exists, which can deliver the same information, the CS is able to utilize this AS as service endpoint. Due to altering infrastructure conditions this stage monitors service behaviour and performs necessary actions to adapt the composite service infrastructure. Furthermore the monitoring delivers non functional service quality and load information that can be utilized during next iterations of the service life cycle.
Outcomes: Report of service usage and availability, adaptation, QoS adherence, occurred malfunctions and alerts.

Stage L: Run Time Evaluation

Description: The evaluation of stage K reports is used for further life cycle iterations. Furthermore the enquiry of user experience is used to advance the next service versions.
Outcomes: Documentation of suggestions for service or runtime changes. E.g. the replacement of runtime or redevelopment of service if QoS issues occur.

3   Conclusion

The proposed SOA approach lowers the obstacle for integrating IoT resources into existing service architectures and shows a far-reaching applicability in the IoT domain. In combination with a structured development using a service life cycle, which is utilising semantic descriptions, it ensures re-usability of services and facilitates (semi-) automatic test derivation and composition. Next steps will be the automated monitoring and Service Composition Environment (SCE) based tracking of the service life cycle.

Acknowledgments. The research leading to these results has received funding from the European Union Seventh Framework Programme for the IoT.est project under grant agreement n° 257521. http://www.ict-iotest.eu

References

1. Fielding, R.T.: Architectural Styles and the Design of Network-based Software Architectures, University of California (2000)
2. Kuemper, D., Reetz, E.S., Toenjes, R.: Test Derivation for Semantically Described IoT Services. In: 22nd Future Network and Mobile Summit, Lisbon (2013)
3. Cabral Pinto, F., Chainho, P., Pssaro, N., Santiago, F., Corujo, D., Gomes, D.: The business of things architecture. Transactions on Emerging Telecommunications Technologies (2013)
4. Raverdy, P.G., Autili, M., Bertolino, A., Cordier, C., Bhushan, B., Ords, I., Devlic, A.: Service Lifecycle Management, Mobile Service Platforms (MSP) cluster of IST FP6 projects. White Paper (2008)
5. Andrea, J.: Envisioning the next-generation of functional testing tools. IEEE Software (2007)
6. Reetz, E.S., Kuemper, D., Lehmann, A., Toenjes, R.: Test Driven Life Cycle Management for Internet of Things based Services: a Semantic Approach. In: VALID 2012, The Fourth International Conference on Advances in System Testing and Validation Lifecycle, Lisbon, pp. 21–27 (2012)
7. Hadley, M.J.: Web application description language (WADL), Technical report, Sun Microsystems (2006)
8. ETSI, EG 201 873-1: Methods for Testing and Specification (MTS); The Testing and Test Control Notation version 3; Part1: TTCN-3 Core Language (2012)
9. Reetz, E., Kuemper, D., Moessner, K., Toenjes, R.: How to Test IoT Services before Deploying them into Real World. In: 19th European Wireless Conference (EW 2013), Guildford (2013)

Author Index

Aagesen, Finn Arve   173
Alloush, Iyas   245

Bauknecht, Uwe   1
Bauschert, Thomas   13, 292
Bonnin, Jean-Marie   257
Borchert, Kathrin   100
Büsing, Christina   13

Čeleda, Pavel   136
Cuppens, Frédéric   148
Cuppens-Boulahia, Nora   148

de Boer, Pieter-Tjerk   54
Dittawit, Kornschnok   173
Dorn, Jürgen   257
Drašar, Martin   304
Drechsler, Chris   298

Eckert, Marcus   112
Ergen, Sinem Coleri   221

Fabini, Joachim   78
Farkas, Károly   287
Feller, Frank   1
Fioreze, Tiago   54
Fourcot, Florent   148

Gelabert, Xavier   66
Gligoroski, Danilo   161
Globa, Larisa   233
Görg, Carmelita   90, 270
Gulyás, András   274

Hail, Mohamed Ahmed M.   209
Heegaard, Poul E.   25, 124, 185
Hellbrück, Horst   209
Hirschbichler, Michael   78
Hölker, Daniel   314

Jiang, Yuming   25, 66
Jirsík, Tomáš   136

Kermarrec, Yvon   245
Khloussy, Elissar   66

Klein, Dominik   100
Knoll, Thomas Martin   112
Köpsell, Stefan   148
Kot, Tetiana   233
Kralevska, Katina   161
Kuemper, Daniel   314
Kuthan, Jiri   78
Kutschka, Manuel   13

Lange, Stanislav   100
Lehnert, Ralf J.   197

Marwat, Safdar Nawaz Khan   90, 270
Mauri, Giulia   310
Megyesi, Péter   37
Molnár, Sándor   37
Moura, Giovane C.M.   54
Mudriievskyi, Stanislav   197
Mühleisen, Maciej   46

Nizamoglu, Irem   221

Øverby, Harald   161
Ozkasap, Oznur   221

Petersen, Christoph   46
Porsch, Marco   292, 298
Pötsch, Thomas   90, 270
Pras, Aiko   54

Reetz, Eike Steffen   314
Reichl, Peter   257, 282
Rouvrais, Siegfried   245

Schill, Alexander   233
Schmid, Matthias   100
Singeorzan, Vlad   100
Steglich, Uwe   13
Szabó, Dávid   274
Szabó, Róbert L.   287

Teubler, Torsten   209
Timm-Giel, Andreas   46

Tönjes, Ralf   314
Toutain, Laurent   148
Tsokalo, Ievgenii Anatolijovuch   197

Velan, Petr   136
Verticale, Giacomo   310
Villa, Bjørn J.   124

Wäfler, Jonas   185
Weerawardane, Thushara   90

Wiedermann, Werner   78
Windisch, Gerd   298

Xie, Lang   25

Zaki, Yasir   90, 270
Zeiß, Joachim   257
Zinner, Thomas   100
Zwickl, Patrick   282